Match-Fixing in Sport

Match-fixing represents a greater potential threat to the integrity of sport than doping. It has been linked to organised crime, illegal drugs and money-laundering. Law enforcement and sporting authorities are struggling to establish legal and regulatory responses to this emerging threat, particularly in light of cross-border internet gambling.

This book examines match-fixing and the legal responses to it in three key Asian sporting nations: Australia, Japan and Korea. It explores the significance of legal, regulatory and cultural differences, and draws lessons in terms of best practice and enforcement for legal and sporting authorities around the world. Including key insights from players, the betting industry, law enforcement and prosecution authorities, it discusses the strengths and weakness of current anti-corruption strategies in the three jurisdictions.

Match-Fixing in Sport: Comparative Studies from Australia, Japan, Korea and Beyond offers important insights for all students and scholars with an interest in sport studies, law, criminology and Asian studies.

Stacey Steele is Associate Professor and Associate Director (Japan) of the Asian Law Centre at Melbourne Law School, Australia.

Hayden Opie is Senior Fellow and former Director of Studies of the Sports Law Program at Melbourne Law School, Australia.

Routledge Research in Sport and Corruption

Series Editors:

James Skinner
Loughborough University London, UK

Terry Engelberg-Moston
James Cook University, Australia

Match-Fixing in Sport
Comparative Studies from Australia, Japan, Korea and Beyond
Edited by Stacey Steele and Hayden Opie

Match-Fixing in Sport

Comparative Studies from Australia, Japan, Korea and Beyond

Edited by Stacey Steele and Hayden Opie

Routledge
Taylor & Francis Group
LONDON AND NEW YORK

First published 2018 by Routledge

2 Park Square, Milton Park, Abingdon, Oxfordshire OX14 4RN
52 Vanderbilt Avenue, New York, NY 10017

Routledge is an imprint of the Taylor & Francis Group, an informa business

First issued in paperback 2020

British Library Cataloguing in Publication Data
A catalogue record for this book is available from the British Library

Library of Congress Cataloging in Publication Data
A catalog record for this book has been requested

ISBN: 978-0-415-78530-3 (hbk)
ISBN: 978-0-367-40690-5 (pbk)

Typeset in Sabon
by Wearset Ltd, Boldon, Tyne and Wear

Contents

Tables

Contributors

Yuta Ando is an expert on sports and law in Japan. He currently works for the Japan Sport Council ('JSC'), the central organization of the Japanese government specialising in sports promotional activities and the maintenance and enhancement of school children's health. He is a graduate of the University of Tokyo and studied at the Graduate School of Sport Sciences, Waseda University and Sciences Po Rennes, L'institut d'études politiques de Rennes (France). His specialised area of research is the integrity of sport. Recently, he worked with the drafting group of the Convention of the Council of Europe on the Manipulation of Sports Competitions and after the project he contributed to the establishment of the Sport Integrity Unit at the JSC.

Sanjeevan C. Balasingam is the Director for Asia and Oceania at Fédération Internationale de Football Association ('FIFA'), world football's peak body based in Zurich, Switzerland. His previous roles include Director of Member Associations and Director of Legal Services at the Asian Football Confederation ('AFC'). While at the AFC, he established the AFC's Integrity Unit and Strategic plan to curb match-fixing in Asian football. He has served as a member of FIFA's Security and Integrity Committee and from 2007 to 2009 was General Secretary of FIFPro's (the international federation of professional footballers' associations) Asian Division, also encompassing Oceania. He holds a bachelor's degree in law from the University of Glamorgan in Wales, a Master's degree in law from Staffordshire University in England and a Master of Laws (Sports Law) from the University of Melbourne.

Young Ryuel Chung, PhD, teaches sport management at Korea University, where he received the best lecturer award (2013–15). He is a director and paper jury member of the Korean Society for Sport Management (2011–present). He is also a member of the human resources committee for the sports team of the Goyang City, Korea (2013–present). He has published 16 research papers in relation to marketing and human resource management of professional sports organizations. Prior to joining academia, he worked as a pro-athlete agent for five years in Korea and America.

Steven Finocchiaro is a graduate lawyer who holds a Bachelor of Arts (Political Science and International Relations; History) and Juris Doctor from the University of Melbourne. Under the mentorship of the Executive Director of the World Players Association, Brendan Schwab, Steven was formerly a paralegal at Professional Footballers Australia ('PFA'), the players' association for Australian footballers based domestically and overseas, and International Player Relations ('IPR'), a boutique law firm specialising in industrial relations and workplace bargaining consulting. Steven is a member of the Football Federation Victoria ('FFV') Disciplinary Tribunal and is active within the Aeolian-Australian community of Melbourne. He is currently Graduate In-House Counsel at recruitment agency Drake International, specialising in employment law.

Joo Won Jun graduated from Woosung University, Korea, with a major in Physical Education. She competed nationally and internationally for 20 years as a member of the Korean national women's basketball team, which came fourth in the 27th Olympic Games in Sydney and won gold, silver and bronze medals in the Twelfth, Thirteenth and Fourteenth Asian Games respectively. From 2011, she began coaching the Korean national women's team, which in 2014 won a gold medal at the Seventeenth Asian Games. In 2005, she was recognised by the Korean government for her achievements and contribution to sports in Korea. She is currently studying a combined Masters and PhD in Physical Education at Dankook University, Korea. Her area of research is recreation and sports management.

Keiji Kawai, PhD, is a professor of sport law in the Department of Policy Studies at Doshisha University in Kyoto, Japan. His book, *The Legal Status of Professional League Players* (2003), was awarded the Okinaga Prize by the Labor Research Center. He served as visiting researcher at the University of Massachusetts at Amherst from 2007 to 2009. Dr Kawai is the General Secretary of the Japan Sports Law Association, and is also on the arbitrator panel at the Japan Sports Arbitration Agency. He was an executive board member of the Nippon Basketball League ('NBL') from 2013 to 2015. He is currently conducting comparative studies funded by the Japan Society for the Promotion of Science ('JSPS') on labour relations in sport.

Jin Kook Kim graduated from a catholic university with a major in Mathematics. He later completed a Master's and PhD in sports management at Korea University. His contribution to sports in Korea was recognised by an award from the Korean Society for Sport Management. He is qualified as a Sports Management Coordinator and Big Data Business Analyst. He has published over 20 theses in his areas of interest, which include professional sports marketing, sports brand management and sports statistics. He has lectured at Korea University, Namseoul University, Duksun Women's University, Sangji University and Woosong University and is currently a physical education lecturer at Korea University.

Genevieve Lim, BA(Hons)/LLB, GDipLegPrac, LLM, is a legal officer with the Victorian Government where she develops and administers legislation relating to major sporting events. She was a national-level fencer and represented Australia at several international tournaments, and was a Director of Fencing Victoria for five years and the Administration Director for the 2010 Commonwealth Fencing Championships. She is a qualified fencing coach and is passionate about increasing opportunities for participation in sport, protecting the integrity of competitions and promoting good governance in sporting organisations. She has completed an LLM at the University of Melbourne focusing on sports law.

Andrew Menz is the Legal and Corporate Affairs Director for CrownBet and previously held the same position at Betfair Australia. Andrew completed a double degree in Law/Commerce (Accounting) at Monash University and has practiced in the wagering industry since joining Betfair in 2010. Andrew is responsible for managing CrownBet's relationships with regulators and sports controlling bodies and providing assistance in the form of wagering trends and betting records to assist to protect the integrity of Australian sport. Andrew is presently completing his Masters of Laws in the sports law programme at the University of Melbourne.

James Moller is a Financial Analyst with the Victoria Police Sporting Integrity Intelligence Unit ('SIIU'). James is a qualified accountant who has previously worked as a Finance Manager in the university sector, as well as delivering and auditing a number of grant funding programmes with a Federal Government department. His current role focuses on the analysis of betting information in relation to Victoria Police operations and the assessment and analysis of a range of issues relating to organised crime and the integrity of professional sport in Australia.

Kieran Murnane is a Detective Sergeant at the Victoria Police Sporting Integrity Intelligence Unit. Kieran has been a police officer for 17 years, having previously worked general duties in the western suburbs, divisional criminal investigation duties, as well as taskforces targeting middle-eastern organised crime and outlaw motorcycle gangs. Kieran leads the sport integrity team and has successfully investigated soccer and tennis match-fixing and recently completed a successful harness race-fixing investigation.

Hayden Opie is a Senior Fellow at the Melbourne Law School where he established and led the teaching of sports law from 1987 to 2017. He has taught and researched in all areas of sports law and is recognised internationally for his work in the field. He now concentrates on sports integrity and has extensive experience in anti-doping, having served as a legal member of the Australian government's Anti-Doping Rule Violation Panel from 2010 to 2015. Hayden was a Main Contributor to the 2014 Sorbonne-ICSS report, *Fighting against the Manipulation of Sports Competitions*. He is the founding President of the Australian and New Zealand Sports Law Association and is a member of the Court of Arbitration for Sport.

Catherine Ordway is a Senior Consultant (Sports Law) with Snedden Hall and Gallop Lawyers and a Senior Fellow at the Melbourne Law School where she teaches *Sports Integrity and Investigations* with Hayden Opie. Catherine is an Australian lawyer and has a Graduate Diploma in Investigations Management. She has extensive experience in international anti-doping administration, is a sought-after media commentator, and has served on numerous ethics and anti-doping committees in Australia and internationally. Currently writing her PhD thesis, Catherine has presented and published widely on sports integrity topics, and serves on various editorial boards.

Ji Hoon Park is an attorney-at-law and member of the Korean Bar Association. He has defended professional athletes in numerous civil and criminal cases and has a deep understanding of sports law and sports sociology. He was a semi-professional baseball player at Seoul National University. As a member of the Sports Culture Institute, he has designed and participated in numerous seminars and symposiums regarding sport law and culture. He is also an in-house counsel for the Korean Sport and Olympic Committee ('KOC') (2013–present). He has published a translation of *The Legal Status of Professional League Players* from Japanese into Korean.

Brendan Schwab, an Australian lawyer, is the Executive Director of the World Players Association, the Swiss-based global collective of 85,000 professional athletes through major player associations including the Fédération Internationale des Associations Footballeurs Professionnels ('FIFPro'), the Federation of International Cricketers' Associations, the International Rugby Players' Association, EU Athletes, the US National Basketball Players Association, the US National Football League Players Association, the National Hockey League Players Association (US and Canada), the Japanese Professional Baseball Players Association and the Australian Athletes' Alliance ('AAA'). He has 25 years' experience in the collective representation of professional athletes with a large part of that dedicated to Asia. He is a former long-serving Chairman of FIFPro Division Asia/Oceania and FIFPro Board member and Vice President. He is also a former General Secretary of the AAA and Chief Executive of Professional Footballers Australia.

Jess (Hee Sung) Shin completed a Juris Doctor at Melbourne Law School in 2016, and worked as a research assistant at its Asian Law Centre. She holds a Bachelor of Arts majoring in Criminology and Japanese, also from the University of Melbourne.

David Skene is the Head of Legal for Betfair Australia. Before joining Betfair Australia in August 2015, David worked as a regulatory lawyer in a commercial law firm for ten years, during which time he acted for Commonwealth and State regulators and highly regulated entities. He is now responsible for ensuring that Betfair Australia complies with its statutory obligations and its integrity agreements with racing and sports controlling bodies, working closely with Betfair Australia's regulator, law enforcement agencies and racing and sports controlling bodies to ensure that the integrity of Betfair Australia's betting markets is maintained.

Stacey Steele leads the Japanese and Korean Programs at the Asian Law Centre, Melbourne Law School where she has hosted many Japanese and Korean judges, prosecutors and court clerks. Her research interests include the Japanese legal system, law reform, insolvency law in the Asia-Pacific, legal education and banking law. Her publications include *Legal Education in Asia: Globalisation, Change and Contexts* (2010, Routledge, co-edited with K. Taylor), *Internationalising Japan: Discourse and Practice* (2014, Routledge, co-edited with J. Breaden and C. Stevens) and numerous articles. Stacey holds degrees from the University of Queensland (BA (Jap)), Monash University (MA (Jap)) and the University of Melbourne (LLB (Hons) and LLM (by thesis)). She speaks Japanese and is also a practising lawyer specialising in financial services law.

Sarah (Jin Hyung) Yang completed a Juris Doctor at Melbourne Law School in 2016, and worked as a research assistant at its Asian Law Centre. She holds a Bachelor of Biomedicine, also from the University of Melbourne.

Kee Young Yeun, PhD, is a Professor of Law at Dongguk University in Seoul, Founding President of the Korean Association of Sports and Entertainment Law (1999–2013) and Founding President of the Sport, Entertainment, Media & Tourism Arbitration ('SEMTA') Forum (2014). He has been Vice President of the International Association of Sports Law (IASA) from 2006 and Mediator of the Seoul High Court from 2006. He was Founder and President of the Asia Sports Law

Association ('ASLA') (2005–07). He was also Dean of the College of Law, Dongguk University (1997–2003), President of the Korean Association of Buddhist Professors (2001–05), Chairman of the 2006 World Religious Leaders' Conference in Seoul and Board Member and Arbitrator of the Korea Sports Arbitration Committee (KSAC) (2006–10). He studied Law and Buddhism at Dongguk University in Seoul (LLB, LLM), and received a Dr. jur. (Göttingen). He has written many publications about civil law, product liability, sports law, legal philosophy and Buddhism. He recently published *Framework of Sports Law* (2013, YR Publishing), and edited *New Prospects of Sports Law* (2013, YR Publishing).

Foreword

Professional sport plays a pivotal role in modern society whilst also being a multi-billion-dollar industry. An integral aspect of sport is the uncertainty of the outcome of its matches or competitions. Any threat to this would endanger its credibility and public perception as well as jeopardise its very existence.

Match-fixing poses the main threat to the sanctity of professional sport and, with the advent of new technology coupled with illegal or unregulated sports betting providers, a global menace has emerged.

This book presents legal analysis, comparative evaluation, case studies and empirical findings for practitioners and researchers as well as the numerous stakeholders in sport. It provides a detailed examination of the recent legal strategies employed in this field and their impact on curbing the dangers of match-fixing in professional sport.

Australia, Japan and Korea were chosen as subjects because collectively they are Asian sporting powerhouses, both as competitors and hosts of major international events. All three have hosted the Olympic Games, and Korea and Japan co-hosted the 2002 FIFA World Cup. Korea will also host the Winter Olympic Games in 2018 and Tokyo will host the Summer Olympic Games in 2020.

All three nations are strong performers in the final overall medals tally in the Summer Olympic Games, and Australia is or has been world or continental champion in cricket, both codes of rugby, football and netball, to speak of just a few major sporting disciplines.

This trio is also an interesting blend of legal jurisdictions that take varied approaches to combating match-fixing and betting on sport. While sports betting is akin to an Australian pastime, gambling in general is prohibited under the Japanese Criminal Code. Korea on the other hand, which has faced the most perilous incidents of match-fixing in recent years, has an Act of Parliament to promote and protect the integrity of professional sport in the country.

As good team work is an essential prerequisite to on-field success, it is a similar case in order to defeat match-fixing in sport. Thus, close cooperation between sport governing bodies and both domestic and supranational law enforcement agencies is a must.

There is a wealth of academic, operational and practical knowledge inherent in this book, which is gleaned from leading minds in this sphere of sport, an area that melds together various legal disciplines and jurisdictions. Those practising, teaching or researching into match-fixing in sport are bound to find invaluable material within the following chapters.

Match-Fixing in Sport: Comparative Studies from Australia, Japan, Korea and Beyond is an interesting and insightful addition to the growing corpus of research into this fascinating, dynamic and important segment of sports law.

Sanjeevan C. Balasingam
Director for Asia and Oceania
Fédération Internationale de Football Association
Zurich
May 2017

Acknowledgements

First, we thank Professor Pip Nicholson, Director, Asian Law Centre, Melbourne Law School, who initially suggested that we collaborate on a project involving Australia and Korea around the theme of major sports events. Given recent scandals in these jurisdictions and Japan's imminent hosting of significant international sporting events, we decided to focus on match-fixing in sport in these three jurisdictions.

Our collaboration initially resulted in the *Sports Law and Integrity Workshop* which brought together leading practitioners, industry representatives, lawyers, academics and law enforcement representatives to discuss the issue of match-fixing in Australia, Japan and Korea in February 2015. The Workshop was generously hosted by international law firm K&L Gates at its Melbourne office, and we are particularly grateful for the support of Stephen Meade and Chris Nikou, partners at the firm with a keen interest in the law as it relates to sport. We are also grateful for the contributions at the Workshop of Andrew Godkin and Damien Voltz of the Australian National Integrity in Sport Unit, Jo Setright of Football Federation Australia and Sergeant Philip van Dissel of the Australian Federal Police, in addition to many of the contributors to this volume.

The Workshop was also financially supported by the Australia-Korea Foundation and a MLS-Asia Research Collaboration Grant, enabling us to bring our international guests to Melbourne and provide appropriate language support. We thank Jess Shin, Sarah Yang, Yeon Lee, Shojeeb Alam, Hae Jin Kwon and Soo Kyung Lee for language assistance during the Workshop, and the unwavering support of Kathryn Taylor, Manager, and Ade Suharto, Coordinator, both of the Asian Law Centre, Melbourne Law School.

A further MLS-Asia Research Collaboration Grant supported the translation work required to complete this volume. We fondly recall the task of bringing together such a mix of languages, cultures and professional backgrounds which was described by one of the publisher's reviewers as an 'adventure'. The translation, editorial and communication process has been complex, and extremely rewarding. We could not have undertaken this endeavour without the support of our research associates and Melbourne Law School Juris Doctor students, Jess Shin, Sarah Yang and Jeremy Latcham. Jess Shin was crucial to the production of a number of chapters and our communication with our Korean authors. Sarah Yang provided excellent project management support in addition to her author and research roles. Jeremy Latcham's attention to detail, knowledge of the style guide and commitment to producing a high quality final product kept us sane. We are also grateful for financial support from the MLS International Research Visitors Scheme for Professor Kawai's visit to the Melbourne Law School in 2016 to complete his chapter.

We are grateful for various forms of assistance, guidance and inspiration provided by distinguished international sports administrator Malcolm Speed AO, academic colleagues Judy Bourke, Lloyd Freeburn and Björn Hessert, the staff of the Melbourne Law Library and especially the MLS Academic Research Service, the Victorian Racing Integrity Commissioner Sal Perna, and Sam Walch of Codeware. We also thank Yoko Kushida from the Japanese Para-sports Association who attended the Workshop and introduced us to Yuta Ando. We thank Sandra Pyke, Monash University, who compiled the index with speed and efficiency as always.

Finally, we thank the contributors for their cooperation, patience and intellectually stimulating discussions over the course of this project.

This book is dedicated to children who play sport, especially Stacey's son Charlie. May they play with passion and integrity; without fear or threat of interference.

Stacey Steele and Hayden Opie
May 2017

Notes on style

Currency

Monetary amounts are generally described in this volume in the currency in which the amounts were originally specified for transparency and longevity purposes.

For reference, at the time of writing (May 2017), the following currencies were equivalent to US$1. The monetary amounts referred to in this volume, however, may relate to a period of time with different currency conversion rates than those listed below.

- AU$: 1.346
- €: 0.900
- GB£: 0.768
- KR₩: 1130.360
- JP¥: 111.106

Naming conventions

References to 'Korea' in this volume are to the Republic of Korea, commonly known as South Korea.

All individual names, including Japanese and Korean names, appear with a person's given name first and family name last.

Korean names are generally written according to their common spelling in English (e.g. 'Park', which is transliterated as 'Bak' under the Revised Romanisation of Korean system). The names of people are unitalicised except where within a longer extract of Romanised text (e.g. within the Romanised title of a Korean or Japanese newspaper article in an endnote citation).

Transliterations and translations

In this volume, Korean words are Romanised under the Revised Romanisation of Korean system, and Japanese words are Romanised under the Modified Hepburn Romanisation system. Romanised Korean and Japanese words appear in italics, except as noted below.

Words that are already a normal part of the English lexicon appear according to their regular English usage (e.g. Seoul, sumo), without italics or diacritics. Proper nouns such as the names of organisations appear in the format preferred by the organisation itself.

Specific to Chapter 7 by Yuta Ando, references originally written in Bulgarian, Greek, Mandarin Chinese and Russian have been Romanised according to the Library of Congress (US) Romanisation tables.[1]

Although research on Korean legislation for this volume was conducted by reading the official, Korean-language legislation, translated excerpts from Korean legislation in this volume are primarily direct quotations from the unofficial English translations provided by Korea's Ministry of Government Legislation.[2]

Notes

1 Available online at Library of Congress 2017, *ALA-LC Romanization tables*, www.loc.gov/catdir/cpso/roman.html.
2 Available online at Korea Ministry of Government Legislation, *National Law Information Center*, www.law.go.kr/eng/engMain.do.

Abbreviations

ACIC	Australian Criminal Intelligence Commission
AFC	Asian Football Confederation
AFL	Australian Football League
AFP	Australian Federal Police
AML/CTF Act	*Anti-Money Laundering and Counter-Terrorism Financing Act 2006* (Cth)
ARU	Australian Rugby Union
ASADA	Australian Sports Anti-Doping Authority
AUSTRAC	Australian Transaction Reports and Analysis Centre
CA	Cricket Australia
CAS	Court of Arbitration for Sport
Con Ops	Concepts of Operations
FFA	Football Federation Australia
FIFA	Fédération Internationale de Football Association
GR Act	*Gambling Regulation Act 2003* (Vic)
HRV	Harness Racing Victoria
ICC	International Cricket Council
ICSS	International Centre for Sport Security
IGA	*Interactive Gambling Act 2001* (Cth)
IOC	International Olympic Committee
IP	Internet Protocol
JOC	Japan Olympic Committee
JSA	Japan Sports Agency
JSC	Japan Sport Council
MACC	Malaysian Anti-Corruption Commission
MACC	*Malaysian Anti-Corruption Commission Act 2009*
MEXT	Ministry of Education, Culture, Sports, Science and Technology (Japan)
MGA	Malta Gaming Authority
MoU	Memoranda of Understanding
MSE 2015	major sporting events 2015
NBL	National Basketball League (Australia)

NISU	National Integrity in Sport Unit (Australia)
NPB	Nippon Professional Baseball (Japan)
NRL	National Rugby League (Australia)
NSWLRC	New South Wales Law Reform Commission
ORIC	Office of the Racing Integrity Commissioner (Victoria)
POI	persons of interest
SCBs	sport controlling bodies
SIIU	Victoria Police Sporting Integrity Intelligence Unit
TA	Tennis Australia
TIU	Tennis Integrity Unit, International Tennis Federation
UEFA	Union of European Football Associations
VPL	Victorian Premier League

Part I

Conceptualising match-fixing

Chapter 1

Comparing approaches to match-fixing in sport

Revisiting perceptions and definitions

Hayden Opie and Stacey Steele

Introduction: Australia, Japan and Korea in regional and international match-fixing landscapes

The chapters in this volume analyse match-fixing in sport in Australia, Japan, Korea and beyond. Match-fixing may be described as the manipulation of an outcome or contingency of a sports competition by improper means; but there is no universally accepted definition, as this volume demonstrates.[1] The volume emphasises legal and regulatory responses to the threats that match-fixing presents. It also includes important perspectives from players,[2] the betting industry,[3] law enforcement[4] and prosecution authorities.[5] The fight against match-fixing beyond Australia, Japan and Korea is examined through analysis of international typologies for criminalising match-fixing and regulating sports betting,[6] as well as exploring the scope for the *Council of Europe Convention on the Manipulation of Sports Competitions* ('*Convention*')[7] to serve as a model for reform.[8] In recognition of the dynamic environment of match-fixing in the Asian region and beyond, the volume concludes with analysis of some potential future challenges, including whether attributes such as gender have an influence on match-fixing, and the emergence of e-sports which have a strong following among younger generations, particularly in Asian jurisdictions such as Korea.[9]

The approach adopted in this volume of combining analysis of three jurisdictions and providing individual, in-depth chapters devoted to each jurisdiction, helps to avoid the pitfalls of a bilateral or side-by-side examination which tends to highlight one or the other jurisdiction as an outlier on any given issue. As the chapters in this volume show, there are many commonalities between the issues faced in these jurisdictions. Australia, Japan and Korea are democracies with modern, free market economies. Each nation has well organised professional sports leagues, successfully hosts major international sports competitions and has a population that enthusiastically follows national and international sport. Gambling – sports betting in particular – varies in popularity across the three nations, and the extent to which betting on sports is lawful in each of them differs considerably. In recent years, both Australia and Korea have enacted laws to specifically criminalise match-fixing in response to growing international concern and domestic match-fixing scandals. Japan remains more cautious about enacting laws which target match-fixing across a wide range of sports and is less touched by match-fixing scandals than Australia and Korea. Further, the tradition in sumo of *ninjō*, or losing compassionately, helps to support the argument that match-fixing should remain the purview of sporting authorities and not law enforcement, as suggested by Kawai in this volume.[10] This position will continue to come under pressure, however, as Japan prepares to host major international sports events in the men's Rugby World Cup in 2019 and the Olympic and Paralympic Games in 2020. Moreover, recent events suggest that Japan and Japanese players are not immune to match-fixing scandals.[11]

This chapter places the responses of Australia, Japan and Korea within global debates, and regional and international contexts. In particular, the absence of a generally accepted definition of match-fixing at an international level, and even within national jurisdictions such as Australia, is problematic for transnational sports competitions played under the criminal and other laws and regulations of various jurisdictions. The absence of an accepted definition also raises concerns due to the lack of consistency in the rules of sport promulgated by different sport governing bodies at international and national levels. The effectiveness of even the best national frameworks will continue to be impaired unless they are adapted to international mechanisms which help to build consensus about what it means to fix a match. The chapter also considers the roles of key fixers, a number of whom operate from bases in Asia, reflecting the focus of this volume on betting-related match-fixing.[12] Internet-based sports betting makes betting with operators located outside of Australia, Japan and Korea possible; such betting is illegal within all three jurisdictions and presents difficulties for detection and enforcement. Modern communications also enable those who organise match-fixing to operate internationally which forces law enforcement agencies to seek the assistance of their counterparts in other jurisdictions to gather evidence and extradite suspects.

What is match-fixing?

Conceptualising match-fixing: some thoughts on terminology and contexts

This section examines some colloquial meanings of 'match-fixing' and the types of actors which may be involved in fixing. The act of fixing may determine (1) who wins or loses a sporting competition or (2) the happening of a contingency within a sporting competition. Depending on the context, the term 'match-fixing' may encompass both or only the former. The term 'spot-fixing' is often used to describe the fixing of contingencies and can include 'point shaving' which describes fixing the winning margin – a margin smaller than would otherwise be possible. Spot-fixing may also include 'the time and rate of scoring, the score at certain times, the occurrence of particular events such as who scores first [and] the number of penalties awarded'.[13] The use of the term 'match-fixing' is deeply entrenched and, along with spot-fixing, is used in this volume. Even the term 'match-fixing' itself is not universally accepted or used, however. The term 'manipulation of sports competitions' is used, but not necessarily exclusively, in the *Convention* and some policy documents[14] and research documents[15] emanating from Europe, for example.

Match-fixing's greatest threat to the integrity of sport occurs when it is linked to betting.[16] Some commentators argue that the contemporary increase in fixing is driven by developments in the betting industry.[17] Perhaps the most common form of match-fixing is deliberate underperformance by one or more players in a sporting competition. Fixing may also be committed, however, by an umpire, referee, judge or other match official who unfairly favours a player or team. In an extraordinary incident in England, for example, a security guard was bribed to facilitate turning off the lights for a night game of football, forcing it to be abandoned, with the intention of corrupting illegal betting markets in Malaysia.[18] The people who engage in such behaviour are almost universally referred to as 'fixers'.

Intermediaries are one step removed from fixers. Intermediaries arrange for players or other fixers to commit the fix, including by obtaining a fixer's willingness to participate, conveying instructions and making payment. They may also place bets on behalf of other people involved in the fix. Various terms describe these intermediaries including 'brokers' in Korea (see Yeun and others in this volume), 'runners' in South-East Asia and other places[19] and 'facilitators' in Australian legislation (see Opie and Lim in this volume). In many places, these intermediaries are also referred to simply as 'fixers'.

A third and overarching role is filled by those people who conceive and plan the fix. These people have connections to those players (and others) who can commit the fix or to people in the sport who can act as the intermediaries to facilitate it. This third group will also have the connections necessary to arrange finance for the fix. Yeun in this volume refers to such people as 'financiers'. They are also commonly called fixers,[20] but are distinguished by the higher level in the fix at which they operate from other so-called fixers. People in this group may be protected by organised crime or corrupt government officials, or even be members of organised crime gangs themselves.[21] Betting operators (bookmakers) may also be involved in conceiving and planning a fix, although as a general matter betting operators are more likely to be victims of a successful fix.[22]

A fourth role may be filled by the financers of the fix. Usually, they will be a wealthy gambler, a betting syndicate or organised crime gang.[23] The prospect of terrorist groups organising and financing match-fixing and associated betting to fund their activities has been recognised too.[24] Financiers stand to gain the greatest monetary rewards from fixes and are usually the least visible party involved.

These various typical roles for participants in match-fixing may be further divided for complex fixes or they may be combined. The third and fourth roles identified above, for example, are sometimes combined in Korea as suggested by Yeun and Park in this volume. Further, so called lone-wolf players or match officials may bet on game results or contingencies which they fix by their own actions without any involvement of others.[25]

The motivations for engaging in fixing by each type of participant and even amongst certain types of participants are numerous and varied. Money is a key motivation, but rarely the only one, and financial gain does not explain why some people and sports appear to be more susceptible than others.[26] Lower levels of competition are generally recognised as more attractive to fixers than high-level events which are likely to be subject to closer scrutiny from law enforcement and regulators.[27] Furthermore, for the often poorly paid athletes who participate in these competitions a bribe may be less easy to resist. The significance of the fix in a sporting sense can also be an important factor in the eyes of players. Fixes which will not affect overall outcomes such as so-called dead rubbers in a tournament[28] or numerous methods of spot-fixing, especially points shaving, may be more acceptable to players.[29] The inability of vulnerable players to resist pressure from unscrupulous employers and promoters, as highlighted by Schwab and Finocchiaro in this volume, may be an influential factor too. Ordway in this volume argues that match-fixing is also being driven more recently by the desire of organised crime gangs and terrorists to launder money and reap easy profits. Factors such as gender are also largely unexplored in the literature, as highlighted by Steele and Opie in the conclusion to this volume.

International harmonisation: towards a common definition of match-fixing?

Despite widespread agreement that match-fixing is wrong, there is no settled global definition of match-fixing or consensus on penalties. This uncertainty may be largely traced to the circumstance that conduct, even intentional, may not be considered wrong if motivated by a strategic or tactical sporting reason.[30] A further factor is that some actions may arguably be considered wrong in a sporting sense, but may not warrant the imposition of criminal responsibility.[31] The search for an agreed definition is also complicated by the tension between the desire to establish broad policy positions which can attract support and the need for clarity and precision in the wording of criminal laws and sport disciplinary rules.

There are various definitions of match-fixing which incorporate varying standards involving impropriety, dishonesty, negative impact on integrity, undue advantage and unpredictability. Commentators have offered various suggestions including:

> improperly influencing the outcome or any dimension of a sports event for financial or personal benefit;[32]

and

> a dishonest activity by participants, team officials, match officials or other interested parties to ensure a specific outcome in a particular sporting match or event for competitive advantage and/or financial gain which negatively impacts on the integrity of sport.[33]

The *Convention* (art 3.4) says that 'manipulation of sports competitions':

> means an intentional arrangement, act or omission aimed at an improper alteration of the result or the course of a sports competition in order to remove all or part of the unpredictable nature of the aforementioned sports competition with a view to obtaining an undue advantage for oneself or for others.

There is scope for more analysis of how these standards might apply to commonly encountered circumstances in sport where players and teams are inclined to lose intentionally, not to use their maximum endeavours at all times or act in a manner that might involve 'sharp practice' or be considered 'unsporting'.[34]

In June 2016, the United Nations Office on Drugs and Crime and the International Olympic Committee issued *Model Criminal Law Provisions for the Prosecution of Competition Manipulation*.[35] This model offers a further framework for harmonisation and uses the *Convention* as a basis for its recommendations. The recommendation that the specific 'match-fixing offence be independent from betting on a sports event or competition which is fixed' is of particular relevance to Australia and Japan.[36] The match-fixing laws of Australia and Japan are confined to sports where betting is permitted, whereas recent amendments to match-fixing laws in Korea mean that there are offences which apply to all registered sports irrespective of whether they are subject to betting.[37] The limits to the potential harmonisation of laws and definitions relating to match-fixing through the adoption of the *Convention* model are considered further in this volume by Ando and Steele and Opie.

Sporting powerhouses in Asia: why Australia, Japan and Korea?

Beyond Australia, Japan and Korea: wider regional perceptions and challenges

In the world of sports match-fixing many roads lead to Asia, as that region is nebulously and broadly defined.[38] Depending on the political, social, historical, legal and economic context under consideration, Asia may be said to cover a large geographic area stretching from the Middle East to Japan. References to Asia-Pacific are similarly difficult to define comprehensively. Even in sport, there is significant fluidity in the international grouping of member states. The Olympic Movement recognises five continental groups: Africa, the Americas, Asia, Europe and Oceania (which includes Australia).[39] Sporting activities under the oversight of the Olympic Council of Asia now include nations from the Oceania continental region in some instances, however.[40] The membership of the Asian Football Confederation provides another key sporting representation of Asia and encompasses 47 countries from Lebanon in the west to Guam in the east, and from Mongolia in the north to Australia in the south.[41] Based on this definition, the most internationally notorious fixers,[42] immense illegal sports betting markets,[43] large-scale fixes severely damaging to the attractiveness of sporting competitions,[44] and extensive betting-related money-laundering[45] have all resided and occurred in the Asian landscape. Australia, Japan and Korea's standing as Asian sporting powerhouses[46] risks damage from the unfavourable worldwide reputation that Asia, taken as a monolithic whole, has developed for match-fixing.

This volume contributes to a more nuanced understanding of efforts to combat match-fixing in Australia, Japan and Korea, but also suggests that there is a role for these three nations in the region in reversing any undesirable reputation and in protecting their own sporting competitions from regional corrupting influences. Other jurisdictions in Asia, including China and India, are relevant to the fight against match-fixing, but to date they have been a focus of research because of the problems arising from those jurisdictions, not because of their potential to offer solutions. As sporting powerhouses in Asia, Australia, Japan and Korea are among the nations in the region best equipped to address the challenges presented by match-fixing. Australia is considered a leader in this area of regulation and law enforcement, and its experiences may provide ideas for other jurisdictions. Korea is also advancing its measures to combat match-fixing due to its experiences of match-fixing scandals, and may also provide a model. Moreover, Japan and Korea are about to host major international events which are also focusing global efforts on the measures that they have taken, or will take, to align themselves with global commitments in light of domestic considerations and contexts. Accordingly, a goal of the project which led to this volume was to increase awareness amongst law enforcement and reformers of the different perspectives, approaches and contexts in each of Australia, Japan and Korea for combating match-fixing.

Sporting powerhouses focusing on combating match-fixing

In addition to their position of sporting leadership, the three jurisdictions are also of interest because of the different approaches that each has taken to combat match-fixing. In recent years both Australia and Korea have enacted new wide-reaching legislation to criminalise match-fixing and pursued various administrative policies aimed to positively discourage the practice in their domestic sports competitions. Japan has long-standing match-fixing offences, but only in regard to those few sports on which gambling is permitted. Japan is being urged to contemplate policies to combat match-fixing in a wider range of sports in light of its upcoming international commitments.

The various approaches reflect important considerations such as different histories, cultures, sporting and betting norms, social organisation, and political and legal institutions, as highlighted by the chapters in this volume. Despite these factors, there is a need for government, betting operators, law enforcement and sports bodies in the three jurisdictions to work together closely to combat match-fixing. Not only are the three nations confronting a common or similar foe, as discussed further below, there is a strong mutual interest in maintaining the integrity of the sporting contests in which they compete against one another or in which their nationals participate. In football, for instance, national men's and women's teams from Australia, Japan and Korea regularly play against each other in open and age competitions organised by the Fédération Internationale de Football Association and the Asian Football Confederation. Leading professional league teams from the three nations encounter each other in the AFC Champions League and individual professional players participate not only in each other nation's domestic leagues but also across the region.

This increasing interconnectedness highlights the need for mutual understanding and cooperation among Australia, Japan, Korea and other jurisdictions in the region in relation to the approach of others to combating the causes of match-fixing, whether those causes are common or different. Moreover, an understanding of the nature and reach of relevant criminal law and sporting offences, the potential for criminal intelligence gathering and sharing, investigation and prosecution measures, and levels of punishment and deterrence, is also needed to successfully combat match-fixing. The *Convention* identifies three key actors in efforts to promote mutual understanding and cooperation: public authorities (including law enforcement bodies), sports organisations (including competition organisers) and betting operators.[47] This volume contributes to the promotion of such understanding and cooperation, and includes consideration of each of these actors.

Countermeasures in Australia, Japan and Korea compared

The comparative position of Australia, Japan and Korea relative to steps taken to combat match-fixing remains relatively unchanged since a key report by Sorbonne and the International Centre for Sport Security (ICSS) published in 2014 – *Protecting the integrity of sport competition: the last bet for modern sport* ('*ICSS report*')[48] – despite significant developments over the last three years in each jurisdiction. The *ICSS report* classifies and compares countries according to the priority given to sports integrity across a matrix. The matrix is created by a vertical axis along which countries are ranked from strong to weak in terms of the fight against illegal betting, and a horizontal axis along which countries are classified from strong to weak in relation to prioritisation of sports integrity. Australia, Japan and Korea received different classifications, reflecting the fertile ground for comparison between these jurisdictions as further evidenced by this volume.[49]

Australia may still typically be categorised as a 'pioneer' country with 'strict regulations concerning sports bets' and a jurisdiction which protects 'sport integrity in the most effective manner', as it was described in the *ICSS report.*[50] As the chapters by Menz and Skene, Murnane and Moller, Ordway, and Opie and Lim in this volume demonstrate, Australia's governments, sporting organisations, betting operators and regulators, and law enforcement at all levels take the threat of match-fixing seriously, whether they be driven by profit, policy or other goals. Even Australia is not immune from match-fixing scandals, however. The conviction in 2016 of a tennis player for match-fixing at an International Tennis Federation (ITF) Futures tournament[51] and the guilty plea in 2017 of the 18-year-old Australian national boys' tennis champion to fixing an Association of Tennis Professionals (ATP) Challenger event[52] brought match-fixing to the attention of the sporting and general community again. Australia's future challenge is the further harmonisation of its approach to match-fixing across federal borders, and deciding the extent to which it will align itself with an international regime largely driven by European-designed instruments to date.

Japan and Australia sit far apart on the continuum created by the ICSS' matrix, especially in relation to prioritisation of sports integrity. Japan may still be described, as it was in 2014 by the ICSS, as not taking the 'dangers posed by illegal bets' into account and ignoring the risks affecting sports. Ando's chapter highlights the lack of a sense of urgency in relation to match-fixing in Japan at the time of writing, and Kawai's chapter helps to explain why. Japan, however, now has an international imperative to address match-fixing in the form of teams competing in regional competitions based outside of Japan, and Japan's hosting of the 2019 Rugby World Cup and 2020 Tokyo Olympic and Paralympic Games, as discussed by Steele and Opie in this volume. Yet Japan remains largely unperturbed by the dangers posed by match-fixing and hostile to further legalisation of sports betting which may assist better regulation in this area. To date, Japan has avoided a major match-fixing scandal outside of sumo, in contrast to Australia and Korea as highlighted by Moller and Murnane and Park respectively in this volume. This lack of sensational public scandal is a key explanation for Japan's complacency, but cross-border developments and technology surrounding sport and betting in the twenty-first century require a re-examination of long-held traditional values and beliefs highlighted by Kawai, as Ando argues in this volume.

Korea's approach to match-fixing sits somewhere between that of Australia and Japan, according to the ICSS' classification. Korea is noted in the *ICSS report* as 'generally' combating 'illegal bets' and attempting to 'preserve' sports integrity. Of the three jurisdictions, Korea has experienced the most serious and frequent public match-fixing scandals. Korea also has the worst ranking (52nd out of 176) on Transparency International's Corruption Perception Index 2016 when compared with Australia (13th) and Japan (20th), suggesting that on this rough measure Korea is also generally perceived as more corrupt than the other two jurisdictions.[53]

Recent government-sponsored legislative and operational reforms in Korea suggest, however, that Korea is taking match-fixing and integrity in sport ever more seriously, and has moved significantly closer to Australia in terms of its position on the ICSS' matrix since 2014. This conclusion is supported by the analysis of Korea's legal system and prosecutorial system provided respectively by Yeun and Steele, Shin and Yang in this volume. The shortcomings of the Korean system are also highlighted in this volume, however, with a thorough investigation of Korean judicial decisions between 2011 and 2013 by Park. Park suggests that whilst courts take match-fixing seriously and a body of jurisprudence around match-fixing is being developed, there are still relatively unexplored areas, including the culpability of players who match-fix in physically and psychologically threatening environments. Moreover, there are serious concerns for the health and safety of players as demonstrated by Park. Chung, Jun and Kim's survey of player perceptions of match-fixing in Korea suggests that players want more education and the level of understanding of match-fixing differs depending on many factors, including the sport in question, and scandals continue to come to light. Schwab and Finocchiaro's analysis in this volume also highlights the predicament of players who are largely painted as treacherous wrong-doers by sports organisations, media and criminal justice systems.

Role of key fixers: who are they and how do they work?

Australia, Japan and Korea are exposed not only to the risk of homegrown match-fixing, but also to the prospect of fixing activity in their jurisdictions orchestrated by fixers based in other countries in the Asian region or elsewhere. Australia's sporting competitions, for example, have been targeted by people who conceive and plan fixes from abroad. The implementation of countermeasures by law enforcement and sports regulators requires an understanding and monitoring of potential fixers no matter where they are located. Significantly for Australia, Japan and Korea as sporting powerhouses in Asia, however, is that a number of influential fixers operate and are based in the Asian region. Examples from law enforcement and other sources confirm that fixers located in Asia have been involved with fixes in other regions of the world, especially in Europe.[54]

Three Singaporean fixers are notorious in relation to football, for example.[55] They are known as the 'Kelong Kings' meaning 'kings of cheating'.[56] Menz and Skene in this volume highlight a major scandal in football in the cross-border league between Malaysia and Singapore during the early 1990s. Rajendran 'Pal' Kurusamy from Singapore is alleged to have been responsible for conceiving and planning much of the fixing in that league.[57] Europol's announcement in February 2013 of the suspected fixing of over 380 European professional football matches described the ringleaders behind the criminal group alleged to be responsible for the fixes as being 'of Asian origin'.[58] Another of the Kelong Kings, Dan Tan Seet Eng, is alleged to be behind many of these European fixes.[59] The third Kelong King, Wilson Raj Perumal,[60] is suspected of having conceived and planned the Southern Stars' match-fixing scandal in Australia which is discussed by Murnane and Moller in this volume. There are also recent claims that Perumal may have organised fixes involving other Australian football matches around the same time.[61]

Although Kurusamy[62] and Dan Tan[63] are currently in custody in Singapore and Perumal lives in Hungary,[64] their exploits demonstrate that they, and others like them, are sufficiently skilful and resourced to target sports competitions in any of Australia, Japan and Korea. Japanese football referees sent to Thailand to officiate at the 2012 Thai Football Association Cup Final, for example, reported an attempt to bribe them to favour one team in the game.[65] Awareness of match-fixing in football and understanding of the methods of operation of match-fixers has been greatly advanced by the seminal and ongoing investigative studies and commentary undertaken by Hill.[66] Further, FIFPro now includes the issue of match-fixing in its player surveys, as highlighted by Schwab and Finocchiaro in this volume.

Cricket is another popular sport in South Asia and Australia, and ranks second after football as susceptible to match-fixing based on publicly available reports.[67] Dawood Ibrahim Kaskar is the reputed leader of the organised crime gang 'D Company' and is alleged to be involved with match-fixing in cricket in South Asia[68] and is on INTERPOL's wanted list.[69] Understanding of Indian illegal sports betting markets and the methods of operation of match-fixers in cricket in India and beyond has been significantly advanced by the investigative study of Hawkins.[70] The prospect of Australian cricket players becoming embroiled in match-fixing activities in South Asia was demonstrated by the involvement of two leading national team players in a money-for-inside information deal with a bookmaker in Sri Lanka as far back as 1994.[71]

As these examples from football and cricket demonstrate, players and officials from Australia, Japan and Korea are at risk, particularly when travelling to other countries, and need to be appropriately educated, supported and monitored to avoid contacts in person or electronically with fixers in those jurisdictions, in addition to when at home.

Conclusion

As sporting powerhouses in Asia, Australia, Japan and Korea are positioned to advance efforts to counter match-fixing at home, within the region and beyond. Nonetheless, each jurisdiction is at a different stage in its development of measures to combat match-fixing reflecting many different factors, including experiences of match-fixing scandals, existing administrative, institutional and legal frameworks, and cultural, historical and economic circumstances. Common to all jurisdictions are the challenges occasioned by the internationalisation and rapid expansion of betting markets which increase the prospect of involvement by the corrupting influences of international match-fixers, organised crime networks and terrorists. Responses to these challenges are hindered, however, by the different terminology used to describe match-fixing activities and actors, despite international efforts aimed to achieve greater harmonisation of match-fixing laws and regulations.

This volume contributes to these debates by providing in-depth analysis of aspects of each jurisdiction's effort to combat match-fixing, as well as companion chapters designed to highlight contemporary issues such as law enforcement, prevention and player participation in solutions to this global problem. Each chapter makes its own contribution, but the volume is designed to be read as a whole with each chapter complementing others. This volume gives further context to the chapters by dividing them into four parts which reflect the multi-faceted nature of the challenges presented by match-fixing. Part I consists of two chapters, including this introductory chapter, which start to conceptualise match-fixing. It introduces the responses of Australia, Japan and Korea to match-fixing and analyses some foundational concepts and structures, including the nature and definition of match-fixing and the regulation of betting markets. Part II consists of five chapters and examines the substantive legal and regulatory responses of each of Australia, Japan and Korea to match-fixing and includes analysis of legislation, government policies and examples of prosecutions. These responses are placed in an international context by consideration of typologies of match-fixing and betting laws from other countries as well as exploring the scope for the *Convention* to serve as a model for reform. In five chapters, Part III explores match-fixing from the perspective of prevention and enforcement, including analysis of the roles and expectations of players. The enforcement of match-fixing laws by police and regulatory bodies in Australia, and by prosecutors in Korea, is also examined. Part IV contains a concluding chapter, which is not simply a traditional summary of the volume's findings. It extends the analyses in the chapters of this volume by reflecting on the processes of change necessary to combat match-fixing and investigating the connection between gender and match-fixing. The chapter concludes by highlighting emerging issues for law enforcement and regulators, including e-sports and cross-border leagues, and suggesting areas for future research.

Notes

1 The meaning of match-fixing is discussed below.
2 See Schwab and Finocchiaro, and Chung, Jun and Kim in this volume.
3 See Menz and Skene in this volume.
4 See Murnane and Moller, and Ordway in this volume.
5 See Murnane and Moller, and Steele, Shin and Yang in this volume.
6 See Menz and Skene, and Ando in this volume.
7 *Council of Europe Convention on the Manipulation of Sports Competitions*, opened for signature 18 September 2014, CETS no. 215 (not yet in force). The *Convention* is also known as the treaty of *Magglingen* (in German) or *Macolin* (in French), after the place of its conclusion in Switzerland.
8 See Ando in this volume on the *Council of Europe Convention on the Manipulation of Sports Competitions*, opened for signature 18 September 2014, CETS no. 215 (not yet in force).
9 See Steele and Opie in this volume.
10 See also the discussion of debates about criminalising doping in Japan in Steele and Opie in this volume.
11 See Steele and Opie in this volume for a discussion of recent events in Japan, including reform processes and restructuring of the sports bureaucratic apparatus. See also Ando and Kawai in this volume on Japan.
12 C.f. Holden, J.T. and Rodenberg, R.M., 2017, 'Lone-wolf match-fixing: global policy considerations', *International Journal of Sport Policy and Politics*, vol. 9, no. 1, pp. 137–151.
13 Ordway, C. and Opie, H., 2017, 'Integrity and corruption in sport', in Schulenkorf, N. and Frawley, S. (eds.), *Critical issues in global sport management*, Routledge, pp. 38–63, p. 43.
14 United Nations Office on Drugs and Crime and International Olympic Committee 2016, *Model criminal law provisions for the prosecution of competition manipulation*, www.unodc.org/documents/corruption/Publications/UNODC-IOC_Model_Criminal_Law_Provisions_for_the_Prosecution_of_Competition_

Manipulation_Booklet.pdf. Even this document makes use of 'match-fixing' and acknowledges the interchangeability of terms: at p. 6.

15 International Centre for Sport Security and University Paris 1 Panthéon-Sorbonne 2014, *Protecting the integrity of sport competition: the last bet for modern sport*, May, www.theicss.org/wp-content/themes/icss-corp/pdf/SIF14/Sorbonne-ICSS%20Report%20Executive%20Summary_WEB.pdf?lbisphpreq=1.

16 Ibid., p. 37.

17 Forrest, D., 2013, 'Match fixing: an economics perspective', in Haberfeld, M.R. and Sheehan, D., (eds.), *Match-fixing in international sports*, Springer, pp. 177–197, p. 177. See also Ando in this volume.

18 Chaudray, V. and Gregoriadis, L., 1999, 'Floodlights scam to beat bookies' *Guardian*, 21 August, www.theguardian.com/uk/1999/aug/21/linusgregoriadis.vivekchaudhary1.

19 Yusof, Z.M., 2014, *Foul! The inside story of Singapore match fixers*, Straits Times Press.

20 See, e.g. Hawkins, E., 2012, *Bookie gambler fixer spy: a journey to the heart of cricket's underworld*, Bloomsbury.

21 See, e.g. Yusof, above n. 19.

22 See, e.g. Zaman, I., Sharmin, R. and Alam, M.R., 2016, 'Cricket in Bangladesh: challenges of governance and match-fixing', in *Transparency international, global corruption report*, Routledge, pp. 242–249, p. 244.

23 On usual methods of financing, see International Centre for Sport Security and University Paris 1 Panthéon-Sorbonne, above n. 15, p. 5.

24 Yusof, Z.M., 2016, 'Terror networks target sports betting' *The New Paper*, 8 November, www.tnp.sg/news/singapore/terror-networks-target-sports-betting.

25 Holden and Rodenberg, above n. 12.

26 Carpenter, K., 2012, 'Match-fixing – the biggest threat to sport in the 21st century?', *Sweet and Maxwell's International Sports Law Review* Issue 2, pp. 13–24, pp. 16–17.

27 Nonetheless, it has been suggested that the fixing of men's World Cup football and cricket matches might have occurred: Hill, D., 2008, *The fix: soccer and organized crime*, McClelland and Stewart; Hawkins, above n. 20.

28 Carpenter, above n. 26, p. 17.

29 See, e.g. Opie, H., 2009, 'Survey: a global perspective on the most important cases affecting the sports industry', *Villanova Sports and Entertainment Law Journal*, vol. 16, no. 1, pp. 99–122, pp. 100–101. The heavily favoured Vietnamese football team defeated Myanmar only 1–0 in the South-East Asian Games in 2005 – the conspiring players who were bribed to point-shave 'saw nothing wrong with the scheme as long as their team won' at p. 101.

30 Ordway and Opie, above n. 13, p. 43.

31 See also Opie and Lim in this volume.

32 Heron, M. and Jiang, C., 2010, 'The gathering storm – organised crime and sports corruption', *Australian and New Zealand Sports Law Journal*, vol. 5, no. 1, pp. 99–118, p. 99.

33 Carpenter, K., 2013, 'Global match-fixing and the United States' role in upholding sporting integrity', *Berkeley Journal of Entertainment and Sports Law*, vol. 2, pp. 214–229, p. 215.

34 For a brief discussion of some of these terms, see Council of Europe 2014, *Explanatory report to the Council of Europe Convention on the Manipulation of Sports Competitions*, 18 September, pp. 9, 21, https://rm.coe.int/16800d383f.

35 United Nations Office on Drugs and Crime and International Olympic Committee, above n. 14.

36 Ibid., p. 18.

37 See Opie and Lim, Kawai, and Yeun in this volume.

38 On the difficulty of defining Asia, including for the purposes of a multi-jurisdictional comparison such as this volume, see Steele, S. and Taylor, K., 2010, 'Introduction: globalisation, change and contexts', in Steele, S. and Taylor, K. (eds.), *Legal education in Asia: globalisation, change and contexts*, Routledge, pp. 3–19, pp. 6–7.

39 Association of National Olympic Committees, *Continental associations*, www.acnolympic.org/olympic-movement-contacts/continental-associations/.

40 See, e.g. Linden, J., 2014, 'Australia "interested" in joining Asian Games', *Reuters*, 23 September, http://in.reuters.com/article/games-asian-oceania-idINKCN0HI08C20140923.

41 For the membership of the AFC, see Asian Football Confederation 2017, *AFC Membership*, www.the-afc.com/member-associationx.

42 See below in this chapter. See also Yusof, above n. 19.

43 See below in this chapter. See also Murdoch, L., 2013, 'Illegal betting could top $500b each year', *The Sydney Morning Herald*, 17 September, www.smh.com.au/national/illegal-betting-could-top-500b-each-year-20130916-2tv6n.html. See also Menz and Skene in this volume.

44 See below in this chapter. See also Menz and Skene in this volume for reports of match-fixing scandals in Malaysia, Singapore and China.

45 See below in this chapter. See also Ordway in this volume.

46 See Balasingam, and Yeun in this volume. China is the fourth powerhouse in Asia. Specifically, at the 2016 Rio Olympic Games, China ranked third, Japan sixth, Korea eighth and Australia 10th: see BBC 2017, *Medal Table*, www.bbc.com/sport/olympics/rio-2016/medals/countries. In the 2014 Asian Games in Incheon, China ranked first, Japan second and Korea third in the medal tally. Australia does not participate in the Asian Games: see The Times of India 2014, *Asian Games 2014 medal tally*, http://timesofindia.indiatimes.com/sports/tournaments/asian-games-2014/medal-tally/ag2014medaltally.cms.

47 See Ando in this volume.

48 International Centre for Sport Security and University Paris 1 Panthéon-Sorbonne, above n. 15.

49 Ibid., pp. 87–88.

50 Ibid.

51 Dole, N., 2016, 'Match-fixing tennis player Nick Lindahl sentenced but avoids jail', *ABC News Sport*, 18 April, www.abc.net.au/news/2016-04-18/tennis-player-sentenced-over-toowoomba-match-fixing/7334146?section=sport. See also Murnane and Moller in this volume.

52 Asher, N., 2017, 'Oliver Anderson, former boys' Australian Open tennis champ, fined $500 for match fixing', *ABC News Sport*, 23 May, www.abc.net.au/news/2017-05-23/junior-boys-tennis-matchfixing-case-oliver-anderson/8549564?section=sport.

53 For the rankings and explanations for each jurisdiction, see Transparency International 2016, *Australia*, www.transparency.org/country/AUS, Transparency International 2016, *Japan*, www.transparency.org/country/JPN and Transparency International 2016, *South Korea*, www.transparency.org/country/KOR.

54 See, e.g. Chaudray, V. and Gregoriadis, L., 1999, 'Floodlights scam to beat bookies' *Guardian*, 21 August, www.theguardian.com/uk/1999/aug/21/linus-gregoriadis.vivekchaudhary1.

55 Yusof, above n. 19.

56 Ibid., p. 17.

57 Ibid., pp. 49–63. Hill describes Kurusamy as 'a genius' in the context of match-fixing: Hill, above n. 27, p. 196.
58 Europol 2013, *Update – results from the largest football match-fixing investigation in Europe*, press release, 6 February, www.europol.europa.eu/newsroom/news/update-results-largest-football-match-fixing-investigation-in-europe. See also Kelso, P., 2013, 'How German police fell on European football's biggest match-fixing scandal by accident', *Telegraph*, 5 February, www.telegraph.co.uk/sport/football/news/9851507/How-German-police-fell-on-European-footballs-biggest-match-fixing-scandal-by-accident.html.
59 Yusof, above n. 19, pp. 46–47.
60 Perumal has co-written an autobiography: Perumal, W.J., Righi, A. and Piano, E., 2014, *Kelong kings*, Invisible Dog.
61 Brown, A., 2016, 'Southern Stars unlikely to be only team in control of match-fixers in 2013', *Sports Integrity Initiative*, 6 July, www.sportsintegrityinitiative.com/southern-stars-unlikely-to-be-only-team-in-control-of-match-fixers-in-2013.
62 Chelvan, V.P., 2015, 'SEA Games football match-fixing: Singaporean gets 4 years jail', *Channel NewsAsia*, 21 September, www.channelnewsasia.com/news/singapore/sea-games-football-match-fixing-singaporean-gets-4-years-jail-8226360.
63 Associated Press 2015, 'Alleged match-fixing mastermind Dan Tan re-arrested in Singapore' *Guardian*, 2 December, www.theguardian.com/football/2015/dec/02/alleged-match-fixing-mastermind-dan-tan-rearrested.
64 Dhanaraj, J., 2016, 'Movie to be made about Singapore match-fixer Wilson Raj: TNP suggests casting choices', *The New Paper*, 29 January, www.tnp.sg/news/singapore-news/movie-be-made-about-singapore-match-fixer-wilson-raj-tnp-suggests-casting.
65 Reuters 2013, 'Thai FA opens investigation into match-fixing claims', *Eurosport*, 19 February, www.eurosport.com/football/international-football/2010/thai-fa-open-investigation-into-match-fixing-claims_sto3629709/story.shtml; 'Japanese soccer trying to stay clear of match-fixing scandal' 2013, *This Week in Gambling*, 11 September, www.thisweekingambling.com/japanese-soccer-trying-to-stay-clear-of-match-fixing-scandal/.
66 Hill, above n. 27. See also Yusof, above n. 19.
67 International Centre for Sport Security and University Paris 1 Panthéon-Sorbonne, above n. 15, p. 4.
68 See, e.g. Hawkins, above n. 20; Chauhani, N., 2013, 'Dawood Ibrahim personally set IPL betting rates: police papers' *The Times of India*, 27 July, http://timesofindia.indiatimes.com/news/Dawood-Ibrahim-personally-set-IPL-betting-rates-Police-papers/articleshow/21379878.cms.
69 INTERPOL 2017, *Kaskar, Dawood Ibrahim*, www.interpol.int/notice/search/wanted/1993-14193.
70 Hawkins, above n. 20.
71 Speed, M.S., 2011, *Sticky wicket*, Harper Sports, pp. 23–42.

Chapter 2

Betting markets and the roles of private enterprise in combating match-fixing

Andrew Menz and David Skene

Introduction: roles for licensed and regulated betting operators

This chapter analyses the important role that licensed and regulated betting operators can play in assisting sport controlling bodies ('SCBs')[1] and law enforcement agencies to reduce betting-related corruption. In Australia, lawful betting on a sport cannot usually occur without the approval of the applicable SCB and regulated betting operators have a legal obligation to share customer information and betting records with the applicable SCB and law enforcement agencies. This chapter argues that this level of transparency makes the legal betting market largely unattractive for corruptors looking to compromise a sporting event. However, up to 80 per cent of all betting on global sports occurs with illegal betting operators which are subject to little or no regulation.[2] This chapter argues that such a regulatory shortfall poses significant risks to the integrity of sports.

Corruptors are drawn to unregulated and under-regulated betting markets which presently provide for greater liquidity (i.e. greater volume of monies wagered) than regulated betting markets and greater opportunity for financial gain. Illegal sports betting also offers a low-risk and inexpensive opportunity to launder money.[3] These risks have increased due to the internet which has opened access to betting markets and given unlicensed betting operators a false aura of legitimacy. This chapter focuses on the different ways that Australia has mandated transparency for its regulated and licenced betting operators and argues that the way in which these licenced betting operators discharge their transparency obligations is a key tool in combating corruption in sport. The authors draw on their experience of Betfair Pty Limited ('Betfair'), which conducts a pioneering and leading betting exchange in Australia, to inform and illustrate this argument. Betfair is a wholly owned subsidiary of Crown Resorts Limited and operates the 'Betfair' Betting Exchange in Australia.

This chapter commences with a brief analysis of the growth in sports betting and the threat that match-fixing motivated by betting represents to sport. The regulation of sports betting is then considered with particular reference to the impact of under-regulated and unregulated markets. The chapter uses this continuum to categorise types of sports betting markets and operators from highly regulated to under-regulated and then unregulated, before analysing the role of a betting operator in a highly-regulated market such as Australia. The chapter concludes with an analysis of key considerations for governments and other stakeholders when designing a regulatory framework for sports betting.

Sports betting: a rapidly growing global industry

The internet and the rapid uptake by citizens around the world of mobile internet technology have revolutionised the sports betting industry. The internet has also transformed sports betting from a cash-based activity that was largely bound by physical proximity and therefore the local laws of the relevant jurisdiction, to a borderless market that connects operators with customers regardless of their location. Sporting administrators need to be much more conscious of the risks of fixing in the internet age because of internet-based technology. The commercialisation and globalisation of sport has also projected distant and new sports leagues into homes around the world to the extent that star European football players are household names in Asia, for example. Combined, these elements are largely responsible for the unprecedented growth occurring in the sports betting industry.

Consumers also have more choice with access to sports betting providers from all over the world, but this reality brings new challenges for sports. Betting operators and customers from beyond the sport's jurisdiction are wagering on those sports in increasingly large sums. Consumers are no longer forced to wager with local betting operators that offer low returns and poor value. In 2014, research conducted by Gambling Research Australia found that Australians were 'most likely to choose an online betting website based on competitive price and promotions'.[4] The research indicated that 'at least one-third of interactive gamblers were not concerned about gambling with offshore providers'.[5] An operator licensed in the Philippines, for example, can offer odds to a customer in Germany on the outcome of the first-half of a soccer match being played in the New Zealand domestic league. This scenario poses a significant challenge for those responsible for protecting the integrity of the New Zealand soccer game.

Global internet access has also significantly opened wagering opportunities for operators and customers in jurisdictions where wagering is illegal. This chapter argues that it is these markets that represent the most significant threat to the integrity of world sport. The illegal sports betting market in the whole of the United States of America, where gambling is illegal in many States, is estimated to be 100 times larger than the legal

Nevada sports betting market. These estimates value the illegal market at an amount up to US$380 billion.[6] The illegal Asian betting market is believed to be worth between US$500 billion as reported by INTERPOL[7] and US$1 trillion.[8] The internet has also given operators based in unregulated and under-regulated jurisdictions an appearance of legitimacy that was not previously possible. In the majority of circumstances, consumers are unable to differentiate between a legal, highly-regulated sports betting operator and one that has no such standing.

Understanding the risks that illegal betting may pose to sport and the impact of match-fixing

The risks that illegal betting pose to Australian sport were captured as part of the *National Policy on Match-Fixing in Sport*.[9] The Policy was released in 2012 and agreed to by the Federal, State and Territory governments. It states:

> While it is recognised that betting is a legitimate pursuit, illegal or fraudulent betting is not. Fraudulent betting on sport and the associated match-fixing is an emerging and critical issue globally, for sport, the betting industry and governments alike. It has the potential to undermine public confidence in the integrity of sport, sporting events and the products offered by betting agencies. Left unchecked, this corruption will devalue the integrity of sport and diminish the acceptability and effectiveness of sport as a tool to develop and support many aspects of our society.[10]

The policy reflects the basic premise of sport and what makes it so unique. According to former World Anti-Doping Agency President, Richard Pound, the result of any event is 'inherently uncertain and depends on a range of factors, including skill, ability, strategy, conditions and training'.[11] It is the same uncertainty that also makes sport such an attractive product for gamblers to wager on. Sports bodies, legitimate betting operators, spectators and gamblers are therefore united in their desire to ensure that sport remains free of the corrupting influence of match-fixing.[12]

The manipulation of a sporting contest provides a significant advantage to those with knowledge of the manipulation as against the rest of the participants in the betting market. Corruptors or those with knowledge of the fix can wager significant amounts expecting that the result will go their way. The fraud is committed against all those who put their trust in the contest: from the crowd to the club sponsors, the bookmakers and other gamblers. Accordingly, where match-fixing is suspected or publicly proven, the trust placed in that league or competition is likely to be tested, placing at risk attendances, television coverage, sponsorship, media exposure and ultimately the ongoing viability of the competition.[13]

The collapse of a number of Asian professional soccer leagues in the 1990s illustrates the catastrophic impact of match-fixing. In 1989, the football associations in Malaysia and Singapore established a cross-border professional league. The league was well supported in terms of government infrastructure investment, international television coverage and significant corporate sponsorship. In 1994, following an extensive police investigation as a result of widespread media concern, one cabinet minister estimated that 70 per cent of the matches played since the league's inception had been subject to some form of corruption.[14] As a result, 21 players and coaches were sacked, 58 players were suspended and 126 players were questioned over corruption.[15] The revelation of the extent of corruption in the league destroyed public confidence and interest. In the decade following the exposure of the corruption, attendance fell by three-quarters.[16]

Whilst in the Malaysia-Singapore case the corruption was detected at the time it occurred, authorities investigating the Chinese Super League took ten years to instigate prosecutions for alleged match-fixing offences occurring in the 2003 season. Champions Shanghai Shenhua were stripped of their title and 33 players and officials, including the chief executive officer of the league, received life bans and were prosecuted with a range of fraud offences.[17] Most noticeably, however, fans voted with their feet when the corruption occurred. In the 2003 season, an average of 17,701 people attended each match.[18] The average attendance fell to 10,838 the following season.[19] Whilst the authorities took nearly a decade to commence an investigation and obtain the necessary evidence, the fans immediately knew that something was amiss and diverted their attention to other forms of entertainment.

Types of sports betting markets and operators: a continuum

This section analyses the impact of under-regulated and unregulated markets to help better define the analysis of the roles of betting operators which may also be categorised along a continuum of highly-regulated, under-regulated and unregulated. The advent of internet gambling has facilitated the extension of the activities of betting operators beyond the jurisdiction in which they have their home base. A betting operator may be lawful in one jurisdiction (whether highly-regulated or under-regulated), but unlawful in others where it is not registered but nevertheless projects its services via the internet.

Highly-regulated markets and betting operators

In a highly-regulated market, betting operators are subject to rigorous controls over their probity and operations making fraudulent conduct significantly more difficult than in under-regulated or unregulated markets, as discussed below. Highly-regulated betting operators hold all necessary licences and authorisations to conduct business in all countries in which they provide services. They use sophisticated computer software to attempt to block customers in prohibited jurisdictions from utilising their services via the internet.[20] Major highly-regulated betting operators also have 'sophisticated detection and consumer identification systems, restricted stakes, markets closed and bets voided in suspicious cases'.[21] Regulated betting operators in Australia, for example, require proof of the customer's identity to the same standard as major financial institutions, details of all sources of account funding and details of bank accounts to which any funds are withdrawn. These operators also employ sophisticated forensic technologies to verify a customer's location and the devices by which they are accessing the sports betting operator's website.[22] All of this information may be shared with law enforcement agencies and sports bodies authorised under the local laws to obtain this information. This level of transparency is not conducive to fraudulent conduct.

Under-regulated markets

Under-regulated markets are characterised by significantly low standards when it comes to issues such as transparency and reporting, and are sometimes referred to as 'grey markets'. Grey markets are alleged to provide havens for money-laundering with some betting operators believed to have links to organised crime. Many so-called licensing hubs, being jurisdictions that seek to attract online gambling operators to provide a benefit to the local economy via employment and taxes, should also be regarded as under-regulated. This level of regulation is a key part of their attraction to gambling operators, especially when the operators are able to use those hubs as a base from which to offer gambling services via the internet into highly-regulated jurisdictions without the need to pay taxes and fees or meet the higher regulatory standards in those jurisdictions.

The Philippines is sometimes used as an example of a licensing hub which lacks adequate regulatory oversight of its operators. CITIbet is an example of a betting exchange operator based in the Philippines which lacks transparency in its operations. Whilst accurate figures are difficult to obtain, CITIbet is said to be the world's largest betting exchange, offering services via complex and opaque ownership structures to anonymous gamblers who bet through agents.[23]

Licensing hubs are not necessarily problematic for the integrity of sports competitions, however. Malta, for example, is an established licensing hub regulated by the Malta Gaming Authority ('MGA') which licenses 100 operators providing sports betting.[24] The MGA describes its mission as promoting a 'fair and transparent gaming sector' and promotes its intention to 'safeguard against crime and corruption, and to offer protection to minors and vulnerable players'.[25] Malta has developed sophisticated measures to ensure that its regulation is effective. According to its Annual Report, the MGA 'aims to be the best in class and the most innovative regulator, offering proactive and effective supervision of licences, maximising opportunities in existing markets and proactively looking for growth opportunities while ensuring proper protection of players'.[26] The MGA lays claim to being Europe's top gambling regulator[27] and it appeared on the so-called white list of the United Kingdom Gambling Commission. White listing entitled Maltese licensed operators to lawfully offer their services into the UK, implying that the UK accepted Malta as a highly-regulated gambling market at the time.[28]

Under-regulated betting operators

Under-regulated betting operators are typically based in licensing hubs where they hold a licence. The hubs may offer betting operators economies of agglomeration, suitably skilled labour, less expensive premises and competitive licence fees and rates of taxation on turnover. A hub also provides an operator with a home-based regulator who is responsible for the regulation of gambling technology and systems and the probity of shareholders and employees. Under-regulated betting operators typically hold the appropriate licences in their home jurisdiction but offer services via the internet to customers around the world, ignoring the local laws of jurisdictions outside of their home base. Under-regulated operators form a key class of operators from a sports integrity perspective and represent a segment over which sports may seek to significantly improve transparency.

There are a number of variables that differentiate under-regulated operators, including the extent to which:

1. the operator seeks to obtain licences or authorisations in foreign jurisdictions and complies with local laws including the payment of government taxes and any fees to sports authorities for the right to offer betting markets on their sports;
2. the operator is willing to verify the identity of its customers, prevent third-party access[29] and monitor betting markets for suspicious activities; and
3. the operator is willing to share information regarding potentially corrupt betting markets with law enforcement and SCBs – whether proactively or reactively.

A common theme among under-regulated operators is that they all operate certain elements of their businesses illegally.

The extent to which SCBs should put such illegality to one side and seek to engage with under-regulated operators to improve sporting integrity is a key question for SCBs. What is most relevant from a sporting integrity perspective is that these operators undertake due-diligence to accurately identify their customers and assist a SCB conducting an investigation into suspicious betting on its sport by providing information about that betting including the identity of gamblers. These goals could be achieved by agreed cooperation, although some attempts have been rebuffed. Whether under-regulated operators can be successfully encouraged in this direction, perhaps by offering concessions such as so-called official gambling partner status, is problematic. Achieving information disclosure is arguably more likely than those under-regulated operators becoming licensed in a highly-regulated jurisdiction into which that operator currently offers gambling services illegally. Such licensing would defeat the competitive advantages of lesser regulation and non-payment of taxes and fees which they may currently enjoy.

Unregulated markets

Unregulated markets exist primarily in jurisdictions where gambling is prohibited such as China, India and some parts of the US. Betting operators in these jurisdictions are not subject to any regulatory oversight, deal largely with customers on an anonymous basis and do not operate in a manner conducive to providing transparency over betting activity with respect to either law enforcement or SCBs. Organised crime may also be attracted to these markets where there is no regulation. These so-called black markets may also be found operating outside the regulatory framework in highly-regulated jurisdictions and jurisdictions where gambling is permitted to some degree.

Unregulated betting operators

Unregulated betting operators do not hold a wagering licence in any jurisdiction and offer their services to customers regardless of their location. The volumes traded through unregulated betting operators are increasing.[30] According to a recent international report on sport integrity, the 'co-existence of legal, illegal and partially illegal operators' presents a unique challenge for sports administrators, gambling regulators and legislatures.[31] The challenge is to effectively enforce prohibitions against illegal operators and encourage consumers to choose to be with licensed and regulated operators. By removing legitimate customers from unregulated markets, liquidity is diminished and those markets are less attractive to corruptors.

Corruptors are immediately attracted to unregulated betting operators, which lack integrity measures and are largely unwilling to comply with laws that demand transparency of betting information. Further, unregulated operators advertise the anonymity they provide as a way to attract customers. In Asia, unregulated sports betting operators sometimes employ a number of levels of agents who place bets and receive funds with the operators on behalf of the agent's customers, adding further levels of complexity to identifying those placing bets using corrupt information.[32] Even the betting operators do not know who they are betting against. Accordingly, even if there is a willingness to share information, the operator may not be in a position to do so.[33]

Further, the larger (or more liquid) the betting market, the greater is the opportunity for the corruptor to make financial gains by participating in the corruption of that market. Corruptors working in liquid markets are able to place larger bets whilst avoiding detection by betting operators or SCBs.[34] On the other hand, corruptors are often unable to place large bets in illiquid markets as they are likely to be noticed and in certain circumstances not be accepted by a bookmaker for whom such a relatively large bet is too big a risk, especially if there is the prospect of fraud. There is also anecdotal evidence that unregulated markets provide criminals with an inexpensive and low-risk mechanism by which to launder money.[35] Unregulated betting operators also have the advantage of little to no taxation obligations and are therefore able to offer higher payout rates to customers than legal, highly-regulated operators, which are generally subject to significant taxes and licence fees payable to governments, regulators and SCBs for use of their product.

The corruption of sports and sports betting markets is viewed as an activity that carries a lower risk of detection and more lenient sentencing than other crimes of similar gravity. The risk is low due to a lack of sophistication and resources devoted by law-enforcement as well as the use of unregulated betting markets. SCBs, which may devote resources to the task, are unable to impose sanctions on any individual or entity that is not subject to the sport's authority and sports cannot compel the production of evidence from or charge perpetrators in relation to the relevant conduct. Therefore, the assistance of the formal legal system is essential. Few jurisdictions have criminal laws which are aimed at match-fixing connected with gambling, however. Some Australian States and Territories,[36] Spain[37] and the UK,[38] outlaw cheating at gambling on all sports, while others such as Japan[39] outlaw match-fixing only in those sports on which it is lawful to bet. This situation poses difficulties in prosecution. For those jurisdictions which lack specific laws, prosecution under the general fraud provisions of the criminal law has largely proved to be ineffective in dealing with the relevant conduct.[40]

There is also little prospect of local laws being effectively enforced against those who are physically outside the national jurisdiction even if they can be identified and located.[41] That consideration, among others, demonstrates that the pursuit and prosecution of unregulated operators, whilst important, may not be the most effective regulatory mechanism with which to address questions of integrity. Furthermore, unregulated betting does not necessarily pose a threat to the integrity of sport. What constitutes unregulated betting is merely determined by reference to the laws of the relevant jurisdiction. Further, not all customers that wager with unregulated operators are engaged in fixing. However, criminals will seek to utilise unregulated and under-regulated markets when perpetrating match-fixing offences to reduce the likelihood of detection. Therefore, to appropriately manage risks, sporting administrators need to develop a deeper understanding of the rapidly expanding global sports betting market and its link to corruption in sport. The ultimate weapon in fighting corruption in sport is transparency, as highlighted by the Australian experience discussed below.[42]

The Australian regulatory framework

As the analysis of under-regulated and unregulated betting markets and operators suggests, these markets and operators make it easier for corruption to occur in sport than where a market or operator is highly-regulated. It does not follow, however, that highly-regulated markets are immune to unregulated betting or match-fixing. Despite extensive legislative reform and being one of the first nations to implement targeted criminal offences for engaging in match-fixing, Australian sport remains exposed. It has proven difficult to establish jurisdiction and effectively enforce sports betting laws against individuals and entities outside of Australia. Ninety-one per cent of unauthorised operators continue to offer sports betting into Australia.[43] This section analyses the basic State and Territory laws concerning gambling, federal law regulating online gambling, anti-money-laundering legislation, and requirements whereby the controlling bodies of sports and racing may receive a share of gambling revenues generated by their events. An understanding of the complex mix of Federal, State and Territory laws which make up the Australian regulatory framework affords insights into why the vast majority of betting operators offering markets on Australian racing and sporting events operate in contravention of Australian law.

State and Territory-based prohibitions and authorisations

Under the law of each Australian State and Territory, gambling is illegal as a general rule.[44] However, each State and Territory has authorised certain types of gambling to such an extent that there are many and varied opportunities to gamble. The major authorisations are those provided to casino operators, agencies appointed to run totalisator wagering on racing (also known as 'the TAB'), licensed bookmakers, promoters of lotteries and gaming machine operators. The Australian experience highlights some of the issues which may arise in a federated state where legal responsibility for gambling regulation is held by the constituent States.[45] Historically, betting markets corresponded with a State or Territory's geographic limits and generated taxation revenues for the relevant jurisdiction. Betting via telephone and then the internet broke down these borders.

A pivotal development occurred in 2006, when the State of Tasmania issued Australia's first betting exchange licence to the UK-based operator Betfair. On the basis that it held a wagering licence from an Australian jurisdiction, Betfair commenced offering its services to customers around Australia. The State of Western Australia enacted the *Betting and Racing Legislation Amendment Act 2006* (WA) to amend the *Betting Control Act 1954* (WA) to create an offence for a betting exchange to be offered to Western Australian customers.[46] The law also made it an offence for a resident of Western Australia to wager using a betting exchange.[47] The Western Australian government claimed that the purpose of the law was to protect the integrity of Western Australian racing on the basis that it considered betting exchanges posed a higher risk of corrupt activity than did traditional pari-mutuel operators and bookmakers. An argument can be mounted that the purpose of the law was to protect the Western Australian TAB from competition and ensure revenue to the Western Australian government was not affected. The High Court of Australia unanimously declared the law invalid on the basis that it was in breach of s. 92 of the Australian Constitution which guarantees freedom of trade between the States.[48] The High Court found that the Tasmanian government had the right to determine whether appropriate controls were in place and, provided that was the case, then Western Australia was not entitled to prohibit the conduct.[49] It is now accepted that a licence issued by one Australian jurisdiction entitles the licence holder to offer their services in all Australian States and Territories.

Interactive Gambling Act 2001 *(Cth)*

In 2001, the Australian Parliament enacted the *Interactive Gambling Act 2001* (Cth) ('*IGA*') to deal with online gambling generally, and to a lesser extent betting on sport by Australian consumers. The primary objective of the Act was to 'prohibit Australian-based interactive gambling services being provided to customers in Australia and to limit the ability of Australian customers to access internet gambling sites located overseas'[50] largely in order to reduce the potential for gambling harm to consumers as opposed to protect the integrity of sporting contests.

Subject to some exclusions, the *IGA* prohibits the provision of 'interactive gambling services' to Australian customers including all forms of online gambling.[51] The prohibition is targeted mainly at online forms of poker and casino games, with online betting on animal races and sports excluded from the prohibition subject to the qualification that online sports betting is prohibited from the time the event commences.[52]

The *IGA* therefore prohibits betting operators from offering online 'in-play' betting on sporting events to Australian customers. However, this prohibition does not apply to bets placed over the telephone[53] or in cash at retail outlets,[54] and online in-play betting is permitted for animal racing. It is also not an offence for an Australian customer to place a bet with an operator that offers in-play betting. Moreover, Australia is the only nation that permits online sports wagering, but prohibits in-play wagering. Given that the vast majority of in-play wagering by Australian customers is likely to be on Australian sporting events, the prohibition forces Australian customers that wish to engage in in-play betting to do so with operators that offer that service to them in breach of the *IGA*. The implications of this anomaly for sports integrity are considered below.

Anti-Money Laundering and Counter-Terrorism Financing Act 2006 *(Cth)*

The *Anti-Money Laundering and Counter-Terrorism Financing Act 2006* (Cth) ('*AML/CTF Act*') is part of a legislative package which brought Australia into line with international best practice to deter money laundering and terrorism financing. The *AML/CTF Act* places a number of obligations on 'reporting entities' when they provide designated services. Betting operators in Australia qualify as 'reporting entities'[55] and, in accordance with the provisions of the *AML/CTF Act*, they must:

a put in place an *AML/CTF Act* programme for their business, which needs to specify how the operator identifies, mitigates and manages the risk of its services being misused to facilitate money laundering;[56]

b collect and verify customer identification information. A betting operator in Australia must be reasonably satisfied that a customer is who they claim to be;[57]

c comply with a range of record-keeping obligations;[58] and

d submit several types of 'transaction reports' to the regulator (Australian Transaction Reports and Analysis Centre ('AUSTRAC')), including 'threshold transaction reports' and 'suspicious matter reports'.[59] With respect to the latter, a betting operator must submit a suspicious matter report to AUSTRAC if the operator forms a suspicion on reasonable grounds that: (i) a person is not the person they claim to be; or (ii) information the operator has may be relevant to investigate or prosecute a person for an offence against a Commonwealth, state or territory law.[60]

These *AML/CTF Act* provisions require betting operators to identify customers and monitor their financial transactions, ensuring a level of oversight which may also detect behaviour which indicates match-fixing.

Race fields and sports fields legislation[61]

Arrangements are in place across Australia which require betting operators to obtain authorisation from the relevant SCB or animal racing body to offer betting on their respective events. The legal basis for these arrangements is different for sports betting on the one hand and animal racing on the other.

Sports betting approvals are governed by legislation in the two largest states: New South Wales and Victoria, although for commercial reasons the arrangements apply nationally.[62] Section 4.5.22(1) of the *Gambling Regulation Act 2003* (Vic) ('*GR Act*') states that 'a sports betting provider must not, in Victoria or elsewhere, offer a betting service on a sports betting event unless an agreement is in effect ... between the [SCB] for that event and the sports betting provider'. Importantly, under s. 4.5.23(2) of the *GR Act*, an agreement must provide for the sharing of information between the parties for the purposes of protecting and supporting integrity in sports and sports betting. Similarly, s. 18C(1) of the *Betting and Racing Act 1998* (NSW) states that:

> a betting service provider must not, in New South Wales or elsewhere, offer a betting service in relation to a sporting event unless ... an integrity agreement ... is in place between the [SCB] for the sporting event and the licensed betting service provider.

The agreements are typically between regulated betting operators and *national* SCBs because both groups wish for uniform national arrangements even though governing legislation exists in only two states. The agreements provide for a fee to be paid to the SCB and provide for the provision of information by the operator to the sporting body, either upon request or in circumstances where the betting operator notices any suspicious trends in any wagering on the relevant sport. Importantly, the agreements also provide for information sharing that allows betting operators to audit their customer databases for players or officials. The results of these audits are provided to SCBs in order for them to identify whether any players or officials are in breach of the wagering rules or policies of the sport.

With regard to betting on animal racing, authorisation is obtained pursuant to the race fields provisions in State legislation. A race field means information that identifies the names and numbers of horses or greyhounds participating in races. Regulated betting operators must obtain approvals from racing bodies to publish such essential information in the course of their betting operations: so-called race fields approvals. Section 4.2.3A(1) of the *GR Act*, for example, states that:

> a wagering service provider must not, in Victoria or elsewhere, publish, cause to be published, use or otherwise make available, a race field in the course of business unless the wagering service provider has obtained the publication and use approval of the appropriate controlling body.

The race field approvals contain provisions which require a regulated betting operator to, among other things, respond to requests for information and pay race field fees to the racing bodies.

Role of regulated betting operators in combating corruption in Australia

The legislation outlined in the preceding section demonstrates that Australian legislators have determined that strict regulatory requirements mandating transparency are a key way to curb betting related corruption. The legislation addresses the location of the operator (licensing requirements), the location of the customer (licensing requirements and *AML/CTF Act* obligations) and, unique to Australian and New Zealand law, the location of the sporting event.[63] This three-pronged approach seeks to guarantee transparency of all information relevant to Australia. In jurisdictions where any of these elements are lacking, there are weaknesses which render sports more susceptible to match-fixing.

While strict regulatory requirements which mandate transparency in its various respects are a strong counter to corruption, they also impose on Australian licensed wagering operators significant responsibilities in offering their services to Australian customers on Australian sporting events. The manner in which those responsibilities are addressed in practice is considered in this section by examining information sharing agreements, the types of information held by betting operators which can be shared with SCBs and law enforcement authorities, and the data collection and analytical tools that can be deployed.

Information sharing agreements

As noted above, Australian licensed wagering operators enter into information sharing agreements to provide certain information to SCBs. These agreements are pivotal in the fight against betting-related corruption and require the betting operator to:

a comply with any requests for information from a controlling body, including requests for information about the betting that occurred with the operator on a particular event, or information pertaining to a particular customer;

b monitor their betting markets and proactively disclose any suspicious or irregular betting to controlling bodies even in circumstances where the relevant regulator does not make an information request;

c upon receipt of the necessary information, conduct an audit of all betting accounts held by participants (e.g. players, coaches, officials, jockeys, trainers) and advise the controlling body if any of those individuals attempt to wager on their sport/race. This is a vital step in ensuring that participants and others with 'inside information' are not utilising that information for wagering purposes;

d agree to have their systems and records independently audited upon reasonable request; and

e pay 'product fees' to controlling bodies for use of their products, with such fees generally dedicated towards the relevant controlling body investing in integrity resources.

Types of information held by regulated betting operators

The effectiveness of these information sharing agreements depends on the quality and quantity of information that online wagering operators collect and retain about their customers and the wagering activities that occur on their betting platforms. This information generally includes the customer's name, date of birth, address (both current and any previous address), telephone numbers, bank account information and credit card details, and identity verification documents provided by customers (e.g. driver's licence, passport). The information will also detail deposit and withdrawal information of customers, including third-party funding information,[64] and full betting histories for customers, containing details of all bets placed and profits/losses, as well as IP (Internet Protocol) and cookie information for customer logins and bet placement. Data collected also includes conversation histories (e.g. telephone, email) between the betting operator and the customer, and forensic linkage information – betting operators can identify links between multiple account holders. Market-level information collected by betting operators includes: full details of all bets placed on unsettled and settled markets, volumes held on specific markets and selections within a market, biggest winners and losers on a particular event/race, and betting trends.

Major Australian betting providers have a number of staff dedicated to compliance with the information disclosure obligations in information sharing agreements. During the 2015 calendar year, for example, Betfair's Australian Integrity Team responded to more than 400 requests for information which were lodged by SCBs and law enforcement bodies. This Team analyses the flow of money through the Betting Exchange system, win percentages of punters, any transactions that do not correspond with a punter's normal betting pattern and betting trends. All members of the Integrity Team receive extensive training on how to identify suspect betting transactions. Betfair has the ability to monitor all customer account activity including every bet placed or amount withdrawn. On Betfair's Betting Exchange, every click of the mouse is recorded on every event or race every second of every day. In addition, Betfair records all telephone calls to its telephone betting operators.

The information sharing agreements provide SCBs with information to enforce their rules and undertake investigations into any suspected incidents of corruption. Examples of rule breaches uncovered to date include prohibited betting by Australian Football League players[65] and their families,[66] and betting on races which photo-finish judges of the Australian Turf Club were on-duty to judge.[67]

Online and interactive tools used to fight against betting-related corruption

In addition to responding to information requests, licensed wagering operators in Australia undertake the following activities to maintain the integrity of their betting markets:

- a live monitoring before and during events of betting markets and 'high risk' customer accounts;
- b review transactional information daily and investigate irregular betting activity on an exceptions basis;[68]
- c undertake complex forensic analysis to identify linkages between holders of various accounts;
- d if any unusual or suspicious betting trends or transactions are identified, proactively report the matter to the relevant SCB; and
- e provide assistance and support to SCBs and law enforcement bodies that are investigating potential corruption.

Betfair provides SCBs with direct live access to wagers being struck on its Betting Exchange via a secure, online tool known as the Bet Monitor. The Bet Monitor ensures that SCBs are best placed to conduct immediate investigations into potentially corrupt activity. The Bet Monitor is a purpose-built system that permits the user to access details of bets in real-time. The user is able to set up 'filters' of the system to make it easier to monitor particular customers, particular matches/races and/or bets over a particular size.

The Bet Monitor is unique to Betfair in Australia and is provided to SCBs by Betfair on a voluntary basis. It allows SCBs to monitor, in real-time, the wagers being placed on their events/races. The provision of real time betting information is likely to be made compulsory in the short to medium-term future, which would provide significantly enhanced betting information to racing stewards and sports integrity units.

Essential features of regulating sports betting in the digital age

The Australian experience demonstrates that a thoroughly planned regulatory framework is a vital tool in preventing betting-related corruption in sports.[69] There are a number of important considerations that face governments seeking to deal with the issues produced by a sports betting market that continues to migrate online, including reforming outmoded gambling laws, dealing with the possible extraterritorial reach of any regulatory system and where the focus of regulation should rest. This section canvasses those considerations.

Do existing laws need review?

Gambling has been strictly controlled by states around the world because it is regarded as harmful for a variety of cultural, religious and social reasons. Despite some relaxation of controls in some nations in the second half of the twentieth century and the twenty-first century, restrictive gambling laws have been in place for significant periods of time and remain largely unchanged from previous centuries.

However, the advent of internet-based sports betting requires a reconsideration of those laws to determine whether they remain appropriate to meet their aims. Governments are now being forced to determine whether sports betting via the internet 'represents something new and different or whether even the newest of digital innovations can be analysed and controlled in ways that the impact of past inventions have'.[70]

A particular dilemma for states which permit some gambling is how to deal with the advent of the same style of gambling potentially made available over the internet. Major sporting jurisdictions including Australia and the US have adopted the view that there is a need to control online wagering in a manner that is inconsistent with how land-based gambling is treated. In the US, online gambling, including sports betting, is prohibited, whilst terrestrial casinos which offer sports and race betting are viewed as an important source of revenue for nearly 40 States.[71] In Australia, as explained above, in-play betting on sports is prohibited online but not by other means. These prohibitions will encourage gamblers to seek betting opportunities via unregulated or under-regulated operators working illegally and the opportunity to subject any such betting activity to the level of integrity scrutiny applicable to highly-regulated operators will be lost.

Can domestic laws be enforced extraterritorially?

Whether a nation can assert jurisdiction over a sports bet that is only linked to the nation because the relevant sporting event occurs there remains unclear. It is now commonplace for bets on the outcome of Australian sports events to be made in foreign jurisdictions between foreign nationals and residents. Whereas those bets would be subject to the high levels of scrutiny and transparency outlined above if they were, say, placed with Australian licensed operators, there is little that Australian SCBs or law enforcement authorities can do to gather information about those betting transactions which might reveal match-fixing activity in the Australian sports event.

The laws of a state are constrained in their application by the doctrine of territoriality, which deems that laws are prima facie unenforceable beyond a state's borders. Australian State and Federal governments have attempted to extend their jurisdiction by enacting legislation that captures acts wherever committed that cause a 'criminal result' to occur in Australia.[72] The *Interactive Gambling Act 2001* (Cth), for example, applies to the provision of any interactive gambling service to an Australian resident, purporting to cover the hosting of websites anywhere in the world provided that they are accessible to Australian residents.[73] The so-called criminal result occurs in Australia because the customer accesses the prohibited content from within the jurisdiction.

Even where a nation can establish that its laws are applicable, there are significant issues with effectively being able to enforce the laws against entities or individuals who are not located within the jurisdiction. There are difficulties in the collection of evidence, the interviewing of suspects and witnesses, access to information and extradition. Proactive enforcement measures such as financial transactions blocking and internet service provider blocking are often championed as an effective mechanism of preventing illegal activity online. The global evidence suggests that these options are of limited utility and in any event focus primarily on customers that are located within the state's jurisdiction.[74] It is naïve to suggest that Australian governments could compel foreign financial institutions to block transactions between banks and gambling operators because those operators are not meeting obligations to Australian SCBs.[75]

Where should the focus of the regulation lie?

There are essentially three concepts that need to be identified and managed in the development of a regulatory regime that will be most effective in reducing betting-related corruption.

Location of the betting operator

The regulatory regime must deal with whether, and on what terms, it will issue gambling licences. It should contain a regulatory framework that allows for operators to be licensed and regulated by a statutory gambling authority and contain restrictions on all operators (in the case of a blanket prohibition on sports betting) or those operators who are not licensed (in the case of a licence-based regime) from physically operating within that jurisdiction.

Location of the customer

The regulatory framework must also provide adequate rules and regulations around the conduct of wagering customers (i.e. punters) that are located within the jurisdiction. These rules should apply to all betting activities of the jurisdiction's residents even where they wager with an overseas operator. As the so-called criminal result of betting-related corruption occurs where the punter places the bet (and collects their winnings), a regulatory framework dealing with such activity is necessary. For example, the match-fixing provisions in the *Crimes Act 1958* (Vic) apply to anyone that places a bet in Victoria, regardless of whether the operator is unregulated or the betting activity illegal (e.g. online in-play betting on sports). Such requirements may include obligations on punters to participate and produce documents and records as part of regulatory investigations into corruption. This approach would eliminate the requirement for a betting operator to cooperate – which as outlined above is unlikely in respect of unregulated betting operators.

Regulating customer conduct is also important because customers of online wagering operators are often based outside of the jurisdiction in which the betting operator is licensed or where the sporting event is played. It is therefore insufficient to regulate the betting operator only.

Location of the sporting event

The regulatory framework should seek to ensure that operators that are offering betting markets on sporting events occurring in the jurisdiction are required to provide integrity related information to SCBs or gambling regulators. This transparency is the most important element of any framework for SCBs, but also poses the most difficulties from a jurisdiction and enforcement perspective.

Conclusion

A significant unregulated and under-regulated global online sports betting market poses a significant risk to the integrity of sport. Highly-regulated betting operators, like Betfair, play a key role in combating corruption. They provide integrity-related information to SCBs both on request and proactively, and this level of transparency makes legal betting markets less attractive for corruptors looking to compromise a sporting event. Cross-border illegal betting online in particular, however, continues to threaten the integrity of Australian sport and requires further legislative and enforcement focus.

Notes

1 In this chapter unless otherwise indicated or required by the context, the term 'sport controlling body' ('SCB') includes the governing bodies of human sport and animal racing. In later parts of this chapter, the term SCB may adopt the meaning used in New South Wales and Victorian gambling legislation to signify the sports body recognised as controlling a sports event for the purpose of authorising sports betting on the event. See the discussion of race fields and sports fields legislation in this chapter.

2 University Paris 1 Panthéon Sorbonne and International Centre for Sport Security 2014, *Fighting against the manipulation of sports competitions*, Sorbonne-ICSS Programme on Ethics and Sport Security, November, p. 14, http://sorbonne-icss.univ-paris1.fr/presse.

3 See Ordway in this volume.

4 Hing, N., Gainsbury, S., Blaszczynski, A., Wood, R., Lubman, D. and Russell, A., 2014, *Interactive gambling*, Gambling Research Australia, p. xiv, www.gamblingresearch.org.au/sites/default/files/embridge_cache/emshare/original/public/2016/09/76/49eef736f/interactive%2Bgambling.pdf. Interactive betting is discussed further below in relation to the relevant Australian legislation. 'Pari-mutuel betting' refers to a bet type where the odds quoted at the time of the bet are indicative and the final payout is determined upon completion of the event based on the pool of money wagered on the event. This type of betting is in contrast to 'fixed odds betting' (offered by corporate bookmakers such as CrownBet Pty Limited) where the odds agreed to at the time of the bet are used to determine the final payout. A betting exchange (like the one operated by Betfair) is an online platform that enables people to bet against each other on an event at a known price that they set.

5 Ibid.

6 Borghesi, R., 2008, 'Widespread corruption in sports – fact or fiction', *Southern Economic Journal*, vol. 74, no. 4, pp. 1063–1069, p. 1063.

7 Murdoch, L., 2013, 'Illegal betting could top $500b each year', *The Sydney Morning Herald*, 17 September, www.smh.com.au/national/illegal-betting-could-top-500b-each-year-20130916-2tv6n.html.

8 This figure is unproven but is gaining traction among a number of industry experts. Unregulated sports and race betting in Hong Kong accounted for an estimated US$64 billion in turnover in 2013, which one commentator argues, 'represents more than four times the legal turnover at the Hong Kong Jockey Club and exceeds nearby Macau's world leading regulated casino gaming revenues of US$45 billion that year': Foley-Train, J., 2014, *Sports betting: commercial and integrity issues*, Remote Gaming Association, September, p. 11.

9 Australian Government Department of Health 2014, *National policy on match-fixing in sport*, 11 February, www.health.gov.au/internet/main/publishing.nsf/Content/national-policy-on-match-fixing-in-sport.

10 Ibid., art. 1.4.
11 Pound, R., 2011, 'Responses to corruption in sport', paper presented at the Play the Game Conference, 3 October, Cologne, Germany, p. 1, www.playthegame.org/fileadmin/image/PTG2011/Presentation/Richard_Pound_2011.pdf.
12 Forrest, D., McHale, I. and McCauley, K., 2008, *Risks to the integrity of sport from betting corruption*, Centre for Study of Gambling, February, p. 1.
13 University Paris 1 Panthéon Sorbonne and International Centre for Sport Security, above n. 2, p. 20.
14 Hill, D., 2013, 'The big fix is in – global match-fixing has the power to destroy much of the modern sports world', *The Sydney Morning Herald*, 18 September, www.smh.com.au/world/the-big-fix-is-in-20130917–2tx8f.html.
15 'Football: New corruption scandal erupts in Malaysia' 2012, *AsiaOne Sports*, 20 January, http://news.asiaone.com/News/Latest+News/Sports/Story/A1Story20120120-323145.html.
16 'Corruption beyond FIFA – good money, bad money' 2015, *The Economist*, 4 June, www.economist.com/news/international/21653615-cash-corrupts-it-can-also-help-clean-up-sport-good-money-bad-money.
17 Associated Press 2013, 'Shanghai Shenhua stripped of 2003 title in China match-fixing inquiry', *Guardian*, 19 February, www.theguardian.com/football/2013/feb/19/shanghai-shenhau-stripped-match-fixing.
18 Sheringham, S., 2013, 'Didier Drogba and Nicolas Anelka put Chinese football on the map', *BBC Sport*, 8 January, www.bbc.com/sport/football/20894477.
19 Ibid.
20 The effectiveness of these blocks is debatable.
21 Foley-Train, above n. 8, p. 49.
22 Ibid.
23 Industry insiders claim that Philippines' licensed operators using multilayered structures pose serious questions over the probity of those involved. For a CITIbet agent, see Citibet Agent, *Citibet agent*, www.citibetagent.com.
24 Malta Gaming Authority 2015, *Annual report 2015*, p. 39.
25 Malta Gaming Authority, *Our brand*, www.mga.org.mt/about-us/our-brand.
26 Malta Gaming Authority, above n. 24, p. 14.
27 Ibid.
28 'White listing' arrangements were abolished by the *Gambling (Licensing and Advertising) Act 2014* (UK) (amending the *Gambling Act 2005* (UK)) by in effect requiring all operators offering services into the UK to be licensed in the UK.
29 Preventing a third party from using the wagering account of a customer is important, because the identity of the third party may not be known and the third party could be engaged in criminal activities.
30 Hing *et al.*, above n. 4, p. xvii.
31 International Centre for Sport Security and University Paris 1 Panthéon-Sorbonne 2014, *Protecting the integrity of sport competition: the last bet for modern sport*, May, p. 26, www.theicss.org/wp-content/themes/icss-corp/pdf/SIF14/Sorbonne-ICSS%20Report%20Executive%20Summary_WEB.pdf?lbisphpreq=1.
32 Hawkins, E., 2012, *Bookie gambler fixer spy: a journey to the corrupt heart of cricket's underworld*, Bloomsbury Publishing.
33 See, e.g. Cox, M., 2014, '"Amway for gamblers" is easy money for super agents', *South China Morning Post*, 22 November, www.scmp.com/sport/racing/article/1646397/amway-gamblers-easy-money-super-agents.
34 University Paris 1 Panthéon Sorbonne and International Centre for Sport Security, above n. 2, p. 426.

35 See also Ordway in this volume.
36 See Opie and Lim in this volume.
37 See *Ley del Deporte* [Law on Sport], 10/1990, art. 76.1(c) (Spain), which makes it an offence to 'predetermine by payment, intimidation or simple agreements, the outcome of an event or competition'.
38 See s. 42 of the *Gambling Act 2005* (UK). Section 42(1) states that 'a person commits an offence if he: (a) cheats at gambling; or (b) does anything for the purpose of enabling or assisting another person to cheat at gambling'. This provision can cover match-fixing, but that is not its sole purpose.
39 See Kawai in this volume.
40 The failed prosecution of members of a betting syndicate as part of the Ryan Tandy affair in Australia is evidence of the difficulties in successfully prosecuting these offences. See Opie and Lim in this volume.
41 The principal measure available to enforcement authorities in such instances is to block the access of Australian gamblers to websites of off-shore unregulated, illegal operators. However, a number of practical issues work against this approach. See further below and Opie and Lim in this volume.
42 Betfair Pty Ltd 2001, *Submission to the Department of Broadband, Communications and the Digital Economy: interim report – review of the Interactive Gambling Act 2001*, September, p. 14, www.aph.gov.au/DocumentStore.ashx?id=ea52f057-aa0b-4d42-9a5e-1f92f8330f33.
43 Gainsbury, S., 2011, *Internet gambling: current research findings and implications*, Springer, p. 30.
44 See, e.g. *Gambling Regulation Act 2003* (Vic). See also Opie and Lim in this volume.
45 See Opie and Lim in this volume.
46 *Betting Control Act 1954* (WA), s. 27D(1).
47 Ibid. s. 24(1aa).
48 *Betfair* v. *Western Australia* (2008) 234 CLR 418.
49 Ibid., para. 110.
50 See the second reading speech for the Act: Commonwealth, *Parliamentary Debates*, Senate, 21 June 2001, p. 24834.
51 *Interactive Gambling Act 2001* (Cth), s. 15.
52 To be read in conjunction with the definitions of 'interactive gambling service' and 'excluded wagering service': ibid., ss. 5, 8A.
53 See the exception contained in ibid., s. 5(3).
54 The *Interactive Gambling Act 2001* (Cth) applies only to interactive gambling. The issue of physical gambling remains the jurisdiction of each of the States and Territories that licence gambling operators.
55 *Anti-Money Laundering and Counter-Terrorism Financing Act 2006* (Cth), s. 6 extends the definition of designated services to the provision of services for gambling. See also s. 5 (definition of 'reporting entity').
56 Ibid., pt. 7.
57 Ibid., pt. 2.
58 Ibid., pt. 10.
59 Ibid., pt. 3.
60 Ibid., s. 41.
61 On these arrangements, see also Opie and Lim in this volume.
62 See Opie and Lim in this volume.
63 For example, under the *Gambling Regulation Act 2003* (Vic), a betting operator wishing to publish a Victorian thoroughbred race field must first obtain a publication and use approval from Racing Victoria.

64 Third-party funding information will include deposits made by a third party into the wagering account of an existing customer.
65 Walsh, C., 2011, 'Collingwood defender Heath Shaw suspended in AFL betting scandal', *The Australian*, 15 July, www.theaustralian.com.au/sport/collingwood-player-to-tbe-suspended-in-afl-betting-scandal/story-e6frg7mf-1226095384244.
66 Wilson, C., 2011, 'Heath Shaw suspended for betting on football', *The Age*, 15 July, www.theage.com.au/afl/afl-news/heath-shaw-suspended-for-betting-on-football 20110715-1hhe1.html.
67 Australian Associated Press 2014, 'ATC employees sacked over race-day betting', *Just Horse Racing*, 18 November, www.justhorseracing.com.au/news/australian-racing/atc-employees-sacked-over-race-day-betting/268299.
68 Licensed wagering operators in Australia, such as Betfair, investigate irregular betting activity on an 'exceptions basis'. If a wagering transaction falls outside of certain established thresholds (e.g. the bet is much higher in value than is usual for the particular customer), then the wagering operator will be alerted to the 'exception' and will investigate the transaction.
69 Sparrow, M., 2009, 'Can internet gambling be effectively regulated? Managing the risks', 2 December, http://financialservices.house.gov/media/file/hearings/111/sparrow.pdf. On the shortcomings of the Australian framework, see Opie and Lim in this volume.
70 Champion, W. and Rose, I., 2012, 'Gaming law in a nutshell', *Westlaw*, p. 311.
71 Palmeri, C., 2014, 'Local casinos are a losing bet', *Bloomberg Businessweek*, 3 April, www.businessweek.com/articles/2014-04-03/casinos-close-as-revenue-falls-in-gambling-saturated-u-dot-s.
72 Hornle, J. and Zammit, B., 2012, *Cross-border online gambling law and policy*, Edward Elgar Publishing, p. 84.
73 *Interactive Gambling Act 2001* (Cth), s. 15.
74 Department of Broadband Communications and the Digital Economy 2012, *Review of the Interactive Gambling Act 2001 – final report*, June, p. 86.
75 See, e.g. Averill, A., 2013, 'Effective enforcement: is there any such thing?', *iGaming Business*, 1 March.

Part II

Legal theories, frameworks and developments

Chapter 3

Match-fixing and illegal gambling in Japan

Cultural interpretations of integrity

Keiji Kawai[1]

Introduction: linking match-fixing to Japan's prohibition on gambling

Japan views the practice of betting on sports and gambling in general from quite a different perspective compared with countries such as Australia, where sports betting is largely legalised. This chapter argues that it therefore should not be surprising that the approach taken by Japan to ensure integrity in sport is also different. In Japan, there are no general laws or regulations that ban or limit the fixing of matches, games or other competitions. Because gambling is already prohibited by the *Kei hō* [Criminal Code] (act no. 45, 1907 (Japan)) ('*Criminal Code*'), Japan lacks a broadly legalised sports betting market, and traditionally this has negated the need to target match-fixing in Japan with general legislation. Where gambling is legal – the four forms of competitive racing known as *kōei kyōgi*[2] which are operated by the government, and the government-run *toto*, or football pools – match-fixing has been criminalised under special laws.[3] Match-fixing in horse racing (*keiba*), motor boat racing (*kyōtei*, speedboats), auto racing (*ōtorēsu*, track motorcycles) and bicycle racing (*keirin*, track cycling) has occurred on occasion and examples are analysed in this chapter. The prohibition of match-fixing under special legislation is primarily designed, however, to protect the reliability of the betting industry rather than the integrity of the game.

In addition to presenting an overview of the laws and regulations currently in force in Japan pertaining to gambling in general, this chapter also analyses two incidents of match-fixing in professional sports: the 'Black Mist Scandal' of 1969–71 in baseball and the Grand Sumo Scandal of 2011. These incidents are the only publicly known cases of match-fixing in Japanese professional sports outside *kōei kyōgi*. This chapter also argues that the characterisation of gambling within Japanese society, especially gambling on sports, clearly differs from that in many European nations and Australia. This difference creates variations between Japan and other nations in match-fixing regulations.

This chapter argues that Japan is unlikely to legalise betting generally and thus criminalise match-fixing for all sports in the near future for at least five reasons. First, the negative connotations associated with gambling are too deeply rooted in Japanese society at the current time. Second, gambling on sports is widely regarded as having the potential to endanger the health and soundness of sport itself while significantly diminishing its educational value. Third, while illegal gambling does exist in the form of a black market, there have been no gambling cases linked to match-fixing since the 1969 Black Mist Scandal.[4] Fourth, Japanese society historically condones and in fact encourages a culture of *ninjō*, whereby a victory is conceded to one's opponent out of compassion. Fifth, given that sports betting is generally required for match-fixing and similar misconduct to occur in the first place, eliminating sports betting in a sport altogether is seen as an appropriate and even necessary step to combat match-fixing misconduct. The chapter concludes, however, that in the future Japan may move to criminalise match-fixing, particularly in light of international expectations and the participation of Japanese teams in globalised competitions.

Match-fixing and exceptions to the general prohibition on gambling in Japan

Japan's special laws for certain racing industries and match-fixing in kōei kyōgi

The general prohibition on gambling in Japan is set out in art. 185 of the *Criminal Code* and is supported by a Supreme Court of Japan judicial precedent prohibiting the act of gambling.[5] The Court found that gambling was illegal to 'prevent adverse effects on public morals, that is to say, on healthy economic activity and work, as well as the side effect of crime'.[6] Despite the ban imposed by the *Criminal Code*, gambling on government-run racing industries or *kōei kyōgi* is legalised under special laws: the *Horse Racing Act*,[7] *Bicycle Racing Act*,[8] *Auto Racing Act*,[9] and the *Motor Boat Racing Act*.[10] Horse racing began in Japan in 1862 in Yokohama, where races were held by foreign expatriates. In 1948, horse racing became a government-run event as part of economic reconstruction efforts following the Second World War. Bicycle, auto and boat racing were later introduced in part due to their conceptual similarity.[11]

There are specific stipulations built into each special law that carry penalties for the practice of match-fixing. The penalties for match-fixing in arts. 31–34 of the *Horse Racing Act*, for example, include three years' imprisonment or a fine of JP¥3 million, with imprisonment of up to five years for dishonest acts in relation to match-fixing conduct.

At least six cases of match-fixing or misconduct in government-run racing have been dealt with by the courts (see Table 3.1). The athletes

Table 3.1 Cases where match-fixing was established within *kōei kyōgi*[a]

Date of the relevant judgment	*Sport*	*Fine*	*Imprisonment*
22 October 1954	Bicycle racing	JP¥5,000	1 year
9 February 1960	Bicycle racing	JP¥510,500 in total	1 year, 3 months
19 September 1970	Auto racing	None	6 months
30 March 1971	Bicycle racing	JP¥8,267,000 in total	2 years, 6 months
13 March 1984	Horse racing	JP¥400,000 in total	1 year
28 May 1987	Horse racing	JP¥60,000	4 months

Note

a From top-to-bottom: Supreme Court (22 October 1954), *Keishū*, vol. 8, no. 10, p. 1616; Supreme Court (9 February 1960), *Keishū*, vol. 14, no. 1, p. 92; Tokyo District Court (19 September 1970), *Hanrei Jihō*, no. 613, p. 104; Osaka District Court (30 March 1971), *Hanrei Jihō*, no. 640, p. 98; Supreme Court (13 March 1984), *Keishū*, vol. 38, no. 5, p. 1984; Hiroshima District Court (28 May 1987), *Hanrei Times*, no. 639, p. 249.

involved in these incidents were convicted of offences under the applicable special law and received permanent, lifelong bans from participating in racing. Accordingly, they were prohibited from competing or betting on races and entering racecourses. Penalties for criminal fraud were also applied in one case in 1950, where seven cyclists conspired to illegally earn prize money and a payout by fixing the outcome of a race, predetermining who would win first and second places. Given that the entire race had been effectively rigged, the Supreme Court ruled that the conduct constituted criminal fraud.[12] According to the ruling, the criminal conduct began when the cyclists were positioned at the starting line, and finished when the prize money and payout were awarded. The cyclists defrauded the race organiser, Gifu City, as well as the staff and officials from the Gifu Bicycle Racing Association.[13]

From 1962 to 1965, there were a number of incidents in which organised crime syndicates approached cyclists to fix the outcomes of races (see, e.g. Osaka District Court (30 March 1971), *Hanrei Jihō*, no. 640, p. 98). These cyclists would then obstruct other cyclists to ensure the desired order of finishers. Although the conduct in these cases was recognised as a violation of the special law, the charges of criminal fraud and attempted fraud were rejected (see, e.g. Osaka District Court (30 March 1971), *Hanrei Jihō*, no. 640, p. 98). The court found that it was not clearly established that the obstructive conduct in question had in fact brought about the intended outcome. It was difficult, if not impossible, to definitively establish that a cyclist's attempts to intentionally lose, or the cyclist's obstructive conduct, did in fact produce the actual outcome of a race. These cases demonstrate that, though the criminal charge of fraud may apply in cases in which the race as a whole is thought to have been rigged, courts are reluctant to support a charge of fraud when the match-fixing is limited to only *some* of the athletes participating in a particular race or competition.[14]

Many of the match-fixing cases between 1950 and 1987 involved organised crime syndicates who controlled the racers and claimed the dividends from the match-fixing according to media reports.[15] Each of the four publicly regulated racing industries established training schools for athletes, which has helped mitigate against syndicate involvement in recent years. Pupils who wish to become jockeys, for example, must enrol in a training school for three years during which they receive practical training and lectures aimed at countering illegal activity. Moreover, jockeys are secluded in a preparation facility next to the racecourse one day before a race, with strict limitations on contact with people outside the facility.

The Sports Promotion Lottery Act: *introduction and implementation*

A clear distinction should be made between legalised betting in *kōei kyōgi* and the national lottery system for soccer, called *toto*. The Japanese government introduced *toto* in 2000, in order to secure adequate resources for the promotion of sports (*Supōtsushinkōtōhyō no jisshitō ni kansuru hōritsu* [Sports Promotion Lottery Act], act no. 63, 1998 (Japan) ('*Sports Promotion Lottery Act*')).[16] With a JP¥100 betting slip, participants predict the outcomes of designated matches with a chance to win the full prize money. The prize money was initially set at a maximum of JP¥100 million. Later, with the introduction of a prize pool carryover, this maximum payout was raised to its current level of JP¥500 million. Full prize money is awarded if all predictions are correct, and then partial prize money if all but one are correct.[17] An independent administrative entity known as the Japan Sport Council operates and governs the *toto* system.[18] The Council designates a total of 13 matches (a mixture of J1 and J2 League matches) on which patrons can bet on a win, loss or tie for the home team. All 13 matches are normally played on the same day or during a consecutive two-day period. Given the extreme difficulty of fixing the outcomes of multiple matches all at once, holding the matches on the same day or within as short a period as possible is designed to prevent match-fixing.[19]

When first introduced, proponents of *toto* in the National Diet described *toto* as a lottery and not a form of gambling, given that the odds of winning the maximum payoff are exceedingly low – approximately 1.5 million to one.[20] *Toto* is something between a true lottery system, which is predicated solely on random chance, and the type of betting allowed in *kōei kyōgi*, which allows for analysis and prediction. Although the *toto* system benefited from extensive coverage in the media at the time it was introduced, revenue from *toto* began to drop off dramatically in 2004, endangering its continued operation.[21] In response to falling revenue, the Japan Sport Council introduced two new forms of the lottery in 2006: 'mini *toto*', which permits bets with a higher likelihood of success; and '*toto* BIG', which offers participants the chance to win up to JP¥600 million.[22] With the highest-ever cash prize to be offered by a lottery in Japan, *toto* BIG received a great deal of public attention and significantly improved ticket sales. *Toto* became more attractive because the odds of actually winning a top prize (one in 4.8 million) were greater than those for winning the standard *Takarakuji* lottery.[23]

When the *toto* system was first introduced for soccer in 2000, there was no public debate about whether or not to criminalise match-fixing. The *Sports Promotion Lottery Act* stipulates, however, penalties for match-fixing and other dishonest conduct in games subject to the *toto*. Article 37 of the Act states that if an executive or employee of an organisation, a player, or other individual directly involved in a game accepts, demands, or agrees to receive or provide a bribe as mentioned in art. 24, he or she may be sentenced to up to three years of imprisonment with work. If the individual commits a dishonest act or fails to perform his or her required duties, in exchange for a bribe, he or she shall receive up to five years of imprisonment with work. So far, there have been no reported cases of match-fixing involving a *toto*-related game.

Recently, there has been speculation that the Japanese government intends to expand the *toto* lottery system to baseball and rugby. In 2015, it was reported in a major national newspaper that a project group had been established for the purpose of studying major reforms to the current sports lottery system.[24] It was also reported that Toshiaki Endo, the minister in charge of the 2020 Tokyo Olympic and Paralympic Games, was studying the possibility of expanding the scope of the *toto* system.[25] The planned expansion would generate more profits from the *toto* system and, at the same time, bring other sports into scope for *toto*-related criminal sanctions for match-fixing. The public's strong negative reaction against recent reports of professional athletes betting on matches and visiting illegal casinos forced the government and the Japan Sport Council to postpone the expansion of the *toto* system to include baseball and rugby.[26]

The 'Black Mist Scandal' in baseball and regulation of misconduct by self-governing associations

Other than match-fixing cases relating to *kōei kyōgi*, one other publicly reported match-fixing incident in Japan occurred during the 1960s and 1970s. The 'Black Mist Scandal' refers to a series of proven and suspected events in Japanese professional baseball from 1969 to 1971. These scandals involved players fixing games in exchange for monetary rewards. During the 1969 regular season, the Nishitetsu Lions' front office suspected that some of their players were involved in fixing the outcomes of games and, under great secrecy, began an internal investigation.[27] The investigation concluded that Lions' pitcher Masayuki Nagayasu had, at the request of an organised crime group, deliberately lost or attempted to lose a number of games.[28] The club investigated further and found that Nagayasu asked two other players to participate in the effort to fix game outcomes.[29] Some players were also found to have been involved in match-fixing in auto racing, which resulted in 19 active racing drivers being arrested by the police.[30] Furthermore, accused of fixing auto races, Chunichi Dragons' Pitcher Kentaro Ogawa was arrested for violation of the *Auto Racing Act*. Later, he was found guilty and sentenced to three months in prison with probation of three years.[31]

At the time, the *Yakyū kyōyaku* [Professional Baseball Agreement] ('*Professional Baseball Agreement*')[32] stipulated that if any employee of a Nippon Professional Baseball ('NPB') club participating in the Agreement colluded or conspired with others to deliberately attempt to lose a game or fail to put forth his or her best efforts, then the Commissioner would impose a lifetime ban on the individual at the request of the Chairman of the relevant league (*Professional Baseball Agreement*, art. 355(1)).[33] A ban could also be imposed on an individual who was solicited with a bribe and then failed to report this conduct to the Chairman of the relevant league (*Professional Baseball Agreement*, art. 355(2)). A lifetime ban would be imposed automatically if any employee of an NPB club demanded or accepted money or gifts as part of an attempt to cause the opposing team to lose a game (*Professional Baseball Agreement*, art. 356).[34] This article would have applied where causing the opposing team to lose went beyond simply performing at one's best athletically, and instead involved dishonest conduct such as obtaining confidential information from the opposing team.

Nineteen NPB players were sanctioned under the *Professional Baseball Agreement* in connection with the Black Mist Scandal, six of whom received lifetime bans from the sport. Sanctions imposed by the NPB also included reductions in salaries and long-term suspensions from Japanese professional baseball.[35] None of the players involved in the match-fixing faced any criminal charges, however some of the players received summary indictments and were subsequently found guilty of aiding and abetting habitual gamblers.[36] Academics debated whether or not the parties involved should have been charged with fraud or as accomplices to the crime of fraudulent gambling, but the practical probability of successful prosecutions against these parties was thought to be extremely low.[37] The application of these criminal charges is limited to cases in which it can be proven that the player(s) involved were fully aware of the specific methods and other details of the betting scheme in question and, with such awareness, received a payment to engage in match-fixing conduct that actually affected the outcome of the race or game.[38]

Stakeholders are reluctant to enact criminal laws designed to curb the kind of match-fixing and related misconduct exposed in the Black Mist Scandal. Unlike betting on *kōei kyōgi* and *toto* which is an officially recognised practice, misconduct in professional sports not managed by the government has been left to the governing bodies of those sports. In other words, ensuring the fairness of the *kōei kyōgi* and *toto* systems through criminal prosecution is perceived as necessary to protect the general public and those gambling markets. The general public is also perceived as having a financial interest in keeping *kōei kyōgi* and *toto* fair because of their government backing, which also justifies criminal sanctions.[39] Other professional sports, however, have their own internal rules and conventions to which players are expected to conform, one of the most essential being sportsmanship. This understanding applies at both the professional and amateur levels. Accordingly, sanctioning conduct in these sports has historically been left to the self-governing abilities of the sport itself wherever possible.[40]

Moreover, conditions today are much less conducive to the kind of match-fixing that occurred in the Black Mist Scandal. First, the influence of organised crime syndicates in Japanese sport has declined due to the government's crackdown on such groups with the implementation of regulations such as the *Tōkyō-to bōryokudan haijo jōrei* [Tokyo Metropolitan Ordinance for the Elimination of Organised Crime] (ordinance no. 54, 2011 (Tokyo Metropolis)).[41] Second, players found to be associated with organised crime will be subject to sharp public criticism and significant reputational damage. Third, the rise in player salaries in many sports has mitigated the financial incentive to engage in such behaviour. Finally, given that gambling on baseball games itself is illegal in Japan, the baseball betting industry exists as a black market with a limited presence. Sports now generally operate in a domestic environment that is significantly less susceptible to match-fixing than it was in the 1960s and 1970s.

Sumo: culturally based interpretations of match-fixing

Professional sumo in Japan raises an example of match-fixing with issues which differ from those in *kōei kyōgi*, *toto* and professional sports such as baseball.[42] Match-fixing incidents have occurred entirely independent of sports betting and reflect both the nature of sumo as a competitive sport and its long-standing cultural significance in Japan. The example of sumo suggests that Japanese people are traditionally much more likely to be accepting of match-fixing in a certain cultural context. The practice of a sumo wrestler intentionally losing a bout out of consideration for his opponent is referred to as *ninjō zumō*, or 'compassionate sumo'. Though only tacitly acknowledged within professional sumo itself, *ninjō zumō* has been widely accepted by sumo fans and the public as a whole, with some wrestlers occasionally receiving an ovation for this conduct. Well-known historical stories celebrate the practice.[43] Intentionally losing a bout may also be seen as a means of managing a wrestler's physical condition, particularly where there may be concerns over possible injuries resulting from overexertion over the course of several bouts.

The debate over the nature of match-fixing in sumo highlights the complexities involved in defining match-fixing conduct. On one view, believing that match-fixing is an issue in professional sumo is to fundamentally misunderstand sumo itself.[44] This line of thinking does not view sumo as a sport; rather, it suggests that sumo should instead be understood as 'traditional culture' (*dentō bunka*).[45] This culture accepts the fixing of bouts in which the contestants themselves have mutually agreed upon the outcome. Accordingly, sumo should not be judged by modern standards using contemporary doctrines or theories of sport. Historically, however, there have been numerous allegations of match-fixing in professional sumo.[46] *Shūkan Gendai*, a weekly magazine published by Kodansha, published an article alleging match-fixing in 2008.[47] The *Shūkan Post*, a weekly magazine published by Shogakukan, published a report on alleged match-fixing since the 1980s and accused former sumo wrestlers of the practice.[48] The *Nihon Sumō Kyōkai* (also known as the Japan Sumo Association) consistently denied the existence of match-fixing in professional sumo wrestling.[49] Several members of the Association even successfully sued for defamation of character. On 26 March 2009, for example, the Tokyo District Court concluded that there was 'insufficient evidence to support most of [the claims made]' and ordered Kodansha and others (the author and editors) to publish an article denying the allegations and pay JP¥42.9 million.[50]

During a Honbasho (an official Grand Sumo Tournament) in 2011, it was discovered that professional sumo wrestlers had intentionally thrown matches in exchange for money that their opponents paid to them.[51] The Chairman of the *Nihon Sumō Kyōkai* declared that match-fixing had never occurred in professional sumo up to that point, and that the sumo world was facing an entirely new problem.[52] The wrestlers involved corresponded with one another via text messages about fixing the outcome of the match, as well as the specific moves to be used during the match. These facts were uncovered during the examination of mobile phones seized by police as evidence from sumo wrestlers suspected of involvement in a baseball betting scandal in 2010.[53] Unlike the gambling practices discovered the previous year in professional baseball, the rigging of matches by the wrestlers themselves is not prohibited by law. The conduct might have been prosecuted if it were performed in conjunction with betting on those matches, because the wrestlers may have been charged with the crime of aiding and abetting illegal gambling or fraud. However, there was no legal basis to connect the series of bouts for which match-fixing was suspected to the act of gambling. The 2011 scandal was the first ever to be officially recognised as an 'intentionally lethargic bout' (*kōi ni yoru mukiryoku-zumō*).

The match-fixing uncovered in professional sumo in 2011 was a coordinated effort of mutual give-and-take, whereby an 'exchange of victories' (*hoshi no kashikari*) preserves the current rankings of wrestlers from the *Makuuchi* to *Jūryō* divisions.[54] The behaviour is driven by a number of institutional incentives whereby wrestlers act to protect their own ranking and those of certain opponents via a culture of mutual back-scratching.[55] First, there are economic-related incentives to fix a sumo match. Currently, salaries are only provided to a total of 70 sumo wrestlers from the two highest divisions, *Makuuchi* (42) and *Jūryō* (28).[56] The financial incentive for wrestlers receiving a salary who have already secured a winning record to then continue posting wins is small when compared to a wrestler's overall salary (JP¥2,000 per win) (*Nihon Sumō Kyōkai*, *Nihon sumō kyōkai kifu kōi sekō saisoku* [Detailed regulations for executing Japan Sumo Association endowments], art. 92(1)). Wrestlers in training from the *Makushita* and lower divisions receive a small allowance and financial incentives from the *Nihon Sumō Kyōkai* in accordance with the number of wins, but not a salary.[57]

Second, wrestlers and their managers are able to influence rankings by producing a winning or losing record, to the extent that the resulting change(s) in rank can be predicted.[58] There is a significant difference in the way sumo wrestlers in the elite *Makuuchi* and *Jūryō* divisions are treated as compared to those in the *Makushita* and lower divisions. For example, the former are allowed to have the *ōichō* hairstyle, are given their own private quarters and have private attendants.[59] By contrast, the latter are required to wear their hair in the *chonmage* style, share rooms inside the stables and prepare other wrestlers' meals and perform other miscellaneous chores.

An internal investigation determined that 23 wrestlers had been involved in the match-fixing in 2011. All were forced to retire by the *Nihon Sumō Kyōkai*, although 20 of the 23 wrestlers denied any wrongdoing.[60] To prevent further match-fixing, the *Nihon Sumō Kyōkai* reinforced its investigative committee's capacity to look into potentially fixed matches, prohibited the use of mobile phones in sumo tournament sites and prohibited attendants from being present in dressing rooms.[61]

Even though intentionally losing a match has been acknowledged by the Association and commentators as possibly constituting undesirable conduct, establishing match-fixing in sumo remains difficult. It is necessary to show that there was foreknowledge of the outcome of the bout in question. Even if a given sumo bout appears to have been fixed, at least one of the participants involved must admit this foreknowledge. Otherwise, it is very difficult, if not impossible, for such an instance to qualify as match-fixing. In the case study from 2011 described above, there was physical evidence in the form of text messages which allowed the instance to qualify as a match-fixing scheme conducted over a fixed period by a select group of parties collaborating with one another for mutual benefit. In the defamation lawsuits filed up to 2011, however, the courts found that there was no definitive evidence to conclude that match-fixing had in fact taken place, despite multiple accusations made for years by persons involved in professional sumo.[62]

Future trends and developments in Japan

The willingness to consider that match-fixing may occur in sumo perhaps suggests a shift in thinking by at least some stakeholders away from the traditional conceptualisation of the practice of *ninjō*. As Japan's approach to match-fixing in sport suggests, however, protecting the integrity of sport itself is not the same as protecting the integrity of the sports betting industry. Like John Landy who quashed his chances at the world mile record by assisting a fallen competitor during a race at the 1956 Australian National Championships, many sumo wrestlers perform acts of sportsmanship and lose matches to improve their opponent's ranking. This conduct may be praised despite affecting the competition outcome. In contrast to this interpretation, where fans can legally bet on such competitions, the shadow of match-fixing causes such heart-warming moments to be looked upon with suspicion. Japan's approach to match-fixing involves limiting its prohibition to *kōei kyōgi* and *toto*, and otherwise leaving its regulation up to sports governing bodies if it is not related to gambling. It reflects the public's attitude against legalised gambling as evidenced by the backlash against extending the *toto* to baseball and rugby in light of the recent scandals surrounding baseball players[63] and members of Japan's elite badminton squad.[64] The disciplinary actions taken in both cases reflect the widely held belief in Japanese society that gambling itself poses a threat to integrity in sport.

In light of the general community disquiet about further legalising sports betting, it is not surprising that there is yet to be a significant public debate about the need for a holistic, legislative approach to match-fixing. Japan's international commitments and the globalisation of sport, however, suggest that the time is right for further consideration of this important issue. The Japanese government along with the Japan Rugby Football Union, for example, have expressed a commitment to achieving a level of sports integrity that conforms to international standards before the start of the 2019 Rugby World Cup and 2020 Tokyo Olympic Games. Moreover, Japanese teams are competing in jurisdictions where betting is more broadly legalised.

The Sunwolves, a new professional rugby team, joined the international Super Rugby competition in 2016, for example. The Sunwolves team is competing in jurisdictions where betting on rugby is legal: Australia, New Zealand and South Africa. It may no longer be possible to quarantine the prohibition on match-fixing to those sports which are government run and played in Japan. In order to ensure sports integrity on the international stage and for Japanese teams, it has become essential to strengthen cooperation between sporting associations and enforcement organisations in other countries, but there is not yet a clear plan on how this may be done in the context of contemporary, globalised Japanese sport.

Japan's participation in and hosting of international sports events may lead Japan to introduce ad hoc criminalisation of match-fixing, or at least a compulsory investigation system, for some international events such as the 2019 Rugby World Cup and the 2020 Tokyo Olympics. Criminalising match-fixing also inevitably alters the role and standing of any athlete under suspicion of being involved. Sanctions imposed on athletes by sports organisations up to the present would now be replaced with criminal sentences handed down by courts. The sumo-related defamation cases demonstrate the difficulty in establishing whether match-fixing has occurred. Criminalising match-fixing may bolster the viability and effectiveness of investigations into specific incidents. At the same time, it would also significantly impact the privacy and other rights of players. The primary challenge is to strike an appropriate balance between these two conflicting interests.

Conclusion

In Japan, with the exception of *kōei kyōgi* and *toto*, betting on sports is illegal. Accordingly, the practice of match-fixing is not targeted by the *Criminal Code*, and is instead considered a matter of ethics and sportsmanship unless it involves a sport on which betting is legalised. In Australia and many other countries, sports betting is a big, legalised industry. At the very core of the sports betting business is the uncertainty of the outcome, to which match-fixing poses a threat. Where sports betting is legal, countries have introduced very strict regulations to ensure integrity within sports and thus integrity in the related betting markets.[65] For the same reason, Japan tightly regulates *kōei kyōgi*, with the practice of match-fixing in these sectors criminalised under special laws. There are signs that the Japanese government is planning to expand the *toto* sports lottery system to include sports other than soccer, which will extend the criminalisation of the act of match-fixing in relation to those sports. These plans do not currently have the support of the general Japanese public, however. Moreover, the perceived link between gambling and match-fixing, as well as traditional notions such as *ninjō zumō*, have prevented a comprehensive public debate about prohibiting match-fixing generally. Contemporary developments, including the Tokyo Olympics and Japanese teams joining international competitions, may force a new evaluation of match-fixing before any domestic considerations.

Notes

1 This research was partly supported by JSPS KAKENHI Grant no. JP 25301006.
2 *Kōei kyōgi* refers to the four forms of government-regulated racing. It has also been translated as the 'four specific forms of competitive racing' or 'four publicly-managed racings'. See Yamazaki, T. and Mabuchi, Y., 2011, 'Sports betting and the law in Japan', in Anderson, P.M., Blackshaw, I.S., Siekmann, R.C.R. and Soek, J. (eds.) *Sports betting: law and policy*, Springer, pp. 515–520.
3 Japan's long-standing fascination with pachinko or slot machines is also another form of legalised gambling, but beyond the scope of this chapter.
4 The influence of crime syndicates has also declined, as discussed below.
5 Article 185 of the Criminal Code fines habitual gamblers a maximum of JP¥500,000, while art. 186(1) imposes a maximum term of imprisonment of three years on gamblers who are in the habit of gambling. The court determines whether the gambling is habitual by considering circumstances including previous gambling offences, recurrent gambling behaviour, the type of gambling and the amount being bet. See also Supreme Court (10 February 1949) *Keishū*, vol. 3, no. 2, p. 155.
6 Supreme Court (22 November 1950) *Keishū*, vol. 4, no. 11, p. 2380.
7 *Keiba hō* [Horse Racing Act], act no. 158, 1948 (Japan), arts. 31–34 ('*Horse Racing Act*').
8 *Jitensha kyōgi hō* [Bicycle Racing Act], act no. 209, 1948 (Japan), arts. 60–63 ('*Bicycle Racing Act*').
9 *Kogata jidōsha kyōsō hō* [Auto Racing Act], act no. 208, 1950 (Japan), arts. 65–68 ('*Auto Racing Act*').
10 *Mōtā bōto kyōsō hō* [Motor Boat Racing Act], act no. 242, 1951 (Japan), arts. 72–75 ('*Motor Boat Racing Act*').
11 Sasaki, A., 1999, *Kōei kyōgi no bunka-keizai-gaku* [The cultural economics of government-controlled competitions], Fuyōshobō Shuppan.
12 Supreme Court (22 October 1954) *Keishū*, vol. 8, no. 10, p. 1616, p. 1618.
13 Supreme Court (22 October 1954) *Keishū*, vol. 8, no. 10, p. 1616.
14 Ishikawa, W., 1970, '*Puro-yakyū yaochō senshu no keijisekinin* [The criminal liability of players for match-fixing in professional baseball]', *Toki no hōrei* [Law and Ordinances of the Times], no. 715, pp. 22–27, p. 27; Maeda, H., 1970, '*Puro-yakyū no yaochō jiken* [Match-fixing events in professional baseball]', *Keisatsu Kōron* [Police Public Opinion], vol. 25, no. 7, pp. 83–87, p. 87.
15 See, e.g. '*Kondo wa yaochō keirin Osaka de teire bōryokudanra taiho* [This time a fixed bicycle race: police raid in Osaka, several gang members arrested]' 1965, *Asahi Shimbun (evening ed.)*, 20 September, p. 11.
16 For the *toto* website, see Japan Sport Council, *Supōtsu kuji* [Sports lottery], www.toto-dream.com.
17 On the establishment of the *toto* system, see 'J. League bets on Toto' 2001, *The Japan Times*, 9 March, www.japantimes.co.jp/sports/2001/03/09/soccer/j-league/j-league-bets-on-toto.
18 On the Japan Sport Council, see Steele and Opie in this volume.

19 Japan Sport Council, '*Toto keiyaku* [*Toto* terms of agreement]', www.totodream.com/policy/agreement.html.

20 Conference minutes (no. 15), 140th meeting of the Committee on Education, House of Representatives, National Diet of Japan (23 May 1997); Conference minutes (no. 6), 142nd meeting of the Committee on Education, Culture, Sports, Science and Technology, House of Councillors, National Diet of Japan (17 February 1998).

21 Japan Sport Council 2004, *Supōtsu shinkō kuji toto 2004 nen shīzun no hanbai kekka gaikyō ni tsuite* [Regarding the sales results outlook of the sports promotion lottery toto 2004 season], www.jpnsport.go.jp/sinko/Portals/0/sinko/sinko/pdf/happyou161224_1.pdf. See also Japan Productivity Center 1995, *Rejā hakusho* [Leisure white paper]; Japan Productivity Center 2015, *Rejā hakusho* [Leisure white paper].

22 '*Sakkā kuji toto, tōsenkin appu* [Soccer lottery toto, prize money increased]' 2006, *Asahi Shimbun (morning ed.)*, 18 July, p. 34.

23 Brasor, P. and Tsubuku, M., 2010, 'Soccer lottery BIG in Japan', *The Japan Times*, 25 February, www.japantimes.co.jp/news/2010/02/25/business/soccer-lottery-big-in-japan/#.WFji1vmLSUk.

24 '*Puro-yakyū "toto"-an fujō chōtōha giirenmei, seido kentō e* [Professional baseball "toto" plan emerges, nonpartisan Diet caucus investigation into the system]' 2015, *Asahi Shimbun (morning ed.)*, 16 April, p. 4.

25 '*Gorinshō "toto konnan" Kyojin senshu no tobaku mondai* [Tokyo Olympic and Paralympic Games Minister says "toto is difficult" after gambling incident with Giants' players]' 2015, *Asahi Shimbun (evening ed.)*, 6 October, p. 2.

26 Two recent major incidents of gambling in Japanese sports made the front pages: '*Tobaku 3 senshu, muki shikkaku kyojin ni seisaikin 1000 manen yakyūkikō shobun* [3 gambling players, indefinite disqualification, Giants fined JP¥10 million, dealt with by baseball organisation]' 2015, *Asahi Shimbun (morning ed.)*, 11 November, p. 1; '*Fukuta senshu ga yakyū tobaku* [Fukuta, pitcher, gambling in baseball]' 2015, *Asahi Shimbun (morning ed.)*, 6 October, p. 34; '*Urakajino "kitai ya ōen uragitta"* [Underground casino "betrayed expectations and supporters"]', 29 April, p. 22. One incident involved a professional badminton player, who was widely considered to be a medal contender at the Olympic Games in Rio De Janeiro, frequenting an illegal casino.

27 '*Nishitetsu • Nagayasu tōshu ga yaōcho yakyū tobaku kara kane morau kōkyū nage, jigun ni wa sanshin tanomu "eikyū tuihō" shobun kimeru* [Nishitetsu's pitcher Nagayasu fixes match baseball gambling receives money from gang pitch well, but asks his team to strike out; punished by being "banned for sport for life"]' 1969, *Yomiuri Shimbun (morning ed.)*, 8 October, p. 15.

28 '*Yaochō wa jijitsu datta? Puro-yakyū nagayasu mototōshu no yaochō jiken* [Was the match-fixing real? Ex-professional baseball pitcher Nagayasu's match-fixing incident]' 1970, *Asahi Shimbun (evening ed.)*, 7 April, p. 11.

29 Sasakura, A., 2005, *Fukken – Ikenaga Masaaki, 35-nenkan no chinmoku no shinsō* [Restoration – Masaaki Ikenaga, the truth of 53 years' silence], Bungeishunjū.

30 The conduct of these 19 drivers was in direct violation of the *Auto Racing Act*, act no. 208, 1950 (Japan), arts. 65–68. See also '*Puro-yakyū kuroikiri o otte 1~8* [Following the professional baseball Black Mist Scandal, parts 1 to 8]' 1993, *Asahi Shimbun (evening ed.)*, 6 December, p. 3, 7 December, p. 3, 8 December, p. 3, 9 December, p. 3, 13 December, p. 3, 14 December, p. 3, 15 December, p. 3, 16 December, p. 3. See also Sasakura, above n. 29.

31 Tokyo District Court (19 September 1970), *Hanrei Jihō* no. 613, p. 104.
32 Nippon Professional Baseball 1970, *Yakyū kyōyaku* [Professional Baseball Agreement].
33 This agreement is referred to as baseball's constitution, and corresponds to Major League Baseball's Collective Bargaining Agreement. However, teams, not team members, are parties to the Professional Baseball Agreement.
34 Sasakura, above n. 29, p. 24; Shimoyama, E., 1970, '*Yakyū keiyaku to sore o meguru shomondai* [Baseball contracts and various problems concerning them]', *Juristo* [Jurist], vol. 453, pp. 41–47, p. 44.
35 Abe, T., 2010, *Yakyū tobaku to yaochō wa naze, nakunaranainoka* [Why does betting and match-fixing in baseball not go away?], KK Bestsellers, pp. 57–58; '*(Sazaesan wo sagashite) Kuroikiri jiken "haimen nage" no meitōshu no kioku* [(Find Sazaesan) Black Mist Scandal: memories from the "behind-the-back" notable pitcher]' 2011, *Asahi Shimbun (morning ed.)*, 2 April, p. 3.
36 Hayashi, N., 1996, *Soshiki bōryoku no ichi-danmen* [*One cross-section of organised violence*], Tachibana Shobō, p. 296.
37 Ibid., p. 292; Tobita, K., 1970, '*Yakyū tobaku ni tsuite* [On gambling in baseball]', *Keisatsu Kōron* [Police Public Opinion], vol. 25, no. 6 (June), pp. 93–97, pp. 94–95.
38 Ishikawa, above n. 14, p. 27.
39 Maeda, above n. 14, p. 87.
40 Ishikawa, above n. 14, p. 27.
41 Each prefecture has its own ordinances.
42 On sumo's role as a national sport, see Gilbert, H. and Watts, K., 2014, 'Internationalising sumo: from viewing to doing Japan's national sport', in Steele, S., Breaden, J. and Stevens, C.S. (eds.), *Internationalising Japan: discourse and practice*, Routledge, pp. 158–179.
43 See *Ginjō* 2010, '*Rakugo "Sanoyama" no butai o aruku* [Walking the stage of the "Sanoyama" rakugo]', November, http://ginjo.fc2web.com/208sanoyama/sanoyama.htm. Based on a *rakugo* (traditional comic performance), the story of Tanikaze Kajinosuke is illustrative. Tanikaze Kajinosuke, a prestigious Yokozuna-ranked wrestler, threw a match to allow the much smaller Sanoyama to win. Sanoyama was in deep financial trouble and greatly fatigued at the time of the bout from having to care for his mother, who was suffering from a severe illness. After nine losses in nine days and subsisting on water, Sanoyama won when Tanikaze intentionally placed his foot outside of the ring. Sumo fans came to refer to this act as *ninjō zumō*.
44 Sawano M., 2010, '*Ō-zumō ni okeru shinri to wa nanika* [What is the truth about professional sumo wrestling?]', *Gendai Shishō*, vol. 38, no. 13, pp. 114–125; Tamaki, M., 2011, *Ō-zumō yaochō hihan o warau* [Laughing at criticism of match-fixing in professional sumo], Asuka Shinsha; Tamaki, M., 2011, '*Yaochō de nani ga warui* [What is wrong with match-fixing?]', *Shinchō45*, vol. 30, no. 4, pp. 210–217.
45 The professional sumo wrestling system was settled in the seventeenth century as sumo arenas (*dohyō*) and merchant guilds were established, and sumo wrestlers from various domains began performing. By the eighteenth century, amateur performance was prohibited and the training of specialist wrestlers in units was established. Nitta, I., 2010, *Sumō no rekishi* [The history of sumo], Kodansha; Inagaki, M., 2014, '*Geki! Supōtsu hihyō (2) ō-zumō yaochō wa aku ni arazu* [Attack! Sports criticism 2: Grand Sumo: match-fixing is not evil]', *Hiroba Union*, no. 631, pp. 14–16.
46 Recently, researchers using statistical data have alleged match-fixing by wrestlers intent on moving up the ranks to obtain improved salary and conditions.

Kuwamori, M., 2013, *Ō-zumō no mikata [Looking at professional sumo]*, Heibonsha.

47 '*Kesshi no shōgen! Renzoku sukūpu tsuikyū dai-ichi-dan kakukai jōka! Sumō kyōkai wo kaitaiseyo dokusen wakunohō yaochō kokuhaku* [A courageous testimony! Scoop chase series one, cleaning up the sumo world! Demolish the sumo world-exclusive interview on Wakunoho's confession on match fixing]' 2008, *Shūkan Gendai*, 18 October, pp. 16–27.

48 Shūkan Post Editorial Department 2011, *Shinban 'Shūkan Posuto' wa ō-zumō yaochō o kō hōjitekita* [The brand new 'Shūkan Post' reported on match-fixing in professional sumo like this], Shogakukan, Tokyo.

49 Wrestlers may have been issued a warning for so-called 'lethargic sumo' (*mukiryoku-zumō*), however.

50 Tokyo District Court (26 March 2009), *Hanrei Jihō* no. 2039, p. 25.

51 '*Yaochō, Chiyohakuhō · Moto Kasuganishiki · Enatsukasa no san rikishi mitomeru kannyo giwaku sara ni hitori Ōzumō* [Match fixing, three sumo wrestlers, Chiyohakuhō, Moto Kasuganishiki, and Enatsukasa confess while one's involvement still under suspicion: professional sumo]' 2011, *Asahi Shimbun (evening ed.)*, 3 February, p. 11.

52 McNiell, D., 2011, 'Thrown open: the dark side of sumo wrestling', *Independent*, 3 February, www.independent.co.uk/news/world/asia/thrown-open-the-dark-side-of-sumo-wrestling-2202618.html.

53 On the 2010 scandal, see McCurry, J., 2010, 'Sumo wrestles with illegal betting scandal', *Guardian*, 28 June, www.theguardian.com/world/2010/jun/28/sumo-wrestles-illegal-betting-scandal; Tabuchi, H., 2011, 'Before big match, sumo wrestlers appear to text the outcome', *New York Times*, New York, 5 February, A4.

54 Mochidzuki, K., 2013, '*Ō-zumō ni okeru integrity mondai: yaochō mondai o chūshin ni (hōteki kanten kara mita kyōsō supōtsu no integrity: yaochō, mukiryoku shiai to sono taisaku o chūshin ni* [Integrity problems in professional sumo wrestling: focus on match-fixing problems (Integrity of competitive sports from a legal perspective: focus on match-fixing, throwing matches and their countermeasures)]', *Japan Sports Law Association Annual Review*, no. 20, pp. 53–72.

55 Tamaki, above n. 44; Kashihara, M., 2013, '*Gachinko to yaochō: ō-zumō no supōtsu shakaigaku* [Competing in earnest and match-fixing: the sports sociology of professional sumo]', *Bulletin of the Faculty of Sociology, Otemon Gakuin University*, no. 7, pp. 1–16.

56 A total of 629 sumo wrestlers and wrestlers in training participated in the January 2017 Basho tournament.

57 Japan Sumo Association, *Nihon Sumō Kyōkai kifu kōi sekō saisoku* [Detailed regulations for executing Japan Sumo Association endowments], art. 93; Mochidzuki, above n. 54, pp. 64–65.

58 Shūkan Post Editorial Department, above n. 48.

59 Oinuma, Y., 1994, *Sumō shakai no kenkyū* [Study of the society of sumo], Fumaido, p. 63.

60 Retirement is the *Nihon Sumō Kyōkai's* second harshest sanction (expulsion being the harshest). Only three of the wrestlers whose text message conversations were found admitted involvement in match-fixing. They were suspended for two years, receiving a lighter sentence for cooperating with the investigation. These wrestlers also retired soon after the judgment.

61 '*Shitaku-beya e no keitai mochikomi kinshi, sumōkyōkai ga yaochō bōshisaku* [Ban on bringing mobile phones into dressing rooms: Sumo Association

match-fixing prevention measures]' 2011, *Asahi Shimbun*, 4 May, www.asahi.com/special/08020/TKY201105040245.html.

62 ' "*Uradzuke shuzaishiteinai*" *Kitanoumi zenrijichō ga shōso, Kōdansha-gawa ni 1500-man'en baishō meirei* ["The reports aren't corroborated", Former chairman Kitanoumi demands JP¥15,000,000 compensation from Kodansha]' 2009, *Sankei News*, 5 March, http://webs.sankei.co.jp/search/page.do?mode=1&paperNo=1&publishDate=20090306&newsId=20090306100008110f&keyword=.

63 Three Yomiuri Giants pitchers bet on NPB and high school baseball games. One of the pitchers bet on the outcomes of games in which the Giants played. The three pitchers were suspended indefinitely by the NPB Commissioner: '*Tobaku 3 senshu, muki shikkaku Kyojin ni seisaikin 1000-man'en yakyūkikō shobun* [3 gambling players, indefinite disqualification, Giants fined JP¥10 million, dealt with by baseball organisation]', above n. 26. In late April 2016, the Tokyo Metropolitan Police arrested a restaurant owner on suspicion of organising the betting scheme, and former pitcher Shoki Kasahara on suspicion of aiding and abetting the restaurant owner: '*Kasahara hikoku, hatsukōhan yakyū tobaku jiken* [Accused Kasahara, first trial regarding baseball gambling incident]' 2016, *Asahi Shimbun (evening ed.)*, 11 July, p. 12; '*Kasahara mototōshura kiso yakyū tobaku jiken* [Ex-pitchers including Kasahara prosecuted, baseball gambling incident]' 2016, *Asahi Shimbun (morning ed.)*, 25 May, p. 31. Investigations also revealed that some Yomiuri Giants players bet among themselves on the outcomes of Giants regular season games: '*Enjin hassei, kateba 6-man–8-man ni Kyojin, genkatsugi wo kyōchō genkin yaritori ōkō* [Huddle chant: JP¥60–80 thousand to the Giants if won, highlights superstitions, cash exchange rampant]' 2016, *Asahi Shimbun (morning ed.)*, 15 March, p. 39. Such practices were not limited to players in the Yomiuri Giants according to some media reports: '*Hanshin demo kinsen yaritori puro yakyu* [Money exchange in professional baseball, even at Hanshin]' 2016, *Asahi Shimbun (evening ed.)*, 15 March, p. 1; '*DeNa senshu, kōkō yakyū kuji "shūgi" mo* [DeNa player, high school lottery, also at celebrations]' 2016, *Asahi Shimbun (morning ed.)*, 21 March, p. 38; '*Momota senshu, mukigen shutsujō teishi Tago senshu wa tōroku masshō ihō kajino* [Momota faces indefinite suspension, Tago deregistered, illegal casino]' 2016, *Asahi Shimbun (evening ed.)*, 11 April, p. 10.

64 In April 2016, the Nippon Badminton Association alleged that two players frequented an illegal casino. The Association suspended a player indefinitely and removed the name of his more senior teammate from their Athletes' Register, effectively preventing the players from participating in the Rio De Janeiro Olympics: '*Momota-senshu, mukigen shutsujō teishi Tago-senshu wa tōroku masshō ihō kajino* [Momota faces indefinite suspension, Tago deregistered, illegal casino]', above n. 63. The Japan Sport Council was considering requiring the return of sports subsidies paid to the players: see '*Tago・Momota-ryō-senshu no joseikin, JSC "henkan o kentō"* [JSC "considering the return" of Tago, Momota subsidy] 2016, *Asahi Shimbun (morning ed.)*, 16 April, p. 16.

65 See Menz and Skene, and Opie and Lim in this volume.

Chapter 4

The Australian legal framework for countering match-fixing

Hayden Opie and Genevieve Lim

Introduction: achieving a national approach to match-fixing in a federal state

Match-fixing with links to betting is a threat to the integrity of sports competitions worldwide. Recognising this threat, Australian federal, state and territory governments in 2011 jointly decided to implement a range of nationally consistent legislative and regulatory countermeasures which included specific criminal laws aimed not only at match-fixers but others complicit in fixes who seek to benefit financially. Sports betting was to be more closely regulated, with sport governing bodies deciding whether to permit betting on their sports.

This Australian approach has been acclaimed as a guide for other nations seeking to address the problem of match-fixing.[1] However, it has never been completed as envisaged and it is questionable whether the framework is sufficient to respond to the challenges posed by the internationalisation of betting markets. Specifically, the need to assemble and disseminate intelligence about match-fixing and suspicious betting among law enforcement and sports bodies both inside and outside of Australia continues to present difficulties.

This chapter analyses the Australian framework for countering match-fixing including its origins, the role of sports governing bodies in countering match-fixing and approving betting on their events, and new criminal laws which were refined from original proposals to target behaviour intended to corrupt sports betting rather than the act of match-fixing. This framework applies within a federal governance structure[2] in which criminal law and gambling regulation are the responsibility of state and territory governments. Also, in contrast to most countries in Asia, gambling is lawful in Australia in a wide range of circumstances including on animal racing (horses and greyhounds) and human sports. Gambling is therefore conducted openly, provides taxation revenue to governments and fees to sports bodies, and is subject to significant regulation.[3] The chapter concludes by analysing the progress and shortcomings of the Australian framework.

The threat of match-fixing and the origins of the Australian framework

Until 2010, match-fixing was not considered a material threat to Australian sport.[4] In October 2009, when speaking to the annual conference of the Australian and New Zealand Sports Law Association, Canadian academic and investigative journalist Declan Hill[5] claimed that a major match-fixing scandal would affect Australian sport within five years. He warned that Australia was 'ripe for exploitation by an Asian crime syndicate with an established reach into Europe and an eye to expand'.[6] Hill believed that the combination of obsession with sport, numerous sporting codes, a tradition of sports betting, the advent of online gambling and shared time zones with Asia made Australia an obvious target for match-fixing.[7]

This prediction of a major scandal was fulfilled in fewer than ten months, although the fix was alleged to have been initiated in Australia. On 21 August 2010, an incident occurred in a National Rugby League ('NRL') match which suggested an attempted spot-fix.[8] Following investigation by both the NRL and the New South Wales police, a player was charged and, in October 2011, convicted of a fraud-related offence.[9] Others who had bet on the incident were charged with fraud offences, but the prosecutions were not successful for various reasons including a lack of evidence of the involvement of the accused in the attempted fix and the difficulty of establishing a 'deception' when placing a bet, even with knowledge of the fix.[10]

On 5 January 2011, amid growing international concern over match-fixing and following soon after the NRL incident, the New South Wales Law Reform Commission ('NSWLRC') was asked by the Attorney-General for New South Wales to review the criminal law in that State relating to cheating at gambling; specifically, conduct directed at fixing results or individual events in the course of sporting and other activities which might be the subject of spot or spread betting.[11]

While the NSWLRC process was underway, the Australian Council of Sport and Recreation Ministers (from the Commonwealth and all states and territories) adopted a *National Policy on Match-Fixing in Sport* ('*Policy*')[12] on 10 June 2011. The NSWLRC delivered its report on reform of the law relating to cheating at gambling in August 2011.[13] The Council met again on 30 September 2011[14] and agreed on a legislative and administrative model for approval of betting on sports, the sharing of information between betting operators and integrity controls within sports. Arrangements were also put in place to refer to relevant state and territory ministers the question of adopting nationally consistent criminal laws to deal with cheating at gambling (inspired by recommendations in the NSWLRC report).

On 18 November 2011, the Commonwealth, state and territory Attorneys-General supported the development of such laws[15] and New

South Wales was the first state to introduce legislation in August 2012.[16] These measures were accompanied in at least one state by increased police resources devoted to enforcing the new laws[17] and the creation of a National Integrity in Sport Unit ('NISU')[18] to perform a national coordination role including developing policy and liaising with national and international stakeholders.

The creation of the framework placed new and demanding obligations on stakeholders ranging from governments to relatively small sports bodies. The high value that Australians place on sport and its protection from corrupting influences is evident from the expeditious development and implementation of a complex model involving many different bodies.

Overview of the Australian framework

The *Policy* formally acknowledges the threat to the credibility of sport worldwide posed by corruption motivated by 'illegal and irregular sports betting'[19] and represents a commitment by Australian governments to collaborate with sports organisations, betting operators and each other to address match-fixing behaviour. It is underpinned by four principles:

- a nationally consistent approach to deterring and dealing with match-fixing in Australia;
- information sharing and highly efficient networks between governments, major sports, betting operators and law enforcers;
- consistent national code of conduct principles for sport; and
- active participation in international efforts to combat corruption in sport, including an international code of conduct and an international body.[20]

As the platform for collaboration, the *Policy* specifies in detail the expected roles of governments, sporting organisations and betting agencies. '[L]egislation, regulation, codes of conduct and industry standards'[21] were envisaged as the basis of implementation.[22] Specifically, the *Policy* provides for: sports governing bodies establishing codes of conduct prohibiting match-fixing (sporting sanctions); criminal punishment imposed by the justice system within each Australian jurisdiction; and regulating the sports betting industry and requiring betting operators to enter into agreements with sports governing bodies before offering betting markets on their sports events.

The obligations of sporting bodies are set out in cl. 4.2 of the *Policy*. The leading obligation is to 'adopt an anti-match-fixing/anti-corruption code of conduct which aligns with nationally agreed principles'. Sporting organisations are also obliged to: educate players about anti-match-fixing measures; bind officials and others to the code; enter into integrity agreements with betting agencies whereby information about possible match-fixing is exchanged and authority given for the operation of betting markets; and exchange information with various interested parties including law enforcement authorities.

Clause 4.5 of the *Policy* specifies the behaviour which the code of conduct will restrict, as reflected in the nationally agreed principles. This behaviour is wider in scope than the act of match-fixing and includes betting on the sport or encouraging others to do so, revealing inside information about forthcoming team composition and tactics, failing to report others engaging in or suspected of engaging in prohibited conduct and failing to report being approached to engage in prohibited conduct.

To assist sports, especially smaller ones with limited resources, NISU established a template for a code of conduct which reflects the various requirements of the *Policy*.[23] The prohibitions set out in cl. 3 relating to match-fixing and spot-fixing require that the conduct be linked to betting. Conduct engaged in for tactical sporting reasons which incidentally affects betting would appear not to be prohibited under the template.

The next section analyses the second of the principal legal mechanisms under the *Policy*: namely, specific laws to criminalise match-fixing.

Specific match-fixing legislation

The 2011 NRL match-fixing case is regarded as the first of its kind in Australia, although there were two earlier successful criminal prosecutions for fraudulently entering a superior horse in a thoroughbred race using the identity of a less well-performed horse.[24] The 2011 NRL case suggested that existing fraud offences were not sufficient to punish all people involved in dishonest practices related to betting in sport.[25] It also highlighted the fact that sporting bodies may not have authority over all relevant actors for the purpose of imposing sporting sanctions.

For those reasons and others identified in its Report, the NSWLRC recommended, and Australian governments agreed, that new criminal laws were necessary to deal with match-fixing. Specific legislation criminalising match-fixing and related corrupt conduct in sport has been initiated in four states and both territories, although the legislation in Victoria and Queensland contains some significant differences to the other jurisdictions. Western Australia[26] and Tasmania maintain that their existing criminal laws are consistent with the objectives of the *Policy* which acknowledges that states and territories need not necessarily adopt uniform legislation.[27]

New South Wales ('NSW') was the first state to act by creating five new criminal offences. The NSW model is the benchmark against which the legislation of the other states and the territories is measured. The offences encompass the conduct of fixers, facilitators and concealers, those who use knowledge of the fix for financial gain (but are not involved in the fix), and those who use other 'inside information' about sport performance for financial gain.

A key innovation under the NSW legislation was to refrain from prohibiting the fix (or underperformance or 'tanking'[28]) as such and to criminalise it only when there is an intentional link to betting. In general terms, this approach served to insulate from criminality sporting underperformance where it occurs for a sporting reason; for example, resting star performers to conserve their energy for later play. Nonetheless, some instances of underperformance may attract sporting sanctions under a sport's rules even though there is no criminality. This situation might occur where parties to a contest who have qualified for a final series may seek to lose in order to avoid playing an especially strong opponent in an early round of the final series.

The provisions set out in the *Crimes Act 1900* (NSW) ('*NSW Crimes Act*') apply to both the outcomes of contests and any contingency associated with an event (*NSW Crimes Act*, s. 193J). This means that spot fixing – manipulating an otherwise innocuous occurrence within a match – and fixing the ultimate result of a contest are equally prohibited. The inclusion of contingencies is necessary to ensure that criminals are unable to profit from exotic betting, i.e. the betting market that has emerged relating to elements of a match, such as who will kick the first goal or concede the first penalty. Sporting participants may be more easily persuaded to execute a spot fix because it does not affect the final result of the competition and may therefore be rationalised as less morally reprehensible than throwing a match. These manipulations, however, may still achieve significant profit for gamblers who are aware of them.

The first new criminal offence relates to conduct that intentionally or recklessly corrupts the betting outcome of an event with the intention of obtaining a financial advantage or creating financial detriment for someone else (*NSW Crimes Act*, s. 193N), whether or not that advantage or disadvantage is achieved (*NSW Crimes Act*, s. 193L(2)). Two other closely related offences are created for facilitating that conduct (*NSW Crimes Act*, s. 193O) and encouraging its concealment (*NSW Crimes Act*, s. 193P).

A fourth criminal offence was created by the NSW legislation for the use of 'corrupt conduct information' (*NSW Crimes Act*, s. 193Q(1)). This information is knowledge of perpetrated or planned conduct that corrupts the betting outcome of an event. A person commits the offence where she or he uses such information to place a bet, encourages another person to place a bet, or communicates the information to another whom the person knows is likely to bet on the event.

These four offences are underpinned by two necessary conditions (*NSW Crimes Act*, s. 193H(1)). First, the alleged conduct must affect or be likely to affect the outcome of betting on the event or event contingency upon which it is lawful to bet under a law of NSW, another state, a territory or the Commonwealth. The event or event contingency may occur anywhere in the world, but the betting market must be located within Australia in order to fall within the scope of the offence. Second, it must be contrary to the standard of integrity that a reasonable person would expect of a person in a position to affect a betting outcome. As indicated above, this innovative formulation is designed to exclude conduct engaged in for sporting reasons which would likely but incidentally affect a betting outcome, such as 'tactical decisions, honest errors, and even foul play that results in a penalty'.[29] It would be highly controversial to subject this type of conduct to criminal penalty for match-fixing where there is no intention to engage in the conduct for material gain, such as a bribe or gambling profits.

A fifth offence concerns the misuse of 'inside information' (*NSW Crimes Act*, s. 193Q(2)). Inside information is information that is not generally available which would be likely to affect betting choices; that is, the information is sensitive because it may materially affect the likelihood of a result or contingency occurring and therefore provide an individual with an advantage in a betting market which is unavailable to other bettors. A person possessing such information, knowing or being reckless as to whether it is inside information, may be guilty of an offence when she or he uses such information to place a bet, encourages another person to place a bet, or communicates the information to another whom the person knows is likely to place a bet.

The penalty for each of the first four offences is up to ten years' imprisonment and up to two years' imprisonment for using inside information.

South Australia's legislation[30] mirrors that of NSW as does the legislation of the two territories. However, the Australian Capital Territory did not include the offences of concealing or facilitating corrupt conduct[31] and the Northern Territory fixed the maximum term of imprisonment for the first four offences at seven years rather than ten.[32] Victoria's legislation[33] also follows the NSW pattern, but omits an offence for the use of inside information.

Queensland's legislation[34] has some similarities with the NSW pattern but is not framed in terms of 'corruption of a betting outcome'. Rather, it seeks to control 'engaging in match-fixing conduct' or 'match-fixing arrangements' (*Criminal Code 1899* (Qld), s. 443 ('*Qld Criminal Code*')). Match-fixing conduct is criminalised (*Qld Criminal Code*, s. 443A) and occurs if four requirements are met. First, the conduct must affect or be likely to affect the outcome of a sporting event or sporting contingency in Queensland or elsewhere (*Qld Criminal Code*, s. 443). Second, the outcome of the event or the happening of the contingency must be lawfully subject to betting under a law of the Commonwealth or a state (*Qld Criminal Code*, s. 443). Third, the conduct must be contrary to the standard of integrity that a reasonable person would expect of a person in a position to affect the outcome of the event or the happening of the contingency

(*Qld Criminal Code*, s. 443). Fourth, the conduct must be engaged in for the purpose of obtaining pecuniary advantage or causing pecuniary detriment (*Qld Criminal Code*, s. 443A).

Three other closely related offences are created for facilitating match-fixing conduct (*Qld Criminal Code*, s. 443B), encouraging its concealment (*Qld Criminal Code*, s. 443E) and inducing it by means of offering benefits or making threats (*Qld Criminal Code*, s. 443C). Match-fixing arrangements mean agreements between two or more persons relating to match-fixing conduct for the purpose of pecuniary gains or detriments (*Qld Criminal Code*, s. 443). Like most other states and territories, using information about match-fixing (*Qld Criminal Code*, s. 443D) and inside information (*Qld Criminal Code*, s. 443F) is criminalised.

Queensland's legislation differs materially from the NSW model in regard to the match-fixer because it is aimed at conduct intended to achieve pecuniary benefit or detriment *without any requirement that the purpose of the conduct be linked to the corruption of a betting outcome of an event*. Thus, a person paid a bribe to lose in Queensland unconnected with betting may be guilty of a match-fixing offence, but will not be captured under the NSW legislative model.

Gambling regulation and an approval pathway for betting on sport

In addition to requiring laws to address match-fixing, the *Policy* also seeks to limit opportunities for corruption within the betting industry. In essence, the central feature is to prohibit gambling on sport without the consent of the governing body of the sport. While Australia is not the first nation to institute consent arrangements,[35] it is a distinctive feature of the Australian framework, especially when compared with other countries in the Asian region.

The *Policy* requires governments in each jurisdiction to establish legislation which designates a process whereby sports controlling bodies register events for betting and engage with betting organisations to sanction types of wagering.[36] Sports will determine which levels of competition and which contingencies may be gambled upon, and a fee will be paid to the sport in return for permission to provide a betting market on those competitions.[37] Arrangements are also made for betting service providers to supply information to sports in relation to details of suspicious patterns of betting, suggestive of fixing. Being able to veto bet types and competitions helps sports protect more vulnerable participants from approaches by match-fixers.[38]

The Australian Council of Sport and Recreation Ministers agreed to an Approval Pathway for Betting on Sport Events in 2011 based on pre-existing Victorian legislation.[39] This legislation sets out the process by which sport controlling bodies can be recognised and betting approval granted. However, only NSW has since passed legislation[40] to implement the objectives of the *Policy* in this respect. In practice, however, many major sports have developed agreements with betting service providers in relation to national betting markets established in relation to their competitions and to share information. These are a natural development where a betting operator may offer markets on the same sport across many jurisdictions and it is logical to apply the same conditions to competitions in the same league in other locations. Although the agreements are only currently supported by legislation in Victoria and NSW, their national application has meant that there is no pressing need for legislation in the other states and the territories.

Some aspects of the Australian online gambling market are regulated by federal law. The *Interactive Gambling Act 2001* (Cth) is designed to restrain the ability of problem gamblers to access particularly addictive forms of online gambling,[41] but it also limits some types of betting that are believed to be attractive to match-fixers. The legislation, which is not within the scope of the *Policy*, is considered by Menz and Skene in this volume.

Evaluation of the Australian framework

Achievements

Specific match-fixing legislation has been adopted by a majority of Australian jurisdictions in a remarkably short period of time and represents a major strength of the Australian framework. While there have only been a small number of match-fixing prosecutions,[42] these cases demonstrate that the new, specific match-fixing legislation has been sufficient to successfully prosecute corrupt conduct in sporting events. In particular, widely applicable criminal penalties are effective at penalising the external individuals who instigate the corruption of competitions but are beyond the disciplinary authority of sports organisations. Match-fixing prosecutions may complement other investigations into organised crime.[43]

While the criminal penalties imposed have been relatively light,[44] the prosecutions have achieved a greater impact because the major penalty for those participants convicted of match-fixing has been exclusion from their sports and the end of their sporting careers.[45] While this exclusion may be achieved without criminal prosecution through disciplinary measures, sporting organisations would encounter significant difficulties proving the execution of match-fixing without the investigative powers of the police. When combined, the force of the criminal justice and sports systems is more effective in identifying and punishing match-fixing than sports attempting to deal with the issues alone.[46]

The *Policy* has resulted in the successful engagement of sports bodies by government and the promotion of anti-match-fixing codes of conduct through mainstream Australian sports. The federal body NISU plays an important role in this process.[47] Victoria Police has created a dedicated Sporting Integrity Intelligence Unit[48] and some major sports governing bodies have also established integrity units to investigate and prosecute corruption in sport. Educative and regulatory measures have widespread support in the community.

The *Policy* contemplates that betting on sports events should occur only with the approval of the controlling body for the sport. While legislation establishing the betting approval pathway has not been universal, its implementation in the two states (NSW and Victoria) which lead most elite sporting and gambling activity has in practice extended the regime to other Australian jurisdictions. Legal gambling operators enter into agreements with the major sports to gain permission to establish betting markets within NSW and Victoria, but also negotiate for a national market even though there is no legislative requirement to do so. As stated above, this confers on sport controlling bodies an important measure of control over whether betting is conducted on their competitions and events.

The betting approval pathway also contributes to monitoring in relation to match-fixing. Agreements between sports and betting operators not only limit gambling markets to those variables which are less susceptible to corruption, but also provide for information sharing, including suspicious activity. The widespread opportunity to bet lawfully with regulated bookmakers also improves the ability of monitoring agencies to track suspect betting patterns within lawful Australian betting markets.

Shortcomings and challenges

Australia has made an early and decisive start in reforming its laws and government policies and is regarded as a world leader in the field. However, a number of difficulties remain in the formulation and implementation of Australia's match-fixing framework, as outlined below.

Lack of legislative consistency between jurisdictions

Criminal laws specifically prohibiting match-fixing and associated behaviour have not been adopted in all Australian jurisdictions. This lack of consistency is attributable to Australia's federal structure under which no one unit has total or overriding responsibility for criminal law and gambling regulation.[49] Perhaps it is no coincidence that Senator Mark Arbib, the energetic Commonwealth Minister for Sport who championed the *Policy*, departed politics before the process of implementation could be completed. The Australian political system in its federated state requires significant energy and determination from the governments of all jurisdictions to implement agreed objectives, and where this is not present implementation may be fragmented.

Where match-fixing legislation exists, there are some instances of divergence in substance and technical formulation, as demonstrated in this chapter. This lack of legislative consistency gives rise to the possibility that match-fixing may be prosecuted differently across Australia, even where the corrupt conduct is essentially identical. The inconsistency may be particularly glaring if match-fixing is prosecuted with different outcomes within the same leagues or competitions which stage events in a number of states and territories.

This inconsistency is a serious consideration for event organisers seeking to stage large sporting festivals comprising competitions in multiple locations, such as the Cricket or Rugby World Cups. Sophisticated match-fixing syndicates may target jurisdictions where their activities will not attract criminal penalties. Fear of that occurrence may influence the decisions of event organisers in determining which states and territories to include in their event programmes. For governments which are usually keen to attract major sporting festivals for economic reasons, the failure to adopt best practice anti-match-fixing measures may make their bids for hosting rights less competitive. Victoria, Western Australia and Tasmania have not established a specific criminal offence regarding the misuse of inside information. This gap raises the prospect of inconsistencies in prosecutions between jurisdictions. Savvy participants in competitions may inappropriately share inside information and bet in those three jurisdictions where they will avoid criminal penalty. Although sporting sanctions may apply, not all who take advantage of such information will be subject to the disciplinary codes of sport.

Further, despite agreement to adopt consistent legislation to regulate sports betting, only Victoria and NSW have implemented legislation which provides for authorised betting pathways. This regulation is a tangible means of empowering sports and betting operators to minimise integrity risks. It is not apparent that there are material obstructions to the development of consistent betting approval pathway legislation in other jurisdictions. However, the practical effect may be limited given the emergence of commercial arrangements between sport controlling bodies and lawful betting operators which favour nation-wide agreements and this means that enactment of legislation is a low priority.

Restrictions on live betting

The rapid rise of online gambling has been identified as an emerging risk to the integrity of Australian sport.[50] Also, any movement of betting from mainstream operators to unregulated or under-regulated offshore operations creates further risks for Australia.[51] As described above, the *Interactive Gambling Act 2001* (Cth) prohibits online in-game betting on human sports. Consumers seeking this form of gambling may resort to off-shore so-called black and grey betting markets which are easily accessible. A recent report into the operation of the legislation determined that the prohibition was still preferable, despite the rise in popularity and in-play online betting being permissible in animal racing.[52] There is a real danger that permitting in-play online betting on sports might create a greater risk of match-fixing.[53] Alternatively, permitting such betting may redirect it away from international providers to legal Australian outlets where greater regulation and oversight exists. As this form of betting becomes more popular, the case for retaining the prohibition should be reviewed.

Enforcement difficulties

Prosecuting match-fixing offences is constrained in at least three areas: the formulation of the offences, legal restrictions in relation to sharing information and lack of material resources to monitor and investigate suspicious behaviour.

Currently, Australian legislation provides that match-fixing may only be prosecuted where manipulation occurs in relation to an event or event contingency which is the subject of a legal betting market in Australia.[54] An important concern, therefore, is that match-fixing performed to secure gains on unregulated and under-regulated international gambling markets (for example, Asian online betting services not registered in Australia) will not be captured by the main Australian match-fixing offences.

Foreign betting markets are known to be active on lower-level Australian sports competitions[55] where there may not necessarily be a legal Australian betting market. That development renders those competitions attractive to those who organise fixes because Australian match-fixing laws will not apply. To ensure prosecution of match-fixing occurring in Australia which is linked to foreign betting, the offences should be redefined to apply irrespective of where the betting occurs or whether it is lawful or not in Australia.

Sports governing bodies are able to share suspicions regarding match-fixing with law enforcement agencies, but this is a one-way road. In the course of investigating match-fixing, Australian law enforcement agencies collect information via telecommunication intercepts, surveillance, interviews and interrogations, and border protection seizures. There are numerous legal restrictions on sharing intelligence, particularly with organisations other than law enforcement agencies. Consequently, police must not share intelligence to enable sports to disrupt match-fixing, accurately gauge integrity in their competitions or take disciplinary action under sporting rules until the intelligence has been made public through legal processes such as a trial. Evidence collected by a law enforcement agency might be insufficient for criminal prosecution; a sporting body, however, may pursue disciplinary procedures more successfully because of the lower standard of proof applicable to civil procedures. Sports could also utilise intelligence to cancel competitions, reassign officials and prosecute breaches of a range of rules that are not addressed by match-fixing legislation, such as consorting with known match-fixers.

While strong public policy justifications underpin the prohibition on sharing with sporting organisations the intelligence gathered through the use of law enforcement powers, it is regrettable that such information cannot be utilised in some form to address match-fixing in ways other than criminal prosecution, such as in disciplinary proceedings. The limits of, and mechanisms for, any such sharing require further analysis and debate. Arguably, it would be less controversial for agencies to share such information with a newly created government entity designed to investigate and even prosecute match-fixing and integrity breaches, akin to the role of the Australian Sports Anti-Doping Authority in relation to doping. This hypothetical agency could also function as a central clearing house or 'brain' for match-fixing intelligence and relevant data similar to the United Kingdom Gambling Commission's Sports Betting Intelligence Unit,[56] receiving and disclosing intelligence as appropriate. Neither NISU nor the Australian Federal Police[57] currently fulfil a dedicated ongoing, operational role in that respect.

Moreover, the effectiveness of Australian match-fixing legislation will be strongly influenced by whether sufficient law enforcement resources are dedicated to gather evidence and prosecute offences. Determining the total number and allocation of resources may be difficult for those who lead law enforcement, but it is notable that most of the match-fixing cases prosecuted under the new laws have occurred in Victoria which has an organisation dedicated to the task. Any insufficiency in resourcing has the further consequence of making it difficult to estimate the extent of match-fixing in Australia.

Fixers as victims

International studies and experience have demonstrated that the organisers of fixes can intentionally place players in very difficult circumstances to intimidate or coerce players to engage in match-fixing.[58] Non-payment of wages, threats of violence, presence in a foreign country without local support of families and friends, and control over accommodation are forms of coercion employed by fixers to pressure players into corrupt conduct. In this respect, an Australian judge described the predicament of one player as 'modern slavery'.[59] International and Australian experience also demonstrates the impact on players who are convicted of match-fixing, with suicide recorded not infrequently.[60]

Steps to address these vulnerabilities as a cause of match-fixing have received less notice and fewer resources in Australia than other initiatives in this field. More should be done to minimise the impact of factors that lead players to match-fix as a useful, if not potent, preventive measure.[61]

Conclusion

Australia has developed an innovative policy to deal with match-fixing in sport. The *Policy* accommodates Australia's federal nature which divides relevant legal responsibilities between governments. It also operates in an environment where gambling on sport is generally lawful and popular.

The approach taken has been to adopt specific criminal laws to prohibit various forms of behaviour associated with match-fixing and to encourage sports to establish disciplinary codes based on a model developed by the government sector and coordinated by a federal agency, NISU. Betting on sports events requires the consent of controlling bodies which betting operators are encouraged to obtain via a specified pathway. Arrangements for the cooperative exchange of information and intelligence especially between sports bodies and gambling operators are encouraged.

There have been significant achievements in the implementation of the *Policy*, but the framework as originally envisaged remains incomplete and perhaps stalled. With a growing threat of corruption linked to internet betting, there is a need to ensure that the Australian framework is as strong as originally envisaged.

Notes

1 In 2013, when addressing the Federation of Indian Chambers of Commerce and Industry on a proposed Bill to implement new match-fixing laws (which lapsed upon a change of government), Mohan Parasaran, the Solicitor General of India, said '[t]his Bill has been drafted after studying the laws of different countries especially from European Union like Denmark, Finland, Germany, etcetera. Australian model is so far the best.': 'Sporting fraud prevention bill styled on laws in many countries' 2013, *Business Standard*, 13 October, www.business-standard.com/article/news-ians/sporting-fraud-prevention-bill-styled-on-laws-in-many-countries-113101300521_1.html. See also, Ross, S.F., Gorman, J., III and Mentzer, R., 2015, 'Reform of sports gambling in the United States: lessons from down under', *Arizona State Sports and Entertainment Law Journal*, vol. 5, no. 1. pp. 6–50.

2 The Australian federated body is known as the Commonwealth. The federating bodies are the six states: (in order of population size) New South Wales, Victoria, Queensland, Western Australia, South Australia and Tasmania. There are two self-governing federal territories: the Australian Capital Territory and the Northern Territory.

3 See Menz and Skene in this volume.

4 Some incidents occurred prior to 2010, including the secret (later exposed) disciplining of two leading national team cricketers for having accepted payment from a

suspected overseas bookmaker for inside information about cricket pitch conditions: see Speed, M., 2011, *Sticky wicket*, Harper Sports, pp. 32–42. See also two criminal prosecutions for fraud over the substitution of horses in thoroughbred racing: on the Royal School scandal, see Opas, P. 1982, *The great ring-in*, Wildgrass Books, and on the Fine Cotton affair, see Ellem, W., 1994, 'Fine Cotton affair', in Vamplew, W., Moore, K., O'Hara, J., Cashman, R. and Jobling, I. (eds.) *Oxford companion to Australian sport*, 2nd edn., Oxford University Press, p. 165.

5 Hill is the author of the landmark text: Hill, D., 2008, *The fix: soccer and organized crime*, McClelland and Stewart.

6 *Australian Leisure Management* 2009, 'Australia a target for match-fixing', 9 October, www.ausleisure.com.au/news/australia-a-target-for-match-fixing.

7 Ibid.

8 The implicated player, Ryan Tandy, played for the Sydney-based team, the Canterbury Bulldogs. Within the first few minutes of a game, Tandy appeared to deliberately concede a penalty when the opposition, the North Queensland Cowboys, were in an easy scoring position. A betting plunge had occurred on the outcome of the first scoring point of the match, being that the Cowboys would kick the first score from a penalty. Those allegedly involved in the fix stood to win over AU$100,000 on Tabcorp, an Australian sports betting agency. As the Cowboys had elected to tap the ball and play on to score a try, rather than score from a penalty kick, the bets failed. The irregular nature of the betting caused the NRL to launch an investigation and this led to involvement of the criminal justice authorities: see Davies, L., 2011, 'Ryan Tandy found guilty of trying to fix 2010 match between Canterbury Bulldogs and North Queensland Cowboys', *Daily Telegraph*, 6 October. See generally Massoud, J., 2014, *The penalty*, Allen and Unwin.

9 Davies, above n. 8.

10 'Rugby League match fixing charges dismissed' 2012, *News.com.au*, 18 May; Gardiner, S., 2013, 'NRL match fixing case thrown out', *The Sydney Morning Herald*, 20 June.

11 New South Wales Law Reform Commission 2011, *Cheating at gambling*, consultation paper no. 12. See especially at pp. 15–19.

12 Sport and Recreation Ministers' Council 2011, *National policy on match-fixing in sport*, 10 June, www.health.gov.au/internet/main/publishing.nsf/Content/F6DB8637F05C9643CA257C310021CCE9/$File/National%20Policy%20on%20Match-Fixing%20in%20Sport%20(FINAL).pdf.

13 New South Wales Law Reform Commission 2011, *Cheating at gambling*, report no. 130, August, www.lawreform.justice.nsw.gov.au/Documents/Publications/Reports/Report-130.pdf.

14 Sport and Recreation Ministers' Council 2011, *Ministers endorse proposed model to give effect to the National Policy on Match Fixing in Sport*, communique, 30 September, http://livelonger.health.gov.au/internet/main/publishing.nsf/Content/communique_20110930.

15 Fox, T., 2013, 'Match-fixing: the Australian legislative response', *Australian Parliamentary Library*, 14 March, www.aph.gov.au/About_Parliament/Parliamentary_Departments/Parliamentary_Library/FlagPost/2013/March/Match-fixing_the_Australian_legislative_response.

16 *Crimes Amendment (Cheating at Gambling) Bill 2012* (NSW).

17 See Murnane and Moller in this volume.

18 Department of Health 2016, *National Integrity of Sport Unit*, www.health.gov.au/internet/main/publishing.nsf/content/national-integrity-of-sport-unit.

19 Sport and Recreation Ministers' Council, above n. 12, cl. 1.6.

20 Ibid., cl. 1.5.

21 Ibid., p. 1.

22 Other ways in which match-fixing has been confronted include education and moral suasion of sports participants, disrupting potential fixers by making it known that they are under close observation and closing the international border to suspected operatives.
23 National Integrity in Sport Unit 2016, *Anti-match-fixing policy template*, 1 August, www.health.gov.au/internet/main/publishing.nsf/Content/Anti-match-fixing-policy-template.
24 See above n. 1. Further instances from animal racing of criminal prosecution for conduct amounting to match-fixing from animal racing were cited by the New South Wales Law Reform Commission, above n. 11, pp. 74–75.
25 This conclusion was also reached by the New South Wales Law Reform Commission: New South Wales Law Reform Commission, above n. 11.
26 When questioned about the commitment in 2014, the Western Australian Minister for Sport and Recreation, Racing and Gaming stated that legal advice confirmed that existing legislation adequately addressed the commitments in the *Policy*: Western Australia 2014, *Parliamentary Debates*, Legislative Assembly Estimates Committee A, 20 May, p. E39 (Terrence Keith Waldron, Minister for Sport and Recreation). The Minister did not detail how a match-fixing incident would be addressed under the *Criminal Code Compilation Act 1913* (WA).
27 Sport and Recreation Ministers' Council, above n. 12, cl. 3.4.
28 'Tanking' is a slang term commonly used to describe underperformance regarded as improper. It is sometimes used in official documents.
29 New South Wales 2012, *Parliamentary Debates*, Legislative Assembly, 22 August, pp. 14227–14230 (Greg Smith, Attorney General).
30 *Criminal Law Consolidation Act 1935* (SA), ss.144G-144K.
31 *Criminal Code 2002* (ACT), ss. 363A-363H.
32 This outcome was in keeping with the jurisdiction's standards for serious offences across all crimes: Northern Territory, *Parliamentary Debates*, Legislative Assembly, 16 May 2013, vol. 2, no. 5 (John Elferink, Attorney General).
33 *Crimes Act 1958* (Vic), ss. 195B–195F.
34 *Criminal Code 1899* (Qld), ss. 443–443G.
35 See, e.g. *Racing Act 2003* (NZ), s. 55.
36 Sport and Recreation Ministers' Council, above n. 12, cl. 3.5. See also Menz and Skene in this volume.
37 Ibid. cl. 3.6.
38 For example, minor leagues or youth competitions may be more vulnerable to match-fixing, as opposed to professional adult competitions.
39 *Gambling Regulation Act 2003* (Vic), ss. 4.5.12–4.5.28.
40 *Betting and Racing Act 1998* (NSW), ss. 17A-18D.
41 Explanatory Memorandum, Interactive Gambling Bill 2001 (Cth).
42 See Murnane and Moller in this volume.
43 This relationship may be increasingly relevant as processing illegally gained funds through black gambling markets on fixed matches has been identified as a low-risk and high-profit method for laundering money. Cleaning the proceeds of crime through unregulated bookmakers is particularly difficult to detect. See Ordway in this volume.
44 For the penalties imposed see Murnane and Moller in this volume.
45 See Schwab and Finocchiaro in this volume for discussion of the appropriateness and proportionality of sporting sanctions imposed for match-fixing.
46 See Murnane and Moller in this volume.
47 See, e.g. National Integrity in Sport Unit 2016, *Integrity tools for sporting organisations*, 1 August, www.health.gov.au/internet/main/publishing.nsf/Content/integrity-tools-for-sporting-organisations.

48 See Murnane and Moller in this volume. The NSW Police investigate sports corruption through the Casino and Racing Investigation Unit which was formed as part of the Firearms and Organised Crime Squad to investigate race-fixing and links to organised crime in thoroughbred, harness and greyhound racing: Bricknell, S., 2015, *Corruption in Australian sport*, Australian Institute of Criminology, www.aic.gov.au/publications/current%20series/tandi/481-500/tandi490.html. See also, Lastra, R., Bell, P. and Bond, C., 2016, 'Sports betting-motivated corruption in Australia: an under-studied phenomenon' *International Journal of Social Science Research*, vol. 4, no. 1, pp. 61–82.
49 The Commonwealth could acquire constitutional power to enact match-fixing and related legislation should Australia become a party to the Council of Europe Convention on the Manipulation of Sports Competitions: see Ando, and Steele and Opie in this volume.
50 See Menz and Skene, and Ando in this volume.
51 See Menz and Skene in this volume.
52 O'Farrell, B., 2015, *Review of illegal offshore wagering*, www.dss.gov.au/sites/default/files/documents/04_2016/review_of_illegal_offshore_wagering_18_december_2015.pdf.
53 It is easier to fix minor aspects of a competition that may be the subject of constantly shifting in-play betting, than to manipulate the overall result of that competition.
54 The NSW legislation provides that an event/event contingency means any event or contingency (whether it takes place in NSW or elsewhere) on which it is lawful to bet under a law of NSW, another state, a territory or the Commonwealth: *Crimes Act 1900* (NSW) s. 193J. However, the Queensland legislation makes no reference to a territory: *Criminal Code 1899* (Qld) s. 443 (definition of 'sporting contingency').
55 See Murnane and Moller in this volume.
56 The Sports Betting Intelligence Unit:

> will share, where appropriate, specific intelligence or information with other partners (for example, betting operators, sports governing bodies, overseas regulators, and so on) both nationally and internationally. In some cases this information may then be used by these bodies in their investigations – for example a sports governing body investigating a breach of their sports rules or code.
>
> (Gambling Commission (UK) 2017, *Sports Betting Intelligence Unit (SBIU)*, www.gamblingcommission.gov.uk/news-action-and-statistics/Match-fixing-and-sports-integrity/Sports-Betting-Intelligence-Unit.aspx)

57 See Ordway in this volume.
58 See Schwab and Finocchiaro in this volume.
59 Bucci, N., 2014, 'Nicholas McKoy escapes conviction over southern stars match fixing', *The Age*, 12 December, www.theage.com.au/victoria/nicholas-mckoy-escapes-conviction-over-southern-stars-match-fixing-20141212-125us7.html.
60 See Park in this volume regarding deaths in Korea. Ryan Tandy was Australia's first convicted fixer, convicted for his role in the 2010 NRL match-fixing incident. He was found dead in April 2014 from a reported drug overdose and had a long history of substance abuse: ABC/AAP 2014, 'Former NRL player Ryan Tandy found dead from reported drug overdose', *ABC News* (online), 29 April; Massoud, above n. 8.
61 See Schwab and Finocchiaro in this volume for recommendations related to player protection.

Chapter 5

Legal and administrative frameworks for combating match-fixing in Korea

Kee Young Yeun[1]

Introduction: the environment for sport in Korea and recent match-fixing scandals

This chapter examines the legal and administrative frameworks for combating match-fixing in Korea. Korea's enthusiasm for sport is demonstrated by its achieving the world's sixth 'Sporting Grand Slam' when PyeongChang was chosen to host the Winter Olympic Games in 2018.[2] Fairness, a basic tenet of sport, has been consistently undermined in Korea, however, due to what the Korean government has described as 'four evils':[3] the privatisation of sports organisations,[4] biased or unfair judgments made by referees resulting in parental suicide,[5] physical and psychological assaults by senior players and coaches on junior players,[6] and corruption in relation to athlete school entrance examinations (*chaeyukge hakkyo yiphak shihum*).[7] In this sporting environment, match-fixing has also become a contemporary social problem.[8] Match-fixing scandals which became public from 2011 to 2013 and the Korean public's critical response to those scandals led to a series of major reviews and reforms.[9] The Ministry of Culture, Sports and Tourism, for example, announced comprehensive measures known as the 'normalisation of sports organisations' (*chaeyuk jungsanghwa bangan*) in 2013 and completed a comprehensive audit of 2099 sports organisations by December 2013.[10] Practical and operational approaches to combating match-fixing were subsequently strengthened, including the introduction of a reporting hotline under the auspices of the Ministry of Culture, Sports and Tourism,[11] reorganisation of education programmes[12] and increased investigative resources.[13] The government also expanded the scope of the *Kukmin chaeyuk jinhungbub* [National Sports Promotion Act] (act no. 8344, 2007 (Republic of Korea)) ('*National Sports Promotion Act*') in 2014 to cover all registered sports and e-sports, and not just sports covered by SportsToto,[14] and sports-related people and not just players (*National Sports Promotion Act*, art. 14(3)). The Act was further amended in 2016 with the introduction of support facilities for players and officials.[15]

In addition to specific offences under the *National Sports Promotion Act*, the Korean legal system also provides for other offences under which participants in match-fixing may be liable.[16] Participants may be liable for a breach of criminal or civil law, and even sued on the basis of contract or tort.[17] Because match-fixing involves predetermining the outcome of a sporting activity,[18] it could be said that participants are participating in a fraudulent scheme. They may also be disciplined under administrative arrangements. Accordingly, the analysis of Korea's legal and administrative frameworks to combat match-fixing in this chapter reflects Gorse and Chadwick's broad approach to the definition of match-fixing which includes any illegal, immoral or unethical activity that corrupts the sporting community as well as any deliberate actions to distort results for personal economic benefit.[19] Cases to date have typically been based on offences under the *National Sports Promotion Act* in relation to players, coaches, supervisors or referees, and criminal law in relation to brokers or operators of illegal websites. This chapter highlights that there are a number of sources of legal and administrative liability for match-fixing in Korea.

This chapter divides the sources of liability for match-fixing in Korea into three categories: criminal liability, liability under administrative procedures and the disciplinary power of sporting organisations, and legal liability under civil law. The discussion of criminal liability is further divided into an analysis of laws applying to specific actors, such as financiers, brokers and players, and laws triggered by the type or context of the match-fixing, including fraud, sporting-specific legislation and intimidation. Korea has recently increased its administrative and disciplinary responses to match-fixing and this section of the chapter also highlights the role of sporting organisations such as the Korean Sport and Olympic Committee. Civil liability for match-fixing in Korea may also arise in the context of contractual or tortious liability, and even as anti-competitive conduct. Finally, the discussion in this chapter provides an update on recent reforms and key measures taken by the government to combat match-fixing.

Criminal liability

Application of Korean criminal law based on the status of the alleged criminal actor

Korean criminal law may be invoked to combat match-fixing based on the status of the alleged criminal actor. Financiers (*jeonju*), for example, typically plan the match-fixing and source funds. Brokers transfer money to the players and order bets. Players, coaches and supervisors participate directly in match-fixing and receive funds. Senior players and members of organised criminal gangs intimidate coaches, supervisors and players who do not respond to their demands to fix matches. The Korean legal framework provides a number of avenues to prosecute such alleged offenders.

Financiers and brokers involved in match-fixing are joint principal offenders and have been shown to interfere with the fair execution of sports covered by the Korean SportsToto. SportsToto is a government-sponsored business initially established in 2001 to help fund the 2002 World Cup and Korea Sports Promotion Foundation. Purchasing a SportsToto ticket qualifies a purchaser for a payment and bonus prizes in one of two ways. A purchaser may choose either a fixed refund rate or Toto, which is determined by the number of people who purchased a ticket and make up a pool to be divided between those who correctly predicted the result, or a fixed dividend rate or Pronto, which is determined by multiplying the amount bet by a pre-disclosed payout ratio for selected target games.[20]

Financiers and brokers who provide financial benefits and property interests (*jesansangl eik*)[21] to players through illegal solicitation may be liable for an offence of fraud *Hyungbub* [Criminal Act] (act no. 293, 1953 (Republic of Korea), art. 347) ('*Criminal Act*'), interference with business through deception (*Criminal Act*, art. 314), receiving or giving a bribe by breach of trust (*Criminal Act*, art. 357) or gambling or habitual gambling (*Criminal Act*, art. 246). Article 47 of the *National Sports Promotion Act* is applicable as well as arts. 3(1) and 3(2) of the *Teugjeonggyeongjebeomje gajungcheobeol deunge gwanhan beoblyul* [Act on the Aggravated Punishment, etc. of Specific Economic Crimes] (act no. 3693, 1983 (Republic of Korea)), if the value of the goods or profits on property obtained from the match-fixing exceed KR₩500 million. In addition, if a person has threatened a player who is involved in match-fixing in relation to a sport covered by SportsToto with exposure of that player's involvement in match-fixing and that person receives or gains financial benefits and property interests in return for keeping the information confidential, then that person may be guilty of extortion under the amended *Poglyeoghaengwi deung cheobeole gwanhan beoblyul* [Punishment of Violence, Etc. Act] (act no. 12896, 2014 (Republic of Korea)) ('*Punishment of Violence, Etc. Act*').[22] This offence would only apply to sports covered by SportsToto, because it is the only licensed betting operator in Korea and this provision applies to the extent that financiers or brokers interfere with that business.

A player is obliged to maintain fairness and integrity based on the spirit of fair play in a sporting event. If a player receives money from a broker with a fraudulent request to lose a game, art. 357 of the *Criminal Act* which prohibits receipt or giving of a bribe by a breach of trust (*baeim jungjaeje*) may apply. In addition, embezzlement and breach of trust (*Criminal Act*, art. 355(2)) may apply if a player underperforms for financial benefits and property interests and third parties such as financiers or brokers receive financial benefits and property interests as a result of the player's underperformance. Embezzlement or breach of trust that breaches one's occupational duties may incur a more severe penalty (*Criminal Act*, art. 356). Moreover, a player who is manipulated by financiers and brokers may be guilty of fraud (*Criminal Act*, art. 347) and be in violation of interference with business (*Criminal Act*, art. 314) if the player purposely lost a game and deceived the game's organisers, opponents and even the player's teammates. Article 47 or 48 of the *National Sports Promotion Act* may also apply if a player from a registered sport receives a financial benefit and property interest in return for a dishonest act under an illegal solicitation, and there may also have been a violation of art. 54 of the *National Sports Promotion Act* if the player purchased, arranged or transferred a sports betting ticket or information to a third party.[23] Any coaches and supervisors who are alleged to have been involved in match-fixing will be treated as alleged joint offenders and may be liable in the same way as a player as noted above.

Application of Korean criminal law based on the type of match-fixing

Establishing fraud

The Korean legislative framework may also be invoked to prosecute acts designed to lose a game via a player's mistake or poor performance where compensation is received for such acts and those acts cause damage to the SportsToto operator and purchasers who paid for a betting ticket in the belief that the game was a fair contest. An act of poor performance may be the equivalent of fraud under the criminal law (*Criminal Act*, art. 347). The complainant would have to show that a person acquired a financial benefit and property interest by deceiving others to establish fraud. The players who participate in match-fixed games may be accessories to the fraud and the force behind the match-fixing who designs and supports the match-fixing through illegal websites may be considered to be the main perpetrator of the fraud. Even when match-fixing is unsuccessful, attempted fraud may be able to be established (*Criminal Act*, arts. 347, 352).[24]

Establishing interference with business

The offence of interference with business (*Criminal Act*, art. 314) may be established on the basis of poor performance because poor performance deceives stakeholders, including SportsToto, who trust that there will be a fair game, process and result.[25] This conduct arguably interferes with the work of all who have placed trust in the fair progress and outcome which has been corrupted by the match-fixing.

Violation of National Sports Promotion Act

Match-fixing is prohibited by art. 14(3) of the *National Sports Promotion Act*. Essentially, a person who uses cheating to damage the fairness of sports competitions or obstruct the fair execution of registered sports will be subject to imprisonment of up to five years or a fine of up to KR₩50 million (*National Sports Promotion Act*, art. 48(1) and (2)). If a player, manager, coach, umpire or executive or employee of a registered sporting organisation receives an illegal solicitation or accepts, demands or promises any financial benefit and property interest and participates in the unlawful fixing conduct, he or she shall be sentenced to up to seven years in jail or a fine not exceeding KR₩70 million (*National Sports Promotion Act*, art. 47(1)).

Cases of intimidation leading to match-fixing

In cases where the force behind the match-fixing is an organised criminal gang, including where the broker or a member of an organised crime gang (*jojikpokrykbae*) intimidates or coerces players, coaches or supervisors to take part in match-fixing, then coercion (*Criminal Act*, art. 324) and intimidation, or intimidation in relation to a lineal ascendant (*jonsok hypbak*) (*Criminal Act*, art. 283) may be established. The force behind the match-fixing may provide the money and demand that players make errors in games and, in fear of those threats, retaliation or violence, the players take part in match-fixing. This kind of intimidation is also subject to arts. 2(2)(3) and 3(4) of the *Punishment of Violence, Etc. Act*.

In the investigation of the 2011 K-League scandal, it was found that some brokers were connected with organised criminal gangs and they threatened players who failed to successfully match-fix with the intention of extracting money from those players. The gangs also threatened the players with exposing their involvement in match-fixing unless the players paid money. Such acts may satisfy the requirement of intimidation and may be subject to heavy penalties in accordance with arts. 2(1)(2) and 3(1) of the *Punishment of Violence, Etc. Act* (as applicable in 2011).[26]

Establishment of accessory to match-fixing

The person who directs and plans the match-fixing and puts it into practice is a principal offender and may also violate the *National Sports Promotion Act*. They may also be joint offenders and liable for fraud or interference with business as discussed above.

Criminal liability for setting up illegal SportsToto websites and betting

If a person illegally opens a private SportsToto website or recruits people to make bets, that person may be guilty of setting up a place for gambling (*Criminal Act*, art. 247). Even if the server is located overseas such as in China or the Philippines, the Korean *Criminal Act* may apply if the perpetrator has Korean nationality (*Criminal Act*, art. 2). Also, for those who have bet through these illegal websites, the offences of gambling and habitual gambling (*Criminal Act*, art. 246) may apply. Since most gambling activities will be treated as habitual, gambling and habitual gambling may easily be established (*Criminal Act*, art. 246).[27]

Liability under administrative and disciplinary frameworks

The Ministry of Culture, Sports and Tourism is responsible for administrative guidance (*hangjung jido*) and supervision of efforts to combat match-fixing. The Ministry is an executive agency which may take administrative disciplinary actions, such as reducing a person's salary, and administrative legal restrictions, such as revoking a licence, in accordance with the rule of law. The Constitution also recognises the rights of sports organisations and federations to exercise disciplinary power on the basis of their sports autonomy.[28] In addition, the Korean Sport and Olympic Committee (*Daehan Chaeyukhwe*) arguably has the power to punish match-fixing offenders and exercise its supervisory power to demand that sports federations punish such offenders. Whether the Korean Sport and Olympic Committee has this administrative and disciplinary power to take disciplinary action is a matter of legal debate amongst academics in Korea, as discussed below.[29]

Government's measures against match-fixing and strengthening administrative regulations

As the 2011 match-fixing scandal in professional football became a serious social problem which expanded to embroil professional volleyball and baseball, the Ministry of Culture, Sports and Tourism announced comprehensive countermeasures to combat further match-fixing known as 'creating measures for a fair and transparent sports environment' (*gongjunghago toomunghan suposu hwankyung josungdaechak*) on 21 February 2012.[30]

The key content of the countermeasures was aimed at restoring fairness in sports games through seven steps which were implemented over the following 12 or so months. The first step was strengthening and revising regulations by extending them to all sports-related parties and not just focusing on players. For example, related parties may receive life bans or suspension, and clubs may have their subsidies reduced or be expelled from a league. Second, a constant monitoring system for combating match-fixing was to be constructed and managed by clean sports call centres operated by the Ministry and sports associations. The third step was strengthening preventive education and self-awareness by increasing education sessions to four times a year and specifying it as a player's mandatory obligation in the player's contract. Fourth, the government implemented a policy of leniency for those who voluntarily cooperated with authorities and established a call centre for whistle-blowers as well as significantly increasing rewards for whistle-blowers from KR₩10 million to KR₩100 million. Fifth, the countermeasures aimed to expand the minimum annual salary and pension system for professional players. Sixth, systems for eradicating illegal sports betting sites were enhanced. Seventh, and finally, the government took steps to form a social environment and public consensus to combat match-fixing.

In addition, to ensure transparency in the operation of school athletic clubs and improve the accountability of sports organisations, a unified certification process under the Korean Sports and Olympic Committee was introduced and the procedures for issuing performance certificates were revised to facilitate online certification.[31] Furthermore, the Korean University Sports Federation (*Daehan Sports Chongjang Hyeplhwe*) announced its resolution on the 'normalisation and advanced measures for university sports including prohibiting financial scouting of players and self-awareness resolutions'.[32] Financial scouting refers to the practice of a university paying elite high school players in anticipation of those players coming to the university to represent it in sport. In 2014, the Federation decided to: refuse applications for admission examinations from players who were known to have benefited from financial scouting; increase the consideration given to individual performance evaluations in team competitions; prohibit the submission of documents which may impede equal opportunity or encourage corruption such as recommendations from school principals or representatives of the university; and provide transparency and clarity around admission criteria.[33] Enhancing transparency and fairness in the selection of students is also expected to enhance overall ethical awareness in the sports industry, emphasise compliance with laws and regulations, and thus ultimately help combat match-fixing.

Punishments for producers and operators of illegal gambling sites were strengthened and a reward system for reporting illegal gambling site operators implemented.[34] The government has also recently announced that it will introduce legislation which will suspend the involvement of any host organisation and cancel sponsorships by organisations involved in match-fixing, as well as to stop the distribution of grants to host organisations.[35] The government could take further steps to combat illegal internet gambling sites by introducing an online search system to research and analyse those markets. Currently, the National Gambling Control Commission (*Saheng-sanyup Tonghap Kamdok Wewonhwe*) is in charge of supervising gambling regardless of whether it is online or not. Under the present law, however, the National Gambling Control Commission may only supervise the legitimate gambling industry.[36] Accordingly, supervising and controlling illegal internet sports gambling does not fall under the Commission's current jurisdiction. Moreover, even if the Korea Communications Commission (*Bangsong Tongshin Wewonhwe*) has the authority and willingness to remove illegal internet sports gambling websites, they may only impose administrative sanctions and not criminal punishments.[37] These limitations suggest that further legal reforms are necessary to appropriately deal with illegal internet sports gambling sites.[38] Research and analysis on online gambling must be carried out at a national level, and the jurisdiction of the relevant institution or bureaucratic department should be clarified.

Korea may learn from the precedents set in the United Kingdom, South Africa and the United States of America, for example, where the relevant government department has robust authority to regulate illegal online gambling because they have the authority to regulate illegal gambling as well as the authority to license, investigate, commission and audit.[39] Moreover, on 28 September 2011, the German Federal Court of Justice ruled that private sports betting and gambling on the internet is prohibited by the *Staatsvertrag zum Glücksspielwesen in Deutschland* [German Interstate Treaty on Gambling] ('*German Interstate Treaty on Gambling*').[40] This Treaty was effective from 1 January 2008 and prohibited open gambling on the internet in order to develop and not to interfere with the German provincial governments' gambling industry (*German Interstate Treaty on Gambling*, art. 4(4)). The complainant in this case contended that this Treaty violated European Union law because it restricted the free exchange and distribution of services under the European Union's Human Rights Treaty and European Union market. However, the Federal Court of Justice stated that the Treaty did not violate European Union laws because:

> The aims of the Treaty are the prevention of gambling addiction, the limitation of betting services and the control of passion for gambling, youth protection, fraud prevention [...] and the special risk potential for young and addicted consumers arising from games offered on the internet due to the anonymity and isolation of players.[41]

This precedent from the German Federal Court of Justice may also provide a blueprint for Korea in relation to this issue.

The legal status and disciplinary power of sports organisations including the Korean Sport and Olympic Committee (Daehan Chaeyukhwe)

The Korean Sport and Olympic Committee is a special juridical corporation established by art. 33 of the *National Sports Promotion Act* and is under the supervision of the Ministry of Culture, Sports and Tourism (*National Sports Promotion Act*, art. 43). The Ministry of Culture, Sports and Tourism or the head of the relevant local government may order the Korean Sport and Olympic Committee to report directly to it and allow its officers to enter the Korean Sport and Olympic Committee's place of business to inspect books, documents and other materials (*National Sports Promotion Act*, art. 44(1)). The Korean Sport and Olympic Committee has characteristics similar to a powerful public institution even though it follows its own constitution.[42] The government subsidises the expenses for the maintenance and operation of the Committee (*National Sports Promotion Act*, art. 33(1)), the Committee follows the fiscal year of the government (*National Sports Promotion Act*, art. 39) and approval from the Ministry of Culture, Sports and Tourism is required for budgeting and settlement of accounts for the Committee (*National Sports Promotion Act*, art. 40).[43]

In the event of alleged match-fixing by a player, umpire, referee, judge or other match official, the related sport association or federation's disciplinary committee may take disciplinary action. If the participant who is subject to the disciplinary action does not challenge the result and does not request a re-evaluation, the disciplinary action shall take effect. If the participant appeals to the Korean Sport and Olympic Committee, then the Committee may finalise the disciplinary action.[44]

If the association or the federation in charge of the sporting event does not take disciplinary action or its punishment is considered insufficient, the Korean Sport and Olympic Committee, as the parent organisation, may act as a supervisor by ordering an appropriate disciplinary action and enforcement. The Committee's right to oversee this objection procedure and its disciplinary power reflect its quasi-public and administrative institutional status.[45]

Players, supervisors and coaches involved in match-fixing are subject to disciplinary actions in accordance with the disciplinary procedures prescribed by applicable sports federation, association or club constitutions.[46] Sports organisations may be formed through the freedom of association and sports autonomy guaranteed under the *Daehanminkuk hyungbub* [Constitution of the Republic of Korea] (constitution no. 10, 1987 (Republic of Korea)).[47] These sports organisations exercise their group autonomy and may establish operational and disciplinary measures. The autonomy of this group may be regarded as a self-determination right under the Korean Constitution.[48] Their rules consist of self-governing norms and regulations including disciplinary manuals. The Supreme Court of Korea found that the legal nature of the constitutions of these groups is equivalent to self-governing law.[49] Therefore, disciplinary action in accordance with a sports organisation's disciplinary rules will be binding on its members.[50]

If the rules, including a sports organisation's constitution, contain discriminatory content or conditions for members, the government may be entitled to take legal control and intervene, however.[51] If a disciplinary rule, for example, violates the *Minbub* [Civil Act] (act no. 471, 1958 (Republic of Korea)) ('*Civil Act*') by being a juridical act contrary to social order (*Civil Act*, art. 103), or an unfair juridical act (*Civil Act*, art. 104), the rule will be subject to judicial review and may be found to be null and void.[52] Players, supervisors and referees who have been disciplined by the Korean Sport and Olympic Committee and affiliated sports organisations may also be entitled to relief under judicial processes based on civil litigation.

Liability under civil law

Contractual liability

Players and supervisors participating in major sporting events have a direct contractual relationship with their clubs, and the club may directly claim damages caused by the match-fixing from the offenders.[53] Damages might be awarded for losses such as lost prize money which the player's club might otherwise have received if the match had not been lost. Such losses may be difficult to prove, however, because a successful claim for economic loss requires that the loss be foreseeable (*Civil Act*, art. 393(2)). Moreover, clubs which are damaged by a referee's involvement in match-fixing will find it difficult to recover from the referee because referees typically do not have a direct contractual relationship with the participating clubs; the club would only have a right to claim damages caused by unlawful acts.

Interestingly, however, the German precedent of a 'contract with protective effect in favour of third parties' (*Vertrag mit Schutzwirkung zugunsten Dritter*) may be recognised in Korea to deal with this issue in exceptional cases. Even if the contracting party is an organiser, player or sports organisation, for example, the referee or the spectator may need to be protected by the contract as a third party.[54] In other words, if a referee is involved in match-fixing, the legal relationship, including employment contracts between the association or federation and the referee may have the effect of establishing a right in favour of the allegedly damaged clubs to claim contractual damages.[55] In accordance with art. 391 of the *Civil*

Act, where a referee affects the performance as a performance assistant (*ehangbohojal goui gwashil*), the intention or negligence of the referee shall be deemed as that of the federation or association hosting the sporting event in which case the federation or association may also face liability.[56]

Liability in tort

Article 750 of the *Civil Act* stipulates that any person who causes loss or inflicts injury on the life, body, health, property or other rights of another person either intentionally or negligently, shall be liable for that unlawful act. The type of losses which might be claimed as part of a tort case include lost prize money and ticket revenues, although there have been no cases brought under this type of claim as yet. Such cases may include unlawful acts which are positive acts or passive omissions. Such unlawful acts must be either intentional or negligent and actual damages must have occurred. Applicants would have to show that they would have received a financial benefit or profit had there been no match-fixing, and then prove a causal relationship between the match-fixing, loss and player or referee's actions or omissions.

The liability for unlawful acts in match-fixing applies to anyone including referees, players, coaches and club supervisors. In principle, a decision made by the referee in accordance with his or her opinion and knowledge during the match is final; therefore, even if the referee has made a wrong decision, the referee may not be held responsible. However, art. 750 of the *Civil Act* suggests that liability will be imposed on the unlawful act of fixing matches intentionally. In particular, if the referee accepts a bribe or commits corruption, the referee may be criminally liable and subject to disciplinary proceedings.[57] In contravention of these statutory obligations, if a person accepts, demands or promises a financial benefit and property interest and in return commits an unlawful act such as being involved in match-fixing or being an agent, such an act may violate that person's duty of care and the person may face liability for damages caused by the person's unlawful acts.[58] Even if a person does not violate any legislation, the violation of the obligations stipulated in the constitutions or competition rules of the applicable sports association, federation or union, including the doctrine or norms of good faith, may be treated as a breach of that person's duty.[59]

Finally, federations or associations hosting a competition may be found liable under art. 756 of the *Civil Act* as an employer of a referee. In cases where more than one claim is available, the team which is the victim of the match-fixing may choose the claim most likely to succeed, including liability for being a performance assistant (*ehangbojoja chakim*) under the contract or a claim in tort.[60]

Liability for damages under the Unfair Competition Act *and the* Unfair Competition Prevention and Trade Secret Protection Act

SportsToto has exclusive authority to sell betting tickets in respect of certain sports. Other companies or individuals that issue betting tickets in breach of that authority may be liable for damages based on a violation of the *Bujeonggyeongjaengbangji mich yeongeobbimilbohoe gwanhan bublyul* [Unfair Competition and Trade Secret Protection Act] (act no. 3897, 1986 (Republic of Korea)). Those who operate illegal internet gambling sites or those who gain profits through illegal SportsToto may be liable for unlawful acts under civil law as well as liable for damages caused by the violation of the *Unfair Competition Prevention and Trade Secret Protection Act.*[61] According to empirical research, the total amount of illegal online business in Korea reached KR₩17 trillion in 2012 and the total amount of illegal online sports betting was approximately KR₩7.6 trillion.[62] SportsToto's total turnover in 2012 was KR₩799 billion and it dropped to KR₩693 billion in 2013.[63] This decrease in turnover is at least partially attributable to illegal sports betting operators who attract customers by offering a large dividend rate.[64] Moreover, SportsToto only facilitates online sports betting on certain domestic sports; people who want to bet on popular overseas leagues use illegal online sites which cover all sports competitions around the world, and they can bet at any time and on any day.[65] These online operators also attract bettors with a variety of interesting and competitive products with virtually no limit on the betting amount, and offer a high dividend rate.

Finally, SportsToto is required to pay approximately 27 per cent of total sales to the Korea Sports Promotion Fund and for sport infrastructure. Illegal gambling sites do not have such obligations, and can thus offer a higher dividend rate.[66] This loss of business as a result of illegal online activity may give the SportsToto a claim in damages against the illegal sports betting website owners. Whilst there has never been a case, SportsToto's chances of winning such a case based on art. 750 of the *Civil Act* are also relatively high, because it has the exclusive right to operate a betting operation under the *National Sports Promotion Act* and thus should be able to demonstrate loss and a causal relationship.

Conclusion

The problem of match-fixing is not new, but recently it has developed into a serious social issue in Korea. The K-League scandal of 2011 and the reality of match-fixing and illegal gambling in key sports such as soccer, volleyball, baseball and basketball created an understanding that match-fixing was a structural, social evil in Korea. Whilst legal and administrative action alone will not solve the problem of match-fixing, Korea has numerous legal and administrative mechanisms to combat corruption in sport and specifically match-fixing, as this chapter demonstrates.[67] In response to various scandals and public outcry, the Korean government took numerous measures to combat match-fixing.[68] The Ministry of Culture, Sports and Tourism introduced new measures to create a fair and transparent sporting environment, and the *National Sports Promotion Act* was amended in 2014 and 2016. Looking forward, further legal and administrative reforms are required to clarify administrative responsibilities for regulating illegal gambling, and more consideration should now be given to international developments which may provide models for improvements of the Korean framework to combat match-fixing.[69]

Notes

1 Translation and research assistance provided by Ms Jess (Hee Sung) Shin, Research Assistant, Asian Law Centre, Melbourne Law School.
2 The sporting grand slam refers to the Summer Olympic Games, Winter Olympic Games, FIFA World Cup (soccer) and IAAF World Championships (athletics).
3 Ministry of Culture, Sports and Tourism 2014, '*Suposu 4-dae ak kunjulel wihan munhwabu, kyungchal hapdongsusaban baljok* [Eradication of sports' four evils through developing cooperative investigation with the Ministry of Culture, Sports and Tourism and the police]', *Ministry of Culture, Sports and Tourism*, 19 May, www.mcst.go.kr/web/s_notice/press/pressView.jsp?pSeq=13534.
4 A recent scandal involving the Korea Karate Federation reflects the governance issues involved in privatisation of sports. The Federation became the 'personal property' of the Chung family. The father and daughter took the role of the chairman and vice chairman respectively, and the two sons and brother-in-law became the chief of referees and national chiefs. The board was also filled with family members. There was evidence that family members used players' training allowances, for example. Lee, S., 2014, '*Jojiksayuhwaro shinemhanun chaeyuk danchae* [Players' organisations bemoan the privatisation of their organisations]', *SBS News*, 28 February, http://news.sbs.co.kr/news/endPage.do?news_id=N1002270873&plink=COPYPASTE&cooper=SBSNEWSEND.
5 In 2014, a father who was also a coach of taekwondo committed suicide and left a note which exposed taekwondo sports organisation's culture of privatisation and accepting bribery. This culture formed the basis for a referee's biased judgments which affected the entrance into elite athlete schools by student players and also results in competitions to select national team players. Han, H., 2014, '*Jasal burun pyunpapanjung … hakbumo chiltaklro shijakgyun selbujojak* [Biased judgment which resulted in a parent's suicide … it started from another parent paying a bribe to fix a match]', *Mookas News*, 15 September, www.mookas.com/media_view.asp?news_no=15418.
6 On the effect of match-fixing in male high schools, see, e.g. Lim, S., 2012, '*Nanja gogyo elitsuposu seungbujojakel shilsangga kunjul bangan* [Match-fixing in male high school elite sports and ways to prevent it]', *Suposuwabub* [The Korean Association of Sports Law], vol. 51, no. 4, pp. 55–68.
7 Ibid.; Han, above n. 5.
8 Moreover, the growth of internet gambling and increasing gambling options, such as spread and first scoring betting, are also making it easier to match-fix.

On the Korean government's involvement in combating internet gambling-related match-fixing, see Choi, C., 2012, '*Seungbujojakga bulbubinteonetdobake kwanhan gibubjuk kyuje* [Legal regulations on sports gambling and match-fixing]', *Suposuwabub* [The Korean Association of Sports Law], vol. 15, no. 1, pp. 9–36. Gambling is also not the only driver of match-fixing. Teams may, for example, seek to fix a match with an opponent team to advance that team to the next round of a tournament. See Kim, S., 2006, '*Sports jachikwongwa sportskibonkwone kwanhan yeongu* [Sports autonomy and the enactment of the basic sport law]', *Suposuwabub* [The Korean Association of Sports Law], vol. 8, no. 1, pp. 15–30.

9 The 2011 scandal involving the Korean Football League, also known as K-League, was particularly shocking for Korean people. Numerous football players, supervisors and officials, including current and former national players, were disciplined and punished. Some participants committed suicide. See Seo, H. and Han, S., 2012, '*Klegu seungbujojakga chaeyukjinhyungtopyokwon sayuk yunyoungel mumjejum* [K-League match-fixing scandal and the problem of Korean SportsToto management]', *Hangugcheyughaghoeji* [The Korean Journal of Physical Education], vol. 51, no. 4, pp. 45–54. For examples of other scandals which came to light during this period, see Park and Steele, Shin and Yang in this volume.

10 Kim, S., 2016, '*Hwengryungelhok sooyoungyeonmeng apsususek … isa deng 3-meng chaepo* [Suspicion of embezzlement, Swimming Federation seized search … arrested three people including a director]', *News 1*, 17 February, http://news1.kr/articles/?2576480.

11 The government reporting centre provides for voluntary confessions and whistleblowing from sports officials and players. The 'Sports Four Game Report Centre' (*Suposu 4-Dae Ak Shingocenter, Hapdongsusaban*) started receiving reports of sports corruption from February 2014. From May 2014, a joint investigation team started operating. By December 2014, 274 reports had been received and 192 investigations completed. Of these 192 cases, 2 cases were sent to prosecutors, 2 cases were referred for direct investigation by prosecutors, 25 cases were referred for disposal pending audit results, and the remaining 163 cases were concluded without further investigation. MNB Star News 2014, '*Suposu 4-daeak, chaeyukgye biri junggan josa gyulgwa balpyo … suposu 4-daeakshingocentre, 269gun jupsu* [4 Sports evil investigation results … 269 cases received]', *MBN Star News*, 30 December, http://star.mbn.co.kr/view.php?no=1578410&year=2014. In 2015, 197 cases were reported, 73 were investigated and 124 cases were concluded without further investigation. In 2016, 209 cases were reported, 154 investigated and 55 concluded without further investigation. Statistics provided by *Munhwachaeyukgwangwangbu chaeyukjungchakgwa sportsbirishingocentre* [Ministry of Culture, Sports and Tourism, Sports Policy and Sports Corruption Reporting Centre].

12 The qualifications for sports instructors were reorganised in 2015 and 'sports ethics' (*suposu yunri*) became part of the national test for all professional sport instructors. Current second-level professional sports instructors and future candidates (who teach amateurs or primary or junior high school players) are also now required to study 'Sports Ethics' for the test, which includes the human rights of players, the ethics of players, instructors and referees, anti-doping matters, and anti-violence and fair competition issues. All second-level instructors must have at least three years of experience before they may apply to become a first-level instructor. Korea Sports Education 2017, *2015 Jagukjaedo gepun* [2015 Reform of qualifications], www.ksportsedu.com/index.asp.

13 The resources consist of personnel from the Ministry of Culture, Sports and Tourism and police, and a prosecutor from Seoul Central District Prosecutor's Office: *Munhwachaeyukgwangwangbu* [Ministry of Culture] 2014, '*Suposu 4-dae ag geunjeoleul wihan munchebu, gyeongchal habdongsusaban baljog* [The Ministry of Culture, Sports and Tourism together with the Police launched the joint investigation team for the four major eradication of 4 evils in sports]', press release, 19 May, www.mcst.go.kr/web/s_notice/press/pressView.jsp?pSeq=13534.

14 SportsToto is discussed further below. For information in English, see SportsToto, *Sports Betting*, www.sportstoto.co.kr/en/business/sports.asp. Whilst amateur groups may become registered sports, article 14(3) would typically apply to elite professional sports in practice.

15 On 20 December 2016, a provision was added through the *Kukmin chaeyuk jinhungbub* [National Sports Promotion Act], amending act no. 14426, 2016 (Republic of Korea) to provide for the establishment of reporting and confidential counselling facilities to protect players and sports leaders from violence, intimidation and unfair conduct (*National Sports Promotion Act*, art. 14(5)). Detailed matters in relation to the operation of those facilities would be prescribed by Presidential Decree (*National Sports Promotion Act*, art. 14(6)). The *Kukminchaeyuk jinhungbub shiheryung* [Enforcement Decree of the National Sports Promotion Act] (act no. 27937, 2017 (Republic of Korea)) ('*Enforcement Decree of the National Sports Promotion Act*') requires the facilities to be established at a convenient place, provide internet access facilities and telephones, as well as partitioning and soundproofing to ensure confidentiality (*Enforcement Decree of the National Sports Promotion Act*, art. 15(2)). Reporting and counselling facilities businesses must obtain permission from the Ministry of Culture, Sports and Tourism or head of the local government and may be, for example, an athletic group or non-profit organisation established for the purpose of preventing sexual violence and protecting victims (*Enforcement Decree of the National Sports Promotion Act*, art. 15(3)).

16 In the field of sports corruption, legal measures to combat match-fixing have only started to be discussed relatively recently. See, e.g. Maennig, W., 2005, 'Corruption in international sports and sport management: forms, tendencies, extent and countermeasures', *European Sport Management Quarterly*, vol. 5, no. 2, pp. 187–225.

17 On criminal and civil lability, see, e.g. Kang, G., 2011, '*Klegu seungbujojakga hyunsajuk chaim* [Criminal liability for the K-League match-fixing scandal]', *Suposuwabub* [The Korean Association of Sports Law], vol. 14, no. 4, pp. 173–197; Park, S., 2011, '*Suposu seungbujojakga hungsa chaum* [Criminal responsibilities and Match-fixing]', *Suposuwabub* [The Korean Association of Sports Law], vol. 14, no. 3, pp. 217–242; Moon, H. and Park, Y., 2012, '*Suposu seungbujojakel hyungsa chaimga hyungsabubjuk daechak* [Criminal liability and measures for combating sport manipulation]', *Hangugcheyughaghoeji* [The Korean Journal of Physical Education], vol. 51, no. 3, pp. 1–16.

18 Shon, S., 2013, '*Suposu seungbujojak shiltaeha gu daecho bangane kwanan yungu* [A study on the match-fixing of sports and its prevention]', *Suposuwabub* [The Korean Association of Sports Law], vol. 16. no. 1, pp. 83–103.

19 Gorse, S. and Chadwick, S., 2011, *The prevalence of corruption in international sport*, Centre for the International Business of Sport. Some commentators argue that match-fixing should be recognised as sports corruption when it is conducted to secure a financial benefit and property interest related to illegal gambling activities. Boniface, P., Lacarriere, S., Verschuuren, P., Tuaillon, A., Forrest, D., Icard, M.J.M., Meyer, J.P. and Wang, X., 2012, *Sports betting and corruption: how to*

preserve the integrity of sport, IRIS, University of Salford, Cabinet Praxes-Avocats, CCLS (Université de Pékin) and Sportaccord.

20 SportsToto, *Toto/Proto*, www.sportstoto.co.kr/en/toto/toto.jsp.

21 '*Jesansangl eik*' is typically translated as 'financial benefits and property interests' in the translations provided by the Ministry of Legislation; however occasionally the Ministry's translations also use 'goods or profits on property' or some other formulation. This chapter uses 'financial benefits and property interests' except in relation to the Crimes Act where the Ministry has used 'goods or profits on property'. In summary, the term refers to benefits which move from one person to another, including money.

22 Kang, above n. 17.

23 Article 54 of the *National Sports Promotion Act* provides:

> if the representative of a corporation, or an agent, employee or worker employed by a corporation or individual commits a violation referred to in art. 47(2) in connection with the affairs of such corporation or individual, not only shall such violator be punished accordingly, but also the corporation or individual shall be punished by a fine prescribed under the relevant provisions: Provided, that where such corporation or individual has not been negligent in giving due attention and supervision concerning the relevant affairs to prevent such violation, this shall not apply.

24 Park, above n. 17.

25 Ibid.

26 Ibid. The allegations that gangs were threatening the player who committed suicide, which started the K-league investigation, were not established. Players gave statements about these allegations, but there was insufficient evidence to prosecute the gangs: Park, T., 2017, '*Prochuggu seonsu Yungiwon jugeum nae-sajonggyeol ... seungbujojag, jopog yeonluseol hyeomui moschaja* [Pro-soccer player Yoon Kye-won's death closed its examination ... related match-fixing scandal cannot find any suspicion about the organised gang's involvement]', *Segye*, 13 February, www.segye.com/content/html/2017/02/13/20170213000136.html?OutUrl=naver.

27 Ibid.

28 The Korean government recognises that sports have their own internal organisation and respects a sport's self-determination over its independent domain. See Kim, above n. 8.

29 Choi, above n. 8.

30 Lee, S., 2012, '*Suposu seungbujojak jungbu hapdongdaechak* [Cooperative measures to stop match-fixing]', *Hankuk News*, 2 February, www.newshankuk.com/news/content.asp?fs=12&ss=57&news_idx=201202211218361314.

31 Shon, above n. 18. The online certification system is designed to prevent the making of misleading and false certificates and corruption.

32 Choi, I., 2012, '*Kumjun sukautui kunjeol daehaksuposucholjanghaephae kulel* [Resolution of the University Sports Council to stop financial scouts]', *Chosun News*, 22 May, http://news.chosun.com/site/data/html_dir/2012/05/21/2012052102706.html. The Federation is an incorporated body composed of university deans from all universities in Korea. It was originally intended to be an organisation like the United States' National Collegiate Athletic Association. The Federation is:

> to promote healthy growth and development of university sports, to achieve the advancement of sports by restoring the essence of university sports through cooperating autonomous consultation, research and coordination, to ensure that student athletes have sound mental, physical, and social

leadership through sports activities and education, to contribute to the development of excellent sportsmen by proposing policies necessary for sports development to the government.

(Korea University Sport Federation, *Korea University Sport Federation*, www.kusf.or.kr/index.html)

33 Ibid.
34 *Kukmin chaeyuk jinhungbub* [National Sports Promotion Act], amending act no. 14426, 2016 (Republic of Korea), art. 14(5).
35 Ministry of Culture, Sports and Tourism 2014, '*Suposu 4-dae ak kunjulel wihan munhwabu, kyungchal hapdongsusaban baljok* [Eradication of sports' four evils through developing cooperative investigation with the Ministry of Culture, Sports and Tourism and the police]', *Ministry of Culture, Sports and Tourism*, 19 May, www.mcst.go.kr/web/s_notice/press/pressView.jsp?pSeq=13534.
36 The National Gambling Control Commission, *Wewonhwe sogye* [Who we are], www.ngcc.go.kr.
37 See *Bangsongtongsinwiwonhoeui seolchi mich unyeonge gwanhan bublyul* [Act on the Establishment and Operation of Korea Communications Commission Act], act no. 13202, 2015 (Republic of Korea), art. 25.
38 Choi, above n. 8; Park, H., 2009, '*Gokile ieseo kyungchale ulhan yebangjuk online susak welhunyeobu* [German police's online search and investigation methods]', *Kyungchel yeungu* [The Study of Police], vol. 9, no. 2, pp. 187–209.
39 Korea Productivity Center 2010, *Oegugeseo onlain dobage gwanhan yeongu* [The study on online betting in foreign countries].
40 *Staatsvertrag zum Glücksspielwesen in Deutschland* [German Interstate Treaty on Gambling], signed 31 July 2007 (entered into force 1 January 2008). This Treaty was replaced by a new *Staatsvertrag zum Glücksspielwesen in Deutschland* [German Inter-State Treaty on Gambling], signed 15 December 2011 (entered into force 1 July 2012), but art. 4(4) remains unchanged.
41 Bundesgerichtshof [German Federal Court of Justice], I ZR 92/09, 28 September 2011; Bundesgerichtshof [German Federal Court of Justice], I ZR 93/10, 28 September 2011; Bundesgerichtshof [German Federal Court of Justice], I ZR 43/10, 28 September 2011; Bundesgerichtshof [German Federal Court of Justice], I ZR 30/10, 28 September 2011; Bundesgerichtshof [German Federal Court of Justice], I ZR 189/08, 28 September 2011. From 1 January 2018, online sports betting will be lawfully offered by up to 35 private operators: Boehringer, S., 2017, 'Neue Regeln für Sportwetten [New regulations on sports betting]', *Süddeutsche Zeitung*, 16 March, www.sueddeutsche.de/wirtschaft/gluecksspiel-neue-regeln-fuer-sportwetten-1.3423223.
42 The Korean Sport and Olympic Committee's constitution is not available to the public.
43 Kim, Y., (2010) '*Suposudanchaeel tonghapnonelwa kukminchaeyukhwel bubjukinhwamumjae* [Discussions on the integration of sports organisations and incorporation of the Korean Sports and Olympic Committee]', *Suposuwabub* [The Korean Association of Sports Law], vol. 13, no. 1, pp. 59–83.
44 Choi, above n. 8, p. 13.
45 Because the Korean Sport and Olympic Committee is recognised as a public entity under Korean administrative law, any disciplinary action taken by the Committee should arguably be treated as an administrative action. Kim, above n. 43. However, some commentators argue that administrative law does not appropriately deal with acts by the Korean Sport and Olympic Committee and sports associations and federations, based on their corporate relationship and self-governing constitutions. Kim, S., 2010, '*Suposudanchel bubjukkyuyulbanan*

[Legal regulation of sports organisations]', *Suposuwabub* [The Korean Association of Sports Law], vol. 13, no. 1, pp. 39–58.
46 Nam, K., 2011, '*Chukgushimpanel sungbujojake ddarun chakim* [Liability for match-fixing by soccer referees]', *Chung-Ang Law Associations*, vol. 13, no. 2, pp. 139–162.
47 Jung, S., 2004, *Suposusunsuel kibonkwonbujange gwanhan yeongu* [A study on guaranteeing fundamental rights for sports players], doctoral thesis, Kyung Hee University, Seoul.
48 Kim, S., 2006, '*Suposujachigwunga suposukibonbube ghwanhan yeongu* [A study on sports autonomy and basic sport law]', *Suposuwabub* [The Korean Association of Sports Law], vol. 8, pp. 11–41; Kwon, Y., 2005, *Hunbukhakgyeru* [Constitutional theory], Bommunsa.
49 Supreme Court of Korea (24 November 2000), case no. 99 *da* 12437.
50 Song, H., 2008, '*Suposudancheoel sunsujinggyee daehan bubjukmumjae* [Legal issues concerning the discipline of players by the sports organisation]', *Suposuwabub* [The Korean Association of Sports Law], vol. 11, no. 1, pp. 39–52.
51 Choi, above n. 8.
52 Park, J., 1998, '*Sadanel gusungwone daehan tongjekwonel bubjukkichowa sabubshimsael bumwhi-dokilel haksulga panrel jungshimero* [The legal basis and the scope of the judicial review on the member's power to control]', *The Korean Association of Law*, vol. 7, no. 1, pp. 347–371.
53 Nam, above n. 46.
54 Yeun, K., 2013, *Suposubukhakyeongu* [Study in Sports Law], Yeokrak, Seoul.
55 Signed 31 July 2007 (entered into force 1 January 2008).
56 See *Civil Act*, act no. 471, 1958 (Republic of Korea), art. 391:

> Where a legal representative for the obligor effects performance in lieu of the latter or the obligor effects performance through the other person as an employee, the intention or negligence of the legal representative or the other person shall be deemed as that of the obligor.

Further, art. 756 states:

> (1) A person who employs another to perform a specific affair is liable for compensating for any loss inflicted on a third person by the employee in the course of performing the specific affair: provided, that this shall not apply where the employer has exercised due care in appointing the employee, and in supervising the performance of the specific affair, or where the loss has been inflicted even if the employer has exercised due care. (2) A person who supervises the performance of a specific affair on behalf of the employer shall also assume the same liability as prescribed in paragraph (1). (3) In cases falling under paragraphs (1) and (2), the employer or the supervisor may claim for reimbursement from the employee.

57 For example, *Gyeonglyun, gyeongjeongbeob* [Bicycle and Motorboat Racing] (act no. 12688, 2014), art. 29(1) states that if a racer or umpire receives, requests or promises a financial benefit and property interest in return for any illegal solicitation for favour related to his or her duties, he or she shall be punished by imprisonment with labour for not more than five years, or by a fine not exceeding KR₩15 million.
58 Choi, K., 2011, '*Shimpanelbulbukhwanhwichakim* [Tort liability for referees]', *Suposuwabub* [The Korean Association of Sports Law], vol. 14, no. 3, pp. 37–52.
59 Ibid.

60 Ibid. See also *Civil Act*, act no. 471, 1958 (Republic of Korea) in relation to performance assistants.
61 Nam, S., Kwon, I. and Jung, H., 2014, '*Bulbubsuposudobakga sungbujojaksagunel bipanjukjupgunbangbubel tonghan miraejukhamel* [A critical approach and progressive opinion on illegal sport gambling and match-fixing through civil law]', *Suposuwabub* [The Korean Association of Sports Law], vol. 23, no. 3, pp. 717–727.
62 Ibid.
63 National Gambling Control Commission 2013, '*Je-2-cha bulbubdobakshiltaejosa* [The second survey on illegal gambling]', *Josahongbugwa* [Division of Research and Public Relations].
64 Jung, H., 2011, '*Suposuel onrainbaetingkyujejungchak*, [A policy to regulate online betting in sports-related gambling]', *Suposuwabub* [The Korean Association of Sports Law], vol. 14, no. 4, pp. 199–219, p. 210.
65 Ibid.
66 Ibid.
67 In addition to the legislation discussed in this chapter, see also, e.g. *Bupaebangjikwonikwuibub* [Act on the Prevention of Corruption and the Establishment and Management of the Anti-Corruption and Civil Rights Commission], act no. 6494, 2002 (Republic of Korea); *Gongjikjayulribub* [Public Service Ethics Act], act no. 5108, 1996 (Republic of Korea). It may be difficult to apply this legislation to match-fixing, however, due to the acknowledgement of the autonomous nature of sporting organisations.
68 See Ando and Steele and Opie in this volume.
69 Whilst outside the scope of this chapter, the efforts to combat match-fixing also require the improvement of labour conditions for players, and greater fairness and transparency in the student athlete selection system. Moreover, increasing the ethical awareness of all people including players, referees, association executives and spectators is extremely important. A solution requires a greater focus on sports ethics education programmes. It is also necessary to improve the reporting and whistle-blower system so that it functions as a mutual check between sports organisations and players. See, e.g. Lee, M. and Seo, K., 2013, '*Suposu sungbujojak: yenrimumjehwa haekyungbangan* [Sports match-fixing: ethics issues and solutions]', *Suposuwabub* [The Korean Association of Sports Law], vol. 21, no. 1, pp. 115–125.

Chapter 6

Practical approaches to match-fixing in Korea

Match-fixing scandals, judicial responses and suggestions for change

Ji Hoon Park[1]

Introduction: match-fixing in Korea

This chapter analyses cases of match-fixing in Korea from four key sports: professional football (soccer), volleyball, baseball and basketball. Gallup Korea, a specialist research company, found that these sports are popular in Korea because people are exposed to seeing and playing them from a young age.[2] These sports are also sponsored by large companies such as Samsung,[3] and national professional leagues are held annually all around Korea. Primary school physical education classes incorporate these sports for all students. Educationally, the classes seek to emphasise and develop teamwork through sport.[4] The match-fixing case studies in these sports discussed in this chapter came to light and were the subject of judicial decisions between 2011 and 2013.

The chapter begins by arguing that many match-fixing cases in Korea have common characteristics, including links to illegal gambling websites, brokers who are former players who facilitate financial payments and seek to influence current players, and vulnerable sporting professionals. The personal and organisational consequences of match-fixing in Korea have been enormous. Media articles in May 2011, for example, suggested that the suicide of a goalkeeper from Korea's professional football league, the K-League, was linked to match-fixing.[5] He was found dead inside his car with a large sum of money after ongoing rumours that he had participated in fixing a match due to consistent threats from gangs. The reports led to an investigation by prosecutors which found that at least 10 per cent of players in the K-League were involved in some sort of match-fixing.[6] The resulting public shock at the suspected level of match-fixing was so great that there were discussions about discontinuing the League.[7] The investigation and subsequent match-fixing cases brought the issue of match-fixing to centre stage in Korean society.

This chapter argues that the causes of match-fixing are inextricably linked to other problems in Korean society. Accordingly, match-fixing can only be prevented by taking into account issues facing the society as a whole, not just the individuals involved. Korea modernised in a very short period of time and many Koreans accept economic growth as a key pillar of social stability and prosperity. Sport is also considered a means of enhancing Korea's international standing. Sports policies aim to increase the number of winning outcomes, rather than regulate the manner in which the sports are played. At a personal level, players are not instilled with strong sports ethics and are driven by the desire for financial success. The chapter concludes with suggestions for ways in which match-fixing may be combated in Korea, based on the author's personal experiences as a semi-professional baseball player and lawyer who has represented players accused of match-fixing.

Analysis of match-fixing in Korean professional sports: common characteristics

The cases of match-fixing between 2011 and 2013 in the four main sports of football, baseball, basketball and volleyball typically involved a financier with links to an illegal gambling website. Those who run illegal private sport gambling websites or those who use these sites to make bets are usually found to be the overarching planners of match-fixing crimes by the courts as suggested by the discussion of the judicial decisions in this chapter. The financier gives money to a broker who is typically a former player. The broker then identifies a key player and uses personal relationships and influence as a senior person in the sport to recruit that player. The broker gives that player money to fix a match. The player is also expected to involve other players in the match-fixing. The key player is usually older and more skilful compared with the other players. The key player uses these advantages to find other players to help carry out the actual match-fixing. The key player then divides the money from the financier which is received via the broker amongst the players.

In the event that the match-fixing fails, the financier threatens the players with exposure or violence to force them to try to succeed in fixing subsequent matches. In the event that the match-fixing succeeds, the financier and broker offer an even greater incentive payment and use the guilt of the players, because they are already involved, to threaten and force players to continue match-fixing. Because of these factors, accused players have pleaded that their responsibility for, and involvement in, match-fixing is less than the financier and broker. This argument is yet to be accepted by the courts in Korea in the context of deciding guilt, however.

The cases resulting from the match-fixing scandals discussed in this section were heard in Korea's district courts in the first instance. District courts in Korea handle by far the majority of cases based on a broad jurisdiction involving first instance matters.[8] Cases are typically brought under the *Hyungbub* [Criminal Act] (act no. 293, 1953 (Republic of Korea))

('*Criminal Act*'), which covers acts of fraud, bribery offences and illegal or irregular gambling, as well as specific sport-related legislation such as the *Kukmin chaeyuk jinhungbub* [National Sports Promotion Act] (act no. 8344, 2007 (Republic of Korea)) ('*National Sports Promotion Act*'). The *National Sports Promotion Act* was amended in 2014 to eradicate irrationality and to create comprehensive countermeasures to foster a fair and transparent environment for sports. The revised Act includes a new art. 14(3) which prohibits a player, manager, coaching staff, umpire, executive or other staff member of a registered sporting organisation from: receiving or asking for any economic benefit in return for illegal favours in connection with a sport event; or offering or promising to offer any economic benefit to a third party in return for illegal favours in connection with a sport event. The penalty for the offence depending on the context is a maximum of seven years in prison or maximum fine of KR₩70 million, or a maximum of five years in prison or maximum fine of KR₩50 million (*National Sports Promotion Act*, art. 47 and art. 48 as applicable).

Professional football

A number of cases of match-fixing have been found to occur in football in Korea. Structurally, match-fixing can be brought about fairly easily by bribing the goalkeeper or just a few key players in football.[9] In one case, for example, a broker bribed three or four key players to underperform to purposely lose the match.[10] The Suwon District Court described a typical scenario of match-fixing in professional football by saying that each player did not do his best to defend or attack.[11] For example, a defender and a goalkeeper may not do their best to prevent the opponent's attack or block the other team's shooting, or a midfielder may pass the ball more to a defender on his team rather than to a striker.

Five players from Korean professional football have been convicted of match-fixing and 11 fixed matches have been confirmed at the time of writing.[12] The five players were all given suspended jail sentences.[13] Of the five, a national team player, who was found to have been involved in fixing six matches and received a total of KR₩30 million, was sentenced to three years' imprisonment, which was suspended for five years. The remaining players who were involved in fixing two or three matches were sentenced to six to ten months' imprisonment, which was suspended for two years.[14] The lesser penalties reflected their lesser involvement in the number of matches fixed.

In one match-fixing case, Choi Seong Guk, a national football player, defended his actions by arguing that he was forced to participate in the match-fixing. He argued that his responsibility for match-fixing was mitigated in accordance with art. 12 of the *Criminal Act*, because he was the subject of irresistible force or threats by an organised gang.[15] The Changwon

District Court in a regional part of Korea went so far as to find that, based on the evidence presented, including witness statements:

> the defendant failed in his attempt to fix a match between Gwangju Samgnoo and Sungnam Ilhwa Chunma on 2 June 2010. After his failed attempt, the defendant received multiple phone calls from the financier, telling him to fix the next game. On the day before the game to be held on 6 June 2010, the defendant and goalkeeper B were called to C and D's room at the hotel where their team was staying. In the room, C and several others were present, including someone who spoke Chinese. They said, 'you guys don't know how to rig matches. Next time, just let the other team score or at least put in an own goal. If that doesn't work, get a red card'.[16]

The player and his legal counsel argued that these circumstances required that he be found innocent.[17] The Court held that irresistible force or threat in art. 12 of the *Criminal Act* referred to acts that arise because of violence or threats that cannot be otherwise avoided.[18] Threats were interpreted by the Court to mean threats to harm one's life or a family member's life, or harm to one's body and where there is no way to avoid the harm. Force means preventing the victim from voluntarily making a decision and making them act in a certain way.[19]

The Court concluded that the circumstances facing Choi Seong Guk did not amount to irresistible force or threat:

> [T]aking into account the circumstances of the case, including the overbearing attitudes of C and the others in the room and the coercive situation and atmosphere and the subject matter of the conversation, it is not doubted that the defendant feared for his safety should he reject the others' proposal. However, it cannot be said that there was a direct, urgent danger to the defendant or his family's life or body, nor can the circumstance be seen as one in which the defendant could not make his own decision freely. Therefore, the circumstances of the present case do not fall into the definitions [of coercion or force] under article 12 of the [*Criminal Act*] such that the defendant cannot be said to have been coerced or forced.[20]

Choi Seong Guk was found guilty of match-fixing and received a life ban from the K-League as well as from the Fédération Internationale de Football Association ('FIFA').[21] The brokers and those who paid the money were also prosecuted and were sentenced to a maximum of one and a half years' suspended imprisonment and the involved players were fined with a maximum of KR₩5 million. The K-League and the Korean Football Association also banned the players for life from playing or being associated with soccer in any form. As a result, these players cannot become a coach or trainer within any Korean football club.

Professional volleyball

Volleyball has also been associated with a number of match-fixing incidents in Korea. Unlike football, one of the reasons that match-fixing has arguably been able to occur in professional volleyball is because it is less popular and receives less media coverage and attention than football.[22] There are significantly fewer clubs in volleyball than other professional sports; the number of clubs has increased by only three clubs for men and one club for women over the last eight years.[23] Volleyball players' salaries are also lower than that of other sports players which may also make it easier for volleyball players to be tempted by the additional money that match-fixing represents.[24] The salary cap for men's volleyball in Korea is KR₩230 million per team and for women's volleyball it is KR₩130 million per team. Other professional sports, such as baseball and football, do not have such restraints on the salaries of players.[25]

A typical match-fixing incident in volleyball is based on the point spread which gives a handicap to weaker teams and facilitates an active betting market.[26] From 2007 to 2012, the volleyball team rankings did not significantly change so a simple win or lose outcome did not attract high betting.[27] As a result, match-fixing in volleyball has mainly been brought about by major players in weaker teams such as KEPCO45, based in Suwon,[28] and Sang Moo Shin Hyup, based in Seongnam.[29]

The first case of match-fixing in volleyball involved the prosecution of a player and a broker by the Public Prosecutors in Daegu. At the time of writing, 11 volleyball players have been charged with offences related to their alleged involvement in match-fixing and 42 fixed games have been confirmed.[30] The high number of confirmed fixed games was one of the reasons for the relatively harsher sentences in the volleyball cases when compared with the results in the football cases discussed above.[31] One player was sentenced to two years' imprisonment for having fixed eight games in return for KR₩61.55 million. Another player received KR₩28 million to fix matches and was sentenced to one year in prison. Further, another player received KR₩36 million for his involvement and was also sentenced to one year imprisonment. The other players received suspended sentences.

Court judgments relating to match-fixing cases in volleyball suggest that the ways in which match-fixing occurs are very similar to baseball as discussed below. The courts use similar expressions, such as players not doing their best. Accordingly, a body of case law is developing such that it is likely that other courts will come to similar conclusions if a similar matter is presented.[32] Daegu District Court, which is in a regional part of Korea, heard the following typical case relating to match-fixing in volleyball and handed down its decision on 18 April 2012.[33] According to the judgment, the facts of the case were that:

> in February 2010, the defendant together with his teammate A, met with broker B, and received KR₩10 million to fix a match. The defendant and teammate A later split the money between themselves. Broker B asked the players to lose a game in the V-league by a specific number of points.[34]

The Court found that:

> on 13 February 2010, the defendant and player A, at the game between their team KEPCO45, and Samsung Hwajae held at the Suwon Indoor Stadium, deliberately missed or inaccurately received and tossed the ball, spiked the ball out of the court or into the opponent's blocking to fix the match with the result that KEPCO45 lost the game 0:3 (set score of 23:25, 22:25, 17:25).[35]

The Court found the defendant guilty and sentenced him to two years' imprisonment. Once again, the volleyball player received a harsher punishment compared to the football players discussed above. In addition to the greater number of matches fixed, the sentences may have been higher because the volleyball scandal occurred after the football scandals and were closely related to creating a betting market. The court wanted this harsh sentence to be a lesson for all sports players to deter them from future involvement in match-fixing.[36]

Professional basketball

By way of contrast with football and volleyball, the only known match-fixing case in Korean professional basketball involved the coach and not the players. Kang Dong Hee coached Wonju Dongbu club during the regular seasons in 2011 to 2012. In an interview in 2012, he said that he would mainly use substitute players as the team had made it to a fourth ranking in the season and advanced to the play-off round, and he wanted to maintain the condition of the best players.[37] In other words, the use of substitute players in this case appears to have been a pre-mediated team strategy to manage key athletes.

In a judgment handed down on 8 August 2013, the Uijeongbu District Court in a regional part of Korea found that Kang Dong Hee had replaced the team's main star players with substitute players and this amounted to match-fixing despite the coach pre-determining that he would use substitute players.[38] The Court held that match-fixing in relation to a coach is not only determined by the coach actively procuring match-fixing, for example, by conspiring with players or bribing the referee. The Court found that a coach's omissions can also be considered as procuring match-fixing where the coach received money and then failed to employ potentially game-winning tactics with the deliberate intention of having the team lose. The Court gave the example of a coach playing substitute players rather than the main, key players or a coach who refuses to coach or lay out tactics for players. The Court concluded that the failure to act as a reasonable coach may be considered misconduct and procuring match-fixing.

In this case, the team was alleged to have lost three games as a result of the coach's actions.[39] The Court found that Kang Dong Hee accepted a request to match-fix, and refused to play star players, put them in the game for a much shorter than average period of time, or simply left substitute players on the basketball court when they clearly did not stand a chance against the other team. The Court also found that Dongbu, the relevant team, was very dependent on its star players, compared with other teams. Accordingly, Dongbu clearly had a greater chance of losing the longer their substitute players were playing.[40] In relation to the pre-game interview statements and the suggestion that resting players was a team strategy, the Court found that the list of players was only finalised one hour before the games commenced.[41] Accordingly, the coach would not be held to previous interview statements that he would play substitute players to maintain the key players' condition because the coach's team had already reached play-offs.[42]

The Court's focus on the timing of the team list, that is the list being finalized just before the game, is questionable. The judgment suggests that any consideration of who will play before the list is lodged an hour before the game commences is merely speculation and not fixed in any way, and submission of the team list one hour prior to the game determines who will play. In reality, however, the list does not fix who will play or when a player will participate. The list is purely an administrative step which does not strictly limit a coach's decisions. The coach is still able to substitute players in the middle of a game, and put different players on and off, including depending on injury. The Court in this case placed too much reliance on the list in its judgment. The Court also relied on the fact that in the four matches that were found to have been fixed, the main players played for a significantly shorter period compared to other non-fixed matches in the season. The author's review of the timetable, however, suggests that it is difficult to see a significant difference in the time of play.

Coach Kang Dong Hee was sentenced to ten months' imprisonment, which was a relatively harsh sentence when compared to the cases discussed above in relation to football and volleyball in light of the circumstances. Although the number of matches fixed was relatively small (four games), the amount of money the coach received from the brokers was considered to be a large sum; that is, KR₩47 million. Moreover, the Court also seems to have held him to a higher standard because he was a coach and not (just) a player.

Professional baseball

Match-fixing in baseball in Korea also appears to be less extensive than football to the extent cases have become public. At the time of writing, two players have been charged with match-fixing in baseball, with five fixed games confirmed. These cases came to light because a broker involved in fixing volleyball matches confessed that he was also involved in baseball match-fixing.[43] One player was found to have fixed two of the games and the other player was found to have fixed three games. They received KR₩5 million and KR₩7 million, respectively, to fix matches. In light of these relatively low amounts, these players were given suspended jail sentences.

In the case of professional baseball, the focus of fixing has not been on the outcome of the match; rather, the focus has been on the first pitcher in the first inning 'walking' batters (described under the rules of baseball as a 'base on balls') by intentionally throwing four 'balls' to a batter. These incidents are considered different to the usual case of match-fixing. Courts tend to use the terminology 'spot-fixing' rather than 'match-fixing' in these baseball cases. In the case of Kim Sung Hyun, for example, it was alleged that Kim was asked to facilitate a base on balls in the first innings in exchange for KR₩5 million with the intention of spot-fixing.[44] The Court found that defendant A asked Kim to take this action around mid-May 2011 in Mokdong, Yang Chunggu in Seoul, near the defendant Kim Sung Hyun's residence, before the game between Nexen Heroes and LG Twins which was scheduled for 14 May 2011. Defendant A promised to give defendant Kim the KR₩2 million he had received from Defendant B. The Court found that Kim accepted the scheme and the money. The Court found that, despite Kim's efforts and intention on 14 May 2011 to walk the batters by pitching the ball away from LG Twins Batters (Dae Hyung Lee, Kung Soo Park and Byung Kyoo Lee), the attempt to spot-fix failed because the batters tried to hit every ball. The Korean Baseball Organisation placed a life ban on these players, including Defendants A and B, from playing any professional or amateur games because of their misconduct.[45]

Causes of match-fixing in Korea

The widespread nature and common characteristics of these match-fixing cases, despite elements of difference between individual sports, suggest that match-fixing in Korea needs to be considered as a whole. This section argues that there are four key causes of match-fixing in popular sports in

Korea: first, a victory-first ideology; second, a lack of ethics or integrity in sport; third, the low support for, and payment of, professional sports' players; and, finally, a lack of tools in the legal system to prevent match-fixing.

A mentality that you must win by any means: victory-first ideology

Over the last 50 years, Korea has undergone enormous economic growth.[46] Korea is now a top ten world economic powerhouse and is a member of the Organisation for Economic Co-operation and Development. Korean society has arguably come to perceive wealth as a respectable and valuable goal in life. Korea has also become very modern over a very short period of time, and has come to accept and expect growth as an important national goal.[47] As a result, achievements, including being promoted at work and winning, are a focus of society, regardless of how a person is promoted or wins.[48]

This victory mentality has been carried over into sport. Coaches and players focus on winning by any means necessary. To be accepted into a prestigious university, and to achieve higher social standing and gain financial success, have all become motivating factors for entering the sporting field.[49] Coaches and players alike have departed from the original, inherent values and objectives of sport and now use it as an avenue for economic success.[50] Match-fixing is not a problem arising from one or two individuals; rather, it is a moral and ethical problem inextricably linked to contemporary Korean social values.

A lack of sports ethics and integrity training: focus on achievement amongst students and coaches

Korea's dramatic economic growth has also resulted in education policies that are not centred on equality and cooperation, but instead are focused on outcomes and results.[51] The curriculum of high school students is filled with subjects such as Korean Language, English and mathematics. Physical Education classes are often named on written timetables, but in practice these classes are substituted by Korean, English or mathematics classes because the emphasis is on gaining intellectual knowledge rather than improving physical well-being and the moral mentality of students.[52]

To the extent that students do focus on sport, they are forced to improve and focus only on their sport. The responsibility for educating student sports players lies primarily on a school's coaches. School coaches, however, are driven by the need for their team to perform well in order to renew their coaching contracts, and therefore the coaches encourage players to focus on improving their sporting skills, rather than learning general knowledge, let alone ethical behaviour. Student sports players are often deprived of a basic education and grow up lacking any ethical basis on which to understand the consequences of, or how to avoid, match-fixing. They lack the fundamentals of sports integrity.[53] Students are also not taught to recognise the dangers of being groomed for or otherwise drawn into match-fixing, or to discern between legal and illegal acts.[54]

Lack of support and low pay for professional sports players

Players with lower salaries are typically found to have been involved in cases of match-fixing in Korea. To the extent that there have been cases involving higher paid, national team players, the match-fixing occurred during the period when the player was serving compulsory time in the army and therefore receiving a lower salary. Conscription applies to males between 18 and 35 years old in Korea and the length of service is up to two years. The case studies from Korea suggest that there is a need to consider not just a lack of ethics when it comes to match-fixing, but also the potential vulnerability of players facing financial instability. In 2014, the average salary of a professional football and baseball player in Korea was KR₩193 million and KR₩106.38 million respectively.[55] Although the salary of sports players is rapidly increasing, the average football and baseball player (excluding star players) receives a salary of between KR₩20 and 30 million.[56] The disparity between payments is also relevant to a discussion of match-fixing. The highest earning baseball player in Korea, for example, received a salary of KR₩1.5 billion, but the lowest earning baseball player received KR₩24 million.[57] This example represents a salary differential of 62.5 times. Further, the Korean national average salary is approximately KR₩22 million;[58] accordingly, receiving KR₩20 to 30 million as a professional athlete is no more than an average person's salary. When the shortness of professional athletes' careers is also taken into account, many professional sports players are vulnerable to accepting the financial gains that are offered by match-fixing.

The emphasis that Korean society places on connections and networks that arise from common schools or hometowns also plays a significant part in the occurrence of match-fixing.[59] There is a tendency to pick young stars and separate them from their peers in order to develop them as elite players. Furthermore, there are only a small number of school sports teams that play a large number of games against each other. From a young age, student sports players form what is known as 'a league of their own' (*gudelmanel rigu*) made up of their school and social connections. Accordingly, each sport is a small world where all players are linked, especially hierarchically as senior and junior players. A junior player finds it difficult to refuse the requests of a senior player even where the senior player has become a broker. These interconnected and complex relationships are another reason why match-fixing occurs in Korea.

A failure of the legal system to prevent match-fixing and regulate sport

The Korean legal system has also failed to keep up with developments in the sporting world and prevent match-fixing. With Korea and Japan's hosting of the 2002 World Cup, Korea established its first SportsToto, a legally authorised betting agency.[60] SportsToto covers the sports of football, basketball, baseball, volleyball and golf. The *National Sports Promotion Act* introduced prohibitions and penalties for match-fixing in sports which are covered by SportsToto in order to promote fairness and integrity in those sports. The Act failed, however, to establish any prohibitions or penalties for sports that were not covered by SportsToto with the result that match-fixing in these sports was not illegal per se. The Act was amended in 2014, after the cases analysed in this chapter, to prohibit match-fixing for registered sports and set out penalties for its contravention.[61]

A prevailing culture of paternalism in courts may also contribute to match-fixing in Korea. As the case studies above demonstrate, courts traditionally deal benevolently with individual players.[62] The match-fixing cases from 2011 to 2013 mainly resulted in suspended sentences; very few players went to prison.[63] The courts consider the role of the person who provides the money or the broker to be more serious than the players' role, and therefore the penalties are focused on the financiers and brokers. Most of the players involved in these cases were young and heavily influenced by their seniors; their vulnerability was a significant mitigating factor that caused courts to have sympathy towards those players although it was not found to exculpate their guilt. The courts are also aware that the sports leagues are likely to take severe action against the young players in addition to any punishment ordered by the court, including life bans, with devastating results for players.[64]

Courts have also refrained to date from finding on the basis of other statutory violations in addition to the *National Sports Promotion Act*.[65] In the majority of match-fixing cases, players have been closely linked to gambling internet website operators.[66] These players are arguably also in breach of the gambling sections of the *Criminal Act* (arts. 246–248). Furthermore, players who engage in match-fixing are also arguably misleading and deceiving the spectators who pay to watch a game with an already fixed outcome. Players could also be in breach of misleading and deceptive conduct provisions (*Criminal Act*, art. 347). It is perhaps a culture of paternalism that prevents courts from applying misleading and deceptive conduct and gambling violations to players' conduct. On the other hand, all brokers and website promoters were sentenced to imprisonment.

Preventing match-fixing in Korea: what can and should be done?

Changes to the structure of Korean sport are necessary to prevent match-fixing. Addressing and preventing match-fixing in Korea requires: a thorough education on sports integrity; reducing the influence that players have on each other because they attended the same school; an introduction of a minimum level of education; building a safety net in social welfare for players; holding games only on weekends; broadcasting and recording games on television; improving the system of chair umpires and referee supervisors; and securing the positions of coaches. This section considers some of these proposals in more detail based on the author's experiences as a semi-professional athlete and lawyer who has represented accused players.

Improve players' fundamental education and education on sports integrity

Players must be instilled with a grounded understanding of sports ethics and the notion that fair play is the spirit of sport from an early age. Coaches, referees and players must be educated on match-fixing, including that it is criminal conduct which should never occur. High schools must create programmes that provide education on sports integrity for coaches, players and parents on a regular basis. At universities, the teaching should cover doping, match-fixing, fighting, fair-play, individual ethics and team ethics in mandatory classes. Players must systematically receive training to internalise fair play and good sportsmanship. Professional sports leagues must continue the education of coaches, staff and players so that if they are ever approached to engage in match-fixing, they are able to confidently and decisively refuse. In particular, professional sports players must be aware of their position in the public eye and must be taught to act accordingly and responsibly.

Increase responsibility of professional clubs for their players

Education on match-fixing must include professional sports clubs. Sports clubs could produce written documentation on the prevention of match-fixing as part of this education. As new players are contracted, they could be requested to sign these documents as an acknowledgement of acts that constitute match-fixing and their declaration to avoid engaging in such conduct. Such declarations could also include a provision that states that the individual player will not damage their reputation or the club's reputation by becoming involved in match-fixing behaviour and, if they do, then the player will bear all civil and criminal responsibilities for their actions. Further, individual clubs need to create case-based ethical education programmes so that the negative impact of match-fixing can be widely understood. Moreover, clubs are well placed to determine the factors that make a player vulnerable to match-fixing and which players fall into that category. Clubs must also have in place programmes to protect players, particularly these vulnerable players, from brokers.

Increase regulation by sports leagues

After the cases discussed in this chapter, further plans for reform in Korea emerged. The four professional leagues of Korea analysed in this chapter have the authority to discipline and sanction players involved in match-fixing. Leagues must thoroughly investigate allegations of match-fixing and impose penalties reflective of players' conduct.[67] Each league could establish a department to constantly monitor and investigate allegations of match-fixing. Sports leagues also need to legally and institutionally regulate cases; for example, by implementing procedures to take away money illegally received by players or other entities. Arising from the 2013 case involving the Korean Basketball League, it was proposed by the Ministry of Culture, Sports and Tourism that leagues improve ways of drafting new players, run a 'clean basketball centre'[68] and improve the monitoring of games by encouraging and providing for a process by which players can admit their involvement and also report other players.[69] This centre now plays a critical role for players and related parties to report voluntarily any misconduct including involvement in match-fixing.

Conclusion: working together to prevent match-fixing in future

Korea has already taken steps to improve its response to match-fixing after the scandals of 2011–13. On 13 March 2013, in acknowledgement of the serious crimes in sport and in order to proactively respond to these matters, the Ministry of Culture, Sports and Tourism together with the four main sports leagues of Korea announced a plan to 'cooperatively tackle match-fixing in professional sports'.[70] First, the reward for reporting match-fixing was increased from KR₩100 million to KR₩200 million.[71] Second, the number of undercover people investigating allegations of match-fixing was increased. Third, the plan proposed the formation of a tentatively named '*Prodanchae hyuplhae*' (Pro-Associations Council), which included the four main sports leagues, in order to respond to match-fixing allegations more actively together. Fourth, in order to prevent games from being fixed within leagues, establishing a designated official was recommended as well as a suggestion for monitoring and recording all games.

For these and other, more recent plans to have a real impact, however, the government must provide funds and each sports league must continuously make efforts to regulate and monitor their games and players. Public prosecutors and other law enforcement agencies, in close cooperation with professional sports leagues, must respond actively to prevent the increasingly cunning and diverse ways in which match-fixing occurs. Plans must deal with the systemic and underlying drivers of sport in contemporary Korea, including a victory-first ideology, a lack of sports ethics and integrity created from insufficient early education for players, as well as players' status gap based on low salaries and seniority, and the courts reluctance to severely punish individual players. To combat these issues, there is also a need to improve players' education so that they feel more responsible for their actions as professional players and are trained to resist approaches from brokers.

Notes

1 The author thanks this volume's editors for their advice and Ms Jess (Hee Sung) Shin and Ms Sarah (Jin Hyung) Yang, Research Assistants, Asian Law Centre, Melbourne Law School, for their research and editorial assistance, and assistance with translation into English of Korean sources.
2 Gallup Korea 2015, *Hankukinijoahanunchumimunhwa* [Korea's most favourite hobby culture], www.gallup.co.kr/gallupdb/reportContent.asp?seqNo=634&pagePos=1&selectYear=0&search=2&searchKeyword=%BF%EE%B5%BF.
3 Copyright Statistics Korea 2016, *Chuyoprosportskwanchungchui* [Current professional sports operational status], www.index.go.kr/potal/main/EachDtlPageDetail.do?idx_cd=1662.
4 Shin, K. and Park, S., 2011, '*Chodung chaeyukeseo changel, insung kyoyuk shilchunel ulhan tamsak* [Implementing education for developing "creativity" and "character" in elementary school physical education]', *Kyuyukhakhwe* [Journal of Education], vol. 50, no. 32, pp. 307–338.
5 Kim, M., 2011, '*YunKiwon jukkum, seulbujojak heesengyanginga* [Death of Yun Ji-Won, is it a result of match-fixing?]', *Chung-Ang News*, 7 May, http://news.joins.com/article/5457432.
6 Ibid.
7 Ibid.
8 Supreme Court of Korea 2016, *Organisation Chart*, http://eng.scourt.go.kr/eng/judiciary/org_chart.jsp.
9 Park, J., 2016, '*Yukneonjeonprochukuseungbujojakyogu • heopparkhanburokakiso* [Prosecution of a broker who threatened pro-baseball players to participate in match-fixing six years ago]', *KBS News*, 27 July, http://news.kbs.co.kr/news/view.do?ncd=3319103&ref=A.
10 Ibid.
11 Suwon District Court (1 February 2013), case no. *no* 4977.
12 Choi, S., 2011, '*Prochukuseungbujojak … sunsugajireogocheouckda* [Professional soccer match-fixing … players run to lose the game]', *Hani*, 25 May, www.hani.co.kr/arti/society/area/479768.html.
13 Ibid.
14 Suwon District Court (1 February 2013), case no. *no* 4977.
15 Changwon District Court (9 February 2012), case no. *gohap* 136.

16 Ibid.
17 Ibid.
18 Ibid.
19 Ibid.
20 Ibid.
21 Ibid.
22 Copyright Statistics Korea 2016, *Chuyoprosportskwanchungchui* [Professional sports operational status], www.index.go.kr/potal/main/EachDtlPageDetail.do?idx_cd=1662.
23 Lee, J., 2014, '*10juneon' probaegu, 10neonhu mukpyokwanjung 100manme-ong* [10th anniversary of professional volleyball, it is aiming for 1 million spectators for next 10 years]', *Newstomato*, 13 October, www.newstomato.com/ReadNews.aspx?no=504526.
24 Kim, H., 2016, '*Hansunsu, Yanghyojin, nanneprobaeguneonbong 1wee* [Han Sun-Sun, Yang Hyo-Jin are Men's and Women's Professional volleyball no. 1 salary players]', *Asiae*, 1 July, http://view.asiae.co.kr/news/view.htm?idxno=2016070111072926417.
25 Lee, J., 2015, '*ProyaekyuFAshijang, alhaecheyeokdaechoidae* [Professional baseball FA market, this year was the biggest in the history]', *Newstomato*, 1 December, www.newstomato.com/ReadNews.aspx?no=604864.
26 Moody, A., 2016, 'Sports betting – understanding point spreads', *About Sports*, 31 January, http://sportsgambling.about.com/od/sportsgambling101/a/intro-sprds.htm.
27 Shim, B., 2012, '*Puro baegu gulsan biga gurimja* [2012 Professional volleyball report: Light and Shadow]', *KBS News*, 13 April, http://news.kbs.co.kr/news/view.do?ncd=2462762&source=https://search.naver.com/search.naver?sm=tab_hty.top&where=nexearch&oquery=2012%20????%20??&ie=utf8&query=2012%20????%20??&retRef=Y.
28 The Sports Org 2015, *Volleyball – Suwon KEPCO 45*, www.the-sports.org/volleyball-suwon-kepco-45-results-identity-equ37027.html.
29 Jung, W., 2012, '*Purobaeguseungbujojakpamumhwaksan ... sangmu, samsung, sunsugadam* [Professional volleyball match-fixing scandal expanded to Sangmu and Samsung players]', *EveryDay News*, 11 February, www.imaeil.com/sub_news/sub_news_view.php?news_id=10270&yy=2012.
30 Jo, Y., 2012, '*Prochukkuiyeobaegudoseungbujojakchungkeukbaegugaejunjun-gunggung* [Match-fixing of professional football and volleyball, big shock for volleyball committees]', *Herald Finance News*, 8 February, http://news.heraldcorp.com/view.php?ud=20120208000416&md=20120318160048_BL. For a detailed analysis of this case, see Steele, Shin and Yang in this volume.
31 Ibid.
32 Similarly to other countries which may be categorised as having a civil law tradition, there is no strict rule of precedent in Korea. Courts are likely to follow similar reasoning and give similar outcomes, however, including because judges, lawyers and prosecutors train together, judges are career-judges, and judges have a high respect for a concept of the rule of law which requires consistency.
33 Daegu District Court (18 April 2012), case no. *godan* 136.
34 Ibid.
35 Ibid.
36 Ibid.
37 YeonHwap News 2012, '*Pronongguongbu Kang DongHeekandokajik 6kang annujeossue* [Professional basketball coach, Kang Dong-Hee: "It is not too late for the 6th round"]', *Naver Sports*, 28 December, http://sports.news.naver.com/general/news/read.nhn?oid=001&aid=0006012948.

38 Uijeongbu District Court (8 August 2013), case no. *godan* 700.
39 Ibid.
40 Ibid.
41 Ibid.
42 Ibid.
43 Jung, K., 2012, '*Proyakyukungkijojak Kim Sunghyunjinyuk 10wol* [Professional baseball match-fixing player, Kim Sung-Hyun imprisoned for 10 months]', *Hankookibo*, 29 March, http://news.naver.com/main/read.nhn?mode=LSD&mid=sec&sid1=102&oid=038&aid=0002243191.
44 Ibid.
45 Ibid.
46 Oh, S., 2015, '*Choibinkukeseomuyeokkangkukeulro • paljunkugeophaeonhankookkyungjae* [One of the poorest countries to a trading powerhouse – rapid development of Korea's economy]', *MBC*, 1 January, http://media.daum.net/economic/others/newsview?newsid=20150101083914457.
47 Ibid.
48 Kim, Y., 2012, '*Cheyukchulhak: corea suposumumhwael gomingori: seungbujojak hankukjuk munhwajihyunggael kaungeosung* [Sports philosophy: the trouble with Korean sports culture: relationship between match-fixing and Korean culture formations]', *Hankukchaeyukchulhakhweji* [Journal of Korean Philosophic Society for Sport and Dance], vol. 20, no. 4, pp. 80–100.
49 Ibid.
50 Ibid.
51 Shon, S., 2013, '*Sukosul seungbujojak siltaewa gudaecheo bangane kwanhan yeongu* [A study on the match-fixing of sports and its prevention]', *Hankukchaeyukchulhakhweji* [Journal of Korean Philosophic Society for Sport and Dance], vol. 16, no. 1, pp. 83–103.
52 Kim, E., 2011, '*Cheyukchulhak: hankuk purochukguel sungbujojake daehan dodukjuk rongo* [Sport philosophy: ethical assertion about match-fixing of K-League]', *Hankukchaeyukchulhakhweji* [Journal of Korean Philosophic Society for Sport and Dance], vol. 19, no. 4, pp. 171–192.
53 Ibid.
54 These circumstances may also lead to less resistance to drug use.
55 Park, S., 2014, '*Lee Dongkuk, tojungyeonbongking … purochulgusunsudelulmomgapgongge* [Lee Dong-Kuk, salary king … salaries of professional football players are revealed]', *CBSNoCut News*, 17 April, www.nocutnews.co.kr/news/4008951.
56 Ibid.
57 Kim, Y., 2014, '*NBA.NFLen'yunchabyulchejuyeonbong'ildda* [Within NBN and NFL, there is a presence of lowest annual salary]', *Hani News*, 3 December, www.hani.co.kr/arti/sports/baseball/667352.html.
58 Organisation for Economic Co-operation and Development 2016, *Korea*, www.oecdbetterlifeindex.org/countries/korea. Converted from US$19,372 at exchange rate on 20 February 2017: see Exchange Currency Converter, *US$ to KRW*, www.xe.com/currencyconverter/convert/?Amount=43403&From=USD&To=KRW.
59 Shon, above n. 51.
60 SportsToto 2016, *History*, www.SportsToto.co.kr/en/about/history.jsp.
61 See Yeun in this volume.
62 Lee, S., 2016, '*Suposudenjungchidenonjungjueuleulkyulmaleul* … [The result of paternalism in sports and politics …]', *Hani*, 1 February, www.hani.co.kr/arti/politics/polibar/728774.html. See also Yeun in this volume.
63 Oh, C., 2016, '*Seungbujochak* [Match-fixing]', *Joongboo Newspaper*, 1 August, www.joongboo.com/?mod=news&act=articleView&idxno=1093418.

64 Shon, above n. 51.
65 For other types of possible causes of legal action, see Yeun in this volume.
66 Ibid.
67 The role of educational programmes run by the international federations for these sports, such as FIFA, Fédération Internationale des Associations de Footballeurs Professionnels ('FIFPro') and International Basketball Federation ('FIBA'), is also important. The role of FIFPro in educating players, for example, is discussed by Schwab and Finocchiaro in this volume.
68 The purpose of this centre is to establish a voluntary call centre for players and any sports associates to report any illegal activities that they have been involved in or know details of. See also Yeun, and Steele, Shin and Yang in this volume.
69 Korean Sports Promotion Foundation 2016, *Clean sports tonghap call centre*, http://cleansports.kspo.or.kr/index.do.
70 Lee, J., 2015, '*Jeonjungmoksuposusuta.danchajangdul, sasangchul "cleangulel"* [All sports star players and heads support the first "Clean Sports"]', *Sports Dongha*, 5 June, http://sports.donga.com/3/all/20150604/71651139/3.
71 Ibid.

Chapter 7

Harmonisation and international approaches to match-fixing

Yuta Ando

Introduction

Over the past ten to 15 years, the term match-fixing has come to international prominence following several scandals prosecuted by law enforcement agencies and sports organisations.[1] If left unchallenged, match-fixing could become deeply entrenched behind the scenes of sports all over the world. Several vulnerabilities may explain the targeting of sport by match-fixers, but the development of information technology has played the crucial role. First, the expansion of the internet and mobile telephony has facilitated match-fixing by making match-fixers more accessible to one another. As match-fixing requires communication between players, match-fixers and intermediaries, the development of online and mobile communication has made match-fixing easy to coordinate, even on a global scale. In some cases, fixers in Asia directed intermediaries in Eastern Europe to contact players in Western Europe.[2] Second, the internet has made sports betting more accessible to consumers. The more that the revenue from sports betting grows, the more that sports betting becomes attractive for match-fixers, because the impact of a fix may be less detectable in large (or liquid) betting markets and the profits to be made can be correspondingly greater.[3] Also, match-fixers can choose which sports events to target from a wide variety of options, and their bets on the corrupted event will be less likely to appear suspicious where there are large numbers of gamblers and betting options. In response to the threat of match-fixing linked to increased sports betting, public authorities, sports organisations and sports betting operators have begun to take various countermeasures.

This chapter commences by presenting typologies for the regulation of gambling and the prohibition of match-fixing from around the world. Second, it analyses the *Council of Europe Convention on the Manipulation of Sports Competitions* ('*Convention*').[4] The *Convention's* suitability as a model in the Asia-Pacific for national laws against match-fixing is then assessed with particular reference to Japan and Australia. The chapter argues that Asia-Pacific countries can strengthen their measures against match-fixing to keep sports clean by adopting the *Convention* model. As the Asia-Pacific includes a wide range of national governance and legal systems, economic systems, cultures and local sports, adoption of the *Convention* model would help to bring consensus and harmonisation to the region as well. Moreover, adopting the *Convention* model could help to start to repair the unfavourable reputation that the Asia-Pacific has developed as the epicentre of a series of scandals in recent years.

Typology of the regulation of gambling

In order to understand the complexity of the fight against match-fixing, it is essential to understand the variety of systems for regulating gambling. Generally, gambling is regulated by a national or local government, although the system of regulation differs from jurisdiction to jurisdiction with three main approaches to regulation evident.

General prohibition

Some states, including China,[5] India[6] and parts of the United States of America[7] prohibit most forms of gambling and subject any exceptions to close regulation. Exceptions often apply to lotteries, because they are a means of raising funds for governments or for popular causes (including sports),[8] and horse racing, which has long-established links to gambling, with modern forms of racing clubs, racetracks and betting also a product of European influence or colonial occupation in a number of Asian countries.[9] In the US, gambling on sports is generally illegal,[10] although it is permitted in the State of Nevada, for example.[11]

Monopoly by government

A wider range of gambling opportunities linked to sport is found in other jurisdictions, but a significant degree of social control is maintained because governments in those jurisdictions exercise a monopoly over the supply of betting services.

Jurisdictions where the national or local governments exclusively control betting markets include Japan, Germany,[12] Korea,[13] Portugal[14] and Sweden.[15] In Japan, for example, gambling in general is prohibited by art. 185 of the *Kei hō* [Criminal Code] (act no. 45, 1907 (Japan)). However, several forms of gambling on sport are allowed, each based on a separate act of the Japanese Parliament and distinguished by sport type: horse racing (*keiba*), motor boat racing (*kyōtei*), auto racing with track motorcycles (*ōtoreesu*), track bicycle racing (*keirin*) and football (soccer).[16] Each gambling system is established and strictly regulated by its respective act, and respectively supervised by specific ministries. There is no chance for legitimate private enterprises to enter into the sports betting business or create new types of betting.

Licence system

A licence system exists where a government establishes standards for the betting industry and related administrative organisations. Private companies may apply to an administrative organisation for permission to operate a gambling business. Australia,[17] France,[18] Italy[19] and the United Kingdom,[20] for example, adopt a licence system. A licence is valid only in the jurisdiction of the issuing authority. Accordingly, operators may have licences in several states to operate a gambling business in multiple jurisdictions.[21] Such systems usually offer the widest opportunities to consumers to engage in lawful sports betting.

Challenges

In recent years, these three types of gambling regulation have faced at least one of two significant challenges. First, gambling is an economic activity involving the supply of a service in exchange for financial reward. Any monopoly or exclusionary arrangements affecting gambling services therefore risk being challenged as anti-competitive business practices. The European Court of Justice held gambling to be an economic activity within the scope of the *Treaty on the Functioning of the European Union* ([2012] OJ C 326/47),[22] prompting private betting operators, particularly in gambling hubs such as Gibraltar and Malta, to argue that the state-run gambling monopolies in Europe inhibit the supply (including the cross-border supply) of gambling services. This challenge has been resisted on the basis that state control is necessary to assure both integrity and social responsibility in the conduct of gambling activities.[23] Similarly, the World Trade Organization has been called upon to arbitrate a long-running dispute between the US and the tiny Caribbean nation of Antigua and Barbuda over restrictions placed on US financial institutions processing funds transfers associated with bets on 'unlawful internet gambling' websites.[24] The dispute centres on the right of Antigua and Barbuda to conduct free trade with the US by the supply of online gambling services and the right of the US to bar that activity for the protection of public morals.

The second challenge comes from the rise of online betting and is often linked to the first challenge. The internet has created the opportunity for customers to access betting in ways and on a scale never before experienced, but it also facilitates black-market gambling. In 1999, it was estimated that the illegal sports betting market in the US was worth between US$80 billion and US$380 billion annually[25] and, in 2013, INTERPOL estimated the Asian illegal betting market to be worth in excess of US$500 billion annually.[26] These statistics indicate that foreign-based betting operators have established a de facto presence popular with gamblers within jurisdictions in which those operators are not licenced. This development is forcing a number of nations which have highly restrictive controls over betting to review and possibly amend their regulations as they apply to online gambling in particular. These nations include Germany,[27] Singapore,[28] Sweden,[29] The Netherlands[30] and the US.[31]

Other than to liberalise in varying degrees consumers' lawful access to online betting services, no particular regulatory response has emerged as dominant globally. The considerations which feature in reform debates include restraining the spread of gambling, maintaining some degree of public ownership of betting service providers, protection of gamblers from unethical practices, control of organised crime including money-laundering, preservation of taxation revenue and the fight against match-fixing.[32]

Typology of mechanisms to criminalise match-fixing[33]

Most nations in Europe rely on general criminal law offences of corruption and fraud to punish match-fixing behaviour.[34] In Australia, that is the position too for the States of Tasmania and Western Australia.[35]

Specific national laws against match-fixing exist in some jurisdictions but are of relatively recent origin. A significant stimulus for the adoption or upgrading of specific match-fixing laws has been the hosting of major sports events such as the Summer Olympic and Paralympic Games in London in 2012,[36] the UEFA European Football Championship in Poland and the Ukraine in 2012[37] and the Winter Olympic and Paralympic Games in 2014 and the FIFA World Cup 2018, all in Russia.[38]

Where specific match-fixing laws exist, there is no uniformity to their structure owing to the different legal frameworks and traditions of each jurisdiction. These specific laws may be classified as one of four types: gambling law offences, specific match-fixing offences within the general criminal law, specific match-fixing offences within a national sport law, and as a separate or stand-alone law criminalising match-fixing.[39]

Gambling law offences

The first classification deals with match-fixing within gambling law. Section 42 of the *Gambling Act 2005* (UK), for example, prohibits cheating at gambling regardless of the achievement of the fraudulent purpose. As this provision is applicable to all sports betting, match-fixing as a form of cheating is illegal if the conduct is related to gambling.[40] The specific match-fixing offences in Japan also fall within this category.[41]

Setting a penalty for match-fixing, especially where the offence is created by a law outside the main body of criminal law, can present difficulties in terms of ensuring that the punishment for match-fixing is in harmony with offences imposed for other criminal conduct generally. In the UK, for example, the Sports Betting Integrity Panel appointed by the Minister for Sport called for reassessment of the two-year maximum period of imprisonment for cheating at gambling.[42] That punishment may be compared with penalties for criminal conduct such as possession of controlled drugs (maximum seven years' imprisonment),[43] dealing in controlled drugs (maximum life imprisonment)[44] and bribery (maximum ten years' imprisonment).[45]

Specific match-fixing offences within the general criminal law

The second type of specific match-fixing offences are those contained in the general body of criminal law. Spanish national law, for example, criminalised match-fixing in 2010 as a form of corruption of private persons in sport (as opposed to government officials). The penalty includes imprisonment from six months to four years (*Código Penal* [Criminal Code], 10/1995 (Spain), art. 286bis). In Bulgaria, specific offences for match-fixing are located in the *Nakazatelen Kodeks* [Criminal Code] (in force since 1 May 1968, last amended by SG no. 13 of 7 February 2017 (Bulgaria), art. 307) ('*Bulgarian Criminal Code*'). The penalty is a maximum of six years' imprisonment for the fixer and a maximum three years' imprisonment for any agent concerned. In addition, fixing which involves betting is punishable by a maximum of ten years' imprisonment (*Bulgarian Criminal Code*, art. 327). The specific match-fixing offences in Australia (other than the States of Western Australia and Tasmania) also fall within this category.[46]

Specific match-fixing offences within a national sport law

Numerous jurisdictions worldwide have enacted laws to regulate sport in general.[47] In some countries the sport law contains specific provisions to criminalise match-fixing as a form of corruption. Three examples are Cyprus, Greece and Poland. Cyprus penalises both active corruption which involves the offering or giving of a bribe to fix the outcome of a sporting contest and passive corruption which involves the solicitation or acceptance of a bribe to fix the contest. The maximum penalty is three years' imprisonment (*O perí Kypriakoú Organismoú Athlitismoú Nómos tou 1969* [Cyprus Sport Organisation Law of 1969], 41/69 (Cyprus), art. 24). Greece's legislation includes offences prohibiting conduct intended to 'influence the evolution, the form or the result of a game' (*Erasitechnikós kai epangelmatikós athlitismós kai álles diatáxeis* [Amateur and Professional Sports and Other Provisions Act] (2725/1999, FEK A' 121/17.06.1999 (Greece), art. 132(1))

('*Greek Sports Act*')). The conduct includes both active and passive bribery involving athletes, trainers, referees, administrators and their associates (*Greek Sports Act*, arts. 132(2), 132(3)). The maximum penalty is up to ten years' imprisonment and a fine of up to €1 million where the fixing is successful or linked to betting (*Greek Sports Act*, art. 132(4)).[48] In Poland, specific sports corruption offences are set out in the *Ustawa z dnia 25 czerwca 2010 r. o sporcie* [Law of 25 June 2010 on Sport] (2010 r. Dz. U. Nr 127, poz. 857 (Poland)) ('*Polish Sports Act*'). Both active and passive corruption are prohibited for which the penalty is imprisonment for up to ten years depending on the seriousness of the violation (*Polish Sports Act*, art. 46). Acting as an intermediary or exerting influence on a sporting association official to bring about match-fixing is also an offence with a penalty of up to eight years' imprisonment (*Polish Sports Act*, art. 48). Using inside information about match-fixing to make bets on the sports event is also an offence for which the penalty is imprisonment for up to five years (*Polish Sports Act*, art. 47). Conviction for some offences may be avoided if the perpetrator upon commission of the offence immediately discloses the full circumstances to the law enforcement authorities before they are otherwise revealed (*Polish Sports Act*, art. 49).[49] The match-fixing offences in Korea also fall within this category as analysed by Yeun in this volume.

Separate laws criminalising match-fixing

The last type of legal framework criminalises match-fixing in sport by the enactment of a separate or stand-alone law. There are three main examples in Europe: Italy, Malta and Portugal. Italy has enacted a specific law against sports fraud (law 401/1989 (Italy)). The scope of that law is limited to the official matches of registered sports organisations. This law criminalises both active and passive corruption in regard to match-fixing (law 401/1989 (Italy), art. 1), but it is confined to the results of matches and therefore appears not to criminalise spot-fixing.[50] The offence is punishable by up to two years' imprisonment. Various high-ranking officials of sports organisations are required to report knowledge of match-fixing to law enforcement authorities (law 401/1989 (Italy), art. 3). In Malta, active and passive corruption in regard to match-fixing is punishable by imprisonment for up to two years (*Prevention of Corruption (Players) Act*, cap. 263 (Malta), arts. 3, 9). Players, officials and organisers who become aware of match-fixing must report their knowledge to the Commissioner of Police otherwise they commit an offence punishable by a fine and up to three months' imprisonment (*Prevention of Corruption (Players) Act*, cap. 263 (Malta), arts. 4, 9). Portugal has also enacted offences against passive and active corruption in regard to match-fixing (law 50/2007 (Portugal), arts. 8–9) although the latter attracts the heavier penalty of up to five years' imprisonment compared with up to three years' imprisonment for active corruption. Further, offences apply to intermediaries and those who collaborate to organise match-fixing on an ongoing basis (law 50/2007 (Portugal), arts. 10–11).

Council of Europe Convention on the Manipulation of Sports Competitions

It is evident from these typologies that there is no commonly agreed or settled approach to the regulation of sports betting or combating match-fixing. The position in regard to match-fixing in Europe in particular is characterised by the different nature and structure of match-fixing laws, in turn exhibiting variation in the conduct prohibited, the persons subject to the offences and the penalties which may be imposed.[51] Amid increasing concern over the threat to sport presented by match-fixing linked to gambling as highlighted by recent major scandals,[52] European authorities have sought a comprehensive and coordinated approach to that threat.

Within the European Union (EU) that concern was evidenced by several reports on online gambling[53] and the Nicosia Declaration on the Fight Against Match-Fixing.[54] However, it was the Council of Europe, which covers a wider geographic area and has a larger membership than the EU, which seized the initiative by assuming responsibility for a new convention against match-fixing: the *Council of Europe Convention on the Manipulation of Sports Competitions* ('*Convention*').[55] This initiative is the third convention on sport to be sponsored by the Council of Europe; the two earlier conventions addressed spectator violence[56] and doping.[57]

The *Convention* was concluded on 18 September 2014 and immediately opened for signature by the member States of the Council of Europe, the other States Party to the European Cultural Convention, the European Union, the non-member States which participated in the *Convention's* elaboration or enjoy observer status with the Council of Europe, and, upon invitation by the Committee of Ministers of the Council of Europe, by other non-member States (*Convention*, arts. 32(1)–32(2)). As of 1 May 2017, the *Convention* had not entered into force.[58]

The purpose of the *Convention* is 'to prevent, detect, punish and discipline the manipulation of sports competitions, as well as enhance the exchange of information and national and international cooperation between the public authorities concerned, and with sports organisations and sports betting operators'.[59] In art. 3.4, the *Convention* defines the 'manipulation of sports competitions' as:

> An intentional arrangement, act or omission aimed at an improper alteration of the result or the course of a sports competition in order to remove all or part of the unpredictable nature of the aforementioned sports competition with a view to obtaining an undue advantage for oneself or for others.

The *Convention* calls on governments to adopt certain measures in the fight against match-fixing. Those measures include enacting legislation preventing conflicts of interest in sports betting operators and sports organisations, encouraging sports betting regulatory authorities to fight against fraud, including by limiting the supply of sports bets or suspending the taking of bets if necessary, and acting against illegal sports betting by, for example, prohibiting or restricting consumers' access to the operators concerned, and blocking financial flows between the operators and consumers.[60]

Sports organisations and competition organisers are to be encouraged by governments to adopt and implement good governance principles and rules to combat the manipulation of sports competitions (*Convention*, art. 7(1)). Sports organisations are also to be encouraged to apply 'specific, effective, proportionate, and dissuasive disciplinary sanctions and measures' in the event of offences (*Convention*, art. 7(3)). The *Convention* requires governments to consider adopting legal measures for the effective protection of informants, witnesses and their family members (*Convention*, art. 21). In many cases, the trigger for investigation of match-fixing is information from the players who are invited to join the fraud or people who witness negotiations. It is very important to create a safe environment for informants.

When the drafting process for the *Convention* started, match-fixing scandals in sport were rife and attracting much publicity, especially in football with the announcement in February 2013 of the large-scale Europol investigation into the suspected fixing of over 380 professional football matches in Europe.[61] Not only law enforcement authorities, but also the sports betting industry,[62] sporting organisations[63] and governments[64] expressed their concern about these developments. That concern resulted in the prospect of a Council of Europe convention attracting attention as a potential means for bringing together actors from different fields or stages to achieve the harmonisation of various efforts against the manipulation of sports competitions.

The Council of Europe identified three actors and three key areas of effort for combating match-fixing. The actors are public authorities (including law enforcement bodies), sports organisations (including competition organisers) and betting operators (*Convention*, art. 4). Coordination between the three actors in the key areas of effort is the foundation of the system of measures against match-fixing supported by the *Convention*. Public authorities should protect people from crime and serve the public's well-being. Sports organisations should preserve and advance the integrity of sport, while sport betting operators should strive to instil in the minds of the gambling public an awareness of good market practices and a justified confidence in the proper functioning of betting markets.

The three key areas of effort are prevention, monitoring and investigation. With regard to prevention, raising awareness through education is important. Article 6 requires parties to the *Convention* to 'encourage awareness raising, education, training and research to strengthen the fight against manipulation of sports competitions'.

Information exchange among governments, sports organisations, sports betting operators and other relevant organisations is essential in all three key areas of effort (*Convention*, art. 12). Parties are to encourage sports organisations to 'adopt and implement the appropriate measures in order to ensure … enhanced and effective monitoring of the course of sports competitions exposed to the risks of manipulation' (*Convention*, art. 7.2). Article 5 requires governments to use gathered information for risk assessment and risk management in cooperation with the sports organisations, sport betting operators and others.

Information for exchange includes 'the types and the object of the [sports] betting products' (*Convention*, art. 12.1) and 'illegal, irregular or suspicious sports betting as well as infringements of the regulations referred to or established in accordance with' (*Convention*, art. 9.1(a)) the *Convention*. Specifically, observed suspicious betting or suspicious acts should be reported to appropriate government and law enforcement authorities, to the competition organisers and to the sports betting operators (e.g. *Convention*, arts. 7.2.b–7.2.c, 9.1.a). The *Convention* provides for 'the suspension of betting, according to domestic law' where an appropriate alert has been issued (*Convention*, art. 9.1(f)). Appropriate authorities may also investigate the suspicious acts with the objective of determining whether criminal or sports disciplinary offences may have occurred and should be prosecuted.

As for criminal offences, the *Convention* prescribes that a state party's domestic laws 'criminally sanction the manipulation of sports competitions [as defined in art. 3.4] when it involves either coercive, corrupt or fraudulent practices' (*Convention*, art. 15). The Explanatory Report to the *Convention* states that art. 15 'does not require the establishment of a specific and uniform offence for manipulation of sports competitions'.[65] The purpose of the *Convention* is for State Parties to implement various measures 'to prevent, detect, punish and discipline the manipulation of sports competitions',[66] rather than for the *Convention* to specify offences. Thus, any absence of uniformity among State Parties in that regard does not limit the opportunity for harmonisation because the important consideration is that each State Party will establish any offences for match manipulation in a form appropriate for its jurisdiction.

In a bid to achieve coordination between public authorities, sports organisations and sports betting operators, the *Convention* in art. 13 requires each State Party to identify a 'national platform' to:

a serve as an information hub, collecting and disseminating information…;

b coordinate the fight against the manipulation of sports competitions;
c receive, centralise and analyse information on irregular and suspicious bets placed on sports competitions taking place on the territory of the Party and, where appropriate, issue alerts;
d transmit information on possible infringements of laws or sports regulations...; and
e cooperate with all organisations and relevant authorities at national and international levels, including national platforms of other States.

The *Convention* neither declares the establishment of an international platform to fulfil roles comparable to the national platforms at an international level, nor does it advocate for a body like the World Anti-Doping Agency which is more concerned with regulation-making, standard setting and compliance rather than operational matters such as investigations, prosecutions and punishment. However, a Convention Follow-up Committee is to be established under art. 30 with functions including recommending measures to improve international cooperation between Parties as well as operational cooperation between public authorities, sports organisations and betting operators (*Convention*, art. 31). Other general measures and statements for international cooperation appear in *Convention* arts. 26, 27 and 28.

In addition to the above measures, a further basic requirement for the fight against match-fixing is the need for action against illegal sports betting (*Convention*, art. 11). Match-fixing is more likely to happen in conjunction with illegal sports betting.[67] There are jurisdictions where regulation of the betting industry is under-regulated or unregulated, especially in the case of online betting. Establishing a definition of illegal betting is problematic given that online betting is potentially available to consumers from all over the world. There are many betting websites, for example, available to Japanese consumers but the location of the betting operators is outside Japan. If those betting operators are legal or have licences for online betting in the area of their location, their status within Japan becomes very complicated for the police or other law enforcement authorities, especially if prosecution for unlawful gambling is being considered.[68]

Possible harmonised reaction to the Council of Europe *Convention* outside Europe

The *Convention* is open for signature by States which are not member States of the Council of Europe. Australia and Japan are eligible to sign the *Convention* because 'they took part in drawing it up'.[69] No other States in the Asian region[70] are eligible on that basis, although it is open to the Committee of Ministers of the Council of Europe to invite non-member States to sign the *Convention* (*Convention*, art. 32(2)).[71] The prospect of accession to the *Convention* by Australia and Japan presents two different illustrations of the effect that the *Convention* might produce. The following analysis may also offer guidance for other nations in the Asian region considering regulatory interventions in the area of match-fixing and associated gambling control.

Japan

Although gambling in Japan is in general unlawful, gambling on horse racing, motor boat racing, auto racing (track motorbikes), bicycle racing (track cycling) and football is allowed. The laws which govern these gambling activities make it a criminal offence to engage in match-fixing behaviour. Various administrative measures also aim to prevent match-fixing or minimise the risk of its occurrence. These measures appear to have been very successful with no reported convictions in the past 30 years in the case of the first four sports or football since gambling was introduced in 2000.[72] Furthermore, in the case of football, FIFA's Early Warning System[73] has issued only one alert for match-fixing for Japan since it was introduced in 2011. That alert occurred in 2014 when irregular betting activity was detected among overseas' betting operators concerning a J-League match: Kawasaki Frontale v. Sanfrecce Hiroshima. It was later found that the irregular betting alert was caused by an attempted joke and had no relation to match-fixing.[74] Despite this good record, and bearing in mind the recent increase in match-fixing scandals in the world, the J-League, the Japan Football Association and the Japan Sport Council ('JSC'), which is the only football betting operator in Japan, are cooperating to raise awareness of the risks of match-fixing by holding seminars for football players, club officials and referees.[75]

The peak bodies of Japanese sport, (such as the Japan Sports Agency ('JSA') and the Japanese Olympic Committee ('JOC')) should extend measures against match-fixing to sports other than horse racing, motor boat racing, auto racing, bicycle racing and football.[76] To date, measures against match-fixing have been considered in the context of sports betting in Japan. Accordingly, sports that are open to sports betting have taken measures against match-fixing.[77] Other sports, however, do not have specific schemes to prevent or detect match-fixing. Now that online gambling has become popular and sports betting globally covers almost all sports and leagues, it is necessary for Japan to recognise that sports betting by non-Japanese operators might target *any* Japanese competition. To protect players and to keep sports clean, measures need to be taken soon for the benefit of not only Japanese sports leagues and Japanese players, but also for non-Japanese clubs and players. Host countries of sports competitions should be able to provide conditions that safeguard sports integrity before inviting players or clubs from abroad.

Moreover, in 2016, Japan experienced two gambling scandals in sport. Although both of the scandals were not related to match-fixing, the scandals shocked Japanese society. In the first scandal,[78] professional baseball players from the Yomiuri Giants, one of the most famous baseball clubs in Japan, were found to have bet on baseball games in their own league and in high school baseball. The players were suspended indefinitely by the baseball league Commissioner. The other scandal involved two famous badminton players visiting illegal casinos in Tokyo. They belonged to the same strong badminton club. One was a former ace player of the Japanese men's badminton team, who represented Japan at the London Olympic Games in 2012. That player was dismissed from the club because of the scandal. The other player was expected to win a gold medal at the Rio de Janeiro Olympic Games in 2016, but was suspended from official training and competitions as a result of the investigation and missed joining the Rio 2016 Olympic team. The players said that they visited casinos overseas when they travelled for badminton competitions. In Japan, casinos are illegal. In the course of the investigation, it became public that several other teammates went to illegal casinos in Japan with the two players. Following the scandal, the badminton club ceased activity for six months.[79] Although neither case was directly related to match-fixing, the scandals demonstrate the potential for risky behaviour by Japanese players and such behaviour may be used to cultivate vulnerabilities that may lead to match-fixing.

These concerns are reflected in results from research conducted for the World Football Players' Union, FIFPro.[80] That research in 2011 was on match-fixing in 15 national football leagues in Central and Eastern Europe, where researchers thought that match-fixing was likely to occur. More than 3000 players answered a questionnaire about match-fixing in their leagues and their environments. This research concluded that match-fixing has some correlation with players in weak positions relative to other players. According to the research, more than half of the players who did not receive their salary as scheduled were invited to join in match-fixing. Another example concerned players who experienced violence by their coaches or coaches' associates. These players are vulnerable to targeting by fixers. This research and anecdotal reports show that fixers do not suddenly approach players to fix a match. Fixers do so gradually, at first pretending that they could be good friends or reliable advisors for the player's career. Fixers will look to use such fake 'friendships' or 'advisory roles' to discover secrets which players will not wish to have revealed; for example, extra-marital affairs or previous criminal associations. Fixers may supply players with prohibited drugs, involve them in illegal gambling or lend them money which the players may find difficult to repay. Having identified or created such vulnerabilities, fixers exploit them to blackmail players into match-fixing. The behaviour of the baseball and badminton players involved in the two 2016 gambling scandals could create such vulnerabilities in the context of Japanese expectations of professional players.

After these two scandals, the JSA, which is the governmental agency for sports, researched how many national sports federations made provision in their codes of conduct for the protection of the integrity of their sports. The JSA expected that national sports federations would ban the following: doping, illegal drugs, illegal betting and acquaintances with antisocial characteristics. The results were unexpected and undesirable. Sixty-nine national sports federations of 72 which belong to the JOC or the JSA answered the questionnaire and 64 federations included in their codes of conduct or codes of compliance at least one of the four desired prohibitions. However, only 20 per cent included all four prohibitions.

The five sports on which betting is legally conducted in Japan possess a strong awareness of the threats posed by match-fixing and are well prepared to respond to those threats with the support of laws creating specific criminal offences, a very strict system of control and good education for their drivers, jockeys, cyclists and football players. Many other Japanese sports have not been exposed to the threat of match-fixing because they have no connection in Japan with lawful betting. They are, therefore, not imbued with the same awareness of the potential threats or of the need for prompt action. That attitude might not have been seen as an imminent problem to date. However, the point has been reached where the internet and mobile telephony enable overseas-based betting operators to offer betting markets on any minor Japanese sports competition and in turn that increases the prospect of matches in those competitions being targeted by criminal elements intending to fix match results in order to profit from betting on the outcome of those matches. It is therefore important that Japanese sports organisations, players and other people involved in sports become more aware of the threat of match-fixing and associated gambling and institute their own preventive measures. In particular, players should be made aware of the nature and tactics of fixers who prey on the vulnerable so that the players are equipped to react in appropriate ways should something irregular happen.

The preventive and deterrent measures (such as codes of conduct, emergency reporting hotlines and player education) which have been adopted in those sports where there is established lawful betting might be too strong to adopt for other sports where there is no tradition of betting. But a sense of urgency must be generated and stakeholders need to head in the same direction to develop concrete measures to fight against match-fixing. The *Convention* offers a model for Japan to consider as it develops its response to match-fixing.

Australia

As Australia is a federal state, powers are shared between the various units of government. Sports policy, criminal law and the betting industry are generally within the law-making authority of states and territories rather than the national government. However, in the early 1970s, a national budget for sport was established and a small federal government bureaucracy to set policy for that budget's expenditure was created. Both the budget and the federal bureaucracy for sport have expanded greatly since then.[81] The international importance of sport has also grown which in turn demands a greater role for the national government. The federal Department of Health is now in charge of national sports policy. In the Department, the National Integrity of Sport Unit ('NISU') was established to oversee, monitor and coordinate efforts to keep sports clean from doping, match-fixing and other corruption. The fight against match-fixing is one of the main aims of NISU and cooperation between national, state and territory governments is essential for Australian sport integrity.

Cooperation was the basis of the agreement of the national, state and territory governments in June 2011 to create a *National Policy on Match-Fixing in Sport* ('*Policy*').[82] The *Policy* establishes the respective roles of governments, sporting organisations and betting operators. Under the *Policy*, governments are required to establish nationally consistent criminal laws against match-fixing (*Policy*, cl. 3.4). State and territory governments are required to enact legislation to regulate sports betting in a manner which strongly promotes cooperation between sports organisations and sports betting operators. Before a betting operator can offer betting on a sport, an agreement between the betting operator and a government approved 'Sports Controlling Body'[83] for the sport must be entered into. The agreement identifies the sports events, competition levels and betting product types that are permitted (*Policy*, cls. 3.5–3.6). The *Policy* enables sports organisations to recognise when and where sports betting will happen. This approach makes it efficient for them to take measures against match-fixing. Moreover, sports organisations are able to refuse inappropriate betting, for instance, betting on matches at junior or youth level.

Information exchange is another important feature of the *Policy*. Various types of information are to be shared between Sport Controlling Bodies and betting operators and provided by both of those groups to betting regulators and law enforcement agencies. That information may concern sports betting patterns and other intelligence in the case of suspect matches and identifying details of players, officials and others subject to the jurisdiction of sport organisations as well as identifying details of gamblers and financial transactions (*Policy*, cl. 3.8). For the purpose of implementing the exchange of information, the *Policy* envisages that sports betting operators will 'adopt an industry standard for information exchange and information provision requirements with sports, governments and law enforcement agencies by July 2012' (*Policy*, cl. 5.2.a) and 'guarantee confidentiality of information provided by sports to the betting agencies' (*Policy*, cl. 5.2.c). These provisions make possible and strengthen information storage, information sharing, prevention or risk management based on information analysis, and appropriate responses after alerts of match-fixing. The provisions reflect the fact that information sharing is highly important to preserve the integrity of both sport and betting.

The *Policy* contemplates the payment of fees by betting operators to Sport Controlling Bodies for the right to offer betting on their sports (*Policy*, cl. 3.8) and a share of betting revenue to defray the costs of integrity programmes including information exchange (*Policy*, cl. 5.2). Legislation to regulate these payments should ensure there is sufficient accountability and transparency in arrangements between betting operators and Sports Controlling Bodies to avoid any conflict of interest compromising the integrity of sports competitions or betting markets.

The *Policy* and the arrangements which come within its scope arguably reflect all of the essential elements of the *Convention*. Nonetheless, for Australia, the prospect of accession to the *Convention* offers some advantages. It would afford an opportunity to influence the *Convention's* implementation and further development. Relationships established with other Parties might also help generate specific cooperative arrangements with them. The *Convention* could also provide the basis for enhanced constitutional powers to aid the national government to implement anti-match-fixing measures nationally and internationally as suggested elsewhere in this volume.[84] For other nations contemplating becoming Parties to the *Convention*, the Australian experience in implementing a regulatory scheme based on principles very similar to those in the *Convention* may also prove instructive.

Conclusion

As the two typologies considered above demonstrate, there is no commonly agreed or settled worldwide approach to the regulation of sports betting or combating match-fixing. The key concept of the *Convention* is to harmonise the fight against match-fixing in the world by setting standards which are both necessary and sufficient. The case studies of Japan and Australia demonstrate two types of frameworks which are different and yet have some common elements, and offer lessons for harmonising the global fight against match-fixing.

Although Japan has strong measures against match-fixing, those measures are designed for, and only applicable to, specific types of sports betting which exist in Japan. Japan should consider expanding these measures in an appropriate way to other sports, recognising the increasing risks that match-fixing presents globally. Japan's hosting of the Tokyo Olympic and Paralympic games in 2020 may serve as a strong impetus for Japanese sports organisations to work towards earning the trust of not only Japanese people but also people abroad when it comes to combating match-fixing. The *Convention* could form a blueprint for future reforms.

Australia's federal system grants law-making power over sports policy, criminal law and the betting industry to State and Territory governments, although the national government has emerged as an influential and major source of funding for national sport. The potential for difficulty for harmonisation manifested by this spread of power has been addressed to at least some extent by the *Policy* agreed to by all governments. The *Policy* provides for consistent, efficient and strong measures all around Australia. The problem often seen internationally of a lack of cooperation between sports organisations and sports betting operators receives careful attention under the *Policy*. Adoption of the *Convention* could help strengthen Australia's measures against match-fixing and further harmonise its existing domestic frameworks.

Notes

1 See, e.g. the 2005 Hoyzer scandal in German football: Harding, L., 2005, 'Two years in jail for match-fixing German referee', *Guardian*, 18 November, www.theguardian.com/football/2005/nov/18/newsstory.sport4; the 2006 *Calciopoli* scandal in Italian football: 'Italian clubs punished for match-fixing' 2006, *Guardian*, 15 July, www.theguardian.com/football/2006/jul/14/europeanfootball.juventus2; and the 2011–13 Europol investigation into the suspected fixing of 380 professional football matches in Europe: Europol 2013, *Update – results from the largest football match-fixing investigation in Europe*, press release, 6 February, www.europol.europa.eu/newsroom/news/update-results-largest-football-match-fixing-investigation-in-europe.

2 See, e.g. Europol, above n. 1.

3 See Menz and Skene in this volume.

4 *Council of Europe Convention on the Manipulation of Sports Competitions*, opened for signature 18 September 2014, CETS no. 215 (not yet in force), https://rm.coe.int/16801cdd7e.

5 Huang, S., 'Sport betting and its regulation in China', in Anderson, P.M., Blackshaw, I.S., Siekmann, R.C.R. and Soek, J. (eds.), 2012, *Sports betting: law and policy*, TMC Asser Press, pp. 325–332.

6 Singhania, V., 'Sports betting: is it really illegal in India?', in Anderson, P.M., Blackshaw, I.S., Siekmann, R.C.R. and Soek, J. (eds.), 2012, *Sports betting: law and policy*, TMC Asser Press, pp. 443–452. The author argues that contrary to conventional wisdom, sports betting as a game of skill may not be illegal in India.

7 Anderson, P.M., 'The regulation of gambling under US Federal and State law', in Anderson, P.M., Blackshaw, I.S., Siekmann, R.C.R. and Soek, J. (eds.), 2012, *Sports betting: law and policy*, TMC Asser Press, pp. 854–869.

8 See, e.g. Huang, above n. 5, pp. 325, 326–330. The first state lotteries in China are said to date from the Tang Dynasty (AD 618–907).

9 See, e.g. *Lakshmanan* v. *State of Tamil Nadu* [1996] AIR 1153; Sayta, J., 2013, 'A primer on horse racing laws in India', *GLaws. All about Gambling*, 12 May, https://glaws.in/2013/05/12/a-primer-on-horse-racing-laws-in-india.
10 *Professional and Amateur Sports Protection Act 1992*, 106 USC §§3701–3704; Anderson, above n. 7, pp. 854, 862–863.
11 Anderson, above n. 7, pp. 854, 867–868.
12 Nolte, M., 'Reorganisation of the sports betting market in Germany', in Anderson, P.M., Blackshaw, I.S., Siekmann, R.C.R. and Soek, J. (eds.), 2012, *Sports betting: law and policy*, TMC Asser Press, pp. 410–420. However, from 1 January 2018, online sports betting will be lawfully offered by up to 35 private operators: Boehringer, S., 2017, '*Neue Regeln für Sportwetten* [New regulations on sports betting]', *Süddeutsche Zeitung*, 16 March, www.sueddeutsche.de/wirtschaft/gluecksspiel-neue-regeln-fuer-sportwetten-1.3423223.
13 See Yeun and Park in this volume.
14 Cardigos, P., 'Sports betting and the law in Portugal', in Anderson, P.M., Blackshaw, I.S., Siekmann, R.C.R. and Soek, J. (eds.), 2012, *Sports betting: law and policy*, TMC Asser Press, pp. 634–643.
15 Plogell, M. and Ullberg, E., 'Sports betting in Sweden', in Anderson, P.M., Blackshaw, I.S., Siekmann, R.C.R. and Soek, J. (eds.), 2012, *Sports betting: law and policy*, TMC Asser Press, pp. 763–773.
16 See Kawai in this volume.
17 See Menz and Skene in this volume.
18 Pelletier, P., Verbeist, T. and Lebon, G., 'Betting in France', in Anderson, P.M., Blackshaw, I.S., Siekmann, R.C.R. and Soek, J. (eds.), 2012, *Sports betting: law and policy*, TMC Asser Press, pp. 383–409.
19 Antignani, F., Colucci, M. and Majani, F., 'Betting in sports events: gambling in Italy', in Anderson, P.M., Blackshaw, I.S., Siekmann, R.C.R. and Soek, J. (eds.), 2012, *Sports betting: law and policy*, TMC Asser Press, pp. 495–511.
20 Barr-Smith, A., 'Sports betting: United Kingdom', in Anderson, P.M., Blackshaw, I.S., Siekmann, R.C.R. and Soek, J. (eds.), 2012, *Sports betting: law and policy*, TMC Asser Press, pp. 843–853.
21 See Menz and Skene in this volume.
22 *Her Majesty's Customs and Excise* v. *Schindler* [1994] ECR I-01039. See also Papaloukas, M., 'Sports betting and European law', in Anderson, P.M., Blackshaw, I.S., Siekmann, R.C.R. and Soek, J. (eds.), 2012, *Sports betting: law and policy*, TMC Asser Press, pp. 98–106.
23 Papaloukas, above n. 22, pp. 104–105.
24 *Unlawful Internet Gambling Enforcement Act of 2006*, 31 USC §§5362–5367. See also, Grunfeld, M., 2007, 'Don't bet on the United States's internet gambling laws: the tension between internet gambling legislation and World Trade Organization commitments', *Columbia Business Law Review*, vol. 2007, no. 2, pp. 439–504.
25 National Gambling Impact Study Commission 1999, *Final Report*, 18 June, http://govinfo.library.unt.edu/ngisc/reports/fullrpt.html.
26 Murdoch, L., 2013, 'Illegal betting could top $500b each year', *The Sydney Morning Herald*, 17 September, www.smh.com.au/national/illegal-betting-could-top-500b-each-year-20130916-2tv6n.html. See also Menz and Skene in this volume.
27 Boehringer, above n. 12.
28 *Remote Gambling Act 2014* (Singapore); Kotwani, M. and Chia, L., 2016, 'Government exempts Singapore Pools, Turf Club from online gambling ban', *Channel NewsAsia*, 29 September, www.channelnewsasia.com/news/singapore/government-exempts-singapore-pools-turf-club-from-online-gamblin-7821326.

29 Isaksson, U., 2017, 'Swedish gaming license inquiry proposes sweeping reforms', *Online Gambling Lawyer*, vol. 16, no. 4, www.cecileparkmedia.com/online-gambling-lawyer/article_template.asp?Contents=Yes&from=woglr&ID=2434.
30 Van Weeren, M., 2017, 'License procedure for remote gambling by the Netherlands', *Blenheim Advocaten*, 8 April, www.blenheim.nl/blogs/1376/remote-gambling-Netherlands.
31 Rose, I.N. and Bolin, R., 2012, 'Game on for internet gambling: with federal approval states line up to place their bets', *Connecticut Law Review*, vol. 45, no. 2, pp. 653–694.
32 See, e.g. Isaksson, above n. 29.
33 This typology is adapted from a study for the European Commission (Directorate-General for Education and Culture): KEA European Affairs 2012, *Match-fixing in sport: a mapping of criminal law provisions in EU 27*, March, pp. 23–39. See at pp. 65–109 for the text of the criminal provisions, statement of available penalties and reports of criminal prosecutions for match-fixing for each country surveyed.
34 Ibid., pp. 23–31.
35 See Opie and Lim in this volume.
36 The operation of the *Gambling Act 2005* (UK) was extended to permit the exchange of suspicious betting information with the International Olympic Committee: Gibson, O., 2011, 'New laws proposed to clamp down on corruption at London 2012', *Guardian*, 17 August, www.theguardian.com/sport/2011/aug/17/olympic-laws-corruption-london-2012.
37 KEA European Affairs, above n. 33, p. 37.
38 In July 2013, Russia upgraded its laws against match-fixing by amending art. 26.2 of the Federal law of 4 December 2007, no. 329-FZ, dated 4 December 2007 *O fizicheskoy kul'ture i sporte v Rossiyskoy Federatsii* [On Physical Culture and Sport in the Russian Federation] (Russian Federation): see Yurlov, S., 2015, 'Russia's attempts to tackle unlawful influence over sports results', *The Sports Integrity Initiative*, 4 December, www.sportsintegrityinitiative.com/russias-attempts-to-tackle-unlawful-influence-over-sport-results. Although Yurlov regarded this upgrade as a response to FIFA and Europol investigations into alleged match-fixing in Russian football, it can also be seen as part of the pattern of preparations for hosting the 2014 Winter Olympic and Paralympic Games and the 2018 FIFA World Cup like other countries hosting similar events.
39 This typology is adapted from a study for the European Commission (Directorate-General for Education and Culture): KEA European Affairs, above n. 33, pp. 23–39.
40 Reliance on the general criminal law may still be necessary as demonstrated by the most famous instance of fixing in recent UK history, a case of spot-fixing in international cricket between England and Pakistan: *R* v. *Amir* [2011] EWCA Crim 2914. The three players concerned and their agent were convicted of conspiracy to cheat at gambling which invoked *Criminal Law Act 1977* (UK), s. 1 ('conspiracy to commit an offence'), the offence being *Gambling Act, 2005* (UK), s. 42 ('cheating at gambling'). See Gardiner, S., '*R* v. *Amir & Butt* [2011] EWCA Civ 2914 [*sic*]', in Anderson, J. (ed.), 2013, *Leading cases in sports law*, Asser Press, pp. 287–303, pp. 287, 298.
41 See Kawai in this volume.
42 Sports Betting Group 2010, *Report of the Sports Betting Integrity Panel*, February, p. 13, www.sportsbettinggroup.org/downloads/Report%20of%20the%20Sports%20Betting%20Integrity%20Panel%20-%20Feb%202010.pdf.
43 *Misuse of Drugs Act 1971* (UK), s. 5(2), sch. 4.
44 Ibid., s. 4(3), sch. 4.

45 *Bribery Act 2010* (UK), ss. 1, 2, 6, 11(1)(b).
46 See Opie and Lim in this volume.
47 See, e.g. *Sports Act* (act no. 25, 2013) (Kenya); *Zhōnghuá rénmín gònghéguó tǐyù fǎ* [Sports Law of the People's Republic of China] (People's Republic of China), 29 August 1995. For analysis of the latter, see Nafziger, J.A.R. and Wei, L., 1998, 'China's sports law', *American Journal of Comparative Law*, vol. 46, no. 3, pp. 453–483.
48 Petropoulos, N. and Maguire, R., 'Match fixing: case studies from Greece and Ireland', in Haberfeld, M.R. and Sheehan, D. (eds.), 2014, *Match-fixing in international sports*, Springer, pp. 89–99, pp. 89, 93.
49 KEA European Affairs, above n. 33, p. 37.
50 Ibid., p. 38.
51 These differences are analysed in detail in KEA European Affairs, above n. 33. For a global perspective, see International Olympic Committee and United Nations Office on Drugs and Crime 2013, *Criminalization approaches to combat match-fixing and illegal/irregular betting: a global perspective*, July, www.unodc.org/documents/corruption/Publications/2013/Criminalization_approaches_to_combat_match-fixing.pdf.
52 See above n. 1; KEA European Affairs, above n. 33.
53 *European Parliament resolution of 10 March 2009 on the integrity of online gambling (2008/2215(INI))* [2010] OJ C E 87/30; European Commission 2011, *On on-line gambling in the internal market*, green paper, 24 March, http://ec.europa.eu/internal_market/consultations/docs/2011/online_gambling/com 2011_128_en.pdf.
54 Presidency of the Council of the European Union, European Commissioner responsible for sport and participants in the EU Sport Forum 2012 2012, *Nicosia Declaration on the Fight Against Match-Fixing*, 20 September.
55 *Council of Europe Convention on the Manipulation of Sports Competitions*, opened for signature 18 September 2014, CETS no. 215 (not yet in force). The *Convention* is also known as the treaty of Magglingen (in German) or Macolin (in French), after the place of its conclusion in Switzerland.
56 *European Convention on Spectator Violence and Misbehaviour at Sports Events and in particular at Football Matches*, opened for signature 19 August 1985, ETS no. 120 (entered into force 1 November 1985), www.coe.int/en/web/conventions/full-list/-/conventions/treaty/120.
57 *Anti-Doping Convention*, opened for signature 16 November 1989, ETS no. 135 (entered into force 1 March 1990), www.coe.int/en/web/conventions/full-list/-/conventions/treaty/135.
58 Council of Europe 2017, *Chart of signatures and ratifications of Treaty 215*, www.coe.int/en/web/conventions/full-list/-/conventions/treaty/215/signatures?p_auth=BDmu5HfE. Article 32 of the *Convention* stipulates that 'five signatories, including at least three member States of the Council of Europe … [must express] … their consent to be bound by the Convention' before it can enter into force. Japan enjoys observer status with the Council, but not Australia or Korea, and both Australia and Japan, but not Korea, participated in the *Convention's* elaboration.
59 Council of Europe 2017, *Details of treaty no. 215*, www.coe.int/en/web/conventions/full-list/-/conventions/treaty/215.
60 Council of Europe, above n. 58.
61 Europol 2013, *Update – results from the largest football match-fixing investigation in Europe*, press release, 6 February, www.europol.europa.eu/newsroom/news/update-results-largest-football-match-fixing-investigation-in-europe. See also Kelso, P., 2013, 'How German police fell on European football's biggest

match-fixing scandal by accident', *Telegraph*, 5 February, www.telegraph.co.uk/sport/football/news/9851507/How-German-police-fell-on-European-footballs-biggest-match-fixing-scandal-by-accident.html.

62 The European Lotteries 2013, *Europol uncovers match-fixing scandal: EL calls for new intensification of cooperation between authorities, sportand* [*sic*] *gambling operators to fight match-fixing*, press release, 5 February, www.european-lotteries.org/announcement/europol-uncovers-match-fixing-scandal-el-calls-new-intensification-cooperation-between-?cf=4&page=6.

63 Conn, D., 2013, 'Fifa wants tough sentences for criminals who are caught match fixing', *Guardian*, 5 February www.theguardian.com/football/2013/feb/04/fifa-tough-match-fixing.

64 *European Parliament resolution on match-fixing and corruption in sport* [2016] OJ C 36/137.

65 Council of Europe 2014, *Explanatory report to the Council of Europe Convention on the Manipulation of Sports Competitions*, 18 September, para. 130, https://rm.coe.int/CoERMPublicCommonSearchServices/DisplayDCTMContent?documentId=09000016800d383f.

66 Council of Europe, above n. 58.

67 See Kawai, Opie and Lim, and Park in this volume for examples.

68 See Menz and Skene in this volume.

69 Council of Europe, above n. 65.

70 Using membership of the Asian Football Confederation as a defining criterion for the Asian region.

71 See also, Council of Europe 2017, *Note for information on the participation of non-member States in Council of Europe treaties*, www.coe.int/en/web/conventions/participation-of-non-member-states. This could apply in the case of Korea: see Steele and Opie in this volume.

72 For an analysis of the legal status of match-fixing and sports betting in Japan as well as the main match-fixing controversies, see Kawai in this volume.

73 See FIFA 2017, *FIFA Early Warning System ('EWS')*, www.fifa.com/about-fifa/news/y=2014/m=1/news=fifa-early-warning-system-ews-2261080.html.

74 The original report from the Early Warning System to the J-League is confidential. A brief description is provided in the J-League's public relations magazine: see '*FIFA EWS-sha kara no keihō e no J-riigu no taiō ni tsuite* [About the J-League interaction to the warning from FIFA EWS]' 2014, *J.League News*, vol. 215, p. 4, www.jleague.jp/img/about/document/jnews/215/vol. 0215.pdf.

75 '*JFA, J-riigu, FIFA EWS-sha kyōsai no integuritii seminā o kaisai* [Integrity seminar held, joint sponsored by JFA, J-League and FIFA EWS]' 2015, *JFA.jp*, 8 October, www.jfa.jp/about_jfa/news/00007588; 'JFA・*J-riigu*・*JSC ga 2016 Integuriti seminā o kaisai* [JFA, J-League and JFC hold 2016 integrity seminar' 2016, *JFA.jp*, 22 September, www.jfa.jp/news/00011017.

76 On the establishment of the Japan Sports Agency and the jurisdiction of the JSC, see Steele and Opie in this volume.

77 See Kawai in this volume.

78 The scandal is described in greater detail by Kawai in this volume.

79 Nippon Telegraph and Telephone East Corporation 2016, '*Heisha shain (danshi badominton-bu shozoku) no shobun oyobi danshi badominton-bu no kongo no katsudō ni tsuite* [Disposition in relation to one of our employees (associated with the male badminton team) and the activities of the male badminton team going forward]', press release, 11 April, www.ntt-east.co.jp/release/detail/__icsFiles/afieldfile/2016/04/11/20160411_01_1.pdf; see also Japan Sport Council 2016, '*Supōtsu shinkō kikin joseikin (asuriito josei) no henkan ni tsuite* [On returning sports promotion grant funds (athlete assistance)]', press release, 13 May, www.jpnsport.go.

jp/sinko/LinkClick.aspx?fileticket=eDTXqYthIHE%3D&tabid=36&mid=658; '*Bado Momota wa mukigen shutsujō teishi, Tago wa mukigen no tōroku masshō* [Badminton: Momota given indefinite participation suspension, Tago indefinitely deregistered]' 2016, Nikkan Sports, 10 April, www.nikkansports.com/sports/news/1629615.html.

80 FIFPro, PFA Scotland and SPINS, Slovenia (eds.), 2012, *FIFPro black book Eastern Europe: the problems professional footballers encounter*, FIFPro Services, www.lefigaro.fr/assets/pdf/fifpro.pdf. See also Schwab and Finocchiaro in this volume.

81 Stewart, B., Nicholson, M., Smith, A. and Westerbeek, H., 2004, *Australian sport – better by design?*, Routledge.

82 Sport and Recreation Ministers' Council 2011, *National Policy on Match-Fixing in Sport*, 10 June, www.health.gov.au/internet/main/publishing.nsf/Content/F6DB8637F05C9643CA257C310021CCE9/$File/National%20Policy%20on%20Match-Fixing%20in%20Sport%20(FINAL).pdf.

83 See Menz and Skene in this volume.

84 See Opie and Lim and Steele and Opie in this volume.

Part III

Prevention and enforcement

Chapter 8

'Don't fix it!'

The role of player empowerment in the prevention of match-fixing

Brendan Schwab and Steven Finocchiaro

Players: key to any solution and not objects for punitive punishments

This chapter argues that players are an important part of any solution when it comes to preventing match-fixing, but players are too often the sole focus of simplistic and legalistic measures which are counterproductive in terms of player welfare and combating the root causes of match-fixing. Empirical research conducted by FIFPro, the worldwide representative organisation for all professional footballers, demonstrates the strong ethical condemnation almost all professional players have of match-fixing, the correlation that exists between match-fixing and the abuse of players' rights, including the non-payment of salaries, the recognition that match-fixing begins not with players, but corrupting third parties, and the importance of effective whistleblower protections in any anti-corruption effort.[1] Important player-based research including the questionnaires and responses underlying the *FIFPro black book (Eastern Europe)*,[2] the *FIFPro 'Don't fix it!'*[3] and the *FIFPro buku hitam*[4] reports support and inform FIFPro's three guiding principles to achieve an effective balance between the need to eradicate match-fixing and the welfare of players: individual case management including proportional bans instead of zero tolerance; secure reporting mechanisms with appropriate incentives and protections for whistle-blowers; and good governance in sports organisations.[5]

In responding to media questioning about a 2014 Union of European Football Associations ('UEFA') Congress' resolution to fight match-fixing, then UEFA general-secretary Gianni Infantino noted that internal alerting mechanisms had only produced '0.7 per cent alerts from the 32,000 matches UEFA monitors 365 days a year, 24 hours a day'.[6] In order to lift this detection rate, the Congress agreed to 'harmonise sanctions across Europe as much as possible with life bans issued across the continent, and no statutes of limitations for when sanctions can be applied'.[7] Further to this, UEFA resolved to include 'hard, strict sanctions in every country including life bans'.[8] Commenting on the resolution, Tony Higgins, FIFPro Division Europe board member and FIFPro's spokesperson on match-fixing, noted that despite the cooperative relationship with UEFA on the issue, the approach to eliminating match manipulation that emanated from the Congress was flawed.[9] Backed by research,[10] FIFPro's position is 'that players very often are the victims of match-fixing. Therefore, the "broad-brush" approach isn't always appropriate or productive'.[11] FIFPro's three guiding principles should form the basis for any effort to combat match-fixing.

This chapter begins by examining the role of players' associations such as FIFPro, and their key constituents, players, in the fight against match-fixing to-date, thus providing background to the empirical research discussed in the next section. The frameworks established by sports to eradicate match-fixing based on contractual relationships with players often consist of strict codes of conduct that may result in players receiving mandatory, career-ending bans. Third-party actors are outside of a sports organisations' jurisdiction, requiring government sanction and legislative responses. Current legislative responses, however, also typically focus on internal participants, especially players, and are highly punitive. Sports, governments, prosecutors and media have been quick to publicise lengthy bans on players to demonstrate a so-called zero tolerance approach.[12] Players suffer detriment to their lives and careers, and the consequences in some cases have been tragic.[13] Based on the analysis of recent empirical studies, the chapter then argues that FIFPro's three guiding principles should be adopted in the fight against match-fixing, with reference to case studies from Italy and Malaysia.

FIFPro's strategic approach and advocacy

FIFPro is the worldwide representative organisation for all professional footballers. It has more than 65,000 male and female player members through 58 national players' associations. FIFPro's operations are underpinned by two key principles: *supporting players* and being the *exclusive collective voice of the world's professional footballers*.[14] FIFPro does not believe that match-fixing begins with players. Accordingly, FIFPro has historically supported players who have been banned under punitive approaches to match-fixing. This stand is illustrated by the case of Norbert Mészáros and Vukasin Poleksic (referred to in proceedings as 'N.' and 'V.', respectively), two players from Hungarian club Debreceni VSC, who appealed to the Court of Arbitration for Sport ('CAS') against their convictions for match-fixing.[15] The players were blamed for not reporting to their club that they were approached for match-fixing before a home-game against Fiorentina on 20 October 2009 in the UEFA Champions League. In September 2010, UEFA dismissed appeals by both players, although three teammates and their club, Debreceni VSC, testified on their behalf. Mészáros was suspended until December 2011 and Poleksic until June 2012. Both received a substantial fine.[16]

Mészáros and Poleksic turned to CAS, helped by their club, the Hungarian players' association and FIFPro. Whilst Poleksic was still found guilty, even though he had not responded to the approach, in allowing Mészáros' appeal, CAS considered the lack of evidence that supported the burden of proof being discharged and found that:

> The elements offered by UEFA (the two ambiguous references to the jersey number of N.) are not sufficient to establish to its comfortable satisfaction that there were contacts between N. and the members of a criminal group involved in match fixing and betting fraud. As opposed to V., the involvement of N. has not been confirmed in any declaration in the German Proceedings or before the UEFA disciplinary bodies, save as in the statements of Mr X, on which UEFA no longer relies; and no mention of the name of N. can be found in the telephone conversations recorded by the German authorities.[17]

Whilst the CAS decision affirmed FIFPro's strong belief that cases must be reviewed on a case-by-case basis, CAS uncritically accepted the appropriateness of UEFA effectively dismissing the impact of possible repercussions on the psyche of the player: '[t]he fear of possible reactions by a criminal gang is no excuse under the ... [UEFA Disciplinary Regulations] for a player's failure to report an illicit approach.'[18]

From FIFPro's perspective, this approach is contrary to quantitative data collected from the players. Even though Poleksic 'lent absolutely no ear to the proposals of that criminal gang'[19] he was found guilty for failing to notify UEFA immediately. This case illustrates that players are faced with false choices: their choice could potentially do them immeasurable harm no matter what they do.

FIFPro's empirical research

FIFPro has sponsored and coordinated a number of empirical studies to combat prevailing notions of player fault, and punitive blanket approaches against players, and help evidence the key causes and participants in match-fixing. These studies cover key sporting markets in Europe and Asia and are titled in chronological order: *FIFPro black book (Eastern Europe)*, *FIFPro 'Don't fix it!'* and *FIFPro buku hitam*. The results from each of these studies and implications are analysed in turn in this section.

The FIFPro black book (Eastern Europe)

The results from *FIFPro black book (Eastern Europe)* were published in 2012. The report presented details regarding the violence, abuse, match-fixing, racism, discrimination and many other actions that professional football players in Eastern Europe are exposed to on a daily basis. The results from the *FIFPro black book (Eastern Europe)* investigation allow FIFPro, and participating countries and their football federations and players' associations, to develop strategies to counteract the issues that are currently facing players, including by highlighting the predicament of players to open a dialogue in response to match-fixing. FIFPro invited 15 countries in Eastern Europe to participate. The corresponding players' unions were asked to cooperate and assist in providing information and spreading the anonymous questionnaires to all the professional football players in their leagues. Data collection took place in September and October 2011 in Bulgaria, Croatia, Cyprus, Czech Republic, Greece, Hungary, Kazakhstan, Malta, Montenegro, Poland, Romania, Russia, Serbia, Slovenia and Ukraine. Table 8.1 reflects the overall findings of the *FIFPro black book (Eastern Europe)* survey.[20] As the data in Table 8.1 shows, almost 12 per cent of players stated that they have been approached to consider fixing the result of a match and more than double that number – 23.6 per cent – are aware that match-fixing has taken place in their league.

The data from the survey also shows that there was a correlation between clubs being well-run entities and the prevalence of match-fixing, as set out in Tables 8.2 and 8.3.[21] The players whose clubs pay salaries on time are less commonly approached to consider match fixing. More than half of respondents who said that they have been approached to consider fixing the result of a match also said that their club does not pay salaries on time, as set out in Table 8.2. Among the respondents that have never been approached with a proposal to match-fix, only 39.7 per cent of respondents stated that their club does not pay their salary on time (see Table 8.3).[22] Further, 59.2 per cent of players who have been approached to consider fixing the result of a match do not get their bonuses paid on

Table 8.1 Summary of *FIFPro black book (Eastern Europe)* investigation results

Question	*Yes*	*No*	*Total no. of responses*
Have you ever been approached to consider fixing the result of a match?	375	2774	3149
Are you aware of any match fixing that took place in your league?	735	2374	3109

Table 8.2 Payment of salaries to players who have been approached to match-fix

Question	*Yes*	*No*	*Total no. of responses*
Does your club pay your salary on time?	168	205	373

Table 8.3 Payment of salaries to players who have *not* been approached to match-fix

Question	*Yes*	*No*	*Total no. of responses*
Does your club pay your salary on time?	1624	1067	2691

time. This percentage is much lower for players that have never been approached to consider fixing the results of a match (47.4 per cent).[23]

The story of Dragisa Pejovic who pursued a career in Serbia as a professional footballer is the archetypal match-fixing situation in Eastern Europe. Pejovic testified that:

> For six years, there were many times when players were required to fix matches. Anyone who did not want to do so was removed from the team. I played fixed matches, not because I wanted to, but because I had to. If I refused to play, I would not receive a salary and I would not have funds to support my family. Football in Serbia is full of crime and criminals and I could not cope, nor fight, with them alone. The criminals in Serbian football always look after their own interests first and use all means to achieve their goals, while the players have to keep silent and suffer, since we do not have any protection from the state and its officials.[24]

As his account shows, Pejovic's actions, and those of others in his situation, are the product of the circumstances within which they work and eradicating match-fixing will not be achieved by a zero-tolerance approach to player conduct. Circumstances, including poor governance structures and deplorable working conditions, essentially provide players with an impossible dilemma.[25] Too much of the discussion around detection and punishment is focused on the role of the player in the facilitation of match-fixing, rather than the broader environment which allows players to be easily manipulated by corrupt third parties and organized crime.

FIFPro 'Don't fix it!'

A second project to gather data to inform decisions about the most appropriate way to deal with match-fixing is the *FIFPro 'Don't fix it!'* project conducted in 2013 by FIFPro and co-funded by the European Commission Sports Unit, UEFA and FIFPro. As part of the project, FIFPro affiliates received responses to its survey from 3206 players in nine countries: England, Finland, Greece, Hungary, Italy, Norway, Romania, Scotland and Slovenia. The survey examined players' beliefs on the extent of match-fixing, the instigators and causes of match-fixing, how match-fixing might be prevented, who should deliver preventative education, who they would trust to report information about match-fixing, how they would prefer to report information and the reasons that might prevent them from doing so. The questionnaire was the first large-scale attempt to ascertain the views of current players in regard to the phenomenon of match-fixing in the nine project countries. It significantly added to knowledge about match-fixing and the strategies to prevent it.

To date a number of player education interventions have been developed by external organisations such as INTERPOL,[26] Sport Accord[27] and the International Centre for Sport Security,[28] but none have included the input of players. The findings of the *FIFPro 'Don't fix it!'* project create the opportunity more than ever before to build educational tools which reflect the identified knowledge, beliefs and practices of players.[29] Placing the student at the centre of education is an essential prerequisite in designing effective learning solutions. Keeping a focus on the place of the student in the education process also helps education providers to reflect upon their own knowledge and assumptions about the topic.[30] The process of being able to develop education initiatives and other interventions that take their cue from the state of knowledge, beliefs and practices that players currently have in respect of match fixing in each of the project countries is vitally important for getting to the root causes of match-fixing.

The hypothesis that players are not solely to blame for match-fixing is evidenced by the findings from the survey in relation to Italy, a significant case study given recent match-fixing scandals, as discussed below. Outside influences were cited by respondent players in Italy as the main likely instigators of match-fixing in the questionnaire (44.2 per cent – 106).[31] A large minority of players in Italy who responded to the survey (31.6 per cent – 71) did not know the rules on betting and a similar proportion (32.7 per cent – 74) admitted to not knowing the rules on inside information, highlighting the folly in simply punishing the players without proper educational programmes.[32] A significant proportion of Italian respondents (41.6 per cent – 106) preferred to report approaches to an independent ombudsman or public official, with a further 30.6 per cent preferring the players' union.[33] However, other bodies such as the police, UEFA and the FIGC

(Italian Football Federation) also gained some support suggesting that multiple reporting avenues may be necessary.[34]

Of the Italian respondents, 11.5 per cent (26) said that they had reason to believe that matches in their league may have been fixed in the past 12 months. Of those, 61.5 per cent (16) thought between two and five games had been fixed and a further five respondents indicated that more than five games had been fixed.[35] While financial difficulties (20.8 per cent – 124) and lack of detection (27.1 per cent – 161) were important factors in a decision to fix a match, the high number of respondents who cited outside pressure and threats suggests that enabling players to resist those pressures is important.[36] The disparity of responses about how players can best be prevented from match-fixing suggests that multiple approaches which combine work on wages and better terms and conditions need to be supplemented with education around gambling and match-fixing.

The study concluded that an organised system of prevention involving all the relevant bodies and authorities, combined with integration between sports and the ordinary legal system is needed. Further, rules need to be clear, enforced and lead to appropriate sanctions when breached. In terms of education, the respondents highlighted the necessity to build programmes around the ethics of self-respect, pride and dignity as well as the dangers of becoming involved with organised crime. The benefits of living a life that is safe and happy both privately and professionally should be emphasised.[37] As the survey's executive summary states:

> Match-fixing will be best prevented using a holistic approach that addresses the economic, social and cultural conditions that give rise to match-fixing, the establishment of clear rules on betting and match-fixing, but which also appeals to personal ethics and players' future.[38]

Moreover, the survey underscores to sports administrators that players are a leading stakeholder in condemning the corruption of their sport through match manipulation. The survey's seventh formal conclusion noted: '[p]ersonal ethics remain a key weapon in the fight against match-fixing and are an underestimated aspect of the solution.[39] Players evidenced a strong ethical stance, and a sense of duty for family, friends, team-mates, club and the game.

FIFPro buku hitam

In addition to these two initial surveys in 2012 and 2013, the *FIFPro buku hitam* survey was undertaken in 2015 by select player associations within Asia to highlight the issues faced by footballers within the fastest-growing confederation in world football.[40] Despite superlatives such as the 'future of football must be in Asia', Weinberg argues that 'the political, economic and socio-cultural circumstances have led to different developments of football structures resulting in the emergence of a core and periphery in terms of sporting and commercial success'.[41] Issues such as match-fixing are prevalent in this 'periphery'. The term '*buku hitam*' literally means 'black book' in Malay, and is a follow-up to the *FIFPro black book (Eastern Europe)*, using similar questions and quantitative methods. It surveyed 1078 professional players in nine member association countries of the Asian Football Confederation: Australia, Hong Kong, India, Indonesia, Japan, Korea, Malaysia, Palestine and Singapore. These countries also represent the foundation of the Asian division of FIFPro.

The data from this study showed that 65.8 per cent of players who claimed that they had been approached to consider fixing the result of a match were generally made up of those who did not receive their payments on time.[42] Of the countries surveyed, Malaysia had the highest percentage of respondents who had been approached to fix matches (22 respondents out of 191).[43]

FIFPro's three guiding principles to balance eradicating match-fixing and welfare of players

With the information and examples evidenced by FIFPro's empirical research in mind, this section analyses FIFPro's three guiding principles to appropriately balance eradicating match-fixing and the welfare of players. The principles of *good governance*, *secure reporting mechanisms* and *individual case management* are discussed in turn. To fully empower the players in the fight against match-fixing, these elements must emphasise their integrity and win their trust. A partnership with the players involving their players' association in assisting the player education effort and as a reporting mechanism is more important than citing a simplistic zero tolerance mantra.

Individual case management

Blanket zero-tolerance approaches are counter-productive. Cases must be managed in light of their individual factual matrix, strictly on a case-by-case basis. It makes a difference, for example, whether an individual is forced into match-fixing by other parties or match-fixes by her or his own choice. Players should also have equal treatment before the law, and afforded natural justice, which includes procedural fairness and the presumption of innocence until proven guilty. Match-fixing behaviour may attract the application of the general criminal law in many jurisdictions, including across Asia. In July 2013, the United Nations Office on Drugs and Crime and the International Olympic Committee released a comparative study on the applicability of criminal law provisions concerning match-fixing and illegal and irregular betting ('*UNODC study*').[44] One of the countries analysed was Malaysia, a jurisdiction of particular focus for FIFPro and FIFPro Asia, and a jurisdiction of focus in the *FIFPro buku hitam* report. Malaysia was named as a 'hub for match-fixing in Southeast Asia' by Chris Eaton, 'an independent industry consultant and FIFA's former security chief'.[45]

Section 415 of the Malaysian *Penal Code*[46] states that

> whoever by deceiving any person, whether or not such deception was the sole or main inducement: (a) fraudulently or dishonestly induces the person so deceived to deliver any property to any person, or to consent that any person shall retain any property; or (b) intentionally induces the person so deceived to do or omit to do anything which he would not do or omit to do if he were not so deceived and which act or omission causes or is likely to cause damage or harm to any person in body, mind, reputation, or property is said to 'cheat'.

The maximum term of imprisonment is five years.[47]

The weakness of using this particular provision to combat match-fixing is its ostensible focus on the role of the player, and not the root causes of match-fixing as evidenced by FIFPro's empirical research. As the key element of this offence is the inducement, in a match-fixing scenario, the person most likely to 'induce' is the player. As such, it would be highly unusual for a third party to be charged with this offence. Such potential deficiencies in the general criminal law have prompted interest in legislation that specifically addresses match-fixing behaviour. In Australia, for example, since the release of the *National policy on matching-fixing in sport*[48] in June 2011 there has been a concerted legislative effort to enact consistent laws across the country that deal with this issue.[49] For instance, in the State of New South Wales, the *Crimes Act 1900* (NSW) was amended to incorporate specific provisions related to 'corrupting betting outcomes'.[50] A breach of these provisions attracts a maximum term of imprisonment of ten years.[51] They commenced on 13 September 2012 and incorporate the aim of sending 'a clear message that match-fixing and corrupt conduct will not be tolerated'.[52] Although they afford greater scope to fix responsibility on corrupting third parties, the legislation, and policy that underpins it, still disproportionally focuses on players as the principal offenders.

The *Malaysian Anti-Corruption Commission Act 2009* ('*MACC*')[53] enacts various offences including the prohibition of active and passive corruption involving both private persons and officers of public bodies (*MACC* s. 16). Sports bodies registered under s. 17 of the *Sports Development Act 1997* are classified as public bodies for the purposes of the *MACC* (s. 3). The maximum imprisonment term is 20 years (s. 24). The most concerning aspect of the *MACC* from FIFPro's perspective is that it shifts the burden of proof. Under s. 50, where the impugned transaction is proven to have occurred, it is presumed to be corrupt unless the contrary is proved. In the *UNODC study* this shift of the burden is described by the contributor of the Malaysian section[54] as 'a significant tool for effective work of law enforcement agencies and judiciary'.[55] However, any player charged with an offence under the *MACC* will be denied a key element of justice; namely, the necessity to have the prosecution prove the entire case against him or her. This type of lack of procedural fairness drives FIFPro's efforts to greatly increase individual case management.

Secure reporting mechanism and an obligation to report

FIFPro argues that individuals should only be obliged to immediately notify the competition organiser if approached for match-fixing on the condition that there is a secure information gathering system to allow people to report (if necessary on an anonymous basis) incidents of match-fixing or attempted match-fixing. Historically, football has not done this well. Across many jurisdictions, hundreds of laws exist in order to protect whistleblowers, such as the UK *Public Interest Disclosure Act*.[56] Whilst de jure protection for whistleblowers exists within both general law and sporting regulations, in practice the issue is far more complex. The example of Simone Farina is an illustration of the false choice that exists for players who are caught within a web of criminal activity. Whilst Farina's initial reporting brought to the fore *Calcio Scommesse*, the betting scandal that engulfed Italian football in 2011 and 2012, it would ultimately cost him his career as a professional footballer.[57]

The football community in Italy is no stranger to controversy surrounding the integrity of its professional football leagues. From the *Calciopoli* scandal[58] to the recent troubles with Catania,[59] numerous clubs have been relegated or docked points due to their indiscretions. Accordingly, the responses to the *FIFPro 'Don't fix it!'* questionnaire for Italy in 2013 assume added significance. In particular, the questionnaire occurred at a volatile time because from June 2011 there were match-fixing investigations ongoing in Cremona, Napoli and Bari[60] and a large number of other significant incidents of match-fixing in the country were reported in 2013.[61] The Cremona investigation involved 160 suspects including players, managers and supporters and 40 matches were suspected of having being manipulated in Serie A and other professional leagues.[62] The scandals in Italy also provide a stark highlight of the deficiencies that most concern FIFPro, namely, the high involvement of third parties and the lack protection for whistleblowers who feel the need to report nefarious behaviour. Unlike the *Calciopoli* scandal which involved the activities of club managers and league officials in influencing the selection of match referees, respondents to the *FIFPro 'Don't fix it!'*

questionnaire identified networks of organised crime as playing a large role in the instigation of match-fixing within Italy.[63]

Good governance

UEFA member associations must ensure through their own regulations that the primacy of contracts between clubs and players are followed and enforced. The non-payment and non-monetary breach of contracts increase the susceptibility of players to corrupting influences. As noted in the *2016 FIFPro global employment report*, players in lower income brackets were twice or three times more likely to be approached by match-fixers.[64] Furthermore, 41.3 per cent of players who experienced delayed payments from their clubs were approached to fix matches.[65] Separately, of players who were approached to fix a match, over half had suffered delayed payments from their clubs.[66]

Coupled with criminal legislative provisions, sports have focused on establishing their own regulatory codes without enough attention being paid to the role of good governance in combating match-fixing. Football associations have enacted specific provisions that deal with actors within the sport. The Football Federation Australia ('FFA') National Code of Conduct provides, for example:

> 4.1 A Member must not engage, directly or indirectly, in:
>
> (a) any bet, wager, gamble or any other form of financial speculation where the relevant person stands to win or gain from the win, draw or loss of any Club competing in a Match;
> (b) the throwing or fixing of a Match; or
> (c) any conduct or behaviour intended to unfairly affect the result of a Match, including accepting or agreeing to accept any Benefit connected with or relating to the ability of a Member to exercise control over or influence the outcome of a Match so as to bring about a result other than that which would be achieved in a fair contest between the competing teams.
>
> 4.2 A Player, an Official and an Agent must not:
>
> (a) accept bribes through the offer, promise or acceptance of any Benefit in return for violating his or her duties; or
> (b) provide for a Benefit any information concerning a Club, its team's actual or likely composition, the form or injuries of Players or possible tactics (other than in connection with a bona fide media interview).[67]

The scope of these provisions is extensive including prohibitions on betting on the outcome of matches, fixing matches and supplying inside information as to team performance. The provisions are limited in their application, however, because only certain categories of people come within the contractually conferred disciplinary authority of FFA, for example, players, match officials and agents. Moreover, the regulations fail to deal with governance matters, including those between organisations and players.[68]

The match-fixing scandal involving Southern Stars FC from the semi-professional Victorian Premier League ('VPL')[69] highlighted some of the shortcomings in this player-focused approach to combating match-fixing. Ten players and a manager were charged after police discovered that the players 'were alleged to have been paid thousands of dollars for their involvement'[70] in match manipulation during a season where Southern Stars FC finished last in the VPL. The case showed the modus for crime syndicates, which target low-paying semi-professional leagues, where a combination of willing participants and lower chances of detection create a situation ripe for manipulation.

One media report on this particular case noted that, 'hundreds of thousands of dollars ... were ... wagered on the outcome of the club's games, including the number of goals conceded, by the syndicate in collaboration with the allegedly corrupted players'.[71] Mike Pride, a former Australian Federal Police officer and ex-FIFA sports integrity investigator, had what a reporter described as 'a revealing conversation with the syndicate's kingpin' who was Wilson Raj Perumal. The discussion focused on Perumal's operation in Australia and his syndicate's plans for the 2014 season, and highlights a complete lack of regard for player welfare. According to the report, Perumal can be heard saying in a recording of the call:

> I'm going to dump all these players on a working visa in Australia – especially in Brisbane.... And I'm going to get about three or four boys to play in each club in Brisbane. These boys are all good players, okay. And they are going to voluntarily go to the club and say can I join you, because I'm on a working visa.... So we have another one year to make money.... These players, it's like a horse race, like what I told you. If you let a class one horse race against a class four horse, he's just going to canter and win the race. So if I'm going to put four or five horses down there, I will definitely be able to achieve the result.[72]

One of the players, Nicholas McKoy, escaped conviction. Judge Barbara Cotterell of the County Court of Victoria noted that:

> [McKoy] found himself in a predicament not unlike 'modern slavery', where he wanted to escape the fixing but felt trapped by the syndicate as they controlled his accommodation and he was in a foreign country. He was also not being paid the promised $500 a week.[73]

Judge Cotterell's finding reflects a nuanced understanding of the forces at play in the context of match-fixing. A blanket approach that specifically targets the wrongdoing of players fails to acknowledge that players can quite easily be victims of the external pressures that circle the global game.

Conclusion

Match-fixing is a complex social problem. FIFPro's mandate in this context is to help protect the rights of professional footballers as a worker and human being in the face of organized crime, low-paying and precarious employment, and false choices. The survey and questionnaire results presented in this chapter reflect that, due to a confluence of factors, players are as much a victim of match-fixing as any other stakeholder within sport. Conversations with players suggest that the three guiding principles of *good governance*, *individual case management* and *secure reporting mechanisms* are a better approach than punitive, player-focused rules contained within the general law and sporting regulations. The application of these guiding principles will help engage football's greatest defence to the threat of match-fixing – the ethical condemnation players have of cheating and their deep respect for the game. The consequences of zero-tolerance can not only rob the player of their livelihood, but also their life. Given that players are the centrepiece of football, it is imperative that FIFPro and other players' unions continue to advocate for more nuanced and thoughtful approaches to combating match-fixing, and that such advocacy is heeded by football's governing bodies.

Notes

1 FIFPro, PFA Scotland and SPINS, Slovenia (eds.) 2012, *FIFPro black book Eastern Europe: the problems professional footballers encounter*, FIFPro Services, www.lefigaro.fr/assets/pdf/fifpro.pdf ('*FIFPro black book (Eastern Europe)*'); Harvey, A. and Levi, H., 2014, *Don't fix it!: an education and prevention programme to fight match-fixing in football*, FIFPro, May, www.fifpro.org/attachments/article/5362/Don't%20Fix%20It%20-%20Players%20Questionnaire%20Results%20and%20Analysis.pdf ('*FIFPro "Don't fix it!"*'); FIFPro Asia 2015, *Buku hitam report and analysis: unveiling football issues in Asia* ('*FIFPro buku hitam*').
2 *FIFPro black book (Eastern Europe)*, above n. 1.
3 *FIFPro 'Don't fix it!'*, above n. 1.
4 *FIFPro buku hitam*, above n. 1.
5 FIFPro 2014, 'Players left exposed in match-fixing resolution', media release, 3 April, www.fifpro.org/news/players-need-more-protection-in-match-fixing-resolution/en.
6 Collet, M., 2014, 'UEFA to back Nations League, more match-fixing sanctions', *Reuters*, 26 March, http://uk.reuters.com/article/uk-soccer-uefa-congress-idUKBREA2P0T620140326.
7 Ibid.

8 Ibid.
9 FIFPro, above n. 5.
10 *FIFPro black book (Eastern Europe)*, above n. 1; *FIFPro 'Don't fix it!'*, above n. 1.
11 FIFPro, above n. 5.
12 According to a study of media reporting of instances of match-fixing in print media by Villeneuve and Aquilina, for example, 'the actors most negatively portrayed in the analysis are teams, players and criminals. The authorities and Federation were those most often attributed a positive role': Villeneuve, J.P. and Aquilina, D., 2015, 'Who's fault is it? An analysis of the press coverage of football betting scandals in France and the United Kingdom', *Sport in Society*, vol. 19, no. 2, pp. 187–200, p. 197.
13 See, e.g. Park in this volume noting player suicide in Korea.
14 FIFPro World Players' Union 2017, *About FIFPro*, www.fifpro.org/en/about-fifpro/about-fifpro.
15 *N & V* v. *UEFA* (Award, Professor Luigi Fumagalli, Mr Andras Gurovits and Mr Christian Duve, Court of Arbitration for Sport, CAS 2010/A/2266, 5 May 2011), http://jurisprudence.tas-cas.org/Shared%20Documents/2266.pdf.
16 *FIFPro black book (Eastern Europe)*, above n. 1, p. 140; see also *N & V* v. *UEFA*, above n. 15.
17 *N & V* v. *UEFA* , above n. 15.
18 Ibid., para. 35(vii).
19 FIFPro 2011, 'FIFPro is furious because of match-fixing sanctions', media release, 6 May, www.fifpro.org/news/fifpro-is-furious-because-of-match-fixing-sanctions/en.
20 *FIFPro black book (Eastern Europe)*, above n. 1, p. 37.
21 Ibid., p. 129. This finding supports the FIFPro principle of good governance discussed further below.
22 Note that there is a discrepancy in the report: the total number of respondents who said yes to having been approached was 375 out of 2774 respondents, but when the number is discussed in relation to payment of salaries, the total number is referred to as 373 out of 2691 respondents: ibid., pp. 37, 129.
23 Ibid., p. 130.
24 Ibid., p. 142.
25 The situation is akin to what Hill described during the cycling scandals of the 1990s and early 2000 where there was a zero-tolerance, athlete-focused strategy implemented in response to widespread doping within cycling. Hill, D., 2016, 'Why sport is losing the war to match-fixers', in Transparency International, *Global corruption report: sport*, Routledge, pp. 303–304.
26 INTERPOL 2017, *E-learning*, www.interpol.int/Crime-areas/Crimes-in-sport/E-learning.
27 SportAccord 2015, *Integrity*, www.sportaccord.com/governance-relations-development/integrity.
28 International Centre for Sport Security, *ICSS provides match-fixing education to Premier League clubs and within Africa,* www.theicss.org/en/expertise/view/icss-provides-match-fixing-education-to-premier-league-clubs-and-within-afr.
29 See also Chung, Jun and Kim in this volume.
30 Blackie, M., Jennifer, A.L., Case, M. and Jawitz, J., 2010, 'Student-centredness: the link between transforming students and transforming ourselves', *Teaching in Higher Education*, vol. 15, no. 6, pp. 637–646.
31 *FIFPro 'Don't fix it!'*, above n. 1.
32 Ibid., p. 58.
33 Ibid.

34 Ibid.
35 Ibid., p. 56.
36 Ibid.
37 Ibid., p. 88.
38 Ibid., p. 3.
39 Ibid., p. 87.
40 See FIFPro, *About FIFPro*, www.fifpro.org/en/about-fifpro/about-fifpro.
41 Weinberg, B., 2015, 'Push-and-run between power, participation and performance: political playmaking and the tactics of the Asian Football Confederation', *International Journal of the History of Sport*, vol. 32, pp. 1016–1029, p. 1019.
42 *FIFPro buku hitam*, above n. 1, p. 192.
43 Ibid., p. 250.
44 International Olympic Committee and United National Office on Drugs and Crime 2013, *Criminalization approaches to combat match-fixing and illegal/irregular betting: a global perspective*, July.
45 'Football: Malaysia calls for proof after match-fixing claim' 2016, *The Straits Times*, 9 November, www.straitstimes.com/sport/football/football-malaysia-calls-for-proof-after-match-fixing-claim.
46 (As at 1 January 2015) (Malaysia).
47 Ibid., s. 417.
48 Australian Council of Sport and Recreation Ministers 2011, *National policy on match-fixing in sport*, 10 June, www.health.gov.au/internet/main/publishing.nsf/Content/F6DB8637F05C9643CA257C310021CCE9/$File/National%20Policy%20on%20Match-Fixing%20in%20Sport%20(FINAL).pdf.
49 See Opie and Lim in this volume.
50 See *Crimes Amendment (Cheating at Gambling) Bill 2012* (NSW).
51 See, e.g. *Crimes Act 1900* (NSW), s. 193N.
52 Lander and Rogers Lawyers 2012, *NSW introduces 10 year jail sentences for match-fixing*, 31 October, www.landers.com.au/publications/sport-and-events/nsw-introduces-10-year-jail-sentences-for-match-fixing.
53 *Malaysian Anti-Corruption Commission Act 2009* (Malaysia).
54 The *UNODC study* has not been 'officially edited'; see International Olympic Committee and United National Office on Drugs and Crime, above n. 44, p. 5.
55 Ibid., p. 132.
56 (UK), cl. 23.
57 Farina, S., 2012, 'Remarks by Simone Farina FIFA Ambassador for Play', presented at the *INTERPOL Global Academic Experts Meeting for Integrity in Sports*, 28 November, Singapore.
58 'Italian clubs punished for match-fixing' 2006, *Guardian*, 15 July, www.theguardian.com/football/2006/jul/14/europeanfootball.juventus2.
59 Homewood, B., 2015, 'Catania demoted to Italian football's third tier after match-fixing scandal', *Reuters*, 20 August, uk.reuters.com/article/uk-soccer-italy-matchfixing-idUKKCN0QP1F020150820.
60 *FIFPro 'Don't fix it!'*, above n. 1, p. 53.
61 Ibid.
62 Ibid.
63 Ibid., p. 56.
64 FIFPro World Players' Union 2016, *2016 FIFPro global employment report*, p. 28, www.fifpro.org/images/documents-pdf/2016-fifpro-global-employment-report.pdf.
65 Ibid.
66 Ibid.

67 Football Federation Australia, *FFA National Code of Conduct*, p. 3, www.footballaustralia.com.au/dct/ffa-dtc-performgroup-eu-west-1/National%20Code%20 of%20Conduct_g6t65k0jmtil11v1pfcbymelz.pdf.

68 The regulations do not deal with third-party influencers that can exacerbate integrity issues, which is why legislative and law enforcement efforts are also necessary.

69 See Murnane and Moller in this volume for an account of the police investigation and prosecution in this case.

70 McKenzie, N., Bucci, B. and Baker, R., 2013, 'Victorian detectives bust alleged soccer match-fixing syndicate', *Sydney Morning Herald*, 15 September, www.smh.com.au/sport/soccer/victorian-detectives-bust-alleged-soccer-matchfixing-syndicate-20130915-2tsh5.html.

71 Ibid.

72 Kerr, J., 2016, 'FFA, FIFA, match-fixing and sports integrity', *The Saturday Paper*, 12 November, www.thesaturdaypaper.com.au/sport/2016/11/12/ffa-fifa-match-fixing-and-sports-integrity/14788692003966.

73 Bucci, N., 2014, 'Nicholas McKoy escapes conviction over Southern Stars match fixing', *The Age*, 12 December, www.theage.com.au/victoria/nicholas-mckoy-escapes-conviction-over-southern-stars-match-fixing-20141212-125us7.html.

Chapter 9

A study of professional players' perceptions of match-fixing and prevention education strategies in Korea

Young Ryuel Chung, Joo Won Jun and Jin Kook Kim[1]

Introduction: the need and the purpose of this study into player perceptions of match-fixing and education

A lack of player ethics is evidenced by recent incidents of match-fixing, violence amongst players and doping both within and outside of professional sports in Korea. Korean society's systematic and increasing focus on the results of games, regardless of how those results are obtained, is partly to blame for these problems.[2] The harsh reality of the sporting world is that players may be relegated at any time and are constantly competing against each other. Furthermore, betting on sports has become increasingly popular in Korea. Although this has had a positive effect by encouraging interest in sports, a negative outcome has been the increase of illegal betting websites on overseas servers. Moreover, the issue of brokers and various forms of match-fixing make solutions complicated and match-fixing incidents have now occurred in all major professional sports in Korea.[3] A common theme in match-fixing in Korea is players taking advantage of hierarchical relationships amongst players of the same team to encourage and even threaten them into match-fixing.[4] Recently, players who refuse to engage in match-fixing have had brokers approach their families or friends as a means of forcing the players to become involved.[5]

This chapter argues that the temptation or threat of match-fixing may be mitigated through education.[6] Sporting committees and associations have attempted to combat match-fixing with education over the past several years. The Korea Volleyball Association has tailored an education programme targeted at over 150 male and female players, coaching staff and club staff.[7] The Korea Volleyball Association has also introduced strict regulations to ban anyone found to have been involved in match-fixing. The Korea Baseball Association implemented yearly education sessions for its current and future players, emphasising the importance of players' integrity in order to combat match-fixing.[8] The Korea Basketball Association also provides education for its general, club and coaching staff and players on the reasons for and methods of match-fixing as well as the penalties for being involved.[9] In order for these strategies to have full and proper effect, however, they must be provided on a regular and ongoing basis. During seasons, players do not receive such education as they are encouraged to focus on their sports training and their schedules are filled accordingly.[10] Therefore, the reality is that this current education system is not very effective.

Moreover, to view the players as the only wrongdoers in the context of match-fixing and, therefore, to focus only on improving players' ethics or imposing large penalties on players has limits and overlooks the issues underlying match-fixing. In competitive sports (compared with friendly games), winning gains attractive advantages in the economy, academia, religion, politics, media and in other social aspects such that match-fixing is always at risk of occurring.[11] There are various academic papers which explore different perspectives of match-fixing. However, most academics have only focused on the legal imposition of penalties or focused on an ethical point of view.[12] Due to the difficulty in passing perfect laws or regulations to prohibit match-fixing,[13] the focus is mainly on changing the players' ethics and attitudes.[14] A wider variety of approaches and a greater understanding of players' motivations and contexts are needed in order to combat match-fixing.

In the meantime, with the main preventative focus being on players, it is vital that players' perspectives on match-fixing are understood. The aim of this research is to reveal these perspectives and, further to this, how to implement preventative education programmes for players. This research therefore aims to provide strategies for combating match-fixing based on an insider's perspective, rather than from an outsider's point of view as other previous studies have done. Accordingly, the key research questions for this study were threefold. First, what do professional sports players think of match-fixing? Second, what do professional sports players think of the current education on match-fixing? Third, what do professional sports players consider to be the most effective strategies for their education?

Research method

Sample population

The survey for this research was conducted from 13 April to 2 June 2015. It used a purposive sampling method to choose male and female current top players, approximately 75 of each from professional baseball, football, basketball and volleyball. Four people were engaged to carry out the survey for each professional sport and explain the survey to the players, asking them to answer honestly in a self-evaluation format. Upon collection of the completed surveys, 26 were discarded from the study for incomplete responses such that a total of 274 surveys made up the sample used. The general characteristics of the survey respondents are set out in Table 9.1.

Table 9.1 General characteristics/trends of the survey respondents

Characteristic	*Categories*	*Number*	*Percentage*
Sex	Male	146	53.2
	Female	128	46.8
Sport	Pro baseball	65	23.7
	Pro football	70	25.5
	Pro basketball	78	28.5
	Pro volleyball	61	22.3
Age	20s	196	71.5
	30s	67	24.5
	Above 40	11	4.0
Professional experience (years of professional playing)	Under 3 years	34	12.4
	3–5 years	22	8.0
	5–7 years	25	9.1
	7–9 years	40	14.6
	9–15 years	108	39.4
	15 years and above	45	16.4
Highest level of education	High school	98	35.8
	Current undergraduate	19	6.9
	Entered university but no graduation (i.e. scouted to pro sports teams before graduation)	4	1.5
	Undergraduate degree	140	51.1
	Postgraduate degree	13	4.7
Average monthly income (in KR₩ million)	Under 3 million	95	34.7
	3–4 million	57	20.8
	4–5 million	31	11.3
	5–10 million	47	17.2
	10–20 million	19	6.9
	Above 20 million	25	9.1

Tools and method

This study used paper survey methodology. Ten of the questions were about players' satisfaction with current education and the quality of education, asking players to rate their opinions on five Likert[15] levels ranging from 'completely agree' to 'completely disagree'.[16] The remainder of the questions were required to be answered in a nominal scale. Five questions about match-fixing were asked, based on research conducted by Yong Suk Seo and Hoon Lee on gambling and adjusted by the authors to reflect match-fixing contexts.[17] Eight questions about preventative education were based on research conducted by Sook Yeon Kim.[18] Five questions about preventative education strategy were based on research by Sol Nam[19] and Eun Sook Yoon.[20] See Table 9.2 for further details of the topics surveyed.

Survey analysis

The 274 surveys were encoded and SPSS 18.0 used to analyse the data obtained. Differences in players' opinions on match-fixing in the different sports were analysed using descriptive statistical analysis. Differences in players' satisfaction with current education, quality of education and level

Table 9.2 Topics surveyed

Category	*Question description*	*Number of questions*
Thoughts on match-fixing	Legal implications, sports ethics, experience with illegal sports gambling, players personally approached to match-fix, experience with illegal betting websites	5
Current preventative education	Education experience, when education began, satisfaction with education, quality of education, level of engagement with education, frequency of education per year, duration of education per session, problems with current education	8
Preventative education strategy	Need for clubs to implement education, how education should be carried out, further activities/ideas to supplement education, the ideal number of sessions for effective prevention, what should be emphasised	5
Personal questions	Gender, sport, age, professional experience, highest level of education, average monthly income	6
Total number of questions		24

of engagement in the education were analysed using cross tabulation. The Duncan Test was used for post verification.[21]

Research limitations

There are several limitations to this research and further research could be conducted in order to address these gaps. Players from four main professional sports in Korea were questioned via the survey. However, there is a lack of research in this area and therefore no baseline by which to measure and contrast the research methods and findings. Further, robust results may also be found through research based on real case studies or research conducted through interviews rather than via paper surveys.

Results

Differences in opinion of the legal implications of match-fixing

To determine if there were any differences amongst the sports in terms of players' thoughts on the legal implications of match-fixing, cross tabulation was used.[22] The results suggest that there is little difference amongst the different sports. The majority of players thought that match-fixing was illegal (see Table 9.3).

Differences in sports ethics

Using cross tabulation, data from the different sports was analysed and compared to reveal that there is little difference amongst players' perception of match-fixing as unethical. The majority of all sports players surveyed perceive match-fixing as unethical (see Table 9.4).

Table 9.3 Differences in opinion on the legal implications of match-fixing

Sport	*I think match-fixing is illegal*	*I think match-fixing is legal*
Baseball	60 (92.3%)	5 (7.7%)
Football	66 (94.3%)	4 (5.7%)
Basketball	73 (93.6%)	5 (6.4%)
Volleyball	58 (95.1%)	3 (4.9%)
Total	**257 (93.8%)**	**17 (6.2%)**

Notes
$\chi^2 = 0.455$, $df = 3$, $p = 0.929$.

Table 9.4 Differences in sports ethics

Sport	I think match-fixing is unethical	I think match-fixing is ethical
Baseball	62 (95.4%)	3 (4.6%)
Football	65 (92.9%)	5 (7.1%)
Basketball	72 (92.3%)	6 (7.7%)
Volleyball	59 (96.7%)	2 (3.3%)
Total	**258 (94.2%)**	**16 (5.8%)**

Notes
$\chi^2 = 1.606$, $df = 3$, $p = 0.658$.

Differences in players' understanding of illegal sports gambling

There was little statistical difference amongst the different sports in players' experiences with match-fixing such as hearing about match-fixing from another teammate. However, the analysis of the results suggests that a fairly significant number of players (65 or 23.7 per cent) had some experience or knowledge of how match-fixing occurs. Basketball players in particular evidenced the highest experience or knowledge at 30.8 per cent of the players.

Differences in players' experiences of receiving match-fixing suggestions from other players

Results on the differences in the number of sports players' experiences of being asked to match-fix are set out in Table 9.6. Using cross tabulation, the results showed that there was a significant difference for players amongst the different sports. Nine basketball players (11.5 per cent) revealed that they had been asked to match-fix, which was more than twice the number in each of volleyball, football and baseball players.

Table 9.5 Differences in players' understanding of illegal sports gambling

Sports	I have heard of how to match-fix from teammates	I have not heard of how to match-fix from teammates
Baseball	13 (20.0%)	52 (80.0%)
Football	12 (17.1%)	58 (82.9%)
Basketball	24 (30.8%)	54 (69.2%)
Volleyball	16 (26.2%)	45 (73.8%)
Total	**65 (23.7%)**	**209 (76.3%)**

Notes
$\chi^2 = 4.525$, $df = 3$, $p = 0.210$.

Table 9.6 Differences in players' experiences of match-fixing suggestions

Sport	*I have previously been approached to match-fix*	*I have not been approached to match-fix*
Baseball	1 (1.5%)	64 (98.5%)
Football	2 (2.9%)	68 (97.1%)
Basketball	9 (11.5%)	69 (88.5%)
Volleyball	3 (4.9%)	58 (95.1%)
Total	**15 (5.5%)**	**259 (94.5%)**

Notes
$\chi^2 = 8.452$, $df = 3$, $p = 0.038$.

Differences in players' experiences with illegal sports gambling websites

There was also a statistical difference amongst the different sports players' experiences with illegal sports gambling websites.[23] Basketball had the greatest number of players who had previously accessed illegal sports gambling websites (seven players, 9 per cent), then football (two players, 2.9 per cent) followed by volleyball (one player, 1.6 per cent). In contrast, no baseball players admitted to having ever accessed illegal sports gambling websites (see Table 9.7).

Current education for professional sports players

Players' experiences of education

In order to analyse differences amongst different sports players' experiences with match-fixing education, cross tabulation was again used. The results are summarised in Table 9.8. A statistically significant difference was found amongst the different sports. The sport which provided the

Table 9.7 Differences in players' experiences with accessing illegal sports gambling websites

Sports	*I have accessed illegal sports gambling websites*	*I have never accessed illegal sports gambling websites*
Baseball	0 (0.0%)	65 (100%)
Football	2 (2.9%)	68 (97.1%)
Basketball	7 (9.0%)	71 (91.0%)
Volleyball	1 (1.6%)	60 (96.4%)
Total	**10 (3.6%)**	**264 (5.8%)**

Notes
$\chi^2 = 9.577$, $df = 3$, $p = 0.038$.

Table 9.8 Experiences with match-fixing education

Sport	*I have received education on match-fixing*	*I have never received education on match-fixing*
Baseball	62 (95.4%)	3 (4.6%)
Football	60 (85.7%)	10 (14.3%)
Basketball	73 (93.6%)	5 (6.4%)
Volleyball	60 (98.4%)	1 (1.6%)
Total	**255 (93.1%)**	**19 (6.9%)**

Notes
$\chi^2 = 9.087$, $df = 3$, $p = 0.028$.

greatest amount of education on match-fixing was volleyball (98.4 per cent of players answered to having received some kind of match-fixing education), followed by baseball (95.4 per cent), basketball (93.6 per cent) and then football (85.7 per cent). Significantly, 14.3 per cent of football players indicated that they had never received education on match-fixing, suggesting football provides less education than other sports.

When players first received match-fixing education

There was a significant difference amongst the different sports for when players first received match-fixing education. The majority of baseball players first received education after they became professional players. In football, 17 players (28 per cent) first received education during their university years, while 41 players (68.3 per cent) first received education during their professional playing years. For basketball and volleyball also, the majority of players first received match-fixing education during their professional years. However, compared with other sports, volleyball and basketball players showed greater numbers of receiving education earlier, such as in their high school and university years (see Table 9.9).

Players' evaluation of their match-fixing education

In order to find any differences amongst the different sports players' evaluation of their match-fixing education, one-way ANOVA[24] was used. The results suggest a statistically significant difference amongst the sports (see Table 9.11). Upon post hoc test results, football players responded with a lower overall evaluation of their match-fixing education than basketball, volleyball or baseball.

Baseball players expressed the highest level of satisfaction with their current education system (4.34, 0.991), followed by volleyball players (4.06, 1.041), basketball players (4.03, 0.881) and football players (3.85, 1.005). Baseball players rated the quality of their education the highest

Table 9.9 Timing of first match-fixing prevention education

Sports	*I first received match-fixing prevention education in junior high (early high school years)*	*I first received match-fixing prevention education in senior high school*	*I first received match-fixing prevention education at university*	*I first received match-fixing prevention education as a professional player*
Baseball	0 (0.0%)	0 (0.0%)	3 (4.8%)	59 (95.2%)
Football	1 (1.7%)	1 (1.7%)	17 (28.3%)	41 (68.3%)
Basketball	1 (1.4%)	9 (12.3%)	6 (8.2%)	57 (78.1%)
Volleyball	0 (0.0%)	3 (5.0%)	4 (6.7%)	53 (88.3%)
Total	**2 (0.8%)**	**13 (5.1%)**	**30 (11.8%)**	**210 (82.4%)**

Notes
$\chi^2 = 35.629$, $df = 9$, $p < 0.001$.

(4.29, 1.030), followed by volleyball (4.02, 0.948), basketball (3.92, 0.939) and football players (3.72, 1.043). When asked to rate the energy and passion of their education sessions, baseball players again rated their session the highest (4.42, 1.017), followed by basketball (4.10, 0.945), volleyball (3.92, 0.926) and football players (3.45, 1.141) (see Table 9.10).

Frequency of players' education

For all four sports, the most common rate of receiving education was once a year (48.6 per cent), followed by twice a year (33.7 per cent). Education was not provided during major events. The majority of baseball players reported receiving education once a year (56.5 per cent), football players reported once a year (50 per cent), basketball players reported once a year (42.5 per cent) and volleyball players reported once a year (46.7 per cent). Over 50 per cent of basketball players answered to receiving education more often than twice a year. The cross-tabulation results revealed that there was no statistically significant difference amongst the different sports in terms of the frequency at which the education was delivered (see Table 9.12).

Table 9.10 Sports players' evaluation of their satisfaction with match-fixing education

Factors	*Baseball*	*Football*	*Basketball*	*Volleyball*
Match-fixing education satisfaction	4.34 (0.991)	3.85 (1.005)	4.03 (0.881)	4.06 (1.041)
Match-fixing education quality	4.29 (1.030)	3.72 (1.043)	3.92 (0.939)	4.02 (0.948)
Match-fixing education passion	4.42 (1.017)	3.45 (1.141)	4.10 (0.945)	3.92 (0.926)

Table 9.11 Differences in players' evaluation of their match-fixing education

	SS	*Df*	*MS*	*F*	*Post-hoc*
Education satisfaction	7.580	3	2.572	2.649*	–
	239.416	251	0.954		adc b
	246.996	254			
Education quality	10.490	3	3.497	3.576*	–
	245.448	251	0.978		adc b
	255.937	254			
Education passion	30.043	3	10.014	9.863*	–
	254.859	251	1.015		adc b
	284.902	254			

Notes
* $p < 0.05$.
a = baseball, b = football, c = basketball, d = volleyball.

Table 9.12 Frequency of players' education

Sport	*Match-fixing education session frequency*				
	1 per year	*2 per year*	*3 per year*	*4 per year*	*5 or more per year*
Baseball	35 (56.5%)	22 (35.5%)	4 (6.5%)	0 (0.0%)	1 (1.6%)
Football	30 (50.0%)	15 (25%)	10 (16.7%)	3 (5.0%)	2 (3.3%)
Basketball	31 (42.5%)	28 (38.4%)	13 (17.8%)	1 (1.4%)	0 (0.0%)
Volleyball	28 (46.7%)	21 (35.0%)	9 (15.0%)	0 (0.0%)	2 (3.3%)
Total	**124 (48.6%)**	**86 (33.7%)**	**36 (14.1%)**	**4 (1.6%)**	**5 (2.0%)**

Notes
$\chi^2 = 15.973$, $df = 12$, $p = 0.192$.

Differences in the duration of players' education

There was a statistically meaningful difference in the duration of education amongst the different sports. The most common duration of an education session was one hour. Forty-two per cent of sports players received education for a duration of two hours and only 2.4 per cent of players received education over a period of three or more hours. The majority of baseball players received education over a period of one hour (74.2 per cent), football players received education over a period of two hours (50 per cent), basketball players received education over a period of one hour (57 per cent) and volleyball players received education over a period of two hours (53.3 per cent). Football and volleyball players' education sessions were longer than other sports players' education (see Table 9.13).

Issues with the current match-fixing education system

Of the professional sports players, 55.8 per cent (153 players) answered that they did not have concerns with the current match-fixing education system. In contrast, 44.2 per cent (121 players) responded that there was a problem with the current match-fixing education system, 14.2 per cent responded that the current education was not interesting or stimulating, 12.7 per cent responded that there was no following up of education, 12.4 per cent responded that the education was not attention-grabbing and 4.7 per cent responded that the education was disorganised (see Table 9.14).

Professional sports players' perception of match-fixing education

Sports players' thoughts on the need for more education

There was no statistically meaningful difference amongst the sports in relation to the players' thoughts on the need for more education

Table 9.13 Duration of players' education

Sport	*Match-fixing education duration*		
	1 hour	*2 hours*	*3 hours*
Baseball	46 (74.2%)	16 (25.8%)	0 (0.0%)
Football	29 (48.3%)	30 (50.0%)	1 (1.7%)
Basketball	42 (57.5%)	29 (39.7%)	2 (2.7%)
Volleyball	25 (41.7%)	32 (53.3%)	3 (5.0%)
Total	**142 (55.6%)**	**107 (42.0%)**	**6 (2.4%)**

Notes
$\chi^2 = 16.687$, $df = 6$, $p = 0.011$.

Table 9.14 Concerns about the current match-fixing education system

Description	*Number*	*Percentage*
Not attention-grabbing	34	12.4
Disorganised	13	4.7
No follow up	35	12.7
Not interesting/stimulating	39	14.2
No concern	153	55.8

($x^2=3.700$, $p=0.296$). In general, 65.7 per cent of professional players thought that match-fixing education had to be more thorough than it is now (see Table 9.15). In particular, for all sports, more than half of the players expressed a desire for a more thorough educational programme.

Professional players' suggestions on how to improve the current education system

Professional players' suggestions on how to improve the current education system are set out in Table 9.16. Suggestions include having lecturers with greater expertise (39.1 per cent), having more proactive counselling about match-fixing (23.2 per cent), growing relationships and having a combined education programme with other professional sports organisations (20.6 per cent) and having more regular education (17.6 per cent).

Other appropriate preventative measures

In order to prevent match-fixing, 51 per cent of sports players recommended implementing a systematic match-fixing prevention programme, 19.3 per cent supported proactive counselling, 15 per cent supported a players' self-governing tribunal and 14.2 per cent supported an anti-match-fixing campaign (see Table 9.17).

Table 9.15 Professional sports players' perception/thoughts of match-fixing prevention education

Sport	*I think match-fixing education must be more thorough than it is now*	
	I agree	*I disagree*
Baseball	38 (58.5%)	27 (41.5%)
Football	44 (62.9%)	26 (37.1%)
Basketball	53 (67.9%)	25 (32.1%)
Volleyball	45 (73.8%)	16 (26.2%)
Total	**180 (65.7%)**	**94 (34.3%)**

Table 9.16 Professional players' suggestions on how to improve the current education system

Description	*Number*	*Percentage*
Lecturer's expertise	107	39.1
Combined education with other professional organisations	56	20.6
More proactive counselling	63	23.2
Regular education	48	17.6
Total	**274**	**100**

Table 9.17 Players' recommendations on other appropriate preventative activities

Description	*Number*	*Percentage*
Anti-match-fixing campaigns	39	14.2
Players' self-governing tribunals	41	15
Other preventative education	141	51.5
Counselling	53	19.3
Total	**274**	**100**

Thoughts on the frequency of match-fixing education

The results suggest that professional players generally considered education once a year prior to joining a league to be sufficient (68.6 per cent). However, a fairly significant number of players (30.3 per cent) also expressed a desire for education at least once a month and education during the league season (see Table 9.18).

The focus of match-fixing education

When questioned on the desired focus of match-fixing education, the highest response evidenced that players want to know what the penalties

Table 9.18 Thoughts on match-fixing education frequency

Description	*Number*	*Percentage*
Once a week	3	1.1
Once a month	36	13.1
Once a year prior to joining a league	188	68.6
During league season	47	17.2
Total	**274**	**100**

are for players involved in match-fixing (30.2 per cent). Risks involved with illegal gambling was the next desired focus (21.2 per cent), followed by sports ethics (17.2 per cent), how to report match-fixing (14.6 per cent) and whistleblowing (12.4 per cent). In addition, other areas that players thought should receive attention included illegal sports gambling case studies, education on how brokers approach players and how to respond when brokers approach (see Table 9.19).

Analysis of the survey results

Differences in players' opinions of match-fixing

The Korean government raised match-fixing as a systemic issue in May 2011, leading to a general disapproval of match-fixing in society. Match-fixing education was accordingly implemented for players and players began to associate match-fixing with illegality. Eun Young Kim argued that in the first cases of K-League match-fixing which occurred in 2011, the players involved did not believe that match-fixing was illegal.[25] He argued that match-fixing arises not merely as a result of an individual's beliefs or lack of ethics. Rather, match-fixing is a social issue which requires constant education and reminding of an individual's responsibility. A wider ethical education is required to include topics such as sportsmanship, violence and doping in a more regular and cohesive structure from when players are students so that once they become professional players their ethics are already strongly grounded. Soo Yeun Lim also suggested that one of the ways to prevent match-fixing is to provide thorough ethical education from a high school age.[26]

All players across the four professional sports surveyed in 2015 for this research viewed match-fixing as illegal and unethical. However, there were still differences amongst the sports in terms of players' knowledge of match-fixing information, the number of encounters with match-fixing, and the rate at which they access illegal gambling websites. There was no

Table 9.19 The focus of match-fixing education

Description	*Number*	*Percentage*
Penalties for match-fixing	83	30.2
Risks of illegal gambling	58	21.2
Reporting match-fixing	40	14.6
Whistleblowing	34	12.4
Sports ethics	47	17.2
Other	12	4.4
Total	**274**	**100**

statistical difference amongst the sports in the reporting of hearing of match-fixing from players' teammates. However, 23.7 per cent of the total number of players reported that they had heard about how to match-fix from a teammate, which is not an insignificant number.

In particular, when compared with other sports players, basketball players showed the highest rate of having exchanged or heard of match-fixing from teammates at 31 per cent. Furthermore, basketball has the highest rate of players being approached to match-fix, and also a large number of players accessing illegal gambling websites when compared with other sports players according to the survey results. It is therefore important to ensure that basketball is thoroughly regulated and ways to prevent match-fixing are explored. Once a player is involved with match-fixing, it is arguably difficult for them to disassociate. It is important to ensure that education begins at a young age to prevent players from becoming involved in the first instance.

Current match-fixing education for professional sports players

This study established that football players have less exposure to match-fixing education compared with other surveyed sports players in Korea. The survey further demonstrated that overall, 80 per cent of players first had exposure to match-fixing education after their entry into a professional league, emphasising the need to implement thorough education earlier. Compared with other sports, football had the greatest number of players who had received match-fixing education during university.

These results can be explained by the fact that, first, during early, mid and senior high school, sports students are taught to focus only on winning games and their sports skills with the result that sports ethics and other studies are neglected. Second, in some sports, players may be instructed by their coaches to lose particular games (with no reward) so that other players may graduate and move up to more senior levels of high school. It is possible that players do not learn to associate match-fixing with illegal activity beyond high school because of this background. Third, amateur leagues have limited funds and professionals to support and implement match-fixing education programmes. Although the professional sports leagues are highly financially independent due to corporate sponsorships in Korea, the amateur leagues are dependent on government funding.

Furthermore, most professional leagues only have match-fixing education sessions once per year for a maximum of one to two hours. It is difficult to see how match-fixing education can effectively and realistically be implemented in such a short period of time. Responses to the survey that indicate that the education is dull and not engaging point to the superficial nature of the education, existing only in name but not effect. It follows that there is a need for each league and sport to focus on updating and revamping match-fixing education.

Professional sports players' education strategy

When asked about the implementation of the current education system, 65 per cent of players responded that there needed to be more frequent and longer classes. Players' responses also suggested that they considered the expertise of their lecturers to be the most important factor in their education.

From 2011, nation-wide scandals revealed that in the majority of cases, a broker is involved in match-fixing in Korea.[27] Most cases involved a broker finding players and persuading them to partake in match-fixing, and then distributing the reward money after match-fixing is successfully carried out. Several players have previously recounted that they have not reported match-fixing out of fear of a broker's threats. These concerns highlight the need to educate sports players on how brokers go about fixing matches and how to safely report brokers.

Responses to the survey also suggest that players were interested in learning about the legal consequences of match-fixing. Match-fixing education should cover legal ramifications and what kind of conduct specifically leads to what penalties.

This research evidences a need for Korea to support the development of lecturers to support and enhance its match-fixing education and counselling. The United States and Singaporean governments provide courses on gambling issues so that there are well recognised qualifications and expertise in these areas.[28] In Korea, there is now a 'clean center'[29] set up under the Ministry of Culture, Sports and Tourism. This center should focus not only on responding to match-fixing allegations and providing counselling but also on broader issues such as prevention education and growing the expertise of lecturers in order to become a more effective centre for gambling and related sports issues.

It is very difficult for players to report match-fixing especially when they still have ongoing careers. Furthermore, sports organisations or committees lack professional staff and knowledge and are often made up of coaches and players with close relationships. Sports organisations are therefore less likely to report incidents in an effort to cover up for one of their members.

Furthermore, clean centers currently only respond to match-fixing allegations and counsel players; it is rare for them to run and monitor sport education. Each sporting administrative body should consider establishing a centre or committee which provides education. KTOTO, a company funded by a government grant, is the current body mainly responsible for sports education in Korea.[30] If this company changes in some way, or funding through the grant is no longer provided, then the consistency and continuity of sports education for players cannot be guaranteed. Therefore, there is a need to set up an independent system purely responsible for sports education tailored to meet each sport's different needs.

The current law must also be interpreted more broadly such that match-fixing results in harsher penalties. Most match-fixing scandals have been punished through specifically applying provisions from the *Kukmin chaeyuk jinhungbub* [National Sports Promotion Act] (act no. 8344, 2007 (Republic of Korea)). This trend is insufficient to fully deter players from the temptations of match-fixing. A wider interpretation of the application of the *Hyungbub* [Criminal Act] (act no. 293, 1953 (Republic of Korea)) which would impose harsher penalties on players is needed.

Conclusion and proposals

This study aimed to provide suggestions for preventing match-fixing before it arises based on a survey of professional players in the four main sports, with results calculated using SPSS 18.0. This conclusion summarises our findings and proposals. First, all sports players perceived match-fixing to be illegal. Basketball players answered to having had the most exposure to match-fixing and illegal gambling websites. Second, the majority of players revealed that they had received some match-fixing prevention education. However, the majority had their first education experience after becoming a professional player. Furthermore, although a large number of players reported satisfaction with the current education system, there was also a high number of football players who indicated that they were not content with the education that they had received. The frequency and duration of the education was reported as being typically once a year and one to two hours on average. This highlights the room for more regular, ongoing education. Third, when questioned about the system and strategy of match-fixing education, the majority of players answered that there was room for improvement. Players considered the expertise of lecturers to be important to the education system and thought it vital to be taught the penalties and legal ramifications of being involved in match-fixing.

Notes

1 This chapter is a translated and edited version of Chung, Y., Jun, J. and Kim, J., 2015, '*Prosports sunsoodulae sungboojojakae daehan inshikkwa yaebanggyoy-ook junlakyeongoo* [A study of professional players' perceptions of match-fixing and prevention education strategies in Korea]', *Hangugcheyughaghoeji* [The Korean Journal of Physical Education], vol. 54, no. 5, pp. 273–284. Translation by Ms Jess (Hee Sung) Shin and Ms Sarah (Jin Hyung) Yang, Research Assistants, Asian Law Centre, Melbourne Law School. The editors are grateful to the Journal for its permission to publish this edited translation.

2 Chae, S., Kim, J., Han, S., Yi, H. and Jang, H., 2012, '*Sportsseunsudulae yoonlisung moonjaewa haegyulbangahn* [The ethics of players and alternatives]', *Hankuksportsinryuhakhwe* [Korean Society for Sport Anthropology], vol. 7, no. 2, pp. 73–93.
3 Ji, M., 2014, '*Prosports sseungbujojak saeraeae daehan gochal* [A study on the match-fixing case of domestic professional sports]', *Hankukenterteinmentsanyuphakhwe* [Journal of the Korea Entertainment Industry Association], vol. 8, no. 3, pp. 109–116.
4 Seo, H. and Han, S., 2012, '*K-leaguesungbujojasahkwonka chaeyookjin hongtupyogwonsahup oonyongae moonjaejuhm* [K-League Match-fixing Scandal and the Problem of Korean SportsToto's Management]', *Hangugcheyughaghoeji* [The Korean Journal of Physical Education], vol. 51, no. 4, pp. 45–54.
5 Kim, J., 2014, '*Purononggu sunsuegedo seulbujojak haeppakmumja* [Threat messages sent to professional baseball players to match-fix]', *DongA*, 30 December, http://news.donga.com/Sports/BestClick/3/all/20141230/68826277/1.
6 Go, Y., 2015, '*Ggeliji annun "gunen son" seulbujojak, sunsu jajung norekel ueulhan daean* [Continuous "black hand" to match-fix, players' self-purification effort is the only alternative]', *OSEN*, 8 May, http://osen.mt.co.kr/article/G1110146606.
7 Kim, Y., 2011, '*Baeguyeonmeng, sunsu, kochi daesang seungbujojak yeibang gyoyuk* [Preventative training for volleyball federation, players and coaches against match-fixing]', *Yonhap News*, 9 June, www.yonhapnews.co.kr/bulletin/2011/06/09/0200000000AKR20110609139200007.HTML.
8 Lee, S., 2015, '*KBO, 2015neun shininsunsu kyoyuk silsi* [KBO (Korean Baseball Organisation) conducts educational training for new players in 2015]', *OSEN*, 7 January, http://osen.mt.co.kr/article/G1110046422.
9 Yang, D., 2013, '*Seungbujojak kyoyukbakneun purononggu sunsudel* [Professional basketball players are receiving education on match-fixing]', *News1 Korea*, 29 April, http://news1.kr/photos/449121.
10 Heo, J., 2011, '*Seungbujojak, jisokjukin kyoyukelro kunjulshikyoya* [Eradicate match-fixing by continuous education]', *OSEN*, 25 May, http://osen.mt.co.kr/article/G1105260248.
11 Lee, J., 2015, *Niklas Luhmannel sahwejuk cheagae irone kichohan kyungjengsuposu seungbujojakel kan han yeongu* [Match-fixing in advanced competitive sports on the social system theory of Niklas Luhmann], doctoral thesis, Keimyung University, Daegu.
12 Kang, K., 2011, '*Keilegu seungbujojakga hyungsajuk chaekim* [The criminal liability for the K-League match-fixing scandal]', *Journal of Sports and Entertainment Law*, vol. 14, no. 4, pp. 173–197; Kim, Y., 2012, '*Chaeyukshulhak: hankuk suposumumhwael gomingulri: seungbujojakga munhwajihyunggael kwangyesung* [Sports philosophy: the trouble with Korean sports culture: relationship between match-fixing and Korean culture formations]', *Philosophy of Movement* [The Journal of Korean Philosophic Society for Sport and Dance], vol. 20, no. 4, pp. 87–100.
13 Park, B., 2011, '*Seungbujojak, sunsu byunhaw elsik yopin bakyakmuhyo* [Without change of players' consciousness, match-fixing will be an ongoing issue]', *Segye News*, 14 July, www.segye.com/content/html/2011/07/13/20110713004784.html.
14 Go, above n. 6.
15 The Likert scale measures attitudes by asking people to respond to a series of statements about a topic in terms of the extent to which they agree with a statement. Research Method Knowledge Base, 2006, www.socialresearchmethods.net/kb/scallik.php.

16 (1) completely disagree, (2) somewhat disagree, (3) undecided, (4) somewhat agree, (5) completely agree.
17 Seo, H. and Han, S., 2012, '*K-leaguesungbujojasahkwonka chaeyookjin hongtupyogwonsahup oonyongae moonjaejuhm* [K-League match-fixing scandal and the problem of Korean Sportstoto's management]', *Hangugcheyughaghoeji* [The Korean Journal of Physical Education], vol. 51, no. 4, pp. 45–54.
18 Kim, S., 2009, *Yuchiwon kyosael adong hakdaee kwanhan yebang kyoyuk inssik chosa* [A study on kindergarten teacher's perception of child abuses prevention education], doctoral thesis, Kyung Hee University, Seoul.
19 Nam, S., 2007, *Hakkyopukryak yebangkyoyuke daehan sahwega kyosal inssike kwanhan yeongu* [Study on social studies teachers' perception on school violence prevention education], doctoral thesis, Sungshin University, Seoul.
20 Yoon, E., 2013, *Chulhaksengl hakkyopokryuk yebangkyoyuke daehan inshin* [Middle school students' perception of school violence prevention education], doctoral thesis, Kangwon National University, Chuncheon.
21 Walter, M., 2010, *Social research methods*, Oxford University Press.
22 Cross tabulation is taking two variables and tabulating the results of one variable against the other.
23 See Yeun in this volume on the link between match-fixing and illegal sports betting websites.
24 One-way ANOVA is a technique used to determine whether there are any statistically significant differences between three or more samples.
25 Kim, E., 2011, '*Hankuk pro cukkyul seungbujojake daehan dodukjuk rongo* [Sport philosophy: ethical assertion about match fixing of K-League]', *Hangugcheyughaghoeji* [The Korean Journal of Physical Education], vol. 51, no. 4, pp. 55–68.
26 Lim, S., 2012, '*Namja gogyo elit suposu seungbujojakel shilsangwa keunjulbangan* [Match-Fixing in male high school elite sports and ways to prevent it]', *Hangugcheyughaghoeji* [The Korean Journal of Physical Education], vol. 51, no. 4, pp. 55–68.
27 Kang, above n. 12.
28 Jang, S., Jun, Y. and Kim, S., 2009, 'A comparison of the certification system for gambling addiction counselors in the U.S., Australia and Singapore', *Korean Journal of Stress Research*, vol. 17, no. 1, pp. 53–62.
29 See also Yeun in this volume.
30 See also Yeun in this volume.

Chapter 10

Police and investigative cooperation on match-fixing

An Australian experience

Catherine Ordway[1]

Introduction: the roles of the Australian Federal Police in combating match-fixing

This chapter analyses the Australian Federal Police's ('AFP') approach to match-fixing and reflects on its publicly reported experiences dealing with the threat of match-fixing at selected major international sporting events hosted in Australia in 2015. The Asian Football Confederation ('AFC') men's Asian Cup ('Asian Cup') involved 16 national teams in 32 matches over five Australian cities between 9 and 31 January; the International Cricket Council ('ICC') men's World Cup ('ICC World Cup') involved 14 teams playing in 49 matches over 14 venues across Australia and New Zealand from 14 February to 29 March; and the International Netball Federation women's Netball World Cup was played in Sydney by 16 teams in 64 matches from 7 to 16 August. These major sporting events ('MSE 2015') together attracted an estimated viewing audience of over a billion fans worldwide.[2] The MSE 2015 serves as a useful case study and highlights the coordinating role that a national organisation such as the AFP can play, particularly in a diversified federal system such as Australia's. The numerous government, law enforcement, and sport stakeholders with different perspectives and agendas required strong leadership, particularly around clarity of roles during, and in the lead up to, these major events. The author assisted the AFP as an independent consultant to develop and then co-facilitate event-based scenario planning sessions for the various MSE 2015 stakeholders and this chapter draws on that experience.

This chapter begins by first explaining the jurisdiction and role of the AFP in Australia's federal system. Match-fixing is a relatively new criminal offence in Australia.[3] Specific match-fixing legislation empowers State and Territory police to investigate this crime type. The AFP has jurisdiction to provide support where there is a nexus to money laundering and the international criminal environment which comes within its authority. The AFP also assists in developing national frameworks. Second, the chapter considers why the AFP prioritised its involvement in preventing and deterring match-fixing as part of its overall strategy. Australian sporting codes and events are vulnerable to match-fixing for several reasons, including: the perception that Australian sport is uncorrupted, the close time zone to Asia and the huge volume of online betting, particularly originating from the Asian region.[4] The harm to sport where match-fixing is involved includes reputational issues resulting in the loss of public confidence and sponsors. Third, the chapter analyses the AFP's approach to match-fixing in the context of the MSE 2015, which presented a complex environment of opportunities and threats.

The chapter demonstrates that the AFP, which also participated in Aviation Security and Border Control scenario planning, played a key role as the lead federal agency to marshal the national government's efforts against match-fixing during the MSE 2015. The AFP worked with other law enforcement, government agencies and sporting codes to develop a collective response to protect the integrity of the MSE 2015. Importantly for the findings in this chapter, the AFP strategies focused heavily on prevention and disruption activities rather than investigation. As the chapter highlights, information sharing between law enforcement and sporting codes was the crucial element for collaboration. The chapter concludes that the focus on prevention and disruption was successful. It is understood that law enforcement worked through several incidents with their sport partners, including proactively targeting and disrupting known match-fixers. Following the completion of the events, the AFP concluded, from information gathered from all jurisdictions and agencies, that there was no evidence of match-fixing, including no spot-fixing, during the MSE 2015.

AFP leadership and coordination in Australia's federal system

Formal public–private relationships between governments and sports organisations are now obligatory for any proposal to host a major international sporting event. Submitting a bid book containing detailed plans, funding and guarantees from local, regional and national governments is a common requirement in the competitive world of major event hosting. As part of the bid process to win the right to be a host nation, the Australian Commonwealth and relevant State Governments guaranteed that innovative solutions would be developed to protect the MSE 2015 from integrity threats.[5] To secure the right to host the MSE 2015, the Commonwealth Government committed to guarantees including the enforcement of offences pertaining to intellectual property crime, money laundering and other criminal activity.[6] The Commonwealth Government does not, however, have the constitutional power to create national legislation to criminalise match-fixing, and the AFP does not have direct jurisdiction in relation to match-fixing.

The AFP's role in combating match-fixing during the MSE 2015 was facilitated by a national policy and the AFP's jurisdiction in relation to other criminal activities such as money laundering and criminal activity with an international element. In June 2011, the Commonwealth, State and Territory Sports Ministers jointly endorsed the *National Policy on Match-Fixing in Sport* ('*Policy*').[7] With reporting lines to the Commonwealth Minister for Sport, this *Policy* is monitored and supported by the National Integrity in Sport Unit ('NISU'). The NISU was established in October 2012 and is located within the Commonwealth Department of Health.[8] The State and Territory Governments implemented the *Policy* in a somewhat harmonised manner in their respective jurisdictions in the lead up to the MSE 2015, although the conduct prohibited under the new State and Territory criminal laws differs from the definition of match-fixing under the national *Policy*.[9] A joint working group was also established by the NISU and the AFP in 2014 as a mechanism to discuss and develop integrity related strategies, policies and procedures, and to allow for otherwise confidential intelligence information to be accessed around the time of the MSE 2015.[10]

Although each State and Territory in Australia has a separate police service, the AFP is the principal law enforcement agency for the Commonwealth Government, and it conducts both community policing in the Australian Capital Territory and investigates offences against federal law in Australia and overseas.[11] The AFP's Corporate Plan 2016–17 describes it as 'the Australian Government's primary policing agency' and 'a key member of the Australian law enforcement and national security community, leading policing efforts to keep Australians and Australian interests safe both at home and overseas'.[12] The AFP's mission of 'dynamic and effective'[13] law enforcement nationally requires a coordinated approach across the eight police services, in addition to the Australian Criminal Intelligence Commission.[14] The AFP's primary purpose is 'to enforce Commonwealth criminal law, contribute to combating organised crime and protecting Commonwealth interests from criminal activity in Australia and overseas'.[15] The AFP provides support to investigations in each Australian State or Territory by, for example, providing intelligence and conducting overseas inquiries.

These aspects of the AFP role were important drivers in its participation in preventing match-fixing during the MSE 2015. By employing the core principles of 'prevention, deterrence, partnership and innovation', the AFP works to counter terrorism and promote national security.[16] The Australian community is also familiar with the AFP regularly reporting on its involvement in disrupting and detecting Commonwealth offences, such as serious fraud against the Commonwealth, and transnational crimes such as drug importation, money laundering, terrorism and people smuggling.[17]

The intersection of money laundering and match-fixing was also a key reason that the AFP was able and willing to employ its resources nationally during the MSE 2015, despite match-fixing not being a Commonwealth crime, and therefore not directly within the AFP's 'operational emphasis'.[18] Sport has traditionally managed its own integrity and behavioural issues through internal regulations and tribunals, without recourse to law enforcement agencies, or domestic courts. This segregation however has been shifting, and the recent AFP initiative to assist in protecting the MSE 2015 was reflective of this development. The detection and prevention of money laundering and the financing of terrorism are key focus areas for the AFP, and the Minister for Justice, the Hon Michael Keenan MP, was cognisant that unregulated global sports betting markets, including online betting, presented opportunities for organised crime to launder funds, including through match-fixing. Accordingly, the AFP's involvement in MSE 2015 complemented its core purpose.[19]

Money laundering is a method used by criminals to make illegitimate money sources appear legitimate.[20] Criminals use professional launderers to legitimise their illicit profits and diversify their activities across legal and illegal businesses, thereby reducing the risk of successful law enforcement intervention. The negative impact of organised crime and its associated money laundering is severe and collectively threatens individuals, companies, services, national economies and the security of governments in multiple ways.[21] Lax regulation means that gambling is one of the traditional methods of laundering money worldwide.[22] Criminals can transfer money between casinos globally outside traditional banking reporting systems, for example. The provision of credit by casinos allows for physical or electronic monetary values to be used in one country while debts are paid via poorly regulated casinos in another. Often gambling debts are paid in full by casino gaming chips.[23] Official estimates suggest that almost US$3 billion per week is laundered through sports betting.[24] Transnational organised crime groups view money laundering via online sports betting as an easy, cost-effective method with little risk of detection.

The so-called 'hyper-globalisation'[25] phenomenon in sport also requires a national approach to match-fixing. This phenomenon has been caused through the international expansion of events and tours, many of which are digitally broadcast. This globalisation creates a global market for gamblers, which is enhanced by the growth in sports gambling operators' sponsorship and marketing saturation,[26] and the breadth of online gambling participation modes.[27] These circumstances create opportunities for transnational criminals and present complex problems for jurisdictionally bound legislators, regulators and law enforcers. The federal system in Australia makes combating match-fixing challenging, because the criminalisation of match-fixing is based on State and Territory legislation.

Transnational online gambling operators have also made laundering even more profitable than through traditional methods.[28] Unregulated and under-regulated online sports betting is a recent development in this environment and contributes to betting being an easy, cost effective method to launder money. The amount of money being laundered through sports betting is ever-increasing and already comprises more than 15 per cent of estimated total global illegal income.[29] Most of the betting takes place in Asia, primarily on football and cricket.[30] Unregulated and under-regulated online sports betting sites, many controlled by Asian organised crime entities, actively facilitate money laundering. This method is low risk because it is practically impossible for jurisdictional and technical reasons for any one law enforcement agency to prosecute unregulated and under-regulated online bookmakers based in foreign locations.

These online sports betting sites have the capacity to launder up to 100 per cent of global organised crime proceeds at much lower cost, and almost no risk, as compared with other laundering methods, particularly if the results have been guaranteed in advance through fixing. Police investigations internationally have demonstrated that criminals have infiltrated sport (or are themselves officials, athletes, coaches or referees)[31] to secure an agreed action (such as a red card, no ball or double fault) or outcome (such as a win, margin or draw) for an agreed sum or other inducement such as drugs, prostitutes or deferment of gambling debts to ensure that their so-called investment is safe and, ideally for transnational criminal organisations' purposes, enhanced. In some cases, those markets are established by criminals primarily for the purpose of money laundering.

The risk of match-fixing exacerbated by betting

There is currently no internationally agreed approach or definition for match-fixing, as distinct from the long-established, and internationally harmonised, approach taken to combat doping in sport.[32] The growing awareness that sports results were being determined prior to the event forced sports organisations to be proactive, particularly over the last decade. Hill's seminal research, published in his 2008 book *The fix: soccer and organized crime*, established through hundreds of in-depth interviews with players, referees, coaches, fixers and gamblers that football and cricket are the two sports most under threat from match-fixing in the world.[33] By June 2010, the then-president of the International Olympic Committee ('IOC'), Jacques Rogge, expressed a concern, also increasingly being voiced elsewhere within the Olympic Movement, that 'cheating driven by betting is undoubtedly the biggest threat to sport after doping'.[34]

The link made to gambling by the IOC is instructive, and hints at the further incentive for law enforcement involvement in the solution. In early examples of match-fixing, the motivation for the fix appears to have been financial;[35] that is, prize money or in other cases relating to putting the team or player into a better position for future rounds or seasons (so-called 'tanking'),[36] which are arguably challenges for sports organisations, and not law enforcement agencies, to address. 'Improperly influencing the outcome or any dimension of a sports event for financial or personal benefit'[37] is not new. However, as Anderson suggests, developments in sports gambling, and more recently the ease of accessibility and scope of betting products created through (particularly unregulated and under-regulated) online gambling operators, require a distinction to be drawn between betting-related 'gambling-led corruption' and non-betting related match-fixing.[38] Anderson also highlights that the Australian framework only criminalises match-fixing if it corrupts betting outcomes. Thus, a bribe to lose a match might be match-fixing in a colloquial context, but not be a criminal offence in most Australian States and Territories because of the absence of gambling.[39] The conduct may, however, be an offence under the applicable sport rules. Deliberately losing a match to obtain a more favourable position in a play-off or just resting several players ahead of an important game resulting in a loss to a lower ranked team is not necessarily regarded as match-fixing by many commentators.[40] In contrast, although linked to gambling, the practice of 'pitch or court-siding' is not regarded as match-fixing, and instead results in the offender's ejection from the sporting premises under ticketing conditions.[41]

Moreover, the evolution and expansion in the sports betting market does not directly create a risk to sports integrity, and some commentators would argue there have also been benefits.[42] This view should be contrasted with concerns frequently aired about the partnership between sports organisations and gambling operators[43] and the social harm caused by gambling more broadly.[44] Match-fixing raises the issue of gambling where it impacts on sporting outcomes, that is, the results of a game or an event within a match. Sport integrity is at risk because professional gamblers and, increasingly, transnational criminal organisations, are not satisfied by the uncertainty of outcome that characterises sport competitions.[45] Instead, unscrupulous gamblers and betting operators are happy to exploit the vulnerable and the greedy to ensure the odds are entirely in their favour. Law enforcement agencies have recognised that money from criminal endeavours may be quickly and easily laundered through under-regulated or unregulated, and even regulated, sports betting markets.[46]

MSE 2015 case study: coordination and cooperation

In the context of the high-level national and international governmental dialogue around possible solutions for gambling-related threats to sport integrity, the AFP began to assess and quantify what it ultimately considered to be the severe threat posed to Australia by transnational criminal organisations' involvement in money laundering via unregulated online sports betting. The AFP collected intelligence, built collaborative networks, and first assisted with a match-fixing investigation in November 2013.[47] The potential harm which match-fixing posed during the MSE 2015 was identified by both sports organisations and law enforcement agencies as a priority and was sought to be minimised through an AFP collaborative initiative. The sports industry has recognised for some time that it must work closely with governments and agencies with access to relevant information, knowledge, powers and resources to protect sport from various integrity threats. In relation to match-fixing, for example, INTERPOL accepts that 'no organisation can tackle the problem of match-fixing alone'.[48] Further, INTERPOL advocates for strategies which 'incorporate partnerships' between national 'associations and betting organizations as well as public authorities including law enforcement and regulators'.[49]

Moreover, at the time, Australian men's sport faced unprecedented integrity crises. The Australian Sports Anti-Doping Authority ('ASADA') was investigating Australian Football League and National Rugby League clubs arising out of the Australian Crime Commission's report claiming 'widespread use of prohibited substances in professional sport',[50] the Football Federation Australia and Victoria Police broke up a gambling ring that was corrupting the outcomes of lower-level football (soccer) matches for financial gain, there were public scandals surrounding the conduct of members of the men's Olympic swimming team, and admissions of doping in cycling.[51] These events heightened the reputational risks associated with the MSE 2015.

The AFP's efforts also confirmed that not only was there growing interest by groups of transnational criminal organisations, such as Asian triads, in unregulated sports betting and match-fixing, but there were multiple links between online sports betting and transnational criminal syndicates, casino junkets and influential political and business entities in Asia and Europe. Some of these groups also had business and family links to Australia, and it was possible that the Asian Cup and ICC World Cup would provide the impetus for transnational criminal organisations to increasingly focus on teams participating in these events. In addition to the threat already posed to the public's and sponsors' confidence in all sporting events through illegal betting, money laundering and match-fixing, major sporting events are particularly vulnerable to organised crime as they generate a huge betting volume.

The volume and breadth of betting interest in football and cricket world-wide, coupled with the extent of match-fixing allegations, betting fraud investigations and corruption and governance failings in these sports, led the AFP to establish a dedicated sports integrity team under Major Events Intelligence.[52] In comparison, both the sport of netball generally, and the World Cup event itself, were considered to be of such low risk as to not require dedicated AFP resources. From 1 July 2014, the AFP Integrity in Sport Team, supported by an AFP civilian recruit with elite sport experience, drew on resources of police in Australia and New Zealand as the MSE 2015 drew closer. For the cricket and football events then, the AFP initiative identified potential persons of interest, and facilitated efforts to reduce the threat to sports integrity through inter-agency (law enforcement and sport) cooperation.

The AFP developed a Concept of Operations ('ConOps') outlining its intentions to address the prevention, disruption and prosecution of organised crime involvement in sport through money laundering, illegal betting, match-fixing and related offences in the lead up to, during and following the MSE 2015. This ConOps highlighted that protecting sport requires a multifaceted approach, combining the efforts of sports, law enforcement and government agencies. A focus on investigating money laundering and the prevention and disruption of illegal betting, match-fixing and related offences were identified as necessary to protect major sporting events and maintain faith in the 'contest' – a key element in sport – by the public and sponsors. The intelligence services tapped into international networks and implemented border security disruption strategies with the Commonwealth Immigration and Customs departments (now the Australian Border Force). Strategies included proactively targeting and disrupting persons of interest in terms of match-fixing and related offences and referring them to the then Department of Immigration and Border Protection for inclusion on their person and document alert systems.[53]

The timely and lawful sharing of information and intelligence was a key plank to the strategy. Memoranda of Understanding ('MoUs') were developed to enhance this process, and to supplement the existing arrangements with the New Zealand Police and Australian State and Territory policing agencies. The AFP entered into MoUs on cooperation and information exchange with stakeholders, including the International Cricket Council,[54] Sportradar[55] and others.[56] The MoUs demonstrate the existence of a formal relationship and enable the AFP to deal directly with the sporting organisation's integrity unit, and share information securely with trusted people. MoUs also set out various legislative obligations of the AFP to collect, store, use and disclose information. This information in certain circumstances may be accessed by external bodies such as the courts, ombudsmen and privacy commissioners.

Outcomes and recommendations

The MSE 2015 events were heralded as a success by players, politicians and the public alike.[57] There was also no evidence of match-fixing or related offences.[58] Research into contemporary policing bodies suggests that success can be measured by organisational credibility, stakeholder acceptance, inter-agency cooperation and the development of personnel.[59] The AFP and other stakeholders' focus on preventing and disrupting attempts to match-fix during the MSE 2015 reflect these contemporary policing benchmarks and highlight the important coordinating role that a national organisation can play in a federal system such as Australia's. To ensure the continued success of major events held in Australia, the NISU and the AFP needs to continue to build on this experience and play a role in implementing identified learnings.

Most crucial in achieving organisational credibility for the parties involved, and acceptance by each of the stakeholders, is inter-agency cooperation through partnership building. The MSE 2015 highlighted the success that a coordinated and partnership-driven focus on match-fixing may bring. The 'at risk' sports would benefit from working more closely together throughout the year, even without hosting a major event. Meetings and invitations to local events or conferences, inclusion on media and mailing lists, and the provision of annual reports, help to promote greater mutual understanding of compatible roles, and not insignificant challenges, and can lead to deeper trust and solution-focused anti-corruption outcomes.

To achieve this closer cooperation, particularly in the lead up to major events, partnerships need to be cultivated proactively at many levels – from the executive equivalents, through to the various operational positions, and including national and international contacts. These partnerships need to go beyond the existing law enforcement and government agency structures, and include other sport industry stakeholders, such as player associations, bookmakers (online and shopfront) and regulatory bodies such as those overseeing sports integrity, betting and telecommunications.

Formal documentation of these relationships should be based on a consensus between partners, ideally via information-sharing MoUs. MoUs were acknowledged as being critical in the success of the MSE 2015 anti-corruption strategies. In some settings there may be legislative or policy barriers preventing information-sharing. The earlier that such obstacles are identified, the quicker they may be removed or minimised. In the Australian context, Commonwealth legislation linking sports integrity and the use of other legislation, such as telecommunications and betting-related instruments, could assist the AFP to target criminal methodologies. Such measures may include broadening the *Telecommunications Act 1997* (Cth) to ensure that mobile phone and internet service providers are prohibited from facilitating match-fixing.[60]

Sharing information between government agencies is consistent with the 'Whole of Government' approach,[61] and in this case study it was crucial to include private bodies in the information loop, including appropriately cleared personnel within the organising committees of the relevant sporting bodies. The direct tripartite relationship between law enforcement, the host sport integrity team and Sportradar as the betting monitoring service for the MSE 2015, was very important to the success of the mission. Pre-Games sharing of Persons of Interest ('POI') lists and other information on potential risk methodologies was a key tool for future events.[62] Law enforcement agencies, in consultation with NISU, can also assist sporting organisations to develop whistle blowing mechanisms to provide players with confidential, anonymous, reporting options. Games-time integrity hubs which facilitate the co-location of these stakeholders during events ensure a timely and complete information sharing, evaluation and inquiry generation process. This geographical proximity enables information sharing, including persons-of-interest lists, which are central to disruption strategies and facilitates effective information sharing.

Conclusion

The temptation to pay a participant to 'throw' a sporting match is not new. Far from it merely being another side-effect of the rampant growth in the commercialisation of modern sport as has been suggested by some commentators,[63] there are many examples of cheating in ancient times.[64] Key modern differences include the intersection of illegal and unregulated and under-regulated online betting, hyper-globalisation of sport and money laundering by transnational organised criminals. These drivers led to the AFP's initiative to reduce the threat to sports integrity through broadly scoped inter-agency cooperation as part of Australia's initiative to disrupt and prevent match-fixing during the MSE 2015. It will be of great benefit to Australia as a sporting integrity island that these collaborative tools should continue to be utilised all year round, particularly for those sports of greatest interest to gamblers, and those who seek to pervert sport for criminal gain.

Notes

1 The author acknowledges the support of several AFP officers.
2 This estimate is based on anecdotal evidence. For cricket, it is claimed that the tournament was watched by more than 1.5 billion people worldwide: see Press Trust of India 2015, 'ICC Cricket World Cup 2015 significantly boosted economies of co-hosts Australia and New Zealand', *Cricket Country*, 30 June, www.cricketcountry.com/news/icc-cricket-world-cup-2015-significantly-boosted-economies-of-co-hosts-australia-and-new-zealand-300850. In relation to football see, e.g. Local Organising Committee 2015, *Asian Cup smashes audience numbers*, Football Federation Australia, 30 January, www.footballaustralia.com.au/article/asian-cup-smashes-audience-numbers/pp. 1ebmxdio8k1gibyf93a54dx.
3 See Opie and Lim in this volume.
4 In Canberra in 2009, the Australian and New Zealand Sports Law Association (ANZSLA) annual conference's keynote speaker, Dr Declan Hill, called on those involved in sport in Australia and New Zealand to take the risk of match-fixing seriously, particularly in light of the threat from Asian gambling and organised crime syndicates. Dowling, J., 2009, 'Breaking the rules', *The Sydney Morning Herald*, 7 November, www.smh.com.au/national/breaking-the-rules-20091106-i28k.html.

5 For football see, e.g. AFC and Football Federation Australia, *AFC Asian Cup Australia 2015: information guide*, p. 2, www.ahavic.com.au/LiteratureRetrieve.aspx?ID=100313&A=SearchResult&SearchID=94753213&ObjectID=100313&ObjectType=6; *Football Federation Australia* 2010, 'Australia's bid to host the 2015 AFC Asian Cup', 21 October, www.footballaustralia.com.au/article/australias-bid-to-host-2015-afc-asian-cup/1dycpy337r16q1oop27e6qcu55. For netball see, e.g. *Netball World Cup Sydney 2015* 2013, 'Sydney to host the 2015 Netball World Cup', 11 November, http://nwc2015.com.au/News/sydney-to-host-2015-netball-world-cup-1. For cricket see, e.g. Worldcup.com.au, *2015 Cricket World Cup*, www.worldcup.com.au/cricket-world-cup/2015-cricket-world-cup; ICC Cricket World Cup 2015, *FAQ*, www.icc-cricket.com/cricket-world-cup/about/277/faq.

6 Commonwealth Government refers to the Australian federal or national government and references in this chapter to the Commonwealth refer to the federal system of Australian government.

7 Australian Government Department of Health 2014, 'National policy on match-fixing in sport', 11 February, www.health.gov.au/internet/main/publishing.nsf/Content/national-policy-on-match-fixing-in-sport. See also Godkin, A., 2013, *National Integrity of Sport Unit*, 27 November, www.ors.sa.gov.au/__data/assets/pdf_file/0004/148522/National-Sport-Integrity-Unit-Presentation.pdf. Sport New Zealand adopted a match-fixing policy in April 2014: Sport New Zealand 2014, *New Zealand policy on sports match-fixing and related corruption*, April, www.sportnz.org.nz/assets/Uploads/attachments/managing-sport/integrity/New-Zealand-policy-on-sports-match-fixing-and-related-corruption. pdf.

8 The NISU works closely with the Australian Criminal Intelligence Commission (ACIC). The ACIC was established on 1 July 2016 following the merger of the Australian Crime Commission and CrimTrac: *Minister for Justice* 2015, 'New super agency to tackle emerging threats', 5 November, www.ministerjustice.gov.au/Mediareleases/Pages/2015/FourthQuarter/5-November-2015-New-super-agency-to-tackle-emerging-threats.aspx. See also Murnane and Moller in this volume.

9 Match-fixing in the Australian National Policy is defined as:

> (a) the deliberate fixing of the result of a contest, or of an occurrence within the contest, or of a points spread; (b) deliberate underperformance; (c) withdrawal (tanking); (d) an official's deliberate misapplication of the rules of the contest; (e) interference with the play or playing surfaces by venue staff; and (f) abuse of insider information to support a bet placed by any of the above or placed by a gambler who has recruited such people to manipulate an outcome or contingency.
>
> (Australian Governments 2011, *National policy match-fixing in sport*, 10 June, p. 2, www.health.gov.au/internet/main/publishing.nsf/Content/F6DB8637F05C9643CA257C310021CCE9/$File/National%20Policy%20on%20Match-Fixing%20in%20Sport%20(FINAL).pdf)

See also Opie and Lim in this volume. In NZ, the Crimes (Match-Fixing) Amendment Act was enacted in 2014, to extend the scope of Section 240 of the Crimes Act 1961.

10 In the 2013–14 Budget, the Commonwealth Government committed to provide $3 million over three years to further strengthen the Major Sporting Events Taskforce within the Department of Regional Australia, Local Government, Arts and Sport, to help ensure the successful staging of the 2015 Cricket World Cup and the Asian Football Cup: Commonwealth of Australia 2013, *Budget*

paper no. 2: 2013–14, 14 May, p. 196, www.budget.gov.au/2013-14/content/bp2/download/BP2_expense.pdf.

11 Australia.gov.au, *Police and crime prevention*, www.australia.gov.au/information-and-services/public-safety-and-law/police-and-crime-prevention.

12 Australian Federal Police, *AFP corporate plan 2016–17*, www.afp.gov.au/corporate-plan-2016-17.

13 Australian Federal Police, *Our organisation*, www.afp.gov.au/about-us/our-organisation.

14 In relation to ACIC, see above n. 8.

15 Australian Federal Police, *Corporate plan 2015–19*, www.afp.gov.au/sites/default/files/PDF/AFP-Corporate-Plan-2015-2019.pdf.

16 Australian Federal Police, *What we do*, www.afp.gov.au/what-we-do.

17 Australian Federal Police, *Media releases*, www.afp.gov.au/news-media/media-releases.

18 AFP, www.afp.gov.au/about-us/our-organisation. The AFP has a community policing role in the ACT, which means that its jurisdiction would include enforcing ACT criminal offences against match-fixing.

19 See Australian Federal Police 2015, *AFP annual report 2014–15*, 16 October, www.afp.gov.au/afp-annual-report-2014-15. See also *Minister for Justice* 2015, 'Serious and organised crime costing Australia $36 billion', media release, 18 December, www.ministerjustice.gov.au/Mediareleases/Pages/2015/FourthQuarter/18-December-2015-Serious-and-organised-crime-costing-Australia-36-billion.aspx.

20 Eligo National Task Force, 'Money laundering', www.austrac.gov.au/sites/default/files/documents/eligo_ml_fact_sheet.pdf; Australian Transaction Reports and Analysis Centre 2011, *Money laundering in Australia*, www.austrac.gov.au/publications/corporate-publications-and-reports/money-laundering-australia-2011.

21 Unger, B. and Busuioc, E.M., 2007, *The scale and impacts of money laundering*, Edward Elgar Publishing.

22 See 'Case studies: gambling', in Australian Transaction Reports and Analysis Centre 2013, *AUSTRAC typologies and case studies report 2013*, pp. 61–64, www.austrac.gov.au/sites/default/files/documents/typ13_full.pdf.

23 See Richards, J.R., 1998, *Transnational criminal organizations, cybercrime, and money laundering: a handbook for law enforcement officers, auditors, and financial investigators*, CRC press; Schopper, M.D., 2002, 'Internet gambling, electronic cash and money laundering: the unintended consequences of a monetary control scheme', *Chapman Law Review*, vol. 5, no. 1, pp. 303–330; Reuter, P., 2004, *Chasing dirty money: the fight against money laundering*, Peterson Institute; Schneider, F. and Windischbauer, U., 2008, 'Money laundering: some facts', *European Journal of Law and Economics*, vol. 26, no. 3, pp. 387–404.

24 A key report estimated that '$US140 billion is laundered every year through sports bets, which means that more than 10% of the worldwide revenue of organised crime would gain the appearance of legality in this way': University Paris 1 Panthéon-Sorbonne and International Centre for Sport Security 2014, *Protecting the integrity of sport competition: the last bet for modern sport*, May, p. 29, www.theicss.org/wp-content/themes/icss-corp/pdf/SIF14/Sorbonne-ICSS%20Report%20Executive%20Summary_WEB.pdf?lbisphpreq=1.

25 This phrase is used in the *Protecting the integrity of sport competition* report, and contemplates an extreme scale, 'accompanied by a lack of regulation, control and coordination between States': ibid., p. 10.

26 Operators involved in sponsorship and marketing are often well-regulated and working in partnership with the sports organisations. See also Thomas, S., Lewis, S., Duong, J. and McLeod, C., 2012, 'Sports betting marketing during

sporting events: a stadium and broadcast census of Australian Football League matches', *Australian and New Zealand Journal of Public Health*, vol. 36, no. 2, pp. 145–152.

27 Woolley, R., 2003, 'Mapping internet gambling: emerging modes of online participation in wagering and sports betting', *International Gambling Studies*, vol. 3, no. 1, pp. 3–21.

28 Fiedler, I., 2012, *Online gambling as a game changer to money laundering?*, https://papers.ssrn.com/sol3/papers.cfm?abstract_id=2261266.

29 In 2009, the United Nations Office for Drugs and Crime (UNODC) estimated that transnational organised crime generates US$870 billion a year: United Nations Office on Drugs and Crime 2017, *Transnational organized crime: the globalized illegal economy*, www.unodc.org/toc/en/crimes/organized-crime.html.

30 University Paris 1 Panthéon-Sorbonne and International Centre for Sport Security, above n. 24.

31 Hill, D., 2009 'How gambling corruptors fix football matches', *European Sport Management Quarterly*, vol. 9, no. 4, pp. 411–432.

32 See Ordway, C. and Opie, H., 2017, 'Integrity and corruption in sport', *Critical issues in global sport management*, Routledge, pp. 38–65.

33 Hill, D., 2008, *The fix: soccer and organized crime*, McClelland and Stewart Limited.

34 *IOC News* 2010, 'Sports movement agrees on unified strategy to tackle irregular betting', 24 June, www.olympic.org/news/sports-movement-agrees-on-unified-strategy-to-tackle-irregular-betting. Chappelet cites evidence for the IOC's proactive stance from 2007: Chappelet, J.L., 2015, 'The Olympic fight against match-fixing', *Sport in Society*, vol. 18, no. 10, pp. 1260–1272.

35 In 2014, historians deciphered an AD 267 contract where a wrestler had agreed to yield for '3,800 drachmas' (approximately the price of a donkey at the time): Rathbone, D.W., '5209. Contract to lose a wrestling match', in Henry, W.B. and Parsons, P.J. (eds.), 2014, *The oxyrhynchus papyri: volume LXXIX*, Egypt Exploration Society, pp. 163–167; Jarus, O., 2014, 'Body slam this! Ancient wrestling match was fixed', *Live Science*, 16 April, www.livescience.com/44867-ancient-wrestling-match-was-fixed.html.

36 E.g. in 1900 Burnley FC offered Nottingham Forest FC a bribe to deliberately lose a so-called dead rubber to ensure Burnley would not be relegated the following season: Inglis, S., 1985, *Soccer in the dock: a history of British football scandals 1900 to 1965*, Willow Books, pp. 8–10. Four women's badminton doubles pairs were expelled from the London 2012 Olympic Games for playing to lose, and thereby secure themselves an easier draw: Zaksaite, S., 2013, 'Match-fixing: the shifting interplay between tactics, disciplinary offence and crime', *The International Sports Law Journal*, vol. 13, no. 3, pp. 287–293.

37 Heron, H. and Jiang, C., 2010, 'The gathering storm – organised crime and sports corruption', *Australian and New Zealand Sports Law Journal*, vol. 5, no. 1, pp. 99–118.

38 See, e.g. Anderson, J., 2012, 'Gambling-led corruption in international sport: an Australian perspective', *International Sports Law Journal*, vol. 1–2, pp. 3–6.

39 See Opie and Lim in this volume.

40 In Australian Rules Football (AFL), for example, some coaches support the process of so-called 'blooding' for young players; rather than play the best players throughout the whole match, they will play young players: see, e.g. Morris, T., 2016, 'Hawthorn coach Alistair Clarkson is successfully blooding young players while challenging for fourth premiership', *Fox Sports*, 11 June, www.foxsports.com.au/afl/hawthorn-coach-alastair-clarkson-is-successfully-blooding-young-players-while-challenging-for-fourth-premiership/news-story/8

abfdd7bec6aee0a67dffd7f80cc304b; Ryan, P., 2015, 'The 10 best wins of Mick Malthouse's coaching career', *AFL*, 1 May, www.afl.com.au/news/2015-05-01/the-10-best-wins-of-mick-malthouses-coaching-career. 'Tanking' in the AFL has also been reviewed by economist Dr Liam Lenten following sanctions against the Melbourne Football Club in 2013: see Lenten, L., 2014, 'AFL draft rule change proposal: rank picks not ladder position', *Australian Financial Review*, 31 July, www.afr.com/opinion/our-writers/afl-draft-rule-change-proposal-rank-picks-order-by-finals-exit-not-ladder-position-20140730-jk6q9. In relation to basketball, the Australian national team was accused of not playing its best team to avoid playing the United States of America in the next round and thereby losing unexpectedly to lesser ranked Angola. For an explanation as to why Australia may have chosen this strategy deliberately, see Prada, M., 2014, 'Why Australia probably tanked against Angola', *SB Nation*, 4 September, www.sbnation.com/nba/2014/9/4/6106015/fiba-world-cup-2014-australia-tank-angola-slovenia.

41 E.g. the New Zealand response at the opening of the ICC World Cup: New Zealand Police 2015, 'Police alert to betting cheats', 14 February, www.police.govt.nz/news/release/police-alert-betting-cheats.

42 In an environment where sponsorships from other products are prohibited, particularly when they are seen to be in conflict with the values of the sport (tobacco and alcohol primarily), and the reduced willingness by Governments to provide financial support for many sports organisations, gambling operators have filled a void. See, e.g. Danson, A., 2010, 'Sponsorship by gambling companies in the UK and Europe: the opportunities and challenges', *Journal of Sponsorship*, vol. 3, no. 2, pp. 194–201.

43 See, e.g. McKelvey, S.M., 2004, 'The growth in marketing alliances between US professional sport and legalised gambling entities: are we putting sport consumers at risk?', *Sport Management Review*, vol. 7, no. 2, pp. 193–210.

44 See, e.g. Walker, D.M. and Barnett, A.H., 1999, 'The social costs of gambling: an economic perspective', *Journal of Gambling Studies*, vol. 15, no. 3, pp. 181–212.

45 Pound, R., 2011, 'Responses to corruption in sport', paper presented at the Play the Game Conference, 3 October, Cologne, Germany, p. 2, www.playthegame.org/fileadmin/image/PTG2011/Presentation/Richard_Pound_2011.pdf; Pielke Jr, R., 2013, 'Does uncertainty of outcome define sport?', *The least thing*, web log post, 19 February, http://leastthing.blogspot.com.au/2013/02/does-uncertainty-of-outcome-define-sport.html. Whether sports consumers care is a separate discussion. See Buraimo, B. and Simmons, R., 2008, 'Do sports fans really value uncertainty of outcome? Evidence from the English Premier League', *International Journal of Sport Finance*, vol. 3, no. 3, pp. 146–155.

46 Including through ignoring the outcome of the event altogether. Major illegal online betting firms will write the winning tickets for organised crime (for a fee), as they are not required to demonstrate that a bet even took place. Buying one dollar for 98 cents is very profitable and risk-free in an anonymous environment.

47 See Australian Associated Press 2015, 'Cairns defence suggests AFP offered deal', *SBS News*, 27 October, www.sbs.com.au/news/article/2015/10/27/cairns-defence-suggests-afp-offered-deal. Cairns was ultimately cleared of the perjury charge: Martin, A., 2015, 'Chris Cairns trial: verdict leaves more questions than answers about match-fixing', *Guardian*, 1 December, www.theguardian.com/sport/2015/nov/30/chris-cairns-verdict-questions-matchfixing.

48 INTERPOL 2015, *Improving awareness and understanding of corruption in football*, p. 1, http://sports.growthlab.cid.harvard.edu/files/icss/files/2013.05_leaflet_integrity_in_sport_enweb.pdf.

49 INTERPOL, *Improving awareness and understanding of match-fixing*, para. 2, www.interpol.int/en/News-and-media/Publications2/Leaflets-and-brochures/Integrity-in-sport-Trifold.
50 Australian Sports Anti-Doping Authority 2013, 'Ministerial statement: organised crime and drugs in sport', 7 February, www.asada.gov.au/news/ministerial-statement-organised-crime-and-drugs-sport.
51 Bricknell, S., 2015, *Corruption in Australian sport*, Trends and issues in crime and criminal justice publication no. 490, Australian Institute of Criminology, Canberra, p. 1.
52 See above n. 10 in relation to funding.
53 See Australian Customs and Border Protection Services 2015, *Annual report 2014–15*, www.border.gov.au/ReportsandPublications/Documents/annual-reports/ACBPS-Annual-report-2014-15.pdf.
54 See, e.g. Boyer, S., 2013, 'Police look at sharing cricket info', *NZ Herald*, 12 December, www.nzherald.co.nz/Sam%20-Boyer/news/article.cfm?a_id=912&objectid=11171027.
55 Inside World Football 2015, 'Aussie police open gateway to more match-fixing data with Sportradar hook-up', 3 May, www.insideworldfootball.com/2015/05/03/aussie-police-open-gateway-to-more-match-fixing-data-with-sportradar-hook-up.
56 See 'Combating criminal infiltration of major sporting events', in Australian Federal Police 2015, *AFP annual report 2014–15*, 16 October, www.afp.gov.au/afp-annual-report-2014-15; Australian Federal Police, *Senate file list – January to June 2013*, www.afp.gov.au/about-us/governance-and-accountability/harradine-report/january-june-2013.
57 See, e.g. 'ICC Cricket World Cup 2015 gives economic boost to Australia and New Zealand' 2015, press release, *International Cricket Council*, 29 June, www.icc-cricket.com/news/181588.
58 In relation to football, as an example, see Asian Football Confederation 2015, 'Asian Cup 2015: no evidence of match-manipulation', web log post, 17 February, www.the-afc.com/asian-cup-2015/asian-cup-2015-no-evidence-of-match-manipulation.
59 See, e.g. the analysis of ASADA in Ordway, C., 2011, 'Doping: review of Australia's national anti-doping agency: part 1', *World Sports Law Report*, vol. 9, no. 6, pp. 2–4. Contemporary policing agencies, e.g.: South Australia Police 2014, *Strategic priorities*, www.police.sa.gov.au/about-us/strategic-priorities; National Crime Agency 2017, *NCA annual plan 2017–18*, p. 6, www.nationalcrimeagency.gov.uk/publications/790-nca-annual-plan-2017-18/file; Garda Inspectorate 2016, *Corporate strategy 2016–2019*, www.gsinsp.ie/en/GSINSP/Garda%20S%C3%ADoch%C3%A1na%20Inspectorate%20Corporate%20Strategy%202016%20-2019.pdf/Files/Garda%20S%C3%ADoch%C3%A1na%20Inspectorate%20Corporate%20Strategy%202016%20-2019.pdf.
60 For the current legislation, see Australian Communications and Media Authority, *Law enforcement (telecommunications)*, www.acma.gov.au/theACMA/law-enforcement-telecommunications.
61 Carson, W.G., 2003, 'Whole of government and crime prevention for Victoria', in *Crime prevention for a safer Victoria: making it work – a consultative symposium*, September, University of Melbourne, pp. 29–30; Goldstein, H., 1990, 'Problem-oriented policing: the basic elements', in *Problem-oriented policing*, McGraw-Hill, pp. 32–49, p. 47: '[p]roblem-oriented policing urges the police to be more aggressive partners with other police agencies'.
62 ICC shared POI lists with Australian and NZ law enforcement: Bayer, K., 2015, 'Match-fixing "sickness" not part of tournament – cricket bosses', *NZ Herald*, 11 February, www.nzherald.co.nz/sport/news/article.cfm?c_id=4&objectid=11400146.

63 See, e.g. the discussion in Hong, F. and Zhouxiang, L., 2013, 'The professionalisation and commercialisation of football in China (1993–2013)', *The International Journal of the History of Sport*, vol. 30, no. 14, pp. 1637–1654.

64 The road to the Olympic stadium in Greece is lined with bronze statues of Zeus hurling thunderbolts like javelins. Called 'Zanes', the statues were purchased by athletes who broke the rules: KU Leuven 2012, *The Zanes*, http://ancientolympics.arts.kuleuven.be/eng/TA008EN.html.

Chapter 11

On the frontline

The role and operations of the Victoria Police Sporting Integrity Intelligence Unit ('SIIU')

Kieran Murnane and James Moller

Introduction: Victoria Police's Sporting Integrity Intelligence Unit

This chapter explains the role and function of the Victoria Police's Sporting Integrity Intelligence Unit ('SIIU') based on the authors' personal experience and recent investigations by the Victoria Police. The SIIU is the only dedicated sporting integrity unit with multi-disciplinary resources embedded in a law enforcement agency anywhere in the world.[1] This chapter begins by detailing the drivers for the establishment of the SIIU, and related governing legislation, and provides an overview of the SIIU's activities. The second part of this chapter examines three key investigations led by the SIIU into match-fixing in soccer, tennis and harness racing. These three case studies of investigations reveal the workings of the SIIU and its approach to match-fixing from the authors' perspectives as members of the SIIU.[2] Finally, the chapter uses the 2015 Asian Football Confederation ('AFC') Asian Cup and International Cricket Council ('ICC') Cricket World Cup as examples of successful deterrent projects involving the SIIU.

Victoria's sporting context and the establishment of the SIIU

Victoria hosts a number of significant national and international sporting events each year with the Victorian Government estimating that these events add over AU$1.8 billion to the Victorian economy annually.[3] Annual tournaments and events attract premium sponsors and are vital for employment and tourism. These events showcase Victoria, and Australia, to a global viewing audience of billions,[4] thus the public has an interest in ensuring the integrity of those events. In late January 2013, Victoria Police was provided with reports from the Office of the Racing Integrity Commissioner ('ORIC') and the Australian Crime Commission, now known as the Australian Criminal Intelligence Commission ('ACIC').[5] The reports highlighted the need for law enforcement agencies to provide a greater focus and commitment to investigating issues and concerns with integrity in the sporting industry due to the risk of infiltration by organised crime and money laundering via gambling markets. Intelligence holdings within Victoria Police at the time supported the recommendations, and with the strong support of then-Deputy Commissioner (now Chief Commissioner) Graham Ashton, the response was exceptionally fast.

On 7 February 2013, the Premier of Victoria informed the State Parliament that the Victoria Police was establishing the SIIU.[6] The SIIU is located within Victoria Police's Intelligence and Covert Support Command and began operations on 11 February 2013.

Objectives and roles of the SIIU

When announcing the establishment of the SIIU, the Premier foreshadowed that the role for the SIIU would be underpinned by planned legislation to outlaw match-fixing. Subsequently, on 24 April 2013, the *Crimes Amendment (Integrity in Sports) Act 2013* (Vic) received Royal Assent. The amendment introduced four offences to the *Crimes Act 1958* (Vic) ('*Crimes Act*') directly related to corrupting the betting outcome of an event or event contingency. The four offences are: engaging in conduct that corrupts or would corrupt a betting outcome of an event or event contingency (*Crimes Act*, s. 195C); facilitating conduct that corrupts or would corrupt a betting outcome of an event or event contingency (*Crimes Act*, s. 195D); concealing conduct, agreement or arrangement that corrupts or would corrupt a betting outcome of an event or event contingency (*Crimes Act*, s. 195E); and use of corrupt conduct information for betting purposes (*Crimes Act*, s. 195F).[7] The legislation focused on a new and emerging crime type more generally referred to as match-fixing. Prior to 2013, the Victoria Police had minimal experience in investigating that type of crime, but the Victoria Police *Blue Paper* had already provided an outline of what would be required to establish this specialist unit.[8] The *Blue Paper* sets out the strategic priorities for Victoria Police towards the year 2025 and recognises that a more sophisticated mix of staff is required by the Police. The Victoria Police 'Capability Plan' progresses key elements of the *Blue Paper*, establishing what the organisation requires to continue to be effective and highlights how it will transform service delivery in order to be an agile, responsive, people-focused and connected organisation.[9]

Due to the complex nature of sporting integrity investigations, the SIIU comprises detectives, a financial analyst, a number of senior and junior intelligence analysts, with oversight and reporting to senior management via the chain of command. This combination provides the SIIU with the ability to manage entire investigations from the initial suspicion through to the final outcome. The early stages of an SIIU investigation can involve the collection and analysis of intelligence gathered from various places including the online environment, combined with the ability to examine betting data and financial records in relation to suspicious transactions.

The SIIU was created with a broad range of objectives within Victoria Police, including preventing corruption in sport and sport-related betting in Victoria. As noted above, sport is an important element of life in Victoria. The SIIU also identifies sources of intelligence, collects information and intelligence from a range of local, national and international sources, and seeks intelligence from sporting participants, data monitoring companies and wagering operators to assist with the identification of potential sport corruption issues. It also conducts intelligence-led investigations and seeks to increase the level of understanding and knowledge of issues that impact on integrity in sport, including by creating and strengthening external stakeholder relationships and networks, providing increased knowledge and awareness to sporting codes and their regulatory bodies on identified integrity issues, and informing policy, law reform or alternative response options to assist with crime prevention.

In keeping with the concerns raised by ORIC and ACIC in 2013 over the threat of penetration of sport by organised crime, the SIIU has a range of responsibilities across various aspects of sport. This broad responsibility also recognises the interconnected nature of organised criminal activities in match-fixing, the supply of performance and image enhancing drugs,[10] combat sports and gambling.[11] Those responsibilities extend to providing advice to the Professional Boxing and Combat Sports Board on the suitability of all new and existing applicants, and preparing, issuing and serving casino and racing exclusion orders, with a focus on disrupting organised criminal networks. The SIIU's work with the Professional Boxing and Combat Sports Board and on casino and racing exclusion orders reflects proactive measures aimed at ensuring organised crime figures are unable to conduct their business at casinos and racecourses across Victoria. The SIIU considers the suitability of new and existing applicants for boxing industry licences. Amendments to the *Professional Boxing and Combat Sports Act 1985* (Vic) expanded the SIIU's role in providing advice and assistance to the Board by conducting various checks to establish if an applicant is a prohibited person, a fit and proper person, and whether it is in the public interest to issue the licence.[12] Furthermore, individuals are automatically prohibited from holding a licence for a number of reasons set out in the legislation related to their status or criminal record.[13]

The SIIU also has oversight of Victoria Police casino and racing exclusion orders. Under these orders, the Chief Commissioner of Police can exclude a person from a casino complex or racing venue, pursuant to the provisions of s. 74(1) of the *Casino Control Act 1991* (Vic) and s. 33(1) of the *Racing Act 1958* (Vic),[14] if he or she considers it necessary in the public interest. The SIIU assesses high-risk individuals and makes recommendations to the Chief Commissioner of Police.

In addition to its domestic roles and objectives, the SIIU is keenly aware that it operates in a global sports betting environment. Sports betting market participants are not subject to geographical borders, making popular sporting events the subject of vast amounts of global gambling. Depending on the wagering operator, the level of regulation in relation to Know Your Customer, Anti-Money Laundering and Counter-Terrorism Financing requirements can also vary dramatically. The SIIU is aware that significant domestic and offshore betting occurs on all major sports occurring in Australia including those managed by the Australian Football League ('AFL'), National Rugby League ('NRL'), Australian Rugby Union ('ARU'), the ICC, Cricket Australia ('CA'), Football Federation Australia ('FFA'), Tennis Australia ('TA') and the National Basketball League ('NBL'). In addition, offshore betting markets have been identified on less traditionally popular sports for gambling in Australia such as volleyball, baseball and ice hockey.

The SIIU has identified that sporting events in Australia will be targeted for manipulation by criminal organisations due to a number of factors, including continued global growth in sports betting markets and technological advancements, such as betting applications ('apps') on smart phones and faster internet speeds making betting almost instantaneous. The proliferation of new wagering operators on the internet, often under-regulated and located in tax havens, also increases risks. The number of bet types available is also increasing, some of which create a risk of spot-fixing within sporting events. Insider trading opportunities also exist. The highly liquid betting activity in both pre-match and live betting markets and extensive bookmaker offerings with high staking limits and anonymity afforded to customers also increases betting activity. Pure financial incentives include the relatively low cost of corrupting participants and the tax-free profits which may be extracted in Australia from sports betting activities. The ability for private shareholders to be involved in the ownership of sports teams potentially creates a conflict of interest between players, officials, owners and other interested parties through the gambling markets as high profits can be made compared to match payments particularly in second-tier sports. Finally, favourable time zones compared to Europe, have led to an increase in gambling in Asia on Australian events, with greater gambling pools providing an increased incentive to fix Australian matches due to the possibility of larger profits.

Another example of the SIIU's role in protecting the integrity of sport was its intervention against an illegal betting market. In early 2016, the SIIU became aware of an unapproved betting exchange being made accessible to Australian customers via a wagering operator licensed by the Norfolk Island Gaming Authority which was confirmed to be an interface for a South-East Asian-based betting exchange. Unapproved offshore bookmakers pose a particular risk to the integrity of Australian sport and racing due to the opaque nature of their operations and the lack of cooperation with domestic integrity units and law enforcement agencies. In Australia, gambling licences are issued and regulated at the state and territory level. Given the seriousness of the exposure of Victorian (and Australian) customers to an unapproved betting exchange, Victoria Police Chief Commissioner Ashton was provided advice, resulting in the Federal Minister for Territories subsequently revoking the Norfolk Island Gaming Authority's power to license wagering operators.[15]

SIIU's policy and relationship roles: reviews, submissions, stakeholders and education

Due to the unique nature of the unit, the SIIU is often consulted on various issues relating to sports betting and integrity and places strategic importance on partnerships. These partnerships are crucial in combating match-fixing as the issue requires input from many stakeholders. No one organisation alone holds all of the intelligence, resources and abilities to conduct a successful investigation, thus collaboration, information sharing and real-time communication between agencies are vital. Sal Perna, the Racing Integrity Commissioner of Victoria, noted that, the '[e]xistence of the unit is evidence that VicPol are accepting the responsibility to address crime associated with sport which is a major international issue.'[16]

The SIIU's confidential submission on behalf of Victoria Police to the Federal Government's 2015 Review into the Impact of Illegal Offshore Wagering is one example of the unit's policy-related activities. The submission outlined the current threats to Australian sport and racing, and opportunities for money laundering by organised crime, and provided a number of recommendations to ensure the online sports betting environment did not expose Australian sport and racing to potential corruption. The SIIU also met with the Independent Review Panel established in 2016 by the governing bodies of tennis. The Panel is reviewing all aspects of the sport's anti-corruption protocols, structures and resources in the wake of significant media attention at the 2016 Australian Open. The SIIU advised the panel of its concerns in relation to match-fixing in tennis and provided some recommendations on how the sport may be able to strengthen its integrity response.

Strategic partnerships are also integral to the unit's functioning and the SIIU engages with a wide variety of domestic and international stakeholders. The SIIU and other members of Victoria Police have provided presentations to, and held workshops with, a number of stakeholders, including The Hong Kong Jockey Club, the 2016 Asian Racing Conference in Mumbai, India, the AFL, CA, TA, Netball Australia, Volleyball Australia, Hockey Australia and Bowls Australia, and at Racing Integrity Investigator forums hosted by the Office of the Racing Integrity Commissioner. In an effort to educate future leaders working in the sporting integrity environment, the SIIU regularly provide lectures to undergraduate and master's-level students at the University of Melbourne, Monash University and La Trobe University. Key stakeholders of the SIIU include sporting associations, universities, other police agencies, betting agencies and regulators.[17] Andrew Godkin, a Sports Integrity Advisor at the Australian Government's National Integrity of Sport Unit described the SIIU's activities in this area as being:

> at the forefront of law enforcement efforts to fight corruption in sport. The SIIU has many successful outcomes to its credit, including landmark prosecutions for match-fixing in Australian sport. The SIIU has also been influential in capacity building, policy development, event response preparation, and stakeholder engagement at national and international levels. These activities have made a substantial contribution to Australia's reputation as a leading nation in the fight to protect the integrity of sport.[18]

The SIIU aims to educate its stakeholders to assist with the prevention and disruption of sports corruption and, where appropriate, investigation of potential offending.

The SIIU's sporting integrity symposium is another initiative of the SIIU which supports its educational objective and has been held annually since the SIIU's establishment in 2013. The symposium is the only event of its type held anywhere in Australia. The symposium creates and strengthens relationships between key stakeholders, with a gathering of senior officials from Australian and international sporting and racing organisations, law enforcement agencies, State and Commonwealth government departments, wagering operators and the university sector. Malcolm Speed commented that the symposium is an 'excellent meeting point for this part of the industry and is achieving recognition as a "must attend" seminar'.[19] Local and international experts are invited from around the world to provide an update on international best practice and trends in sports corruption. Past speakers include world-renowned experts such as then Director of Trading at the Hong Kong Jockey Club Patrick Jay, investigative journalist and author Declan Hill, The Sunday Times and Buzzfeed journalists Jonathan Calvert and Heidi Blake and Singaporean senior correspondent at The New Paper, Zaihan Mohamed Yusof. Themes at the event have included: 'fair game: the corruption and infiltration of sport by organised crime', 'preventing sporting corruption through collaboration' and 'disrupting the corruptors'.

Investigations: case studies

The next section of this chapter highlights the SIIU's investigative work through the examination of three case studies. The case studies highlight the breadth and diversity of the SIIU's sporting coverage, and the complexity of fact patterns, analysis and investigative techniques involved in the enforcement of match-fixing offences.

Operation Starlings: Victorian Premier League

In August 2013, the SIIU commenced its first major investigation into match-fixing in what was then the Victorian Premier League ('VPL'), now a part of the National Premier League. Code-named 'Operation Starlings', detectives from the SIIU and Purana Taskforce[20] investigated the infiltration of the Southern Stars Football Club by members of a global match-fixing syndicate with links to a notorious international match-fixer. The Southern Stars were a football club based out of Kingston Heath in south-east suburban Melbourne and have since been renamed the Dingley Stars Football Club.

This investigation was an international operation involving athletes from the United Kingdom and across Europe, and Malaysian and Singaporean middlemen receiving instructions from the Hungarian-based head of the syndicate. The investigation uncovered the largest known case of match-fixing in Australian sports history.

The initial identification that something was amiss with the Southern Stars came via Sportradar, a supplier of sport and betting-related data. Sportradar provides data to the sports media and betting industry, including fixtures, results, odds compiling and in-running services, as well as statistics and live scores. Sportradar's Integrity Services make use of its Fraud Detection System to provide sports federations and law enforcement agencies with expertise and services in identifying betting-related manipulation across a range of sports.

During 2013, Sportradar identified potential concerns relating to the Southern Stars. Sportradar then monitored and analysed all matches involving the Southern Stars, as well as retrospective analysis of previous matches. Sportradar identified a number of matches with movements in odds with predominantly Asian-based bookmakers whilst matches were underway that could not be explained by the events unfolding on the pitch. These movements suggested that whoever was placing the bets on these matches was particularly confident about how many goals would be scored against the Southern Stars. On some occasions, bets were placed with only minutes remaining in matches when the likelihood of further goals should have been minimal. Sportradar had experience in identifying bets such as these and flagged them as suspicious.

In early August 2013, Sportradar advised FFA of its concerns. The following day FFA contacted Victoria Police and provided the SIIU with reports detailing the suspicions. In one match identified, the SIIU was advised that one of the larger Asian bookmaking operations had taken the trading decision to remove its main market from live betting during the second half of the match. In addition to this, another well-known Asian-based bookmaker had refused to offer a competitive betting market on the match by only offering relatively low odds on a particular outcome. The SIIU was advised that such trading decisions by Asian-based bookmakers are generally only witnessed in matches where there are integrity concerns. On another occasion, it was identified that there was particularly strong confidence by gamblers on the Southern Stars to concede a further goal in a match that had only ten minutes remaining until full-time.

The SIIU was also advised that whilst betting on the VPL was minimal with domestic bookmakers, betting turnover on the league by offshore bookmakers, particularly those based in South-East Asia, was estimated to be in the millions of dollars across the season. Unlike Australian and European bookmakers, Asian-based bookmakers allow customers to continuously place bets meaning there is effectively no limit to the amount that can be wagered.[21] Various betting types were available on Southern Stars matches, including options such as match winner, total number of goals to be scored as well as what is known as 'Asian handicap' betting, a particularly popular bet type across the Asian region. This bet type is used as a way of evening up the two competing teams by giving the underdog a head-start before kick-off. This bet type also eliminates the possibility of the draw, a common result in soccer matches.

On 12 August 2013, Victoria Police commenced a criminal investigation that would last five weeks. The operation was conducted in the same manner as any organised crime investigation and included the use of a number of covert police methodologies. Throughout the investigation police monitored the activities of the players, the head coach and local and international match-fixing syndicate members. The investigation clearly identified the manipulation of Southern Stars matches for betting purposes. Of particular interest was that depending on the betting markets being offered on each match, instructions to the players could vary between winning, losing or drawing in order to maximise the profits that could be achieved. In a number of circumstances, the arrangement was for the Southern Stars to lose by a certain number of goals to take advantage of the offshore 'Asian handicap' markets.

Given that this case was the SIIU's first investigation into match-fixing, it was a significant learning experience and it was surprising for investigators to learn that on at least one occasion players were actually instructed to win the match as the Southern Stars were the underdog and a win would be more lucrative to the match-fixing syndicate than a loss. This scenario occurred on Sunday 18 August 2013 when the Southern Stars were sitting on the bottom of the VPL ladder and were up against the top team, Northcote City. Given their superior skills and experience, the Southern Stars' international players were able to choose to perform and won the match 1–0, with odds of up to 13 to one available on some betting markets. When these two teams had previously met on 25 May 2013, Northcote City had won the match 4–0. Also surprising to investigators was how few spectators were at some matches.

It also became clear to investigators that fixing matches is not foolproof and that matches would not always go to plan, with the Southern Stars not conceding enough goals in a match against Green Gully on 31 August 2013. The syndicate lost a significant amount on unsuccessful bets that had been placed on this match. Interestingly, there were even instructions given to players for this match in relation to when they were to receive yellow and red cards, although these instructions were not always followed either. The players were subsequently punished by the match-fixing syndicate and were not paid what they had been promised, thus providing an incentive for them to follow the syndicate's instructions in future matches. Bonus payments were also often offered to players to encourage their continued involvement in the manipulation of matches but these payments rarely, if ever, seemed to eventuate.

Investigators identified that the match-fixing syndicate had targeted certain positions within the team that would be crucial to manipulating matches. For example, the coach was a key part of the operation; without his assistance, the poor performances of the overseas players would otherwise have resulted in them being dropped from the team, thus restricting the syndicates' ability to manipulate play. Similarly, the goalkeeper was vital to control when bet selections required numerous goals to be scored against the Southern Stars at particular times throughout matches. In some cases, players would be unaware of the specific instructions until just prior to kick-off, depending on when betting markets opened offshore on Southern Stars' matches.

The overseas players had been manipulated into joining the team through the offering of sponsorship support and the suggestion that an opportunity may exist for them to perform well with the potential to be recognised by A-League clubs who may have required their services. Some players were provided with air fares, accommodation, rental cars and signed contracts but were not always aware of what they would be asked to do once they arrived in Australia. Airfares did not always include return flights and match payments were often delayed or not made at all, with players strung along with the promise of salaries and bonuses provided they continued to do as the syndicate asked. The investigators learned that those Australian-based players involved in a number of fixed matches were totally unaware of the manipulation that was occurring. These players questioned why the overseas players could perform at such a high standard at training but could not bring this form to matches, but put it down to them struggling under the pressure of match day.

The final corrupt match identified was played on Friday, 13 September 2013, and on Sunday, 15 September 2013 simultaneous warrants to search for evidence were executed at various properties across Melbourne. Police seized a number of communication devices, computers, documents and receipts relating to financial transactions and arrested a number of players, the coach and one member of the match-fixing syndicate. Partial admissions from some of the arrested parties were then obtained during the interview process. Following the arrests, FFA Chief Executive Officer David Gallop 'welcomed the investigation by the Sporting Integrity Intelligence Unit'.[22]

Throughout the following year, six offenders pleaded guilty to the match-fixing offences. They were fined between AU$1500 and AU$3000 and all were convicted in the Melbourne Magistrates Court. The Malaysian middleman was sentenced to three years' imprisonment, with two years suspended. On release from prison he was deported back to Malaysia. In the time since, one player has been successful in having his conviction overturned. As is often the case in match-fixing investigations, the penalties imposed by the sport's governing bodies were far in excess of those issued by the court. Subsequent to the court proceedings, FFA imposed sanctions. The players and coach were then issued with worldwide lifetime bans by international governing body FIFA, preventing them from taking part in any soccer-related activity ever again.

In May 2014, Victoria Police detectives travelled to Finland to interview a key suspect in the investigation, with enquiries still ongoing. Overall, the investigation attracted global media attention and is often referred to in international media as the blueprint for how to effectively conduct a match-fixing investigation. The learnings and relationships developed by the SIIU from this investigation was the ideal beginning for the Unit, exposing it to one of the more complex match-fixing operations with links around the world. This experience provided the template for how future SIIU investigations into match-fixing in Victoria would be conducted.

Operation Outshouts: tennis

In October 2013, the SIIU received information from the Tennis Integrity Unit ('TIU') (of the International Tennis Federation) and TA and commenced 'Operation Outshouts', an investigation into match-fixing and betting corruption at Futures and Challenger-level tennis tournaments. The suspicious matches were played in Toowoomba, Queensland and Traralgon, Victoria. The investigation highlighted some of the difficulties in relation to investigating and prosecuting match-fixing offences, particularly in a sport such as tennis where athletes are constantly travelling both domestically and internationally.

The player involved was an Australian who never achieved top 150 player status and who had earned limited prize money over his career. The player was believed to have indirectly approached his opponent, an unranked Australian player, and offered to 'tank' (deliberately lose) the match in exchange for money. The offer was declined and the opponent proceeded to win the match in straight sets.

The betting patterns on the match caused suspicion due to a number of gamblers who were either new or inactive suddenly placing wagers for the short-priced favourite to lose the match in straight sets. The betting plunge on such a minor tournament caused one wagering operator to suspend betting on the match. The bookmakers suspected that the gamblers were privy to inside information based on the amounts they were attempting to wager, and on the previous betting activity of one customer in particular.

The operation was a success with the key associate to the player involved being charged with using corrupt conduct information for betting purposes, and convicted and fined AU$3500 in Victoria in December 2014. Due to cross-jurisdictional legal issues, the Victorian investigation was forwarded to New South Wales Police investigators who interviewed and charged the player involved.

The player pleaded guilty in Burwood Local Court, New South Wales and was fined AU$1000 and given a community service order for 150 hours. Once the criminal investigation was complete, the TIU were then in a position to take further action under the Tennis Anti-Corruption Program, banning the player for seven years and issuing him with a US$35,000 fine.[23] The TIU acknowledged the work of the SIIU, stating that they had, 'worked closely with Australian law enforcement agencies on the case'.[24]

Operation Lumberjacks: regional harness racing

In March 2014, the SIIU commenced the successful 'Operation Lumberjacks', an investigation into harness race-fixing in the Mildura region of Victoria. This investigation was the first successful prosecution in any form of racing throughout Australia for such offending under the new match-fixing offences enacted in various Australian States and Territories.

The SIIU worked closely with both Harness Racing Victoria ('HRV') and ORIC throughout the investigation. The operation uncovered collusion between a father and son team who were manipulating the outcome of races and passing this information on to a betting syndicate which would place wagers on their behalf. Manipulation included not just the race winner, but on one occasion went so far as to successfully orchestrate a trifecta (first, second and third place in the race, in the correct order) in the fifth race at Mildura on 12 November 2014. Once again, a number of investigative techniques were used to gather significant evidence to support criminal convictions, with community corrections orders issued to both men for a combined total of 500 hours.

Comments from the Magistrate and industry highlight the importance of the investigation. His Honour Magistrate Lethbridge noted, for example:

> a hundred dollar bet it really isn't here nor there it's the effect that it has on the whole industry ... how it threatens the whole industry if the public believed that it's corrupt, the public won't support it, that threatens the whole industry that hundreds if not thousands of people rely on for their livelihoods.[25]

Moreover, the HRV's Racing Appeals and Disciplinary Board said:

> conduct which had the significant potential to adversely affect the financial viability of the Harness Racing Industry in general, and therefore, that of all the countless people who are engaged in that industry in some way or another and who in part or wholly depend upon for their livelihoods. Consequently, there is an obvious and compelling necessity to deter all persons from engaging in such conduct or similar.[26]

Following the criminal convictions, HRV imposed significant disciplinary penalties for breach of the rules of racing.[27] Both parties involved were disqualified from having any involvement in the harness racing industry for a period of 12 years.[28] The HRV Board found that:

> the corrupt act of race fixing is one of the most serious offences that can be committed by participants involved in the harness racing industry and that any person found guilty of committing such offences should be disqualified for an extended period.[29]

In a media release following the convictions, HRV highlighted the success of the investigation stating:

> HRV particularly wish to acknowledge the significant efforts and dedication of the Sporting Integrity Intelligence Unit in investigating this complex matter.... HRV Stewards look forward to continuing their strong working relationship with the Victorian Police Sporting Integrity Intelligence Unit who lead the law enforcement response to matters of race fixing in sport.[30]

With confidence returning to harness racing in the region, a number of positive flow-on effects to the community have since been observed. Unexpected benefits have varied from an anticipated increase in interest in future horse auctions that have previously had minimal sales, to local stock-feed stores reporting increases in turnover due to trainers and owners returning to the industry. Increases in betting turnover have also been identified, suggesting gamblers have more confidence in the integrity of races in the area.

Deterrence: AFC Asian Cup and ICC Cricket World Cup

Between January and March 2015, in addition to Victoria playing host to the Australian Open Tennis Grand Slam event, Formula 1 Australian Grand Prix and Cricket Australia Big Bash League and One Day International cricket matches, Australia had also won the rights to two marquee back-to-back tournaments – the AFC Asian Cup and ICC Cricket World Cup, with a number of matches to be played in Melbourne. Soccer and cricket are the two sports that attract the highest volume of betting across global gambling markets, and international tournaments are subject to even greater turnover. The SIIU received intelligence from Sportradar projecting over AU$90 million in turnover per match on the AFC Asian Cup and total turnover on the tournament of close to AU$3 billion. The ICC Cricket World Cup was predicted to have an average of approximately AU$85 million in turnover per match, and over AU$4 billion across the tournament. Due to the quality of players and the nations competing in addition to a favourable time zone, 90 per cent of this turnover was expected to occur in Asian gambling markets. Irrespective of whether these funds were legitimate or not, the sheer size of these markets and the returns that could be achieved would provide organised crime not only with opportunities for money laundering, but also with a significant incentive to attempt to fix matches.

The Australian Federal Police ('AFP') hosted a number of workshops gathering state and territory law enforcement agencies, FFA, the Asian Football Confederation, CA, the ICC, Sportradar, the Australian Sports Anti-Doping Authority ('ASADA'), the National Integrity of Sport Unit ('NISU') and the Department of Immigration and Border Protection to collaborate on the most appropriate integrity action plans in preparation for these tournaments. Various scenarios were outlined to discuss potential law enforcement response options to any integrity concerns that might eventuate, with a focus on prevention, disruption and deterrence. The SIIU was frequently called on during these workshops due to the specialist experience members had in intelligence gathering and investigating sporting corruption offences. In addition, the SIIU liaised with the Crime Stoppers network on behalf of the AFP and State and Territory law enforcement agencies to produce 'match-fixing is a crime' posters. These were placed in team hotels and changing rooms to highlight, particularly to overseas players who may not have been aware, that match-fixing was a criminal offence in Australia.

Both tournaments were a resounding success and the effective implementation of the action plans was considered to be a blueprint for future sporting events and sports governing bodies. The AFC and ICC commented positively on the work of Australian law enforcement bodies. The AFC General Secretary Dato' Alex Soosay commented, for example:

> It is extremely encouraging to see that the detailed integrity planning and collaboration for our premier tournament, the AFC Asian Cup, was a success. This would not have been possible without the support and focused efforts of each stakeholder and in particular Australian law enforcement and Sportradar, who worked hand-in-hand with AFC's Integrity Unit throughout the tournament.[31]

Furthermore, David Richardson, Chief Executive Officer of the International Cricket Council, noted that 'on the corruption side, it's safe to say we're the best prepared we've ever been. Our Anti-Corruption personnel have done a lot of work ... with the local police and law enforcement agencies in both New Zealand and Australia'.[32] These comments from key stakeholders evidence the importance of planning, communication and collaboration with law enforcement in protecting the integrity of major sporting events.

Conclusion: future direction for the SIIU

The SIIU continues to increase its knowledge of corruption in sport, with the global sports betting environment ever changing. Those seeking to manipulate events are finding new ways to conceal their attempts to profit from fixed matches. The SIIU continues to receive valuable intelligence in relation to match-fixing from its extensive network of stakeholders, and regularly meets with sporting codes in Australia to educate them on how they can strengthen and protect themselves against this threat. Since the establishment of the SIIU, other law enforcement agencies across Australia and the globe have gradually been directing more resources toward investigating match-fixing. Given the global nature of sport and sports betting, and the complexities involved in investigating sports corruption offences, dedicated law enforcement units are vital to successfully deterring offences and protecting sport from this type of corruption.

Notes

1 Based on the best knowledge of the Victoria Police at the time of writing.
2 Since the release of the Australian Criminal Intelligence Commission's (formerly the Australian Crime Commission) report in 2013 on organised crime and drugs in sport, the SIIU has also been involved in a number of drug-related investigations and conducted intelligence probes into the supply of steroids in Victoria. See Australian Crime Commission, *Organised crime and drugs in sport: new generation performance and image enhancing drugs and organised criminal involvement in their use in professional sport*, February, www.medsafe.govt.nz/consultations/acc-pieds.pdf.
3 State Government of Victoria 2016, 'Major sport events', *Health and Human Services*, web log post, 4 July, http://sport.vic.gov.au/about-sport-in-victoria/major-sport-events.
4 See, e.g. Local Organising Committee 2015, 'Asian Cup smashes audience numbers', *Football Federation Australia*, web log post, 30 January, www.footballaustralia.com.au/article/asian-cup-smashes-audience-numbers/pp.1ebmxdio 8k1gibyf93a54dx.
5 Australian Crime Commission, above n. 2.
6 Parliament of Victoria 2013, *Parliamentary debates: Legislative Assembly*, 7 February, pp. 239–240.
7 See Opie and Lim in this volume.
8 Victoria Police 2014, *A vision for Victoria Police in 2025*, 2 June, www.police.vic.gov.au/content.asp?Document_ID=42063 ('*Blue Paper*').
9 Victoria Police 2016, *Victoria Police Capability Plan 2016–2025*, 6 October, www.police.vic.gov.au/content.asp?Document_ID=48.
10 Australian Crime Commission, above n. 2.
11 For example, an athlete who has been supplied with performance enhancing drugs or has accumulated gambling debts through criminal groups is at increased risk of being pressured to fix matches.
12 *Professional Boxing and Combat Sports Act 1985* (Vic), s. 6A.
13 Ibid.
14 In making such orders, there is a tension between according the subject person procedural fairness on the one hand and not disclosing sensitive criminal intelligence on the other. In a challenge to an exclusion order brought by a prominent former jockey with a criminal and racing disciplinary record as well as a propensity to violent and intimidating behaviour, the Victorian Supreme Court of Appeal decided that the Chief Commissioner had acted properly in not making disclosure: *Chief Commissioner of Police* v. *Nikolic* [2016] VSCA 248. The High Court in Canberra has since rejected Nikolic's application for special leave to appeal and awarded costs to the respondent, Victoria Police's Chief Commissioner.
15 See Senator the Hon Fiona Nash 2016, *Norfolk Island Gaming Authority report and action*, 7 November, http://minister.infrastructure.gov.au/nash/releases/2016/November/fn086_2016.aspx.
16 Cited with permission.
17 For example, the AFC, the ACIC, the AFP, the AFL, the ARU, the ASADA, the Australian Sports Commission, the Australian Taxation Office, the Australian Transaction Reports and Analysis Centre, Basketball Australia, CA, Crime Stoppers, Crown Melbourne Ltd, the Department of Immigration and Border Protection, Europol, FFA, Genius Sports, Global Sports Integrity, Greyhound Racing Victoria, HRV, the Hong Kong Jockey Club, the ICC, INTERPOL, the NISU, Netball Australia, the New Zealand Police, ORIC, Racing Victoria

Limited, the Royal Society for the Prevention of Cruelty to Animals Victoria, Sport and Recreation Victoria, Sportradar, state and territory law enforcement agencies, TA, the TIU, the United Kingdom Gambling Commission, Victorian universities, the Victorian Commission for Gambling and Liquor Regulation, wagering operators and World Rugby.

18 Cited with permission.

19 Speed is the former CEO of the International Cricket Council and current Executive Director of The Coalition of Major Professional and Participation Sports. Cited with permission.

20 The Purana Taskforce was formed in 2003 to investigate an infamous period in Victoria's history commonly known as 'The Gangland Killings'. Early success was followed by a second phase of operations which resulted in the dismantling of an organised crime enterprise known as 'The Company'. The Purana Taskforce entered its third and fourth phase of operations, conducting targeted investigations to disrupt, disable and dismantle organised crime enterprises or networks predominantly involved in major fraud, money laundering, tax evasion, extortion, murder, drug manufacture, trafficking and importation.

21 Asian-based bookmakers adopt a model of balancing their books by accepting wagers on all possible outcomes of the event (and hedging with other bookmakers), thus profiting from a commission built into the odds on offer. In contrast to this model, traditional European bookmakers take a position on the event and are therefore exposed, dependent on the result. Due to the balanced books style of bookmaking, and because Asian gambling pools are much larger than European and Australian pools, Asian-based bookmakers are essentially able to accept an unlimited number of wagers from their customers as their model relies on turnover rather than the result, limiting their exposure to excessive payouts, even where a match has been fixed: Forrest, D. and McHale, I., 2015, 'An evaluation of Sportradar's fraud detection system', University of Liverpool and University of Salford: Manchester, September, pp. 14, 29.

22 McKenzie, N., Bucci, N. and Baker, R., 2013, 'Victorian detectives bust alleged soccer match-fixing syndicate', *The Age*, 15 September, www.theage.com.au/sport/soccer/victorian-detectives-bust-alleged-soccer-matchfixing-syndicate-20130915-2tsh5.html.

23 *Tennis Integrity Unit* 2017, 'Nick Lindahl, Brandon Walkin and Isaac Frost sanctioned for tennis corruption offences', 9 January, www.tennisintegrityunit.com/media-releases/nick-lindahl-brandon-walkin-and-isaac-frost-sanctioned-tennis-corruption-offences.

24 *Tennis Integrity Unit* 2016, 'Tennis integrity unit briefing note April 2016', 22 April, www.tennisintegrityunit.com/media-releases/tennis-integrity-unit-briefing-note-april-2016.

25 Unreported hearing, 3 September 2015, Melbourne Magistrates' Court.

26 *Shayne Cramp and Gregory Cramp and Harness Racing Victoria Board* (23 February 2016), Racing Appeals and Disciplinary Board, p. 12, www.harness.org.au/userfiles/34/Cramp%20Shayne%20and%20Greg%20RAD%20Board%20hearing%2023%20Feb%2016.pdf.

27 Harness Racing Australia, *Australian Harness Racing Rules* (at 21 October 2016), r. 267(1).

28 Harness Racing Victoria 2015, 'Shayne and Greg Cramp disqualified for 12 years', *Australian Harness Racing*, 30 October, www.harness.org.au/news-article.cfm?news_id=27972. This decision on penalty was appealed to, but confirmed by the Racing Appeals and Disciplinary Board in *Cramp and Harness Racing Victoria Board* (unreported, Racing Appeals and Disciplinary Board, Collis (Chairman), Osborne and Denahy (Members), 26 February 2016), www.

harness.org.au/userfiles/34/Cramp%20Shayne%20and%20Greg%20RAD%20Board%20hearing%2023%20Feb%2016.pdf. A further appeal on penalty to the Victorian Civil and Administrative Tribunal was heard on 6 February 2017. See Harness Racing Victoria 2017, 'VCAT review – Shayne and Greg Cramp', *Australian Harness Racing*, 7 February, www.harness.org.au/news-article.cfm?news_id=32437.

29 Harness Racing Victoria 2015, 'Shayne and Greg Cramp disqualified for 12 years', *Australian Harness Racing*, 30 October, www.harness.org.au/news-article.cfm?news_id=27972.

30 Ibid.

31 Asian Football Confederation 2015, 'AFC Asian Cup Australia 2015 Integrity Action Plan successfully implemented', 17 February, www.the-afc.com/media-releases/afc-asian-cup-australia-2015-integrity-action-plan-successfully-implemented.

32 *ICC Cricket World Cup 2015* 2015, 'David Richardson says ICC Cricket World Cup 2015 will be "bigger and better" than ever', 20 January, www.icc-cricket.com/cricket-world-cup/news/2015/media-releases/84619/david-richardson-says-icc-cricket-world-cup-2015-will-be-bigger-and-better-than-ever.

Chapter 12

Match-fixing and the roles of public prosecutors in Korea

Stacey Steele, Jess (Hee Sung) Shin and Sarah (Jin Hyung) Yang

Introduction: distinctive features of Korea's prosecutorial system

This chapter analyses the roles of Korean public prosecutors in investigating and prosecuting match-fixing offences in Korea. It provides further political, institutional and cultural context for other chapters in this volume and highlights different and similar approaches to investigative and law enforcement methods.[1] The chapter draws on English and Korean-language literature, a published court judgment and anecdotal evidence to provide insights into practices in Korea. It is important to highlight these differences and similarities to help avoid misunderstandings amongst enforcement agencies, especially when they are working with each other on cross-border cases, and reformers arguing in favour of harmonisation of investigative, prosecutorial and legislative practices in this nascent area of criminalised activity. Much has been written on recent match-fixing scandals in Korea, but there is little consideration in English about how cases are investigated and prosecuted. As the United Nations Office on Drugs and Crime noted recently, 'the investigation of match-fixing is a relatively new field without strongly established norms, methods or protocols' and suggestions from multiple jurisdictions may be 'adopted and adapted to fit the specific circumstances of interested law enforcement agencies'.[2] A recent partnership development meeting held by INTERPOL and the International Olympic Committee in Korea to promote cooperation on integrity in sport also emphasised the need to deepen understanding across jurisdictions.[3]

The Korean criminal justice system is historically based on the structure of the German criminal justice system with contemporary influences from jurisdictions such as Japan and the United States of America, as well as indigenous characteristics.[4] In 1948, Korea adopted the basic structure for its current criminal justice system and promulgated the *Kumchalchungbub* [Public Prosecutors' Office Act] (act no. 81, 1949 (Republic of Korea)). The criminal justice system may be divided into four main institutions:

courts, the public prosecutors' office, the police and special investigation agency (*ttulbyel susakwan*), and correctional institutions.[5] In practice, police may provide significant investigative assistance in certain cases, but criminal investigations and prosecutions are formally driven by the direction and discretion of a prosecutor who may be the investigator, director of the police investigation and public prosecutor.[6]

The Korean criminal justice system is also characterised by an extremely high level of confessions and convictions, and robust prosecutorial detention powers.[7] Moreover, Korea's legal education system produces an elite cadre of highly trained prosecutor-litigators who typically learn their investigative techniques on-the-job. Another distinctive feature of the Korean prosecutorial system is an individual prosecutor's heavy caseload, with individual prosecutors often being responsible for hundreds of cases at any one time.[8] These resource constraints were formally recognised recently with the *Gumsajungwonbub* [Prosecutors' Quota Act] (act no. 12952, 2014 (Republic of Korea)) being amended to provide for a gradual increase in prosecutorial numbers.[9] There were 2121 prosecutors in 2016. The increased quota means that there will be 2292 prosecutors in 2019.[10] The increase is designed to give prosecutors more resources to combat business corruption, sex offences, and domestic and school violence in regional areas.[11]

After this introduction, the chapter begins by analysing the Korean prosecutorial system and its institutional structure. Second, the chapter examines the context of sport and prosecutions in Korea, and the legal education system which produces Korea's elite prosecutors.[12] The focus of this chapter is the broader social, historical and economic contexts of prosecutions, rather than the drivers for match-fixing which are analysed by others in this volume.[13] Traditionally, and in line with some other jurisdictions with civil law traditions, prosecutors in Korea trained with the judiciary after passing highly competitive entrance examinations.[14] Ultimately, a prosecutor may even serve on the Supreme Court of Korea, the highest court in Korea.[15] Recent reforms to Korean legal education have not changed the elite nature of the prosecutorial service.

The chapter then uses a case study from volleyball and baseball in Korea to highlight the key role that prosecutors play, and the methods that they use, to investigate and prosecute match-fixing cases. The case was chosen because it was high profile and occurred during the height of tensions surrounding the scandals between 2011 and 2013 which led to reforms in Korea. The case is also generally illustrative of the prevalence of brokers and senior players in match-fixing in Korea. As Park's analysis of this and other cases in this volume suggests, however, not all investigations and prosecutions will follow the same trajectory or focus on the same issues. The findings in Park and Chung, Jun and Kim in this volume also suggest that there is variation amongst sports when it comes to match-fixing in

Korea's domestic context. The only known match-fixing case in Korean professional basketball, for example, involved the coach and not the players.[16] Finally, the chapter identifies the reliance on whistle-blowers and retrospective investigations as a potential limitation of existing methods used in Korea and suggests that a more active approach involving other stakeholders, such as SportsToto, sporting associations and governing bodies, would better help to detect and prevent match-fixing conduct, in addition to other recent legislative and practical reforms introduced in the aftermath of match-fixing scandals in 2011–13.

The Korean prosecutorial system

The United Nations' *Resource Guide on Good Practices in the Investigation of Match-Fixing* recommends that investigation and prosecution should be conducted by separate bodies to ensure proper administration of justice.[17] The guide highlights different roles and motives for investigators and prosecutors:

> The role of an investigator in a match-fixing allegation is to concentrate on discovering the facts relevant to that allegation and whether they believe they can prove a charge against a suspect or not. The role of the prosecutor is to assess both the strengths and weaknesses of the case and make an informed decision on whether to bring charges with regard to an offence.[18]

Whilst acknowledging different jurisdictional approaches, an underlying assumption in the Guide is that 'investigators from law enforcement agencies' are the principal personnel investigating allegations of match-fixing and operate separate to 'prosecutors, the judiciary, policy-makers and legislators'.[19] The Guide goes on to recommend that investigators and prosecutors should cooperate and communicate regularly and at an early stage.[20]

The Korean investigatory and prosecutorial systems do not align well with the Guide's assumptions in relation to investigation and prosecution, because of the key role that prosecutors play in both of these processes in Korea. The demarcation between investigation and prosecution is a question of degree in any jurisdiction, but the conflation of these activities in Korea is institutionalised and legislatively mandated.[21] Commentators argue that historically the police operated as a government organisation for keeping public order and peace rather than being involved in criminal investigations.[22] The high degree of prosecutorial influence is not without critics in Korea.[23] Moreover, restraints which apply to police are not equally applicable to prosecutors, and prosecutorial interview practices, for example, have been questioned.[24] Prosecutors and police are also administratively separate, with the police being a national organisation within the Ministry of Internal Affairs.[25] The Public Prosecutors' Office is an affiliate of the Ministry of Justice which is an executive branch of the government.[26] In contemporary practice, judicial police officers (*sabup kyungchel*) perform investigative roles, but are still required to seek instructions and comply with a prosecutor's orders.[27]

The Korean Public Prosecutors' Office consists of the Supreme Prosecutors' Office, the High Prosecutors' Offices, and the District Prosecutors' Offices each corresponding to a court within the same geographical jurisdiction.[28] The Supreme Prosecutors' Office, located in Seoul, is headed by the Prosecutor General.[29] The Prosecutor General is in charge of the affairs of the Supreme Prosecutors' Office, and is vested with the responsibility to 'exercise the overall control over prosecutor affairs, and direct and supervise the public officials in prosecutors' offices'.[30] Structurally, the Public Prosecutors' Office is highly centralised and facilitates a uniform system, similarly to the institutional context for prosecutorial institutions in Japan.[31] Individual prosecutors, however, typically only act within their local jurisdictional reach within Korea. The centralisation and uniformity in structure reflects Korea's unitary national government and has advantages. The central government and Supreme Prosecutors' Office do not have to deal with constitutional and jurisdictional impediments arising out of a federal framework such as Australia's, as highlighted by Opie and Lim in this volume. This top-down, centralised system enabled the Korean government to respond after scandals in 2011–13 with amendments to the *Kukmin chaeyuk jinhungbub* [National Sports Promotion Act] (act no. 8344, 2007 (Republic of Korea)) ('*National Sports Promotion Act*'), for example.

Uniformity and consistency are also enforced in the Korean prosecutorial system by the so-called Principle of Uniformity (*gumsadoilchal wonchik*). The Principle requires prosecutors to 'obey the prosecutors in higher office in prosecutorial affairs'[32] and is designed to ensure the uniformity and fairness of prosecutorial authority.[33] The already hierarchical nature of Korean society is embodied by this principle and codified in law for prosecutors.[34] In practice, uniformity is also underpinned by close ties amongst the career prosecutors developed during their legal education, training and work rotations. Prosecutors control how key investigations are run and direct police who assist the prosecutors.[35] Whilst the involvement of prosecutors in any investigatory process may be a question of degree, Korea clearly evidences a prosecutorial function which is much more involved in the investigatory stages of match-fixing than the Guide anticipates, reflecting its historical development and civil law tradition.[36] Accordingly, consideration of the roles of prosecutors is particularly important when thinking about preventing, investigating and prosecuting match-fixing in Korea.

Contexts for sporting investigations and prosecutions in Korea

Rapid economic development and well-connected institutions

The development, understanding, funding and regulation of sport in any jurisdiction are inextricably linked to its contemporary history, and local political, economic, cultural and social experiences and traditions, in addition to other factors such as international influences.[37] Korea's contemporary national experience has been tumultuous. As Hyug Baeg Im, a professor at Korea University, concludes, Korea has:

> compressed the multiple stages of industrialisation and democratization into a few turbulent decades of national division, the ruins of war, the repression of military dictatorship, and the constraints of a massive military standoff between the opposing states on the peninsula.[38]

These contexts also provide a lens for understanding the environment in which prosecutors work in Korea, including in relation to the investigation and prosecution of match-fixing cases.

Hong convincingly argues that Korean elite sport has been nurtured through its links to projects fostering nation-building and national identity, and has a special relationship with Korea's military and big business, including *chaebols*[39] such as Samsung and Hyundai, as well as historically being used to legitimise dictatorial political leadership.[40] Hong is an academic and board member of the Korean Football Association, as well as being a former Asian Football Confederation referee (2014–15) having refereed women's soccer at the Olympics (London and Beijing).[41] She concludes that 'the Korean sport community was not formed organically with people who have similar beliefs and values, but on the contrary was manufactured'.[42] Moreover, funding for sports in Korea is guaranteed through the *Kukmin chaeyuk jinhungbub* [National Sports Promotion Act] (act no. 8344, 2007) which established the Korea Sports Promotion Fund (*National Sports Promotion Act*, art. 19). The Fund promotes and supports the development of the Korean sports industry and sports infrastructure.[43] Together with private sponsorship and ownership by leading Korean businesses, the Korean sporting industry enjoys special financial and social standing, at least at the elite levels.[44] Connections with the military also help to facilitate elite sport in Korean society.[45] Male athletes are required to serve in the Korean military for a designated time, but there are special exemptions and some athletes may attend elite sporting facilities administered by the armed forces.[46] Male Korean prosecutors are also required to serve in the Korean military, although they may be given special assignments reflecting their particular skills.

Some commentators argue that Korean prosecutors may be pressured to not investigate or to cease investigating cases due to pressure from more senior prosecutors who are in turn pressured by the ruling political party.[47] The independence of prosecutors in relation to high-profile and politically related cases was called into question recently by political scandals involving the former President Park Geun Hye. On 16 March 2017, 88 Daejeon community organisations protested in front of the Daejeon Prosecutor's Office calling for the prosecution of Park Geun Hye and her alleged accomplices in relation to allegations of bribery, extortion and abuse of office.[48] These community organisations believe that true prosecutorial independence will be evidenced by prosecuting Park Geun Hye. On 20 March 2017, prosecutors called Park Geun Hye to their Office and questioned her to establish whether there was sufficient ground to ask a court to issue a warrant for her arrest.[49] According to one media report, prosecutors cannot properly execute on law and order because of the connections between politicians and the prosecutors' office.[50] Candle-light vigils were commenced for the prompt prosecution and punishment of Park Geun Hye.[51] It's not clear what effect this public pressure had on prosecutors, if any, but the former President was arrested on 31 March 2017, and the case at least suggests the potential for public pressure to be brought to bear on prosecutors, especially in high profile cases.

Intense scholastic competition to become a prosecutor

Prosecutors in Korea are part of an elite and well-educated fraternity and are the product of intensive educational competition. A person who is qualified as an attorney-at-law may become a prosecutor.[52] The majority of current prosecutors were educated under the old legal education system prior to reforms in 2009.[53] These prosecutors were required to pass the notoriously competitive Korean National Bar Examination. The pass-rate for the examination in 2006 was less than 1 per cent.[54] After passing the examination, candidates traditionally trained at the Judicial Research and Training Institute for 24 months with other prospective prosecutors, judges and lawyers.[55] A law degree was not required to sit the examination, although most examination candidates studied law as undergraduates at university as well as so-called cram schools.[56] After sitting a final examination to graduate from the Institute, a prosecutor began her or his career as a prosecutor.[57] This undergraduate model of legal education was severely criticised for placing too much pressure on high school students to enter a highly ranked undergraduate law degree requiring too much focus on memorising answers. Similarly, the rote-learning required to pass the National Bar Examination was criticised as unconducive to a genuine legal education.[58] In 2017, the last candidates under the old system who graduated from the Institute and became prosecutors totalled 25 out of 234 candidates at the Institute.[59]

The Korean legal education system was transformed in 2009 with the staged abolition of undergraduate LLB degrees and the National Bar Examination, and the introduction of a postgraduate juris doctor law degree, an English test and Lawyer Admission Test (*bubmubu byunhosa shihum*).[60] Today, prosecutors must have graduated from an undergraduate degree other than law, passed the competitive entrance examinations for one of the government-accredited 25 law schools, graduated from the law school, passed the Lawyer Admission Test and successfully navigated independent written tests and interviews conducted by the Supreme Prosecutors' Office. The Lawyer Admission Test was designed to cover practical legal knowledge and examine application of legal principles, rather than doctrinal or philosophical legal knowledge which was assessed under the previous National Bar Examination.[61] The pass rate for the Lawyer Admission Test for 2016 was 55.2 per cent (1581 successful candidates out of 2864).[62] After passing the Lawyer Admission Test, candidates no longer attend the Institute, but are required to undertake six months' practical legal training at a law firm, court or prosecutors' office. Undertaking practical legal training at a prosecutors' office does not guarantee that a candidate will be entitled to become a prosecutor. Prosecutors are typically recruited from candidates who graduated from an elite Korean university and performed well in subjects related to prosecution practice.[63] Accordingly, prosecutors remain a highly trained and specialised legal elite in Korea.[64] Law school in Korea is also still viewed as a way of becoming financially prosperous and successful in society.[65] Lee argues that the new postgraduate model has enhanced this elitist perception of lawyers, prosecutors and judges.[66]

The consequences of this educational system for the investigation and prosecution of match-fixing cases in Korea include the focus on criminal procedure and legal aspects of investigations. Prosecutors are highly legally trained, and it appears that to date they have not relied on outside experts for further technical expertise in relation to match-fixing. They are also career prosecutors who may not specialise in any one area and are transferred regularly throughout Korea.[67] Despite allocation of resources across various focused administrative departments, the current prosecutorial system makes it difficult to develop expertise in investigative methods associated with criminal cases relating to sport, betting or match-fixing, or develop deep geographical focus and local expertise.[68]

Korean prosecutorial investigative methods: a case study

This section of the chapter examines Korean prosecutorial investigative methods by using a high-profile case study prosecuted in the Daegu District Court relating to match-fixing in volleyball and baseball in 2012.[69] Daegu is a regional city of approximately 2.5 million people located in southern Korea. In 2012, 15 former and active male and female volleyball players were found to have been involved in fixing matches in the 2009–11 seasons. Five brokers and one financier were investigated for charges of paying players to make deliberate mistakes in games. One of the brokers involved in fixing volleyball matches ('Broker B') also approached a former baseball player ('Former Player J') to fix professional baseball matches.[70] The publicly available information, including the court judgment and a report published on the website of the Daegu District Prosecutors' Office,[71] evidences the methods used to investigate and prosecute match-fixing at the time in Korea. Information from a broker arising out of an investigation into volleyball-related match-fixing led to an investigation into alleged match-fixing in the baseball code.[72] Both the volleyball and baseball cases were heard together and resulted in a single judgment involving numerous defendants.

Summary of facts of the case

The facts of the volleyball case as set out by the District Court in its judgment are as follows.[73] It is instructive to set out the complicated factual scenario to demonstrate the detail of the information presented by prosecutors to the Court. The facts also demonstrate the involvement of brokers and former players as also highlighted by Park and Yeun in this volume. In mid-February 2010, a broker ('Broker E') approached two former players ('Former Player A' and 'Former Player C') from a volleyball team ('KEPCO45') with an arrangement to provide money in exchange for KEPCO45 losing a particular game in the 2009–10 volleyball season.[74] Former Players A and C agreed and used their influence to convince a current KEPCO45 player ('Player D') to deliberately aim the volleyball out of court, receive or hit it incorrectly, or deliberately spike the ball so it would be blocked. They succeeded in fixing the match on 13 February 2010, which KEPCO45 lost to Sang Moo Shin Hyup (0:3).[75] Former Player A and Former Player C each received KR₩10 million in total from Broker E for the successful fixing which they split with Player D. Also in February 2010, another broker ('Broker F') approached Former Players A and C to fix a game in return for KR₩10 million. Former Players A and C convinced Player D to participate once more. Former Player A, Former Player C and Player D fixed the game between KEPCO45 and Sang Moo Shin Hyup on 23 February 2010 so that KEPCO45 would lose to Sang Moo Shin Hyup (1:3).[76] Former Player A, Former Player C and Player D split KR₩10 million between them.

Around this time, Former Player A telephoned a third individual ('Insider AH') to inform him that he would fix a match and demand a proportion of any betting money that Insider AH may win from his tip off. Insider AH bet KR₩10 million on the match occurring on 23 February

2010 via SportsToto and transferred KR₩5 million from the winnings into his personal bank account. Insider AH then met at Former Player A's accommodation and gave Former Player A his bank card which Former Player A used to withdraw the KR₩5 million from the account.[77]

In early March 2010, Broker F paid Former Player A, Former Player C and Player D KR₩15 million to fix another volleyball match between KEPCO45 and Sang Moo Shin Hyup on 9 March 2010. Former Player A, Former Player C and Player D received a further KR₩15 million from Broker F to fix another match on 4 March 2010. Former Player A called Insider AH to tip him off regarding the 4 March match-fixing. Broker B provided money to Insider AH to allow Insider AH to bet KR₩50 million on the match via SportsToto. From the winnings, Insider AH transferred KR₩5 million into his personal bank account and Former Player A, already in possession of the account card, withdrew the cash. On 12 and 27 March 2010, at the request of Broker F, Former Player A, Former Player C and Player D fixed another two matches in exchange for KR₩10 million per match. Former Player A called Insider AH once again to tip him off and, financed by Broker B, Insider AH bet KR₩50 million on each match via SportsToto. From each of the winnings, Insider AH put KR₩5 million into his bank account which Former Player A then withdrew via the account card.

From January 2011, Broker F and Broker B also worked together to bribe and fix games in the 2010–11 NH V League season.[78] Broker F researched which games to fix and which players to approach to carry out the fixing, and Broker B arranged the betting and bribery money. Broker F approached Former Player A knowing that Former Player A had previously agreed to fix matches with successful results.[79] Former Player A agreed to participate once again and was paid KR₩20 million. Former Player A then convinced Player D and two other players who had recently joined the KEPCO45 (Player O and Player P) to fix a match on 24 January and they agreed to split the KR₩20 million amongst them. In March 2011, Broker B arranged with Former Player A through Broker F that he would pay KR₩20 million in exchange for another fix. Former Player A took the money and split it amongst Player D, Player O and Player P. On 13 March 2011, the players fixed the game between KEPCO45 and 'AP Team' so that KEPCO45 lost 0:3. The Court found that Broker B, Broker F, Former Player A and the current players also fixed matches on 23 December 2010, 27 December 2010, 29 December 2010, 4 January 2011, 6 January 2011, 17 January 2011, 27 January 2011, 28 February 2011 and 10 March 2011.

At about the same time as these fixes were occurring in the volleyball code, Broker B was also involved in fixing baseball matches. Broker B and Former Player J approached current professional baseball players, 'Pitcher K' and 'Pitcher L'. Former Player J arranged for Pitcher K to throw four balls in the first innings on 24 April 2011 and gave Pitcher K KR₩2 million which was provided by Broker B. Broker B gave Former Player J a further KR₩5 million to give to Pitcher K to throw four balls in games on 14 and 29 May 2011. Former Player J also arranged for Pitcher L to throw four balls in exchange for KR₩5 million, which was also provided by Broker B, to fix games on 24 May and 9 June 2011.

The Daegu District Court reserved its harshest sentences for Broker B and Former Player A, giving each two years' imprisonment. The Court reasoned that Broker B was a key figure in the match-fixing. He collected money from financiers and, through Broker F, passed that money to players. Broker B also provided his place for another broker, Broker G, and Former Player J to design the match-fixing. Broker B's sentence was mitigated, however, due to his confession and active cooperation with the prosecutors.[80] Former Player A was also found to be an active participant in the act and design of the match-fixing with Broker B and Broker F, and to have forced other players to participate. His sentence was also mitigated, however, because the Court took into consideration his financial difficulties and uncertain future resulting from an injury.[81] Broker F was sentenced to one year and two months. The Court found that although Broker F actively assisted Broker B and Former Player A, he admitted all charges, showed remorse, and had already repaid Broker B and Broker G.[82] Broker E was sentenced for the lesser term of ten months. Although he introduced Broker F to Former Player A, Broker E voluntarily stopped his participation. His sentence was also reduced as a result of his family responsibilities: he was required to take care of his disabled father.[83] Player C and Player D were sentenced to one year imprisonment. The Court took their financial difficulties into account when sentencing, but the Court gave them a custodial sentence because they were the captain and a senior player and thus should be role models for junior players. Both Player C and Player D took a part in a significant number of instances of match-fixing at Former Player A's instigation, and engaged other players to match-fix.[84] The other volleyball players involved were given suspended sentences or 200 hours of community service or both presumably because of their lesser involvement. In the case of the baseball match-fixing, the Daegu District Court handed down suspended jail sentences to the two pitchers.

The Court took a number of mitigating factors into account when sentencing the participants, as this summary shows. As Schwab and Finocchiaro argue in this volume, however, the sporting sanctions were more devastating for the players than these court-imposed sentences. The Korean Volleyball Association also imposed lifetime bans on the four key players on 22 February 2012, before the judgment was handed down on 14 March 2012.[85] The Korean Baseball Association had also already imposed lifetime bans.[86] The sports organisations took action after the players were charged and instituted their own sanctions without necessarily having regard to the prosecutions or the court outcomes.

What can these cases tell us about investigation and prosecution methods in Korea?

The prosecutors investigating these cases were based within the Daegu District Prosecutors' Office.[87] As noted above, there is no special match-fixing unit within the Public Prosecutors' Office.[88] Prosecutors investigate allegations within the territorial jurisdiction of the prosecutorial office to which they are assigned. However, they may carry out their duties outside their jurisdiction if required for an investigation.[89] The authors understand that match-fixing cases often come to light through tip-offs or during the investigation of another case, which appears to have happened in these cases. Ongoing rumours about match-fixing in professional sport appear to have led the prosecutors to investigate, and the connection between volleyball and baseball was made as a result of questioning one of the brokers.[90]

Korean prosecutorial practice and the authors' knowledge of the case suggest that the prosecutors led the investigations into the match-fixing allegations.[91] The police may have begun the investigation at the initial stage, but they would have been under the supervision of prosecutors and the prosecutors would have directly questioned witnesses, created prosecutorial interview documents and examined other documents and evidence.[92] In the volleyball and baseball match-fixing cases, prosecutors questioned all of the accused. The witness statements of the accused and Insider AH were submitted to the court.[93] Choe notes that, 'courts rarely question the prosecutorial interview documents and as a result, they are routinely accepted into evidence'.[94] The evidence at trial also included screenshots of personal blogs from social media, team player profiles and information from team websites. The prosecutors also used Insider AH's bank account history, Broker B and Former Player A's joint account confirming the betting transactions, and the account histories of all the accused. The precaution taken by Insider AH and Former Player A of having Former Player A use Insider AH's bank card to withdraw funds from Insider AH's account did not work in this instance. Details of the specific scores for each fixed match and who played in each fixed match were also presented in evidence, as were car registrations. Mobile phone data, including text messages sent and received by all the accused, was also used to evidence connections and instructions.[95] Mobile phone and social media also play an important role in Australian investigations as discussed by Murnane and Moller in this volume. It's not surprising that prosecutors look to these sources for evidence in Korea where it was estimated in 2013 that over 90 per cent of smartphones use Kakaotalk, a Korean-language application for smartphones which offers free calls and text messaging services.[96]

Judicial warrants were obtained for the investigations of both the volleyball and baseball allegations.[97] Prosecutors must obtain judicial warrants for search and seizure.[98] Police officers may make a request for a warrant to prosecutors who may then make an application to a judge.[99] The warrants in these cases were requested by the prosecutors. If there is a probable cause to believe that someone has committed a crime and will not cooperate with authorities to present themselves at a police station, prosecutors may also request an arrest warrant from a judge.[100] If prosecutors wish to detain a suspect for longer than 48 hours, they must apply for a preliminary hearing whereby a judge will decide whether or not to grant a detention warrant to facilitate questioning.[101] Judges routinely agree to these prosecutorial requests. It appears that most of the accused in this case admitted to the claims made against them by the prosecutors, and confessed and cooperated with the investigations.[102] Only two of the accused, Pitchers K and L, initially denied their involvement.[103] According to the District Court, they both admitted their involvement and began cooperating with the prosecutors after increasing media pressure describing Korean society's disappointment in the pitchers.[104]

Insider AH does not appear to have been prosecuted as part of this case, even though the judgment makes it clear that Insider AH was very active in most of the match-fixing. It appears that Insider AH, who previously operated with Former Player A as a broker in other match-fixing incidents not related to this case, was the first to be caught, and sought to avoid prosecution by assisting prosecutors. Prosecutors have discretionary power to decide whether or not to prosecute even if there is sufficient evidence for prosecution.[105] This power is referred to as the Principle of Discretionary Indictment (*Kisoyuye*).[106] In deciding whether or not to institute proceedings, prosecutors may take into account factors such as the age, character and conduct of the offender, the intelligence and environment of the offender, the offender's relation to the victim, the motive for the commission of the crime, the means and the result, and the circumstances after the commission of the crime.[107] After criticism of prosecutors for non-prosecution decisions, the *Hyungsasosongbub* [Criminal Procedure Act] (act no. 14179, 2016 (Republic of Korea)) was amended so that complainants may appeal to the High Court for a review of the appropriateness of non-prosecution of all crimes.[108] Before seeking such a review, complainants should first request that the Prosecutors' Office review a decision not to prosecute.[109] If the High Court considers the non-prosecution to be inappropriate, the Prosecutors' Office must prosecute.[110] In practice, complaints do not get to this level, with prosecutors typically deciding to prosecute before a court requires them to do so.

Future trends in investigating and prosecuting match-fixing in Korea

Decreasing prosecutions and reports to clean sports centres

After match-fixing scandals between 2011 and 2013, the government devoted greater resources to combating match-fixing in Korea and took many other legislative, administrative and practical steps to address the so-called four evils.[111] According to the crime statistics published by the Supreme Prosecutors' Office, these measures may be working. The number of incidents under the *National Sports Promotion Act* decreased recently, as shown in Table 12.1. Data in relation to *National Sports Promotion Act* cases was split out as a separate category in the crime statistics in 2014 and 2015, but match-fixing is still not separately reported. Even so, the statistics by themselves suggest that sport-related offences may be on the decline in Korea. Violations of the *National Sports Promotion Act* about halved between 2014 and 2015 and the number of people prosecuted overall under the Act substantially reduced in 2015. These decreases may be a result of the reforms introduced in 2014, and analysed by Yeun in this volume, after various scandals in 2011–13. Although the application of the Act in relation to match-fixing offences was expanded, the legislative reforms also increased the penalties for sport-related offences. These amendments and other reforms also increased awareness of the possible offences and consequences.

Another part of the explanation for decreasing formal prosecutions, however, may be that reporting to the Korean Sport and Olympic Committee's Clean Sports Reporting Center is providing sports associations with opportunities to deal with incidents internally and incidents are not being reporting to police and prosecutors.[112] Established in 2007, the Committee's Center is focused on player welfare and does not require that incidents be reported to police or prosecutors.[113] This approach has drawn criticism in Korea.[114] There are no publicly available statistics on the number or type of incidents being reported to the Center. A lack of transparency makes it difficult to ascertain if it is making a difference in the

Table 12.1 National Sports Promotion Act prosecution statistics

Year	*Number of reported cases*	*Number of people prosecuted*	*Number of cases prosecuted*	*Rate of prosecution (%)*
2014	1895	2452	1477	77.9
2015	776	1449	735	94.7

Source: Supreme Prosecutors' Office Republic of Korea 2016, '*2016 bunjebunsuk* [2016 analytical statistics on crime]', www.spo.go.kr/spo/info/stats/stats02.jsp.

number of prosecutions, and a recent scandal relating to the daughter of a confidant of former President Park Geun-Hye has brought public attention to the shortcomings of the Center's processes and approach.[115]

The Ministry of Culture, Sports and Tourism also set up a call centre to promote 'fair and transparent sports policies' in 2014.[116] Its telephone hotline receives reports about conduct that undermines sports fairness. Exposing match fixing is a key purpose. In June 2015, the Center was renamed the Sports Corruption Reporting Center and it became possible to also make a report anonymously online.[117] Six police and one prosecutor have been assigned to the Center to help investigate reports.[118] Accordingly, a report to the Sports Corruption Reporting Center may lead to criminal prosecution. In 2016, 206 incidents were reported to the Sports Corruption Reporting Center, with 154 incidents being investigated by the team of police and prosecutor, and 55 concluded without further investigation.[119] The Sports Corruption Reporting Center provides rewards ranging from KR₩1 million to KR₩3 million for an informant if the informant provides her or his name and information results in disciplinary action or criminal punishment.[120]

Further reforms in Korea?

Despite successful prosecutions and reform efforts, match-fixing scandals in Korea continue to occur. A team sponsored by Hyundai Motors,[121] for example, was banned from participation in the Asian Champions League due to allegations that a Jeonbuk Hyundai Motors' club scout paid referees bribes worth KR₩5 million to influence the outcome of matches during 2013–14 K-League seasons.[122] In May 2016, prosecutors charged the two referees for accepting bribes.[123] Jeonbuk Hyundai Motors was fined by the K-League's disciplinary committee and lost nine points in September 2016.[124] This section suggests three ways in which recent measures may be further developed to help combat match-fixing in Korea.

First, a dedicated investigative or prosecutorial unit along the lines of the Victoria Police Sporting Integrity Intelligence Unit may assist Korea's fight against match-fixing.[125] Match-fixing investigations can be complex and require detailed knowledge of global betting markets and sporting codes, and benefit from close relationships with key stakeholders, such as the sporting codes and betting agencies. As Korea moves towards the PyeongChang 2018 Winter Olympics, organisations such as INTERPOL and the International Olympic Committee are interested in further reform in Korea. INTERPOL's press release about its recent partnership development meeting in Korea noted that:

> Key areas for discussion during the meeting were the mechanisms in place for a national coordinated framework and identifying ways to

> overcome obstacles to cross-sector cooperation for efficient investigations. Exercises with real-life scenarios allowed the participants to experience how specific operational collaboration between sport, law enforcement and betting regulators and operators can be achieved.

Moreover, according to INTERPOL, the participants, which included police and prosecutors, 'also discussed setting up a Joint Intelligence Integrity Unit' which would provide help to protect the integrity of the PyeongChang Olympics.[126] INTERPOL also expressed the hope that such a Unit 'could also serve as a lasting legacy to protect sport' in Korea 'from integrity breaches'.[127] The participation of police and prosecutors in investigating reports to the Ministry's Sports Corruption Reporting Center and Korea's prosecutorial, and existing administrative divisions focusing on matters such as drugs and organised crime, could form precedents for a new unit.[128] The issues of regulating betting markets,[129] the independence of any special unit, relationships with sporting associations and their autonomy, sports governance and information sharing also become important in this context.

Proactive approaches based on concentrated expertise in an investigative unit should also provide opportunities to gather contemporary intelligence and evidence. Reports from call centres and telephone hotlines are akin to the tip offs that Korean prosecutors already rely on and should not be considered as a panacea for match-fixing prevention such that it detracts from developing other effective investigatory techniques. The initial success of the hotline may also mean that prosecutors become stuck in a reactive position as they deal with many reports and limited resources, and sporting associations use the opportunity to take action themselves without involving law enforcement. Further, collecting evidence is more difficult with reactive approaches such as relying on whistleblowers. Depending on when an offence occurs, there is a risk that evidence will no longer be available.[130] Further research into the effectiveness and roles of these call centres and reporting mechanisms will be instructive for sports administrators and law enforcement in Korea and globally.

Second, Korean law enforcement could create deeper partnerships with other stakeholders. Such partnerships were important in the lead up to major events in Australia in 2015, and Ordway in this volume recommends that they also be cultivated and maintained outside of major event cycles. The judgments and literature reviewed for this article do not evidence cooperation between prosecutors and other stakeholders, including the volleyball and baseball associations,[131] and the judgment itself does not suggest that they provided evidence. There is also no mention, for example, of interactions with, or evidence from, Korea's SportsToto.[132] SportsToto permits betting on football (soccer), basketball, baseball, volleyball, golf and traditional Korean wrestling.[133] SportsToto does not have any public information sharing agreements such as with the Korean government, national sport federations or prosecutors and police.[134] In Australia, match-fixing investigations may arise through a licensed betting agency detecting and reporting suspicious betting activity.[135] Whilst controversial, Korea could also consider further regulation of betting operators in its jurisdiction and thus create a new source of evidence.[136]

Third, preventive measures from other jurisdictions may be instructive. The practice of disruption, for example, may provide a new opportunity for Korean prosecutors and police to prevent match-fixing during a large, international event such as the PyeongChang Olympics. Disruption was used to protect the integrity of major sporting events in Australia in 2015 as discussed by Ordway in this volume. The police in Australia are likely to choose disruption as a preventive technique where the focus is on attempting to ensure that such large sporting events are free of match-fixing; it would not be a technique used in every instance. Disruption may not, for example, be appropriate where a fix is in progress and the police are focused on continuing to gather evidence for conviction, which was the case in Southern Stars as discussed by Murnane and Moller in this volume.

Conclusion

Ultimately, prosecutors in Korea and elsewhere are not able to single-handedly deal with failures in institutional design or governance in competitions, sporting organisations or betting regimes, a lack of player education or an absence of community and personal responsibility for the various drivers for match-fixing.[137] Where match-fixing allegations have been made in Korea, the strong investigative powers and intense focus of prosecutors have brought results in the courts as evidenced by the volleyball and baseball examples examined in this chapter and also Park in this volume. As Yeun in this volume shows, there are also numerous legislative avenues to prosecute match-fixing in Korea. Korea's next steps in relation to investigating and prosecuting match-fixing are likely to be focused on national coordination as it prepares for international events and integration into international frameworks designed to combat match-fixing.

Notes

1 On Japan's prosecutorial approach, see the seminal work of David Johnson. See especially Johnson, D., 2001, *The Japanese way of justice: prosecuting crime in Japan*, Oxford University Press. In Australia, the investigative process is typically carried out by the police as evidenced by the narratives presented by Ordway and Murnane and Moller in this volume; prosecutors are comparatively more limited to the subsequent court-driven prosecution processes. Victoria Police's Sporting Integrity Intelligence Unit can manage entire match-fixing investigations from the initial suspicion phase to the final

outcome, as discussed by Murnane and Moller in this volume. Police in Australia also carry out summary criminal offence work in lower courts. In Korea, although judicial police officers may conduct investigations, they are officially supervised by a public prosecutor as discussed further below.

2 See United Nations Office on Drugs and Crime 2016, *Resource guide on good practices in the investigation of match-fixing*, p. 1.

3 INTERPOL 2017, 'INTERPOL and IOC meeting in Seoul promotes sports integrity', press release, 16 March, www.interpol.int/en/News-and-media/News/2017/N2017-030. According to INTERPOL, the meeting was attended by 'representatives from law enforcement, the federal prosecutor's office, the PyeongChang 2018 Winter Olympics Organising Committee, the Korean Sport and Olympic Committee, national sports federations, the National Gambling Control Commission, and the sports and justice ministries'.

4 On the history of the Korean legal system, see Chung, H., 1982, 'The criminal justice system in Korea – the role of public prosecutor', *The Korean Journal of Comparative Law*, vol. 10, no. 1, pp. 21–57 p. 53; Park, E.Y., 2011, 'The rule of law in the Republic of Korea', *National Taiwan University Law Review*, vol. 6, no. 1, pp. 301–318, pp. 303–306. From 1910 to 1945, Japan occupied Korea and applied the Japanese criminal justice system to Korea. In 1948, after Japan surrendered to the Allied Forces and three years of United States of America military administration, Korea established its current criminal justice system. Park argues that Korea's legal system has also been substantially influenced by globalisation, particularly after the Asian Financial Crisis (in 1997). See also Supreme Prosecutors' Office Republic of Korea 2011, *History*, www.spo.go.kr/eng/service/history3.jsp.

5 The special investigation agency is akin to the Federal Bureau of Investigation in the United States of America. See Ministry of Justice Republic of Korea 2010, *Affiliates*, www.moj.go.kr/HP/ENG/eng_02/eng_2030.jsp.

6 Comparative research on roles for prosecutors often contrasts prosecutorial powers with the powers of the police and the tension between these two parts of criminal justice systems. See, e.g. Fonda, J., 1995, *Public prosecutors and discretion: a comparative study*, Clarendon Press, p. 6. See also Hall Williams on the introduction of the Crown Prosecution Service in England and Wales in 1986 which was designed to 'restate the relationships between police and prosecutor'. Williams, J.E.H., 'Introduction: the role of the prosecutor', in Williams, J.E. (ed.), 1988, *The role of the prosecutor: report of the international criminal justice seminar held at the London school of economics and political science in January 1987*, pp. 1–26, p. 1. Those reforms concerned reducing the influence of police over the prosecutorial function and making prosecutors more independent.

7 Choe, D.H., 2013, 'The prosecutor's interview with suspects in South Korea', *International Journal of Law, Crime and Justice*, vol. 41, no. 1, pp. 322–342. Based on 20 interviews with legal professionals in Korea, Choe argues that criminal trials rely too heavily on prosecutorial interview documents, and suggests a stronger guarantee of the right to counsel, electronic recording of interviews, limiting the length of interrogation, prohibiting promises of inducements such as leniency, and protections for vulnerable interviewees are needed.

8 The number of cases prosecuted in 2015 was 2,020,731: Supreme Prosecutors' Office Republic of Korea 2016, *2016 bunjebunsuk* [2016 analytical statistics on crime], www.spo.go.kr/spo/info/stats/stats02.jsp.

9 Article 1 of the Act provides that 'the quota of public prosecutors under art. 36 (1) of the *Public Prosecutors' Office Act* shall be 2292 persons': see

also *Gumsajungwonbub* [Prosecutors Quota Act], act no. 12952, 2014 (Republic of Korea). The Act was amended on 8 November 2016 and the amendments came into force on 1 March 2017. The Act provides for an increase in 350 prosecutors: an increase of 90 from 1 January 2015; 80, from 1 January 2016; 70, from 1 January 2017; 70, from 1 January 2018; and 40, from 1 January 2019: *Gumsajungwonbub* [Prosecutors Quota Act], act no. 12952, 2014 (Republic of Korea), art. 1.

10 On the increase, see also Park, K., 2016 '*Jin kyungjin Hong manpyo, Kim hyungjun ... Nanun daehanminkuk kumsada* [Jin Kyung Jin, Hong Man Pyo, Kim Hyung Jun ... I'm a Korean Prosecutor]', *NoCut News*, 22 September, www.nocutnews.co.kr/news/4657200.

11 On the reasons for the amendment, see, *Kumsajungwonbub shihangryung* [Enforcement Decree of the Prosecutors Quota Act], act no. 27868, 2017 (Republic of Korea).

12 Fonda argues that any 'attempt to draw conclusions about the operation of a prosecution system' must take into account 'the contextual features, whether legal, social, political, or historical' of that jurisdiction: Fonda, above n. 6, p. 6. She also notes that changing political leadership and trends, as well as the 'extent and type of criminality' in a jurisdiction are also important considerations: at pp. 10–11.

13 See, e.g. Park in this volume.

14 This aspect of legal education still exists in Japan. On public prosecutors in Germany from a comparative perspective by way of further example, see Gilliéron, G., 'Overview of public prosecutors in Germany: position, powers, and accountability', in Gilliéron, G., 2013, *Public prosecutors in the United States and Europe: a comparative analysis with special focus on Switzerland, France, and Germany*, Springer, pp. 263–286.

15 A justice of the Supreme Court must have at least 20 years' experience as a judge, prosecutor or lawyer and be over 46 years old: see *Bubwonjojinbub* [Court Organisation Act], act no. 12780, 2014 (Republic of Korea), art. 42(1). In reality, most Korean prosecutors are likely to enter private practice if they retire from their prosecutorial position. The opportunities to become a judge are more limited in number and less financially attractive.

16 See Park in this volume. Chung, Jun and Kim's survey in this volume indicates that basketball has the highest frequency of education, which suggests the value of education in countering match-fixing.

17 United Nations Office on Drugs and Crime, above n. 2, p. 55. The resource guide is designed to 'help officials detect and investigate match-fixing' and provides a comprehensive discussion on the meaning of match-fixing with examples from real cases, and analyses issues relating to investigations: at p. iii.

18 United Nations Office on Drugs and Crime, above n. 2, p. 55.

19 Ibid., p. 1.

20 Ibid., p. 56.

21 See, e.g. Gilliéron, above n. 14.

22 Chung, above n. 4, p. 57.

23 See, e.g. Choe, above n. 7.

24 Ibid., pp. 328–330.

25 Korean National Police Agency, *Kyingchelchungjojik kyusungdo* [Organisation of the Korean National Police Agency], www.police.go.kr/portal/main/contents.do?menuNo=200220. This is similar to Germany's federal system, where state police forces are 'subordinate to the Ministers of the Interior' and 'the public prosecution services are under the Ministers of Justice', see Gilliéron, above n. 14, p. 266. Gilliéron describes German public prosecutors as

'the master of criminal investigations'. Gilliéron notes that in practice the German police:

> conduct the great majority of criminal investigations on their own and submit the files to the public prosecutor only at the point at which charges would have to be brought. The public prosecutor is only informed from the very beginning in serious matters.
>
> (At p. 267)

26 The Office is a quasi-independent agency: see Chung, above n. 4, p. 56; Yun, L., 2012, '*Gunchalgaehukga dokrilpdeun tulbulsusakikwanel shinsule gwanhan sogo* [Prosecution reforms and a new investigation on the establishment of independent special investigation agencies]', *Hongik bubhak* [Hong Ik Law Journal Review], vol. 12, no. 1, pp. 49–73; Kim, J., 2013, '*Gumsal kisodokjumkwon tongje bangane kwanhan yeongu* [A study on the control systems over the prosecutor's exclusive right on prosecution]', *Daejin bubhak* [Daejin University Law Journal], vol. 107, no. 1, pp. 1–83.

27 See *Hyungsasosongbub* [Criminal Procedure Act], act no. 341, 1954 (Republic of Korea), art. 196 ('*Criminal Procedure Act*'). Specifically, art. 196 states:

> (1) Investigators, police administrative officers, police superintendents, superintendents, police captains, or police lieutenants shall receive instructions from a prosecutor with regard to all investigations, while serving as senior judicial police officers. (2) Where senior judicial police officers recognize that a person is suspected of having committed a crime, they shall launch and conduct investigation into the offender, the facts of the offense, and the evidence. (3) Judicial police officers shall comply with a prosecutor's instructions. Details of the prosecutor' instructions shall be determined by Presidential Decree. (4) Where senior judicial police officers have investigated a crime, they shall send, without delay, the relevant documents and evidence to the prosecutor. (5) Police sergeants, senior patrol officers, or patrol officers shall assist in the investigation of crimes, as junior judicial police officers. (6) Judicial police officers other than persons prescribed in paragraph (1) or (5) may be determined by Acts.

28 Ministry of Justice Republic of Korea, above n. 5.

29 *Kumchalchungbub* [Prosecutors' Office Act], act no. 14582, 2017 (Republic of Korea), art. 12(1) ('*Prosecutors' Office Act*').

30 Ibid., art. 12(2).

31 See, generally, Johnston D.T., 2012, 'Japan's prosecution system', *The University of Chicago Press Journals*, vol. 41, no. 35, www.journals.uchicago.edu/doi/pdfplus/10.1086/665409.

32 *Prosecutors' Office Act*, art. 7(1).

33 Cho, K., 2010, *Litigation in Korea*, Edward Elgar Publishing, p. 63.

34 Gladwell's research on Korean Air exemplifies the hierarchical aspect of Korean culture. Gladwell, M., 2008, *Outliers: the story of success*, Little Brown. In relation to the impact of hierarchical structures on match-fixing, see also Park in this volume.

35 *Prosecutors' Office Act*, art. 4(1).

36 On the historical reasons for involvement of prosecutors in investigation and prosecution in Korea and the risks associated with this conflation of roles, see, e.g. Choe, above n. 7, p. 332. Choe states that, '[t]he prosecution service has turned into an investigation agency employing inappropriate interviewing tactics'.

37 On the causes of match-fixing in Korea, see Park and Yeun in this volume.

38 Im, H.B., 'From affiliation to association; the challenge of democratic consolidation in Korean industrial relations', in McNamara, D. (ed.), 1999, *Corporation and Korea capitalism*, Routledge, pp. 75–94, p. 75.

39 '*Chaebols*' refers to large conglomerate corporations that exert considerable influence on the economy.

40 See Hong, E., 2011, 'Elite sport and nation-building in South Korea: South Korea as the dark horse in global elite sport', *The International Journal of the History of Sport*, vol. 28, no. 7, pp. 977–989. On the causes of match fixing in Korea, see also Park in this volume. As discussed by Yeun in this volume, the Korean government is also considering introducing legislation that would strip sponsors of their rights. Armstrong and Hodges-Ramon suggest that, 'the close-knit relationship between sporting administrators, politicians, business people, sponsors, and the media can create a high-risk environment for corruption', implying that the issues faced by Korean sport are not unique: Armstrong, G. and Hodges-Ramon, L., 2015, 'Sport and crime', *Oxford Handbooks Online*, November, doi:10.1093/oxfordhb/9780199935383.013.87.

41 For Hong's profile, see Ewha Womans University, *Hong Eun Ah* [Hong Eun Ah], www.ewha.ac.kr/mbs/ewhakr/jsp/sprofile/sprofile_View.jsp?id=ewhakr_030101010000&sabun=MTUyOTE2#.

42 Hong, E., 2012, 'Applying a Western-based policy community framework to the analysis of South Korean elite sport policy: the role of businesses and armed forces', *International Journal of Sport Policy and Politics*, vol. 4, no. 1, pp. 23–37, p. 35.

43 For information about the Fund, see KSPO 2013, *About KSPO*, http://english.kspo.or.kr/?menuno=347.

44 See similarly, Tak, M., 2016, 'Too big to jail: match-fixing, institutional failure and the shifting of responsibility', *International Review for the Sociology of Sport*, January, pp. 1–19.

45 Hong, above n. 42.

46 On the special privileges given to elite athletes, see Hong, above n. 42, p. 27. Hong analyses the role of the Armed Forces Athletic Corps (*sangmu*). Exemptions for gold medal winners, for example, are possible.

47 Cho, above n. 33, p. 63.

48 Ji, S., 2017, '*Daejeon 88-gae Gunchal, Park Geun Hye koosok susahara* [Daejeon: 88 organisations called for the Prosecutor's Office to prosecute Park Guen Hye for the investigation]', *DT News*, 16 March, www.dtnews24.com/news/article.html?no=417118.

49 Choe, S.H., 2017, 'Prosecutors question Park Geun Hye, former South Korean leader, in corruption inquiry', *New York Times*, 20 March, www.nytimes.com/2017/03/20/world/asia/south-korea-ousted-president-park-prosecutors.html?_r=0&module=ArrowsNav&contentCollection=Asia%20Pacific&action=keypress&region=FixedLeft&pgtype=article.

50 Ibid.

51 Choi, C., 2017, '*Dashi taoreun chokbul taneki ttuk annida. Park Geun Hye rl kosukhara* [Restart of candle rally, impeachment is not over. Prosecute Park Geun Hye]', *News Tomato*, 26 March, www.newstomato.com/ReadNews.aspx?no=741218.

52 *Prosecutors' Office Act*, art. 29.

53 Kim, H., 2017 '*Byunhosa gwaingbaechul sengjonkwon chimhae nulran … hunjae "sengjonkwon jaehan anida"* [Controversy of oversupply of lawyers and viability … "It is not about survival"]', *Herald Corp News*, 17 April, http://news.heraldcorp.com/view.php?ud=20170417000465.

54 See Lee, S.S.R., 'Legal education in Korea: new law school reforms', in Steele S. and Taylor, K. (eds.), 2010, *Legal Education in Asia: Globalization, change and contexts*, Routledge, p. 170.
55 Ibid., p. 169.
56 Ibid., p. 170.
57 Ibid.
58 Ibid., p. 172.
59 In 2017, 234 people graduated from the Institute, including 69 women. Of these, 23 joined law firms, 24 became law associates at courts, 25 became prosecutors, five opened their own firms, and four were employed by companies. The remaining graduates were yet to find employment at the time of the survey; in other words, only 45 per cent were employed: Park, H., 2017 '*Sabupyeonsuwondo muk pihan chulup hanpa … julban isangi michulup* [Even the Institute graduates cannot escape from unemployment … more than half of them are unemployed]', *Asiae News*, 16 January, http://view.asiae.co.kr/news/view.htm?idxno=2017011615554463921.
60 Ministry of Justice Republic of Korea 2017, '*Byunhosa Shihum* [Lawyer Admission Test]', 25 March, www.moj.go.kr/HP/lawyer/main/index.jsp.
61 Lee, above n. 54, p. 174.
62 Lee, S., 2016, '*Je-6-hwe byulhosashihum 3,306myung chulwon … hapkukyul 50% choban?* [6th Lawyer Admission Test, 3,306 candidates applied but the pass rate is only 50 per cent?]', *The Law Journal News*, 28 December, www.lec.co.kr/news/articleView.html?idxno=42714. Pass rates for highly ranked universities are higher.
63 In 2016, 35.4 per cent of newly appointed prosecutors (17 people) were from Seoul National University, 18.8 per cent from Yeonsei University (nine people), and 12.5 per cent from Korea University (six people); that is, 66.7 per cent of prosecutors came from the top three most prestigious universities in Korea: Lee, S., 2016, '*All law school shinyimkumsa chulshin daehak, chulsin law school bunsukhekduni* [Analysis of all new prosecutors' graduated universities and law schools]', *The Law Journal News*, 5 May, www.lec.co.kr/news/articleView.html?idxno=40384. Traditionally, the Prosecutors' Office has preferred to hire a person at the very start of their career.
64 For criticism of the elite nature of the Korean prosecutorial system, see Kim, J., 2013, '*Kumsal kisodokjumkwon tongje bangane kwanhan yeongu* [A study on the control systems over the prosecutor's exclusive right on prosecution]', *Daejin bubhak* [Daejin University Law Journal], vol. 107, no. 1, pp. 1–83.
65 Lee, above n. 54, p. 172.
66 Ibid., p. 174.
67 Any prosecutorial lack of specific expertise may be compensated for by local court staff. Transfers are designed to promote independence and avoid conflicts of interest amongst prosecutors. Judges are similarly regularly transferred.
68 There are, of course, areas of specialisation, and prosecutors in district and branch prosecutors' offices are divided into investigation and prosecution during their rotations. Resources are further allocated based on expertise across the 'Criminal, Special Investigation, Criminal Trial, Public Security, and Narcotics and Organized Crime Investigation' departments: Supreme Prosecutors' Office Republic of Korea 2011, *Organization*, www.spo.go.kr/eng/service/organization.jsp. Police similarly have areas of specialisation through which personnel are rotated: Korean National Police Agency, *Kyungchalchungjojik koosungdo* [Organization chart of National Police Agency], www.police.go.kr/portal/main/contents.do?menuNo=200220.

69 This case is also analysed by Park in this volume.
70 The alphabetical references to the various actors in this summary of the case are taken from the Korean-language judgment which does not refer to the actors, including teams, by name.
71 Supreme Prosecutors' Office 2015, *Pro sports (Baegu, yakyu) seulbujojak sakwun susakylgwa* [Analysis of professional sports (volleyball and baseball) match-fixing cases], 11 March, www.spo.go.kr/spo/info/issue/spo_history01.jsp?mode=view&board_no=63&article_no=592686.
72 Lee, S., 2012, '*Seulbujojak yagyuro bulddong … sudokwon ace yeonryu* [Matching-fixing in baseball … Metropolitan Ace team is involved']', *SBS News*, 14 February, http://news.sbs.co.kr/news/endPage.do?news_id=N1001088438&plink=OLDURL.
73 The summary of the case below is taken from the relevant judgment: Daegu District Court (18 April 2012), case no. *godan* 136, pp. 3–13. See also Park in this volume.
74 Daegu District Court (18 April 2012), case no. *godan* 136, p. 3.
75 Ibid., p. 4.
76 Ibid., p. 5.
77 Ibid.
78 Ibid., p. 9.
79 Ibid., p. 9.
80 Ibid., p. 44.
81 Ibid.
82 Ibid., p. 45. By repaying the other brokers, the Court found that Broker F showed that he was trying to remove himself from the criminal activity and had learnt from his mistake before he was caught.
83 Ibid., p. 45.
84 Ibid., p. 44.
85 Choe, S.H., 2012, 'South Korea cracks down on match-fixing epidemic', *New York Times*, 21 February, www.nytimes.com/2012/02/22/sports/22iht-fixing22.html.
86 Daegu District Court (18 April 2012), case no. *godan* 136, p. 46.
87 Supreme Prosecutors' Office, above n. 71.
88 Contrast this with Australia: see Moller and Murnane in this volume.
89 *Kumchalchungbub* [Public Prosecutors' Office Act] (act no. 213, 1948 (Republic of Korea)), art. 5.
90 Supreme Prosecutors' Office, above n. 71.
91 Prosecutors are vested with the authority to investigate crimes, file prosecutions and conduct matters necessary for the maintenance prosecutions: *Criminal Procedure Act*, art. 196.
92 Choe, above n. 7, p. 323. Typically, prosecutors will take over investigation of serious matters: at p. 328.
93 On the accusations as to how the match was fixed, such as spiking in the wrong direction, see Park in this volume.
94 Choe, above n. 7.
95 Daegu District Court (18 April 2012), case no. *godan* 136, p. 36.
96 See Frier, S., 2013, 'With $200 million in revenue, South Korea's top messaging app is all smiley faces', *Bloomberg*, 22 December, www.bloomberg.com/news/2013-12-22/with-200-million-in-revenue-south-korea-s-top-messaging-app-is-all-smiley-faces.html.
97 The judgment lists judicial warrants as part of evidence obtained for cases: Daegu District Court (18 April 2012), case no. *godan* 136, p. 39.
98 *Criminal Procedure Act*, art. 215.

99 Cho, above n. 33, p. 65.

100 *Criminal Procedure Act*, arts. 200–202(1). Exceptions exist under the *Criminal Procedure Act* arts. 200(3)(1) (emergency arrest) and 212 (arrest of flagrant offender). Article 211(2) defines 'flagrant offender' as an offender who is pursued by hue and cry; where a person carries stolen goods, or a weapon or other things recognized as being used in connection with a crime; where there is any apparent evidence on the body or clothes of a criminal suspect; where a person attempts to flee when challenged.

101 *Criminal Procedure Act*, arts. 200–202(5). Choe notes that, 'prosecutors can detain suspects generally up to 480h for investigation, which includes interrogation'. Choe, above n. 7, p. 330.

102 Daegu District Court (18 April 2012), case no. *godan* 136, p. 44.

103 Ibid., p. 46.

104 Ibid.

105 Lee, J.S., 1998, *The characteristics of the Korean prosecution system and the prosecutor's direct investigation*, UNAFEI, resource material series no. 53, February, pp. 83–102, p. 84.

106 *Criminal Procedure Act*, art. 247.

107 Ibid., art. 51. Article 247 of the *Criminal Procedure Act* says '[a] prosecutor may decide not to institute a public prosecution, considering the matters under Article 51 of the Criminal Act'.

108 Ibid., art. 260(1). Prior to 2007, only the non-prosecution of three specific crimes could be appealed to the High Court: crimes of abuse of power; illegal arrest and detention; and battery and cruel treatment.

109 Ibid., art. 260(2).

110 Ibid., art. 262(6).

111 See Yeun in this volume.

112 To the extent that a case is referred to prosecutors, and despite their wide discretion to decide whether to prosecute a case in Korea, prosecutors appear to have prosecuted almost all of the cases which were referred to them (94.7 per cent) under the *National Sports Promotion Act*. This prosecution rate is relatively high when compared to the overall number of cases prosecuted. In 2015, 1,638,549 out of 2,020,731 cases were prosecuted (81.1 per cent) involving the prosecution of 1,948,966 people in total (Supreme Prosecutors' Office Republic of Korea 2016, *2016 bunjebunsuk* [2016 analytical statistics on crime]', www.spo.go.kr/spo/info/stats/stats02.jsp). Some commentators suggest that the conservative exercise of this discretionary power not to prosecute discourages other organisations from taking steps to combat match-fixing: see, e.g. Brooks, G., Lee, J. and Kim, H., 2012, 'Match-fixing in Korean football: corruption in the K-League and the importance of maintaining sporting integrity', *International Journal of Contents*, vol. 8, no. 2, pp. 82–88, p. 86. The authors make a number of suggestions in relation to prevention of match-fixing in the Korean Football Association in light of K-League match-fixing scandals. The authors note the difficulty of separating sport from politics in Korea and that some of their suggestions 'might be regarded as irrelevant to the KFA' because 'prosecutors possess the power to continue or discontinue with a case': at p. 86.

113 The Korean Sport and Olympic Committee's Reporting Center also focuses on the four evils but deals with these matters internally. After a report, the Committee seeks fact confirmation and opinions by transferring the matter to the relevant sports federation or organisation. Then, with the report provided by the sports federation or organisation, the Committee conducts further investigation and then sets out an action for the federation or organisation to take: see Korean

Sport and Olympic Committee 2016, *Clean sport shingo center* [Clean sports reporting centre], www.sports.or.kr/home/010303/0010/main.do.

114 Kim, D., 2017, '*Chaeyukwe, je2el jungyura chulhyun makelsuikkelkka* [Can the Korean Sport and Olympic Committee prevent emergence of the second refinery of Jung Yu-ra?]', *MaeilkyungjelNews*, 18 April, http://mbnmoney.mbn.co.kr/news/view?news_no=MM1002782741. Cf. Schwab and Finocchiaro in relation to player welfare in this volume.

115 Ibid.

116 Ministry of Culture, Sports and Tourism 2014, *Sports biri shingo centa* [Sports corruption reporting centre], www.mcst.go.kr/usr/minwon/eSports/intro/introReport.jsp. The Korean Sports Promotion Fund also has a call centre for reporting of illegal gambling websites on 30 April 2012. See The Korean Sports Promotion Fund, *Seupocheutonghab kolsenteo* [Sports Clean Call Centre] http://cleansports.kspo.or.kr/index.do.

117 Ministry of Culture, Sports and Tourism, above n. 117.

118 Ministry of Culture, Sports and Tourism 2014, *Suposu 4dae ak kunjulel wihan munhwabu, kyungchal hapdongsusaban baljok* [Eradication of sports' four evils through developing cooperative investigation with the Ministry of Culture, Sports and Tourism and the police], 19 May, www.mcst.go.kr/web/s_notice/press/pressView.jsp?pSeq=13534.

119 Correspondence between Kee Young Yeun and authors.

120 See Ministry of Culture, Sports and Tourism 2014, *Sports biri shingo centa* [Sports corruption reporting centre], www.mcst.go.kr/usr/minwon/eSports/intro/introReward.jsp.

121 Hyundai Motors, *Jeonbuk Hyundai Motors*, www.hyundai-motorsfc.com/english/main.asp.

122 Asian Champions League 2017, 'Jeonbuk Hyundai ineligible for AFC Champions League 2017', press release, 18 January, www.the-afc.com/afc-champions-league-2017-media-releases/jeonbuk-hyundai-motors-ineligible-for-afc-champions-league.

123 One of the referees reportedly received three payments of KR₩1 million each and the other referee received two payments of KR₩1 million each. The scout was sentenced to a six-month suspended jail term for bribery by the Busan District Court: Ganguly, S., 2017, 'Asian champions Jeonbuk disqualified from 2017 Asian Champions League over bribery case', *Reuters*, 18 January, http://in.reuters.com/article/soccer-asia-jeonbuk-idINKBN1521RX.

124 Ibid. On the role of the Asian Football Confederation generally, see Weinberg, B., 2015, *Asia and the future of football: the role of the Asian Football Confederation*, Routledge; Kwon, H., 2017 '*Shimpan maesu, jeonbuk. Championleague chachul jungjingye* [Bribing referee, Jeonbuk to withdraw from Champions League]', *Newsis*, 18 January, www.newsis.com/view/?id=NISX20170118_0014649553&cID=10503&pID=10500. JeonBuk Club appealed to the Court of Arbitration for Sport, without success: see Court of Arbitration for Sport 2017, 'CAS procedure between Jeonbuk Hyundai Motors and the Asian Football Confederation has concluded', press release, 17 February, www.tas-cas.org/fileadmin/user_upload/Media_Release_4957_termination_order.pdf; Court of Arbitration for Sport 2017, 'Court of Arbitration for Sport (CAS) rejects the request for provisional measures filed by Jeonbuk Hyundai Motors', press release, 3 February, www.tas-cas.org/fileadmin/user_upload/Media_Release_4957_decision_on_request_for_stay.pdf.

125 On global calls for more resourcing, see United Nations Office on Drugs and Crime, above n. 2. Two representatives of the Ministry of Justice of the Republic of Korea are noted in the acknowledgements as having contributed

expertise and experience, although their specific titles and roles are not identified: at p. iv.

126 INTERPOL, above n. 3.

127 Ibid.

128 See the discussion above in relation to the division of prosecutors across administrative departments and areas of expertise and above n. 6.

129 On the general prohibition on gambling and negative public perceptions towards gambling, see Shon, S., 2013, '*Suposu seungbujojak shiltaeha gu daecho bangane kwanan yungu* [A study on the match-fixing of sports and its prevention]', *Suposuwabub* [The Korean Association of Sports Law], vol. 16, no. 1, pp. 83–103. Article 48(3) of the *National Sports Promotion Act* extends the general prohibition on gambling to sporting events. See also Williams, R.J., Lee, C.K. and Back, K.J., 2013, 'The prevalence and nature of gambling and problem gambling in South Korea', *Social Psychiatry and Psychiatric Epidemiology*, vol. 48, no. 5, pp. 821–834. The authors' research shows that there are few opportunities for Koreans to gamble and little inclination to do so. They suggest that low participation rates by females contribute to the comparatively low prevalence of gambling.

130 In Korea, prosecutors already rely heavily on confessions. See Choe, above n. 7; Park, above n. 4.

131 As discussed above, the judgment provided details of the evidence relied on by prosecutors which included statements by the 20 accused persons, personal phone and bank account records, and information from social media.

132 SportsToto was established under the Ministry of Sports, Culture and Tourism as a way of raising funds for Korea's hosting of the FIFA World Cup in 2002. It was officially launched in October 2001 and continues to operate as the only licenced sports betting agency in Korea: OnlineBetting.com 2017, *3. The laws and types of sports betting in Korea*, www.onlinebetting.com/legal/korea/sport-lottery. See also International Center for Sport Security and University Paris 1 Panthéon-Sorbonne 2014, *Protecting the integrity of sport competition: the last bet for modern sport*, May, pp. 14, 35, www.theicss.org/wp-content/themes/icss-corp/pdf/SIF14/Sorbonne-ICSS%20Report%20Executive%20Summary_WEB.pdf?lbisphpreq=1.

133 Williams *et al.*, above n. 130, p. 825.

134 Won, H.J. and Hong, E., 2015, 'The development of sport policy and management in South Korea', *International Journal of Sport Policy and Politics*, vol. 7, pp. 141–152, p. 150.

135 See Menz and Skene in this volume. Betting activity which is heavily monitored provides an opportunity for law enforcement to gather evidence where the betting operator contacts law enforcement as soon as suspicious bets are placed.

136 See also Yeun in this volume in relation to monitoring illegal sports betting in Korea.

137 On the failure of institutional design and Korean motorboat racing and football, see Tak, above n. 44.

Part IV

Findings and observations

Chapter 13

Preventing match-fixing and promoting integrity in sport

Reflections on experiences in Australia, Japan and Korea

Stacey Steele and Hayden Opie[1]

Comparing and contrasting approaches to match-fixing in Australia, Japan and Korea: commonalities

This chapter takes stock of experiences of match-fixing in Australia, Japan and Korea as reflected in this volume. It further compares and contrasts the contexts for approaches to combating match-fixing in each jurisdiction and potential future trends in each jurisdiction, as well as the need for harmonisation in this area of law and regulation in the context of developments such as cross-border leagues and e-sports. Many of the chapters in this volume tease out differences between the jurisdictions. This chapter focuses on commonalities amongst the three jurisdictions, but even within these commonalities there are distinctions and it would be wrong to conclude that there are no counter debates in each jurisdiction. It is common, for example, that each jurisdiction is keen to combat match-fixing; experience in each jurisdiction suggests that the issue should not be ignored. There are different degrees of priority and various processes and approaches, however. There are also differing views on matters such as to what extent match-fixing should be a sporting or criminal offence. There is also a common concern about regulating betting on sports. As the typologies described by Ando and Menz and Skene in this volume suggest, however, there are many ways to achieve this goal.

After this brief introduction, the chapter examines three key common areas highlighted by the narratives in this volume. First, the chapter argues that, in the context of a crowded international and domestic policy agenda, strong leadership is required on the issue of match-fixing if substantive reform is to be achieved. The impetus for legislative and other reforms in many jurisdictions has required a domestic shock or scandal, or international pressure from organisations such as the International Olympic Committee. Japan is used as a case study to highlight this point in light of its recent reforms to sports law policy development and governance to try to achieve better leadership. Second, the chapters in this volume reflect the understanding that debates about match-fixing in all three jurisdictions to date have typically been focused on men's sport. Recent scholarship and also experience in Korea suggest that women's sport and female players are not immune, although the key offenders are still typically men. Third, the chapter argues that each jurisdiction faces common future challenges. It examines three trends facing all three jurisdictions: increasing pressure to achieve international harmonisation, the rise of cross-border leagues, and technology-driven developments such as e-sports. These complexities will challenge law enforcement and sporting associations as they seek to adapt to this dynamic area of sports.

Leadership: avoiding bureaucratic traps

Developments in Australia and Korea underscore the importance of political commitment and leadership to combating match-fixing. In Australia, the major scandal in 2010 discussed by Opie and Lim in this volume was instrumental in bringing the issue of match-fixing to the attention of policy-makers, and a subsequent key New South Wales Law Reform Commission report contributed significantly to creating a political and bureaucratic environment where action was recognised as desirable and feasible. The support of key political figures such as then Commonwealth Minister for Sport, Senator Arbib, was also instrumental to the reforms analysed in Opie and Lim, and Ordway in this volume. Even in countries such as Australia, where there is a high level of consensus about the importance of sport and betting on sports is popular, strong leadership was required to overcome Australia's federal system. Moreover, amongst Australia's states and territories divergent approaches to legislative reform were taken despite a nationally agreed policy.[2] Similarly, Korea evidenced strong political leadership on match-fixing emanating out of widespread public disgust at scandals which became public and were successfully prosecuted in 2011–13 and beyond, as highlighted by Park, Yeun, and Steele, Shin and Yang in this volume. Korea also continues to reassess and improve its measures for combating match-fixing, as highlighted by Yeun, and Steele, Shin and Yang in this volume. In light of the new trends discussed below and unresolved issues highlighted by Opie and Lim, Australia is due for a general review of its measures to combat match-fixing.

Strong political and sports leadership is also required to overcome perceptions that eradicating match-fixing is too hard or not important enough, or that it is acceptable to turn a blind eye to the issue such as was allegedly the case in cricket and football (soccer) for many years.[3] Player leadership is also important. As Schwab and Finocchiaro assert in their chapter in this volume, player involvement is an important but under-rated resource for combating match-fixing. Even in this area of leadership, the results are uneven across and within jurisdictions and sports. In football, Australia and Japan have FIFPro-affiliated player unions with strong leadership, for example.[4] Korea has observer status with FIFPro, but no properly organised union. As Chung, Jun and Kim in this volume highlight, education is also part of the solution to encourage player leadership.[5]

Of the three jurisdictions which form the focus of this volume, Japan is the least prepared to deal with match-fixing in sport, and law reform in relation to sport has been relatively slow to date. Strong leadership will also be necessary in Japan to effect change, but match-fixing is not yet a legislative or policy priority despite recent bureaucratic restructures and imminent major international events being hosted in this jurisdiction. There are four key, related reasons for this delay. First, Japan is yet to experience a contemporary, significant match-fixing scandal outside of the traditional sport of sumo; although it may only be a matter of time before a major scandal emerges publicly as highlighted by Ando and Kawai in this volume. Second, Japanese policy-makers and society are yet to reach a consensus on the place of betting on sport in Japan, as evidenced by Kawai's analysis in this volume. Third, Japan is only now starting to prepare to host major international events for the first time since the issue of match-fixing came to serious international and academic prominence. Finally, contemporary sport in Japan has been under the policy purview of the Ministry of Education, Culture, Sports, Science and Technology ('MEXT').[6] Accordingly, it has often been overshadowed by other important matters in that portfolio.

Two new institutions in Japan have been established to directly and indirectly promote sports policy and law reform in Japan. First, the Japan Sport Council ('JSC') is an independent administrative corporation established on 1 October 2003 in accordance with the *Dokuritsu gyōsei hōjin tsūsoku hō* [Independent Administrative Corporation General Law] (act no. 103, 1999 (Japan)) and the *Dokuritsu gyōsei hōjin Nihon Supōtsu Shinkō Sentaa hō* [Law on the Japan Sport Council], act no. 162, 2003 (Japan)) ('*Law on the Japan Sport Council*'). The JSC has a broad portfolio and over 400 permanent staff and many more project-based staff.[7] Its initial objectives were to promote sports and to enhance and maintain school children's health. It operates sports facilities, provides necessary assistance for the promotion of sports, covers injury and accidents involving children under school care, and conducts research regarding sports and the maintenance and enhancement of children's health. The JSC is also focused on the development of people's physical and mental health based on sporting activities.[8] Finally, the JSC also operates Japan's *toto*.[9] Accordingly, it has a direct interest in protecting the integrity of sports betting. In light of Japan's upcoming international event commitments, the *Law on the Japan Sport Council* was amended in May 2013 to extend the JSC's responsibilities to ensuring fair and proper implementation of sporting activities. The JSC established the Sport Integrity Unit in April 2014 in response to its new responsibilities. The Unit is focused on developing measures for combating doping, harassment and match manipulation in sport, and the promotion of good governance in Japanese sports organisations.[10] The JSC will launch a new website for anonymous reporting of alleged doping in May 2017 at the time of writing, with reports going to the JSC.[11]

The second newer institution is known as the Japan Sports Agency. The Agency has its genesis in continuing bureaucratic tensions which helped to drive a group of politicians to establish the Bipartisan Sports Parliamentary Association (*Supōtsu Giin Renmei*) in June 2014.[12] The Association's aim was to establish a Japan Sports Agency which had been anticipated since 2011 by the *Supōtsu kihon hō* [Basic Act on Sports] (act no. 78, 2011 (Japan), supplementary provisions, art. 2).[13] Conceptually, such an agency was to be autonomous from MEXT and have the capacity to set its own legislative and operational reform agenda in the hope of further progressing reforms relating to sport in Japan. The Japan Sports Agency was eventually established in October 2015 and has approximately 120 staff.[14] It is specifically designed to enhance coordination between MEXT, the Ministry of Economy, Trade and Industry, the Ministry of Health, Labour and Welfare, and the Ministry of Foreign Affairs to prevent bureaucratic overlapping and to improve efficiency and create new synergies.[15] The Agency is an external bureau (*gaikyoku*) of MEXT, giving it a degree of independence from the Ministry.[16] The Agency also has its own legislative advisory council (*shingikai*), separate to that of MEXT, which investigates policies and legislative reform, and advises the government.[17] *Shingikai* are very important consensus-building bodies for planning and executing ongoing law reform in Japan, and are typically made up of leading academics and representatives of the relevant ministry or ministries as well as other key stakeholders.

Despite these developments, progress in Japan in relation to match-fixing has been slow when compared to how quickly momentum was gained in Australia and Korea between 2011 and 2014. Japan still has no public plan or draft legislation in relation to match-fixing, for example. Moreover, the Agency's *shingikai* met seven times between December 2015 and March 2017, and there has been no formal discussion on match-fixing so far.[18]

Debates about anti-doping legislation reflect bureaucratic tensions in Japan which can delay legislative developments and suggest that the pathway to legislative reform in relation to match-fixing will not be easy despite the new bureaucratic structure and political support. Any new anti-doping legislation is likely to require support across ministries, not just MEXT, including the Ministry of Health, Labour and Welfare.[19] To develop consensus in relation to legal and non-legal measures needed to ensure a clean Olympic Games in 2020, an ad hoc 'taskforce towards formulating and strengthening the anti-doping system' (*anchi-dōpingu taisei no kōchiku, kyōka ni muketa tasukufōsu*) was established within the Japan Sports Agency on 14 December 2015. The Taskforce consisted of a panel of sports professionals including representatives from the Japan Anti-Doping Agency, The Tokyo Organising Committee of the Olympic and Paralympic Games, Japan Sports Agency, and the JSC, as well as legal, medical and pharmaceutical professionals. It held hearings with key stakeholders such as players, player support staff, the Japanese Olympic Committee, and the Japan Paralympic Committee in preparation for the 2019 Rugby World Cup and 2020 Tokyo Olympic and Paralympic Games.[20] The Taskforce discussed measures to prevent anti-doping, including whether doping should be a criminal offence.[21]

The Taskforce's Report was submitted to the Japan Sports Agency on 8 November 2016, after which the Taskforce was dissolved.[22] The Report reflected the view that measures against doping are required because Japan will host players and other stakeholders from all over the world. The Taskforce decided, however, that whether doping involving otherwise legal drugs should be a criminal offence was a matter that should be decided by the Japanese Government, because it involves serious consideration of citizen's rights under the Constitution.[23] The Report suggested that anti-doping legislation should be in force by 1 April 2019.[24] In response to the Report, the Bipartisan Sports Parliamentary Association discussed drafting anti-doping legislation with the JSC. The draft anti-doping law has been approved within the Bipartisan Sports Parliamentary Association, and is likely to be submitted to the Japanese Parliament (Diet) in the near future.

It is likely that the JSC will also play a role in drafting any proposed match-fixing legislation. Representatives of MEXT and the JSC observed the meetings which led up to the *Council of Europe Convention on the Manipulation of Sports Competitions* ('*Convention*') which called on governments to adopt measures, including legislation, notably to prevent conflicts of interest in sports betting operators and sports organisations, and to encourage the sports betting regulatory authorities to fight against fraud.[25] As Ando notes in this volume, international precedents may play a role in informing Japanese debates, but the legislation relating to *toto* and *kōei kyōgi* sports show that there are already indigenous examples on which Japan could build. To the extent that any reform is coming, a key issue to consider will be what, if any, distinction should be drawn between match-fixing relating to sports on which it is legal to bet – that is, currently soccer under *toto* and the four *kōei kyōgi* sports – and other types of match-fixing. As the specific match-fixing legislation in Australia suggests, it is possible to focus criminal sanctions on betting-related match-fixing and allow sports associations to continue to regulate other types of match-fixing, including so-called tanking behaviour, on the basis of sporting sanctions.[26] As many chapters in this volume show, it is often the sporting sanction which is most harsh for players, but criminalisation of match-fixing conduct is necessary to combat other elements such as organised crime, financiers and insiders. Kawai's contribution in this volume suggests that the line between these areas will be just as difficult for Japan to draw as any other jurisdiction.

In the meantime, the JSC's practical approach to anti-doping whilst it awaits anti-doping legislation may give some clues as to how it could seek to combat match-fixing, at least initially. The JSC could, for example, expand its anonymous anti-doping hotline to include reporting of incidents of match-fixing. Another non-legislative mechanism for enforcing anti-match-fixing rules is codes of conduct. As part of its *National Policy on Match-Fixing in Sport*, Australia expects sports organisations to adopt a code of conduct which aligns with nationally agreed principles;[27] and the National Integrity in Sport Unit has issued a model to guide implementation.[28] As Ando notes in this volume, a recent review by Japanese sports authorities suggests that the majority of codes of conduct in Japan do not include prohibitions on each of doping, illegal drugs, illegal betting and acquaintances with antisocial characteristics. Although the codes may deal with some of these issues, it seems that there is room for improvement in relation to governance practices in Japan which may help increase awareness of the danger of match-fixing amongst players and other stakeholders, as well as give sports associations authority to take disciplinary action if codes are breached.

Gender: are women's sports different?

Another common element between the three jurisdictions examined in this volume is that the connection between gender and match-fixing, if any, is not yet well understood or clearly identified. Major studies on match-fixing do not even note the absence of women's involvement. In one of the rare explorations of the issue, Douglas argues that the lack of consideration of the 'involvement of women athletes in match-fixing' in 'numerous inquiries, investigative reports and academic papers' is 'remarkable'.[29] The lack of interest to date may relate to the low status of women's sports compared with men's sports, the lack of large and liquid betting markets on women's sports,[30] and the absence of women players in significant global and public match-fixing scandals to date.

Whether the lack of a major global scandal in women's sport has been the result of good fortune, or perhaps based on ignorance and insufficient regulatory vigilance and monitoring, is a key future research question. Are the dynamics of women's sports different when it comes to match-fixing? Whilst specific drivers for women and men may be different, at least for the time being, it would be naive to believe that there is any overall difference in attitudes towards match-fixing amongst women without further empirical research.[31] Women's competitions may also be targeted precisely because they are mostly under any regulatory and law enforcement radar and salaries and benefits are typically not as great as for men's competitions. Moreover, three examples touched on in this volume suggest that a lack of monitoring and prejudiced assumptions may be more compelling reasons for the lack of public scandals relating to women's sports than any particular female traits in the jurisdictions examined.

First, Chung, Jun and Kim's survey analysed in this volume included both male (146) and female (128) players. The authors' findings did not differentiate between male and female perceptions of match-fixing, although the authors originally planned to look at differences between gender. Ultimately, they felt that examining the differences between the types of sports would be more valuable in the first stage of their research.[32] Experience suggested, at least until the time that the survey was administered, that match-fixing seemed to be more prevalent in male sports and influenced by the types of sports rather than by gender. Chung also speculates that to date male players in Korea have been more exposed to brokers because of their various networks, including through their socialising over alcohol, and living in school dormitories where strong bonds are created between senior and junior players which senior players then exploit. Chung plans to conduct further research on the issue of women's professional sports and match-fixing in Korea.

The volleyball case study discussed in Park and Steele, Shin and Yang is a second example where the issue of gender arises in this volume. Two of the accused were professional female volleyball players who received KR₩5 million each for their participation.[33] The two women players were charged but did not face trial apparently because they were only involved in one or two fixes.[34] The Korea Volleyball Association, however, banned both players for life.[35] Brokers play a key role in instigating match-fixing in Korea, but none of the brokers (or financiers) in the case study were women. This observation is consistent with Douglas' review of research on gender and corruption generally which found that 'female offenders in economic crimes are typically influenced by a close personal relationship with a male partner or "occupying a strategic position within an organisation where they are manipulated by men"'.[36] Moreover, as Douglas also notes, women to date are less likely to have been considered as match-fixing targets by criminal gangs who are typically prejudiced against women and thus women have lacked the opportunity to participate, even if women wanted to.[37]

The issue of funding and resources highlights the third example of gender-bias in combating match-fixing to be found in this volume. Douglas argues that 'sports organisations should ensure that they have allocated sufficient resources to scrutinise women's competitions for suspicious betting behaviour'.[38] Whilst the International Netball Federation women's

Netball World Cup was part of the major sports events hosted in Australia in 2015, it was not the focus of funding to combat match-fixing efforts. Ordway in this volume notes that the Australian Government committed to provide AU$3 million over three years to further strengthen the Major Sporting Events Taskforce within the Department of Regional Australia, Local Government, Arts and Sport. The funding was to help ensure the successful staging of the 2015 Cricket World Cup and the Asian Football Cup.[39] It appears that the Australian Federal Police itself decided that netball was 'of such low risk' that it did not require 'dedicated AFP resources'.[40] This approach may be different in 2017 at the time of writing in light of the watershed of interest and development in Australian women's professional team sports in the last 12 to 24 months, and increasing interest in betting on women's sports.

Internationally and regionally, tennis and football are sports of potential risk. Tennis may be described as a sport made for match-fixing and spot-fixing. Women players face similar economic issues as men: if a player is outside the top 100 ranked players, it is a difficult sport financially.[41] Moreover, a large number of women professional players are from Eastern Europe where organised crime is strong and there is a chance that it has at least tried to manipulate players. Allegations of match-fixing at the Australian Open in 2016 provided a rare public example of match-fixing perhaps involving women players.[42] Women's football is also at risk as it gains momentum in the region. Japan featured in the final of the last two World Cups, winning over the United States of America in 2011[43] and losing to the US in 2015.[44] Globally, Japan is currently ranked sixth in the world, Australia eighth and Korea seventeenth.[45] Within Asia, the rankings are as follows: Japan first, Australia second and Korea fifth.[46] Accordingly, the three principal jurisdictions analysed in this volume constitute a powerhouse in Asian and world women's football. Given the rapidly rising popularity and commercial significance of women's football, in combination with unregulated and under-regulated betting markets in the Asian region, women's football should be looked at closely. After the success of the surveys conducted amongst male players discussed in Schwab and Finocchiaro in this volume, FIFPro is surveying its female player members, including asking questions relating to match-fixing at the time of writing, with the results anticipated in the second half of 2017.[47]

Future trends and developments: international harmonisation, cross-border leagues and e-sports

Australia's hosting of various major sporting events in 2015 and the 2018 Gold Coast Commonwealth Games,[48] and Korea and Japan's upcoming international events highlight another common theme for all jurisdictions. They all operate within a growing body of international practice in measures to combat match-fixing and cross-border match-fixing activity. How each jurisdiction responds to international developments will be crucial to its ability to operate in a global sporting paradigm, attract and maintain the best talent and most committed fans, and avoid the influence of third-party actors such as organised crime and terrorists.[49]

The value of the *Convention's* blueprint discussed by Ando in this volume as a tool for further harmonisation in Asia is likely to be significantly restricted because it assigns an active integrity role to highly regulated betting operators, whereas most betting in the region involves unregulated or under-regulated operators. Even in jurisdictions where betting is highly regulated, existing licensed betting operators may be resistant to further regulation which reflects the requirements in the *Convention*. Obtaining agreement on the concept of match-fixing and whether it includes conduct motivated by strategic or tactical sporting reasons or requires a financial benefit or link to benefit, as well as the extent to which criminal sanctions must be applied, may also be problematic. Australia's example in this regard may prove useful to galvanise harmonisation in Asia, but Australia's openness to sports betting stands at odds with Korea and Japan.[50]

Korea may provide a more useful example for Japan and others to follow in the first instance, with the establishment of a specific, match-fixing law for professional sport which co-exists with minimal legalisation of gambling. As Yeun in this volume demonstrates, the Korean legislation is wider than Japan's existing framework which focuses on *toto* and *kōei kyōgi* sports, even though Korea also severely limits legal betting. In the longer term, however, Asia may follow trends in European jurisdictions which are abandoning government-run monopolies to keep people within their jurisdictions gambling with local operators despite rising internet offerings, and thus raise tax revenue and provide employment within that jurisdiction. If these trends are seen in Asia, despite gambling being a very controversial social issue in some jurisdictions, then it will become even more necessary to appropriately regulate betting operators in those jurisdictions and the Australian example may provide a model for a way forward.

In both Korea and Japan, the International Olympic Committee's ('IOC') policies and preferences may end up prevailing over local concerns in any event. The IOC's Code of Ethics will apply to match-fixing in Korea in 2018 and similarly in Japan in 2020.[51] The Code will only apply, however, as a sporting sanction, and not to anyone outside of the IOC's authority, such as match-fixing financiers and brokers. This exclusion will not be so problematic in Korea where the government amended its legislation in 2014 to include more sports, although some review may be necessary to ensure that all of the winter Olympic sports are within the scope of the new legislation which applies to registered sports. In Japan, however, the lack of specific match-fixing legislation beyond the *toto* and *kōei kyōgi* sports means the law enforcement and regulatory gaps are wide. Moreover, match-fixing may be closer to home than many Japanese would like to think. In 2015, Japan's national football team manager was accused of match-fixing[52] and subsequently dismissed as manager.[53] As this chapter was being finalised, a Japanese tennis player received a life-time ban and fine for match-fixing and gambling on tennis matches.[54] Japanese players and other sporting actors involved in Japanese sport may become the focus of match-fixing by unscrupulous parties looking for unsuspecting jurisdictions if it further delays action.

In the meantime, events are overtaking Japan and other jurisdictions' capacities to respond effectively to match-fixing even if they have domestic legislation. A hypothetical match-fixing scenario involving the team of the Sunwolves from Super Rugby referred to in Kawai's chapter in this volume is illustrative of the challenges that cross-border leagues present.[55] How would an alleged match-fixing incident be dealt with even by a specialised unit like Victoria's Sporting Integrity Intelligence Unit? It would depend on many issues, including where the match and betting took place, whether the match-fixing involved Australian or Japanese players or other actors, details of the Australia–Japan extradition regulations, and the identity of the person placing the bets (which would currently be illegal in Japan). If the betting took place on a match in Japan via a non-Australian betting operator in an unregulated jurisdiction, how would the incident even be discovered? These endless hypothetical fact scenarios underscore the need for an international approach to match-fixing and appropriate sharing of information. Even domestically, Ordway recommends that ongoing information sharing between governments, sporting organisations and betting operators is important to combating match-fixing.

The advent of electronic sports or e-sports is another trend which will challenge law enforcement and policy-makers combating corruption in sport and, in particular, match-fixing. E-sports involve playing electronic games competitively. Players participate for money and sponsorships. Challenges for regulators, law enforcement, betting operators and other stakeholders (even the betting public) are many, and include the anonymity of players, lack of controls or player licensing by tournament organisers, inconsistent rules, constant evolution and close relationships between game developers, vendors and sponsored players. E-sports are immensely popular in Korea, which is ranked number one globally according to the Seoul-based International e-Sports Federation.[56] Korea has already experienced a match-fixing scandal involving e-sports and an illegal betting site.[57] Moreover, gender-based concerns are already an issue in the e-sports industry, with earnings disparity and bullying reports making mainstream news, reinforcing the stereotypes and challenges highlighted above in this chapter.[58]

A key question for the regulation of e-sports is whether they come within traditional definitions of sport and thus should attract regulation, funding and oversight in the same way as traditional sports such as horse racing or football. The focus of this chapter is not to answer this question, but it is important to note that there is still a large gap in perceptions. Given the popularity of e-sports in Asia, it's not surprising that the Olympic Council of Asia officially recognises electronic sports as a sport.[59] There are media reports that e-sports will be a medal event at the 2022 Asian Games.[60] Chess and bridge are already recognised as sports by the International Olympic Committee[61] with the potential for inclusion in an Olympic Games' programme, setting precedents for non-traditional sports such as e-sports to build on.[62]

Notably, the Australian Sports Commission does not recognise e-sports, chess or bridge as sports for the purpose of supporting them based on notions of physical exertion and skill.[63] If e-sports were found to be a sport for the purposes of the Australian Approval Pathway for Betting on Sport Events with an approved sport controlling body,[64] then approval to bet on e-sports events held in Australia would be required from that body (or from the regulator). It appears, however, that there has not yet been an application by an e-sports governing body to regulators in the states of Victoria or New South Wales for recognition as a sport controlling body, suggesting that e-sports in Australia are yet to develop the governance structures usually found in traditional sports. On the other hand, the Northern Territory Racing Commission approved its licence holders for a limited number of overseas-based e-sports leagues after detailed investigations into the integrity of the contests and probity checks into the organisers.[65] Betfair and Sportsbet.com.au are licensed and regulated by the Northern Territory and provide platforms for e-sports betting, for example.[66]

Conclusion

Match-fixing is a sport-related issue which has come to prominence in the last decade spurred on by seminal investigative work by Hill, public scandals, international organisations and sporting events, and increasingly sophisticated betting opportunities in highly regulated, under-regulated and unregulated markets which enhance payouts, and attract criminals seeking to launder and make money. These interrelated issues have brought match-fixing to the attention of the public and law enforcement agencies in many jurisdictions. Out of Australia, Japan and Korea, the awareness of match-fixing problems amongst the general public is lowest in Japan. A major public scandal would change that situation quickly as the public's reaction to recent gambling scandals in Japan and experience of match-fixing in Australia and Korea suggests.[67] All three jurisdictions continue to face challenges combating match-fixing and it will be necessary to maintain the leadership evidenced by legislative changes in Australia in 2012–14, Korea in 2014–16 and Japan in 2013–15. New contexts, such as the impact of player attributes including gender on match-fixing and differences between sports and jurisdictions, will continue to keep researchers and reformers in this area busy, as will international convergence, cross-border leagues and e-sports. Like this volume, future comparative research needs to consider technology-driven innovations such as processes, people and institutions.[68]

Notes

1 We thank Ms Kaori Kano, Principal Research Assistant at the Asia Law Centre, Melbourne Law School, for her research assistance.
2 See Opie and Lim, and Ordway in this volume.
3 See, e.g. Staff and agencies 2001, 'Cricket corruption exposed by report', *Guardian*, 24 May; Speed, M.S., 2011, *Sticky wicket*, Harper Sports, pp. 117–120; Hill, D., 2008, *The fix: soccer and organised crime*, McClelland and Stewart, pp. 45–53.
4 FIFPro 2013, *About FIFpro*, 11 October, www.fifpro.org/en/about-fifpro/about-fifpro.
5 Park in this volume also argues that educating players earlier and more frequently about match-fixing is important. Interestingly, in relation to the role of education and sport in Asia, Szymanski argues that the emphasis on education in Asia is potentially an obstacle to the development of national soccer leagues. He suggests that young people who want to become professional players typically debut at about 17 years of age and have been playing for at least four to five years before, but these types of players are unlikely to emerge from Asian cultures where they have not been given the opportunity to devote all of their efforts to sport rather than education: Szymanski, S., 2016, 'Professional Asian football leagues and the global market', *Asian Economic Policy Review*, vol. 11, no. 1, pp. 16–38, p. 34. The authors of chapters relating to Korea in this volume seem to be indirectly advocating that less sports training and more normalised education is what is needed in Korea.
6 Ministry of Education, Culture, Sports, Science and Technology, *About MEXT*, www.mext.go.jp/en/about/index.htm.
7 Japan Sport Council 2015, *Yakushokuin no jōkyō* [Personnel circumstances], 1 October, www.jpnsport.go.jp/corp/koukai//tabid/67/Default.aspx.
8 *Law on the Japan Sport Council*, art. 3.
9 Ibid., art. 15(5).
10 The Unit also established a Japan anti-doping disciplinary panel (*Nihon anchi-dōpingu kiritsu paneru*) in April 2015. The panel hears disputes between players and the Japan Anti-Doping Agency, to decide whether there was an infringement. See Japan Sport Council 2016, *Supōtsu ni okeru dōpingu bōshi katsudō no suisen*, www.jpnsport.go.jp/corp/gyoumu/antidoping/tabid/772/Default.aspx. The Unit is not an enforcement unit.
11 Correspondence with Yuta Ando.
12 The Association was led by Taro Aso. See *Sangiingiin Ōie Satoshi* [Satoshi Ōie, member of the House of Councillors] 2013, *Supōtsu giin renmei* [Bipartisan Sports Parliamentary Association], 21 February, http://oie-satoshi.com/?p=7684.
13 The *Supōtsu kihon hō* [Basic Act on Sports], act no. 78, 2011 (Japan), replaced the *Supōtsu shinkō hō* [Sports Promotion Act], act no. 141, 1961 (Japan). On the establishment of the *Basic Act on Sports*, see Japan Sports Law Association (ed.)

2011, *Shōkai supōtsu kihon hō* [Explanation of the Basic Act on Sports], Seibundoh; Kiku, K. *et al.* (eds.), 2011, *Supōtsu seisaku ron* [Sports policy theory], Seibundoh, www.mext.go.jp/a_menu/sports/kihonhou/attach/1336024.htm.

14 Japan Sports Agency was established by *Monbu kagaku shō secchi hō no ichibu wo kaisei suru hōritsu* [Law amending parts of law in relation to the establishment of the Ministry of Education, Culture, Sports, Science and Technology], act no. 21, 2015 (Japan), which amended the *Monbu kagaku shō secchi hō*: http://law.c gov.go.jp/htmldata/H11/H11HO096.html. For the staff quota at the Japan Sports Agency, see *Monbu kagaku shō teiin kisoku* [Regulation on staff quota for the Ministry of Education, Culture, Sports, Science and Technology], ordinance of MEXT no. 17, 2001, which was amended by ordinance of MEXT no. 22 of 2015 to include a staff quota for the Japan Sports Agency effective as of 1 April 2015: http://law.e-gov.go.jp/htmldata/H13/H13F20001000017.html.

15 See Japan Sports Agency 2016, *Kankei shōchō to renkei shita supōtsu gyōsei no sōgōteki na suishin* [Comprehensive promotion of sports administration amongst the coordinating relevant ministries and government offices], July, www.mext.go.jp/sports/b_menu/soshiki2/1373932.htm. On the establishment of the Japan Sports Agency, see Japan Sports Agency 2015, *Japan Sports Agency background of establishment*, October, www.mext.go.jp/sports/en/about_us/background/index.htm.

16 See Japan Sports Agency 2015, *Soshiki zu* [Organisational chart], October, www.mext.go.jp/sports/b_menu/soshiki2/1362177.htm.

17 See *Monbu kagaku shō soshiki rei* [Order for Organisation of Ministry of Education, Culture, Sports, Science and Technology], Cabinet order no. 251, 2000 (Japan). The September 2015 amendment to the Order added art. 92, which establishes a legislative advisory council on sports (*supōtsu shingikai*).

18 Some minutes of the meetings are currently publicly available, and the materials distributed for each meeting to date have already been uploaded. See Japan Sports Agency, *Supōtsu shingikai kiji yōshi • gishiroku • haifu shiryō* [Sport Council summary of proceedings, record of proceedings, handout documents], www.mext.go.jp/sports/b_menu/shingi/001_index/giji_list/index.htm. *Toto* has been discussed in meetings: see e.g. Japan Sports Agency, *Supōtsu shinkō tōhyō (supōtsu shinkō kuji: toto) no seido gaiyō* [Sports promotion poll (sports promotion lottery: *toto*) system summary], www.mext.go.jp/sports/b_menu/shingi/001_index/shiryo/__icsFiles/afieldfile/2016/01/06/1365658_09.pdf, which are the materials for the first meeting held on 24 December 2015. See also the discussion in Kawai about abandoned proposals to expand *toto*.

19 The Ministry of Health is involved because any anti-doping legislation for sporting purposes may require amendments to existing drug-related laws: see, e.g. *Kakuseizai torishimari hō* [Stimulants Control Law], act no. 252, 1951 (Japan); *Mayaku oyobi kōseisinnyaku torisimari hō* [Narcotics and Psychotropics Control Law], act no. 14, 1953 (Japan); *Taima torisimari hō* [Cannabis Control Law], act no. 124, 1951 (Japan); *Ahen hō* [Opium Law], act no. 71, 1954 (Japan); *Iyakuhin iryōkiki no hjnshitsu yūkōsei oyobi anzensei no kakuho ni kansuru hōritsu* [Pharmaceutical Affairs Law], act no. 145, 1960 (Japan).

20 Pavitt, M., 2016, 'Japanese Government considering adopting anti-doping law ahead of Tokyo 2020', *Inside the Games*, 4 January, www.insidethegames.biz/articles/1032954/japanese-government-considering-adopting-anti-doping-law-ahead-of-tokyo-2020. Japan Sports Agency 2016, *Supōtsukai no tōmei sei, kōhei, kōseisei no kōjō* [Improving transparency, fairness and impartiality in the

sports world], November, www.mext.go.jp/sports/b_menu/sports/mcatetop10/list/detail/1375009.htm.

21 Other issues included increasing doping test facilities and resources, and anti-doping education for medical professionals and athletes, and improving testing methods. The group also discussed legal measures, including regulations relating to sharing information and intelligence (e.g. with the JSC and the Japan Anti-Doping Agency). See *Anchi-dōpingu taisei no kōchiku, kyōka ni muketa tasukufōsu* [Taskforce towards Formulating and Strengthening the Anti-Doping System] 2016, *Anchi-dōpingu taisei no kōchiku kyōka ni tsuite – Dōpingu no nai kuriin na supōtsu no jitugen ni mukete – hōkokusho* [In relation to the formulating and strengthening of the anti-doping system – towards realisation of clean sports without doping – report], 8 November, p. 20, www.mext.go.jp/sports/b_menu/sports/mcatetop10/list/detail/__icsFiles/afieldfile/2016/11/08/1375009_3_2_1.pdf.

22 Ibid.

23 *Anchi-dōpingu taisei no kōchiku, kyōka ni muketa tasukufōsu*, above n. 21, pp. 20–21.

24 Ibid., p. 23.

25 *Council of Europe Convention on the Manipulation of Sports Competitions*, opened for signature 18 September 2014, CETS no. 215 (not yet in force), https://rm.coe.int/16801cdd7e.

26 As noted by Opie and Steele in this volume, however, the new *Model Criminal Law Provisions for the Prosecution of Competition Manipulation* suggests that the specific 'match-fixing offence be independent from betting on a sports event or competition which is fixed'. United Nations Office on Drugs and Crime and International Olympic Committee 2016, *Model Criminal Law Provisions for the Prosecution of Competition Manipulation.* p. 18, www.unodc.org/documents/corruption/Publications/UNODC-IOC_Model_Criminal_Law_Provisions_for_the_Prosecution_of_Competition_Manipulation_Booklet.pdf.

27 Sport and Recreation Ministers' Council 2011, *National policy on match-fixing in sport*, 10 June, www.health.gov.au/internet/main/publishing.nsf/Content/F6DB8637F05C9643CA257C310021CCE9/$File/National%20Policy%20on%20Match-Fixing%20in%20Sport%20(FINAL).pdf.

28 National Integrity in Sport Unit, *Anti-match-fixing policy template*, www.health.gov.au/internet/main/publishing.nsf/Content/Anti-match-fixing-policy-template.

29 Douglas, L., 2016, '"Say it ain't so … Josephine?" The risk of match-fixing in women's sport', *The Commentator*, vol. 97, pp. 3–16. *The Commentator* is a publication of the Australian and New Zealand Sports Law Association.

30 Observations from gambling research are useful in relation to Korea on this point. Research shows that there are few opportunities for Koreans to gamble and little desire to do so. Interestingly, it also suggests that low participation rates by females contribute to the comparatively low prevalence of gambling. See also Williams, R.J., Lee, C.K. and Back, K.J., 2013, 'The prevalence and nature of gambling and problem gambling in South Korea', *Social Psychiatry and Psychiatric Epidemiology*, vol. 48, no. 5, pp. 821–834.

31 Douglas, above n. 29, pp. 9–13. Douglas argues that as women's sports become more like men's sports, for example, drivers may converge. Douglas also shows that many of the risk factors for match-fixing identified by Hill in 2008 apply to women and women's sports including 'the presence of illegal gambling networks', 'financial vulnerability', and low remuneration and lack of benefits such as paid maternity leave for women players.

32 Correspondence from Young Ryuel Chung, 12 May 2017.

33 Daegu District Court (18 April 2012), case no. *godan* 136, pp. 21–22.
34 Ibid.
35 Ibid.
36 Douglas, above n. 29, p. 13.
37 Ibid., p. 9.
38 Ibid., p. 14.
39 Commonwealth of Australia 2013, *Part 2: expense measures*, 14 May, p. 196, www.budget.gov.au/2013-14/content/bp2/download/BP2_expense.pdf.
40 See Ordway in this volume.
41 On tennis players' incomes, see Bane, M. and Gescheit, D., 2015, 'Rich rewards for those at the top in tennis, but what of the rest?', *The Conversation*, 19 January.
42 Douglas, above n. 29, p. 3. The allegations were subsequently dismissed: Reuters 2017, 'Three Australian Open matches cleared of suspicions of corruption after TIU investigation', *ABC News Sport*, 8 April, www.abc.net.au/news/2017-04-08/three-suspicious-matches-at-australian-open-cleared-by-tiu/8427702?section=sport.
43 Casert, R., 2011, 'Japan edge out USA on penalties to lift women's World Cup', *Guardian*, 18 July, www.theguardian.com/football/2011/jul/18/japan-usa-womens-world-cup-final.
44 Lutz, T., 2015, 'Women's World Cup 2015 final: USA beat Japan 5–2 – as it happened', *Guardian*, 6 July, www.theguardian.com/football/live/2015/jul/05/womens-world-cup-2015-final-usa-v-japan-live.
45 FIFA.com 2017, *Women's ranking: all confederations*, 24 March, www.fifa.com/fifa-world-ranking/ranking-table/women.
46 FIFA.com 2017, *Women's ranking: AFC*, 24 March, www.fifa.com/fifa-world-ranking/ranking-table/women/afc.html.
47 Correspondence with Brendan Schwab, 13 May 2017.
48 The Major Sporting Events Taskforce has also been assigned to oversee the Commonwealth Games in 2018. See Australian Government Department of Health, Major Sporting Events Taskforce, 20 November 2013, www.health.gov.au/internet/main/publishing.nsf/Content/major-sporting-events-taskforce. See also Ordway in this volume. The Commonwealth Games Federation has traditionally not been as active in relation to match-fixing as organisations such as the International Olympic Committee and FIFA, but it is pursuing integrity initiatives. See Brown, A., 2016, 'ICSS signs integrity agreement with Commonwealth Games', *Sports Integrity Initiative*, press release, 26 January, www.sportsintegrityinitiative.com/icss-signs-integrity-agreement-with-commonwealth-games; The International Centre for Sport Security (ICSS), *Commonwealth Games Federation and ICSS EUROPE sign agreement to protect and safeguard sport*, www.theicss.org/en/news/read/commonwealth-games-federation.
49 Yusof, Z.M., 2016, 'Terror networks target sports betting', *The New Paper*, 8 November, www.tnp.sg/news/singapore-news/terror-networks-target-sports-betting.
50 On negative public perceptions about gambling in Korea, see Williams *et al.*, above n. 30. In relation to perceptions of gambling in Japan, see Ando and Kawai in this volume.
51 For the Rio 2016 version, see International Olympic Committee 2016, *Ethics*, https://stillmed.olympic.org/media/Document%20Library/OlympicOrg/Documents/Code-of-Ethics/2016/Book-Code-of-Ethics-2016.pdf#_ga=1.222150808.1286866280.1486549827, p. 73.
52 An influential Japanese daily newspaper reported that 'a Valencia court has accepted a claim filed by Spanish prosecutors alleging Japan manager Javier Aguirre and 40 others were involved in fixing a match between his former club

Real Zaragoza and Levante in 2011': 'Court accepts match-fixing claim involving Japan manager Aguirre' 2015, *The Japan Times*, 14 January, www.japantimes.co.jp/sports/2015/01/14/soccer/international-soccer/court-accepts-match-fixing-claim-involving-japan-manager-aguirre/#.WPRj2fVOLIU.

53 Agencies 2015, 'Japan sack coach Javier Aguirre due to ongoing match-fixing investigation', *Guardian*, 3 February, www.theguardian.com/football/2015/feb/03/japan-sack-coach-javier-aguirre-investigation.

54 Tennis Integrity Unit 2017, 'Lifetime tennis ban and fine for Junn Mitsuhashi following match-fixing convictions', media release, 16 May, www.tennisintegrityunit.com/storage/app/media/Junn%20Mitsuhashi%2016%20May%202017.pdf; Palmer, D., 2017, 'Japanese tennis player banned for life over match-fixing charge', 16 May, www.insidethegames.biz/articles/1050406/japanese-tennis-player-banned-for-life-over-match-fixing-charge. The player reflects the profile of other tennis players found to have fixed matches: low ranking, and participating in low-level tournaments.

55 SANZAAR, *Super Rugby Sunwolves* 2017, www.sanzarrugby.com/superrugby/teams/?competition=205&season=2017&team=19700.

56 International e-Sports Federation 2016, *Total rank*, www.ie-sf.com/en/record/rank.php. The Federation's membership includes Japan and Australia, and many Asian nations: International e-Sports Federation, *Member Nations*, www.ie-sf.com/en/about/nations.php.

57 Noble, R., 2016, 'eSports parallels with traditional sport: governing bodies', *The Roar*, 15 September, www.theroar.com.au/2016/09/15/esports-parallels-traditional-sport-governing-bodies. Noble's article also highlights issues with performance enhancing drugs in e-sports.

58 Ong, T., 2017, 'The female gamers fighting bullying in eSports', *ABC News*, 11 May, www.abc.net.au/news/2017-05-11/women-fighting-pay-disparity-bullying-in-esports/8515202?section=technology.

59 Olympic Council of Asia 2009, *Electronic sports*, www.ocasia.org/Sports/SportsT.aspx?AMPuohtNGyxFinVzEIKang==. E-sports were incorporated into the Asian Indoor Games in 2007.

60 'Esports will be a medal event at the 2022 Asian Games' 2017, *ABC News*, 19 April, www.abc.net.au/news/2017-04-19/e-sports-to-be-medal-event-at-asian-games/8452458.

61 Association of IOC Recognised International Sports Federations, *Members*, undated, www.arisf.org/members.aspx.

62 Usmani, B., 2016 'Is it time for eSports gamers to be recognised as athletes?', *Guardian*, 8 June, www.theguardian.com/technology/2016/jun/08/esports-pro-video-gamers-recognised-athletes.

63 Australian Government, Australian Sports Commission 2017, *Application for Australian Sports Commission National Sporting Organisation recognition*, www.ausport.gov.au/supporting/nso/asc_recognition/recognition_of_nso. This Australian attitude may change for reasons which include e-sports' addition to the medal programme for the 2022 Asian Games and the possible participation of Australia and Oceania in the Games.

64 As envisaged by the *National Policy on Match-fixing in Sport*, see Opie and Lim in this volume.

65 See Northern Territory Government 2017, *Bookmaker licences and permits*, 30 March, https://nt.gov.au/industry/gambling/bookmaker-licences-and-permits/declared-sporting-events-for-bookmaking.

66 See, Betfair Pty Ltd 2017, *Sport highlights*, www.betfair.com.au/exchange; Sportsbet Pty Ltd 2017, *E-sports*, www.sportsbet.com.au/betting/e-sports.

67 On the gambling scandals in 2016, see Ando and Kawai in this volume.

68 Comparisons of black-and-white regulations are important, but require context to reach their ultimate potential. See, e.g. Council of Europe 2012, *Match-fixing in sport: A mapping of criminal law provisions in EU 27*, March, www.keanet.eu/docs/study-sports-fraud-final-version_en.pdf.

Index

www.ingramcontent.com/pod-product-compliance
Ingram Content Group UK Ltd.
Pitfield, Milton Keynes, MK11 3LW, UK
UKHW010957180926
475701UK00004B/421
9780367406905